Rapid Recipes and Tips—Over 600!

WITH TODAY'S busy lifestyles, just about every family cook needs menu ideas that are not only delicious and satisfying, but also fast to fix. And there's no better source than the ever-popular *Quick Cooking Annual Recipes* collection.

The twelfth edition in this series, *2010 Quick Cooking Annual Recipes* gives you every single speedy dish that appeared in *Simple & Delicious* magazine during 2009. Plus, you get dozens of the magazine's helpful hints and how-tos. It all adds up to more than 600 recipes and tips—right here in one convenient cookbook!

With hundreds of gorgeous, full-color photos showing the prepared dishes, this can't-miss collection makes it as easy as ever for you to serve scrumptious, home-cooked foods every day of the week.

Here's what else you'll find inside:

Chapters That Meet Your Needs. We've divided the recipes in this book into 20 chapters that make sense for time-crunched cooks. Just turn to whichever chapter fits your needs, and you'll discover an array of mouth-watering options. (See page 3 for a complete list of chapters.)

For instance, when you have only 10 minutes to spend in the kitchen, try Mushroom Beef Tips with Rice, Chicken Pesto Clubs, Cordon Bleu Potato Soup, Glazed Pear Shortcakes or any of the 16 other done-in-a-dash dishes in the "10 Minutes to the Table" chapter.

Or, on nonstop weekdays when the kids are clamoring for dinner and time's at a premium, rely on the "30 Minutes to Mealtime" chapter for 26 complete menus—all table-ready in half an hour or less!

Six-Week Menu Planner. The home economists in our Test Kitchen gathered 6 full weeks of Monday-through-Friday entrees, complete with a shopping list for each week. Simply follow these handy meal plans to enjoy weeks of stress-free suppers.

Contest-Winning Dishes. You get all of the standout specialties that earned honors in the six national recipe contests held last year: Make It in 10!, Lotsa Pasta, What's Fresh?, Beat the Heat, Kiddin' Around and Go Nuts. Turn to page 4 to "meet" the Grand Prize winners and see where each contest-winning recipe is located in this book.

Special Sections Built for You. In the "On-the-Go Odds & Ends" and "Test Kitchen Secrets" chapters, we've grouped recipes by theme. Featuring grilled fare, leftover makeovers, cooking for two and more, these extra sections give you even more options to suit your lifestyle.

Two Helpful Indexes. See the General Recipe Index to locate a recipe by category and/or major ingredient, and check the Alphabetical Index when you're looking for a specific dish. In both indexes, you'll find a red checkmark (✓) next to recipes that include Nutrition Facts.

Every time-saving recipe and kitchen tip in this collection was specially selected with on-the-go cooks in mind. So no matter how full your schedule is, you and your loved ones will be able to enjoy this indispensable cookbook right away—and for many years to come!

taste of home quick COOKING
2010
ANNUAL RECIPES

Vice President/Books: Heidi Reuter Lloyd
Senior Editor/Books: Mark Hagen
Editor: Michelle Bretl
Art Director: Gretchen Trautman
Layout Designers: Nancy Novak, Kathy Crawford
Proofreaders: Linne Bruskewitz, Vicki Soukup Jensen
Recipe Asset Management Systems: Coleen Martin
Administrative Assistant: Barb Czysz
Cover Photo: Lori Foy (Photographer),
Suzanne Breckenridge (Food Stylist), Jenny Bradley Vent (Set Stylist)

• • •

U.S. Chief Marketing Officer: Lisa Karpinski
Vice President/Book Marketing: Dan Fink
Creative Director/Creative Marketing: Jim Palmen

• • •

Taste of Home Books
©2010 Reiman Media Group, Inc.
5400 S. 60th St., Greendale WI 53129

International Standard Book Number (10): 0-89821-764-4
International Standard Book Number (13): 978-0-89821-764-3
International Standard Serial Number: 1522-6603

PICTURED ON FRONT COVER: Cheese & Onion French Bread (p. 98), Triple Chocolate Cake (p. 28) and Italian Pork Skillet (p. 133).

PICTURED ON BACK COVER: Maple Mustard Chicken (p. 163), Home-Style Stew (p. 165), Party Meatballs (p. 161), Chocolate-Orange Scones (p. 182), Herb-Roasted Turkey (p. 37), Mushroom-Rosemary Turkey Gravy (p. 37) and Banana Sundae Dessert (p. 237).

For other *Taste of Home* books and products, visit
www.ShopTasteofHome.com.

taste of home simple & delicious

Editor in Chief: Catherine Cassidy
Creative Director: Ardyth Cope
Food Director: Diane Werner RD
Executive Editor: Christian Millman

• • •

Editor: Mary Spencer
Managing Editor: Mary C. Hanson
Art Director: Kristen Johnson
Food Editor: Amy Welk-Thieding RD
Associate Editors: John McMillan, Elizabeth Russell
Recipe Editors: Mary King, Christine Rukavena
Copy Editor: Susan Uphill
Editorial Assistant: Marilyn Iczkowski
Executive Assistant: Marie Brannon

• • •

Test Kitchen Manager: Karen Scales
Associate Food Editors: Alicia Bozewicz RD, Tina Johnson, Marie Parker, Annie Rundle
Recipe Specialists: Jenni Warren RD, Katie Bartnicki
Test Kitchen Coordinator: Kristy Martin
Test Kitchen Associates: Rita Krajcir, Laura Scharnott, Erika Schmitt

• • •

Photographers: Rob Hagen, Dan Roberts, Jim Wieland, Lori Foy
Set Stylists: Jenny Bradley Vent, Stephanie Marchese, Melissa Haberman, Dee Dee Jacq, Deone Jahnke
Food Styling Manager: Sarah Thompson
Food Stylists: Kaitlyn Besasie, Alynna Malson, Shannon Roum, Diane Armstrong, Ronnie Day, Leah Rekau (Assistant)
Photo Studio Coordinator: Kathy Swaney

• • •

Vice President, Publisher: Lora Gier
Marketing Director: Kym Blanchard
Advertising Traffic Specialist: Kristine Jacobson

• • •

President and Chief Executive Officer: Mary G. Berner
President, U.S. Affinities: Suzanne M. Grimes
SVP, Global Chief Marketing Officer: Amy J. Radin

⏱ Contents

Recipe Contests Yield Quick Winning Dishes

EVERY TIME *Simple & Delicious* magazine held one of its national recipe contests during the past year, busy cooks from across the country submitted their very best time-saving recipes.

Want to know which scrumptious, fast-to-finish dishes were deemed tops in those contests? You can find out by checking the special section here.

On these two pages, we've featured the six talented cooks who won the Grand Prize in a 2009 contest. We've also let you know where to find their first-place recipes in this book, so you can turn to those celebrated dishes right away...and even prepare them for your family tonight!

Plus, we've added the 11 other recipes that were honored in each contest. You get a complete listing of dishes—all 72 of them—that our panel of judges selected as contest winners during the past year.

Because we've included the page numbers for all of the runners-up, too, you'll easily be able to locate each prize-winning recipe in this book. Dozens of top-honor dishes are right at your fingertips!

From Garden Produce to Pasta

The contest topics during the past year yielded a wide range of reader recipes. But all of those dishes have one thing in common—they're quick-to-fix foods that suit busy cooks' lifestyles.

In the "Make It in 10!" contest, readers shared the super-fast fare that gets their families through the most hectic of weekdays. And "Lotsa Pasta" brought oodles of noodles to the forefront in main courses, side dishes, salads and more.

When summer gardens are overflowing with ripe produce, look to the bountiful choices from the "What's Fresh?" contest. Then keep your cool by turning to the "Beat the Heat" winners to get even more options for warm weather.

Cooking for children? The "Kiddin' Around" contest features youth-inspired foods guaranteed to get smiles from even the pickiest eaters. And you'll please everyone with the variety of entrees, snacks and other nutty delights from "Go Nuts."

Simply pick your favorites from this exciting array of prize-winning recipes...or go ahead and try each one. Either way, you'll have standout sensations you and your family are sure to love.

Count Down to a 10-Minute Winner

A BUSY stay-at-home mom, Veronica Callaghan fixes meals most days of the week for her husband, Daniel, and three children. Her "go-to" dishes include Peachy Shrimp Tacos, which won top honors in the "Make It in 10!" recipe contest.

"My family really loves it, so I make it every few weeks," she says from Glastonbury, Connecticut. "Sometimes I replace the shrimp in the recipe with whatever leftover meat is in the fridge. For example, pork makes a great substitute."

'Make It in 10!' Contest Winners

She Used Her Noodle in the Kitchen

COOKING is one of the ways Judy Armstrong of Prairieville, Louisiana relaxes after a long day working as the principal of a grade school.

"My kids and husband, Tim, are my food critics," she says. "They were excited when the Grand Prize in the 'Lotsa Pasta' contest went to my Barbecue Pork and Penne Skillet.

"To me, it's simple 'comfort food' for a hectic weeknight—nothing too fancy," she notes. "But my son reminded me that the easiest recipes are often the best."

'Lotsa Pasta' Contest Winners

Grilled Sandwich Stacks Up with the Best

A HIGH SCHOOL chemistry teacher, Diana Tseperkas has cooking down to a science. Her exceptional Grilled Vegetable Sandwich proves it!

"During summer, I make that colorful creation often for my husband, Peter, myself and guests," Diana says from her home in Hamden, Connecticut. "People always tell me it's light and delicious."

Our judging panel agreed, awarding it the Grand Prize in the "What's Fresh?" recipe contest.

She Tossed Together a Cool Winner

THOUGH Terri McCarty and her husband, Dan, are retired, family and hobbies can keep their schedules hectic. So Terri looks for fast fare such as Balsamic Chicken Pasta Salad—the top winner in the "Beat the Heat" recipe contest.

"When time is tight, I try to come up with something quick, simple and fresh," explains the Oro Grande, California cook. "My cold pasta dish couldn't be much easier to put together and really hits the spot on warm-weather days."

Kid-Pleasing Cookies Are Child's Play

CHOOSING an entry for the "Kiddin' Around" recipe contest was easy for Rebecca Clark of Warrior, Alabama. "From working with kids at church and being with my relatives' children, I know Oatmeal Surprise Cookies are a hit with youngsters," she says.

Full of chocolate-covered raisins and pumpkin pie spice, her treats ended up receiving the Grand Prize. "They go over big with adults, too," Rebecca notes, "including myself and my husband, Eric."

She Got Crackin' on a Standout Snack

WITH A JOB that requires lots of travel, Heidi Blaine Hadburg makes the most of the time she's able to spend at home with her husband, Bruce, in Safety Harbor, Florida.

"We entertain as much as our schedules allow," Heidi relates. "Because holidays are a slow time for work, I cram in as many parties as I can."

Elegant and rich, her French Quarter Cheese Spread impressed guests—and our judges. They named it the top entry in the "Go Nuts" recipe contest.

Chapter 1

EVER FIND yourself wondering what kind of dinners on-the-go cooks like you put on the table for their own families? You'll get a great idea just by paging through this chapter!

Here, you'll "meet" six fellow cooks and see their best fast-to-fix meals. Each menu is ready to eat in just 30 minutes...or less. In fact, one will be on the table in only 15 minutes!

Pick the meals that would appeal to your family as well. In no time, you'll all be enjoying delicious fare such as Pizza Pasta Toss, Buttery Parmesan Garlic Bread, Easy Chicken Strips and Vegetables with Cheese Sauce.

Plus, you'll get a delectable dessert with each menu. Yum!

TOP CHOICE. Mock Stroganoff and Lemon Green Beans (both recipes on p. 12).

She Makes the Most of Dinner With Fast Fare

AT HOME in Beverly, West Virginia, Lori Daniels' daughters Hannah and Heidi keep her on the go. But in addition to Girl Scouts, basketball and other activities, Lori fits in days at the office, too. "As a realtor, I need to be flexible with my schedule to accommodate out-of-state customers and clients," she says.

Luckily, husband Steve lends a hand with meals. A machinist and welder, he also raises cattle and has a garden, from which he harvests much of the produce Lori uses to make nearly 10 meals weekly!

One of her favorite menus is featured here. Pizza Pasta Toss is a kid-friendly recipe that came to her one busy night. "I needed a one-skillet dish and thought if I added pizza seasonings, pepperoni and cheese, it might appeal to Heidi's 'selective palate.' I was right!"

Alongside, Lori serves Salad Greens & Creamy Sweet Dressing. "Salads are a quick side and healthy, too," Lori notes. "Plus, my children like them."

She finishes the meal with a dessert as special as it is speedy. "I simply top freshly baked chocolate chip cookies with ice cream and a drizzle of chocolate syrup. I love how it makes everyone's eyes light up!"

Pizza Pasta Toss

Prep/Total Time: 30 min.

2 cups uncooked spiral pasta
1 pound ground beef

Cookie Sundaes

1 cup sliced fresh mushrooms
1/2 cup chopped green pepper
1 can (15 ounces) tomato puree
1/2 cup diced pepperoni
4-1/2 teaspoons sugar
1 teaspoon Italian seasoning
1/2 teaspoon salt
1/2 teaspoon garlic powder
1/2 teaspoon dried oregano
1/4 teaspoon onion powder
2 cups (8 ounces) shredded part-skim mozzarella cheese

Cook spiral pasta according to the package directions. Meanwhile, in a large skillet, cook beef, mushrooms and green pepper over medium heat until meat is no longer pink; drain. Add the tomato puree, pepperoni, sugar and seasonings; cook and stir for 5 minutes.

Drain spiral pasta; stir into the meat mixture. Heat through. Sprinkle with mozzarella cheese. Remove from the heat; cover and let stand until cheese is melted. **Yield:** 4 servings.

Salad Greens & Creamy Sweet Dressing

Prep/Total Time: 5 min.

☑ This recipe includes Nutrition Facts and Diabetic Exchanges.

1/4 cup sugar
1/4 cup sour cream
6 tablespoons sliced green onions
2 tablespoons cider vinegar
4 cups torn mixed salad greens

Place the sugar, sour cream, green onions and vinegar in a jar with a tight-fitting lid; shake well. Divide salad greens among four bowls; drizzle with dressing. **Yield:** 4 servings.

Nutrition Facts: 1 cup salad greens with 2 tablespoons dressing equals 91 calories, 3 g fat (2 g saturated fat), 10 mg cholesterol, 23 mg sodium, 15 g carbohydrate, 1 g fiber, 2 g protein. **Diabetic Exchanges:** 1 vegetable, 1/2 starch, 1/2 fat.

Cookie Sundaes

Prep/Total Time: 20 min.

8 refrigerated ready-to-bake chocolate chip cookies
2 cups peanut butter ice cream with peanut butter cup pieces
2 tablespoons chocolate syrup
Whipped cream in a can and chocolate sprinkles, optional

Bake the chocolate chip cookies according to package directions. Remove to a wire rack to cool. Divide cookies among four dessert dishes. Top each with 1/2 cup ice cream; drizzle with chocolate syrup. Garnish with whipped cream and sprinkles if desired. Serve immediately. **Yield:** 4 servings.

Salad Greens & Creamy Sweet Dressing
Pizza Pasta Toss

Hot Sandwich Creates a Quick Yet Fun Supper

WHEN time-strapped moms need a go-to dinner that's sure to be a hit, they can look to Katherine Desrosiers' menu with confidence. From Trail, British Columbia, she provides a spread that's perfect for hectic weeknights.

Ham & Cheese Roll-Ups are a fun twist on the traditional hot ham-and-cheese sandwich. And children like helping to make them as much as eating them!

While the kids are busy layering the tortillas with sandwich fixings and rolling them up, you can put together the easy yet tasty Romaine Salad. It takes a mere 5 minutes to toss together using bagged greens and a simple homemade dressing.

For a twist on her salad recipe, Katherine sprinkles the lettuce with salt, pepper and sugar substitute, then mixes the oil, malt vinegar and balsamic vinegar together before topping the salad.

Whichever way you choose to make the salad, be sure to save room for dessert. Katherine's Rum Banana Sauce is delicious served over scoops of vanilla ice cream. In fact, it's so good that you'll be tempted to forgo the ice cream altogether!

Ham & Cheese Roll-Ups

Prep/Total Time: 20 min.

- 2 tablespoons olive oil, *divided*
- 4 flour tortillas (10 inches)
- 1/2 cup grated Parmesan cheese, *divided*
- 1/4 pound thinly sliced deli ham
- 1/4 pound thinly sliced provolone cheese
- 1/4 pound thinly sliced hard salami
- 1/2 cup roasted sweet red peppers, drained and julienned
- 1 cup (4 ounces) shredded part-skim mozzarella cheese

Marinara sauce, optional

Brush 1 tablespoon oil on one side of tortillas. Sprinkle with 1/4 cup Parmesan cheese. Layer tortillas with deli ham, provolone cheese, salami, red peppers and mozzarella cheese. Fold in the sides of the tortillas; roll up.

Place seam side down on a parchment-lined baking sheet. Brush with remaining oil; sprinkle with remaining Parmesan cheese. Bake at 425° for 9-12 minutes or until golden brown. Serve with marinara sauce if desired. **Yield:** 4 servings.

Romaine Salad

Prep/Total Time: 5 min.

- 3 tablespoons olive oil
- 1-1/2 teaspoons malt *or* rice vinegar
- 1-1/2 teaspoons balsamic vinegar
- 1 teaspoon sugar
- 1/2 teaspoon salt
- 1/2 teaspoon coarsely ground pepper
- 4 cups hearts of romaine salad mix

In a small bowl, whisk together the oil, vinegars, sugar, salt and pepper. Pour over the salad mix; toss to coat. **Yield:** 4 servings.

Rum Banana Sauce

Prep/Total Time: 15 min.

- 3/4 cup packed brown sugar
- 1/4 cup butter, cubed
- 1/4 cup heavy whipping cream
- 2 tablespoons maple syrup
- 2 large bananas, cut into 1/2-inch slices
- 1/2 teaspoon rum extract

Vanilla ice cream

In a small saucepan, combine the brown sugar, butter, cream and maple syrup. Cook and stir over medium heat for 4-5 minutes or until sauce is smooth. Stir in bananas; heat through. Remove from the heat; stir in extract. Serve over ice cream. **Yield:** 4 servings.

Ham & Cheese Roll-Ups
Romaine Salad

Home-Cooked Comforts Make Mealtime Easy

EVERY NIGHT at about 6 p.m., Terri Wetzel of Roseburg, Oregon finds her table filled with at least four hungry mouths to feed. "When my son Timothy comes home, it's five, including my husband Jim, son Joe and daughter Madie. If Tim's fiancee or friends accompany him, we make room for even more!"

To tempt their taste buds and keep things stress-free for herself, Terri often relies on the great flavor and simplicity of Mock Stroganoff for the main dish. "It's a family favorite," Terri relates.

Lemon Green Beans and Microwave Apple Crisp round out her rapid menu. "The crisp is the perfect ending," she notes, "and especially good in fall."

Mock Stroganoff

Prep/Total Time: 25 min.

3 cups uncooked yolk-free noodles
1 pound ground beef
1/4 cup chopped onion
1/4 cup sliced fresh mushrooms
1-1/2 cups water
2 envelopes brown gravy mix
2 cups (16 ounces) sour cream

Cook the noodles according to the package directions. Meanwhile, in a large skillet, cook the beef, onion and mushrooms over medium heat until meat is no longer pink; drain.

Stir in the water and gravy mix. Bring to a boil; cook and stir for 2 minutes or until thickened. Remove from the heat; stir in sour cream. Drain noodles. Serve with meat mixture. **Yield:** 4 servings.

Lemon Green Beans

Prep/Total Time: 10 min.

☑ This recipe includes Nutrition Facts and Diabetic Exchange.

1 package (16 ounces) frozen cut green beans, thawed
2 tablespoons water
1-1/2 teaspoons dried minced onion
1 tablespoon lemon juice
1-1/2 teaspoons real bacon bits
1/4 teaspoon salt
1/4 teaspoon pepper

Place the beans, water and onion in a 1-qt. microwave-safe dish. Cover and microwave on high for 4-5 minutes or until crisp-tender; drain. Stir in the remaining ingredients. **Yield:** 4 servings.

Editor's Note: This recipe was tested in a 1,100-watt microwave.

Nutrition Facts: 3/4 cup equals 40 calories, trace fat (trace saturated fat), 1 mg cholesterol, 305 mg sodium, 8 g carbohydrate, 3 g fiber, 2 g protein. **Diabetic Exchange:** 2 vegetable.

Microwave Apple Crisp

Prep/Total Time: 20 min.

☑ This recipe includes Nutrition Facts.

4 medium tart apples, peeled and thinly sliced
1/3 cup all-purpose flour, *divided*
1/4 cup sugar
2 teaspoons lemon juice
3/4 teaspoon ground cinnamon, *divided*
2/3 cup old-fashioned oats
1/2 cup packed brown sugar
3 tablespoons cold butter
Vanilla ice cream, optional

In a large bowl, combine apples, 1 tablespoon flour, sugar, lemon juice and 1/4 teaspoon cinnamon. Pour into a greased 9-in. deep-dish pie plate.

In a small bowl, combine the oats, brown sugar and remaining flour and cinnamon. Cut in butter until crumbly; sprinkle over apple mixture. Cover with waxed paper. Microwave on high for 5-7 minutes or until apples are tender. Serve with vanilla ice cream if desired. **Yield:** 6 servings.

Editor's Note: This recipe was tested in a 1,100-watt microwave.

Nutrition Facts: 1 cup (calculated without ice cream) equals 252 calories, 7 g fat (4 g saturated fat), 15 mg cholesterol, 66 mg sodium, 49 g carbohydrate, 3 g fiber, 2 g protein.

Microwave Apple Crisp

Italian Menu Satisfies Her Need for Speed

WHOLESOME yet fast Italian food is a favorite with Talena Keeler, her husband Dustin and son Sage in Siloam Springs, Arkansas. So when they found a meal they especially enjoyed at an Italian restaurant, Talena tried duplicating it at home. The fabulous menu here was the result...and a big hit!

"My family actually prefers it to the restaurant's version," says Talena of her creamy and colorful, all-in-one Chicken Fettuccine Alfredo with Veggies. "And it's such an easy dish to serve when we have company drop by unexpectedly."

Talena loves the fact that it goes together in just minutes with a handful of convenience items almost always found in her pantry. She rounds out her pasta entree with a crusty loaf of golden-brown Buttery Parmesan Garlic Bread.

And for a summery finish, Talena adds Berries & Cream Desserts. A marshmallow and cream cheese topping is the crowning touch for this treat, which also makes a great addition to a Fourth of July party.

"I use ready-made pound cake from my local bakery to speed things up," Talena says, "but you can bake your own if you have more time."

Buttery Parmesan Garlic Bread
Chicken Fettuccine Alfredo with Veggies

Chicken Fettuccine Alfredo With Veggies
Prep/Total Time: 15 min.

2 quarts water
1 package (9 ounces) refrigerated fettuccine
3 cups frozen mixed vegetables
1 package (10 ounces) ready-to-serve roasted chicken breast strips
1-1/2 cups Alfredo sauce
1/2 cup shredded Parmesan cheese

In a Dutch oven, bring water to a boil. Add fettuccine and vegetables; return to a boil. Cook on high for 2-3 minutes or until fettuccine and vegetables are tender; drain. Stir in chicken and Alfredo sauce; heat through. Sprinkle with Parmesan cheese. **Yield:** 4 servings.

Buttery Parmesan Garlic Bread
Prep/Total Time: 15 min.

1/4 cup butter, softened
2 tablespoons shredded Parmesan cheese
1 teaspoon garlic powder
1 loaf (8 ounces) French bread, halved lengthwise

In a small bowl, combine the butter, Parmesan cheese and garlic powder. Spread mixture over cut sides of bread. Place on an ungreased baking sheet.

Bake at 400° for 10-12 minutes or until the bread is golden brown. Serve warm. **Yield:** 4 servings.

Berries & Cream Desserts
Prep/Total Time: 15 min.

1 loaf (10-3/4 ounces) frozen pound cake, thawed
1 package (3 ounces) cream cheese, softened
1 cup marshmallow creme
1 cup sliced fresh strawberries
1 cup fresh blueberries

Cut cake in half. Cut one half into 1/2-in. cubes (save remaining cake for another use). In a small bowl, beat cream cheese and marshmallow creme until smooth.

In four small serving dishes, layer the cake cubes and berries. Top with the cream cheese mixture. Chill until serving. **Yield:** 4 servings.

Fresh Take

WHEN fixing Chicken Fettuccine Alfredo with Veggies (recipe at top), Talena Keeler likes to use frozen California-blend vegetables. If you'd prefer to use fresh garden vegetables, start them in boiling water before adding the fettuccine. Add the fettuccine during the last 3 minutes of cook time.

Berries & Cream Desserts

Both Kids and Adults Enjoy Her Tasty Trio

WHEN IT COMES to clever shortcuts and quick kitchen techniques, Crystal Sheckles-Gibson of Beespring, Kentucky is a pro. She has to be!

Not only does she run a housecleaning service and work part-time for the U.S. Census Bureau, but she also has to make meals that accommodate her husband's schedule and her daughter's dietary needs.

"My daughter Cheyenne has quite a few food allergies, so I plan menus around them, as well as what's on sale at the store," Crystal says. "Because my husband Wayne is busy, I try to prepare dinners that also reheat well or can stay warm in the oven."

Her slow cooker, which she uses several times a week, is an invaluable tool. And her backyard garden keeps her fridge stocked with plenty of fresh veggies. "I'm learning how to can them, too," she adds.

One of Crystal's favorite meals is the kid-friendly menu here, which she loves serving to family and friends. "I came up with Easy Chicken Strips one night when I was looking for a new, fast way to serve chicken," she relates.

"They also make great appetizers, especially when served with barbecue or sweet-and-sour sauce for dunking. I've been told they're restaurant-quality."

Winning Crystal even more compliments is Vegetables with Cheese Sauce, which pleases even picky eaters. "The sauce is good with other veggies, too, such as summer squash and potatoes," she notes.

End the meal on a fun and refreshing note with Lime Milk Shakes. The recipe is so simple, even kids can fix them.

"Cheyenne likes to make them in our blender," says Crystal. "I turn them into popsicles by freezing them...or I use orange juice concentrate and orange or rainbow sherbet to switch up their flavor."

Easy Chicken Strips
Prep/Total Time: 30 min.

✓ This recipe includes Nutrition Facts and Diabetic Exchanges.

- 1/4 cup all-purpose flour
- 3/4 teaspoon seasoned salt
- 1-1/4 cups crushed cornflakes
- 1/3 cup butter, melted
- 1-1/2 pounds boneless skinless chicken breasts, cut into 1-inch strips

In a shallow bowl, combine flour and seasoned salt. Place cornflakes and butter in separate shallow bowls. Coat chicken with flour mixture, then dip in butter and coat with cornflakes.

Transfer to an ungreased baking sheet. Bake at 400° for 15-20 minutes or until chicken juices run clear. **Yield:** 6 servings.

Nutrition Facts: 1 serving equals 281 calories, 12 g fat (7 g saturated fat), 87 mg cholesterol, 430 mg sodium, 18 g carbohydrate, trace fiber, 24 g protein. **Diabetic Exchanges:** 3 very lean meat, 2 fat, 1 starch.

Vegetables with Cheese Sauce
Easy Chicken Strips

Vegetables with Cheese Sauce
Prep/Total Time: 15 min.

- 2 packages (16 ounces *each*) frozen California-blend vegetables
- 1 package (8 ounces) process cheese (Velveeta), cubed
- 3 tablespoons milk

Microwave vegetable blend according to package directions. In a small saucepan, combine cheese and milk. Cook and stir over low heat until melted. Serve with vegetables. **Yield:** 6 servings.

Lime Milk Shakes
Prep/Total Time: 10 min.

- 2-1/4 cups milk
- 3/4 cup limeade concentrate
- 3 cups lime sherbet, softened

Place all ingredients in a blender; cover and process until smooth. Pour into chilled glasses; serve immediately. **Yield:** 6 servings.

Special Spread Makes Mealtime Quality Time

WITH a husband who works far from home, Cassie Gourley of Prescott Valley, Arizona knows that their time together is precious. "Howard is at the Grand Canyon for his job most days," she says. "I like to cook for him when he's home, but I'd rather spend more time with him than in the kitchen."

One of her favorite go-to menus features a main course of Creamy Tomato Shrimp with Penne, which takes a mere 20 minutes to prepare. "People love the taste and think it's complicated," Cassie notes. "But jarred sauces make it so fast."

An entree this special is best paired with an easy yet well-flavored side, and that's just what you get with Cassie's Pea Pods and Peppers. "I fix this about once a month. It's a modification on a recipe I found in a cookbook."

Although the name might not sound fancy, her Mud Pies are a delightful way to cap off this show-stopping menu. "I had seen recipes that used pre-made individual pie crusts and ice cream, and then one day just made up this combination," Cassie relates. "I love that it doesn't require any baking."

Mud Pies

Creamy Tomato Shrimp With Penne
Prep/Total Time: 20 min.

 2 cups uncooked penne pasta
 1 pound uncooked medium shrimp, peeled and deveined
 1 teaspoon minced garlic
 1/2 teaspoon crushed red pepper flakes
 2 tablespoons olive oil
 1-1/2 cups spaghetti sauce
 1 carton (10 ounces) refrigerated Alfredo sauce
 2 tablespoons butter
 1/4 teaspoon salt
 1/8 teaspoon pepper
 2 tablespoons minced fresh parsley

Cook the pasta according to the package directions. Meanwhile, in a large skillet, saute the shrimp, garlic and pepper flakes in oil until shrimp turn pink. Stir in the spaghetti sauce, Alfredo sauce, butter, salt and pepper; heat through.

Drain the pasta; serve with shrimp mixture. Sprinkle with parsley. **Yield:** 4 servings.

Pea Pods and Peppers
Prep/Total Time: 15 min.

☑ This recipe includes Nutrition Facts and Diabetic Exchanges.

 2 packages (6 ounces *each*) fresh snow peas
 1 medium sweet red pepper, julienned
 1/2 small onion, sliced
 1/4 teaspoon garlic salt
 1/8 teaspoon pepper
 1 tablespoon canola oil
 1 tablespoon butter

In a large skillet, saute the snow peas, red pepper, onion, garlic salt and pepper in oil and butter until vegetables are tender. **Yield:** 4 servings.

Nutrition Facts: 1 cup equals 102 calories, 7 g fat (2 g saturated fat), 8 mg cholesterol, 138 mg sodium, 9 g carbohydrate, 3 g fiber, 3 g protein. **Diabetic Exchanges:** 2 vegetable, 1 fat.

Mud Pies
Prep/Total Time: 10 min.

 2/3 cup chocolate hazelnut spread
 4 individual graham cracker tart shells
 1 pint coffee ice cream
Whipped cream and chocolate-covered coffee beans

Spoon the chocolate hazelnut spread into the graham cracker tart shells. Top each with ice cream; garnish with whipped cream and chocolate-covered coffee beans. **Yield:** 4 servings.

Chapter 2

⊛ Holiday and Seasonal Pleasers

FROM Pecan Pumpkin Pie and Herb-Roasted Turkey to Spiced Cider Punch and Eggnog Tube Cake, some recipes just "say" holiday. And those are the kinds of dishes you get in this extra-big, extra-festive chapter!

We've featured memorable fare for special occasions year-round. Surprise your loved ones on Valentine's Day with Chocolate Pizza Heart...scare up Black Cat Cupcakes for Halloween... and delight everyone at Christmastime with cute-as-can-be Rudolph Treats.

You'll discover unforgettable spreads for Thanksgiving, Easter, Father's Day and the Fourth of July, too. So go ahead—start the celebrating!

FIT FOR A FEAST. Ham with Apple Raisin Sauce p. 25).

A Very Sweet Valentine's Day

WHETHER you want to treat someone special on February 14 or just want to brighten up a brisk winter's day, you'll discover something perfect here. From chocolaty candies to a golden pear pie, each of these temptations will be ready to enjoy in a heartbeat!

Nutty Chocolate Truffles

(Pictured below)

Prep: 10 min. + chilling

With just five ingredients, these no-bake bites couldn't be easier to make. For variety, use different fruit preserves.
—LeeAnn Karnowski, Stevens Point, Wisconsin

✓ This recipe includes Nutrition Facts and Diabetic Exchanges.

  1 package (8 ounces) cream cheese, softened
  1 cup (6 ounces) semisweet chocolate chips, melted and cooled
  1 cup crushed vanilla wafers (about 30 wafers)
  1/4 cup strawberry preserves
1-1/4 cups chopped almonds, toasted

In a large bowl, beat cream cheese until smooth. Beat in the chocolate, vanilla wafer crumbs and strawberry preserves. Cover and refrigerate for at least 1 hour or until easy to handle.

Shape into 1-in. balls; roll in almonds. Store in the refrigerator. **Yield:** 4 dozen.

Nutrition Facts: 1 truffle equals 68 calories, 5 g fat (2 g saturated fat), 5 mg cholesterol, 22 mg sodium, 6 g carbohydrate, 1 g fiber, 1 g protein. **Diabetic Exchanges:** 1 fat, 1/2 starch.

Raspberry Dessert Sauce

Nutty Chocolate Truffles

Raspberry Dessert Sauce

(Pictured above)

Prep: 10 min. + chilling

Pretty as a picture, this ruby-red dessert sauce is a simple but sensational way to dress up vanilla ice cream, frozen yogurt or angel food cake. Prepare an extra batch to keep in the freezer for drop-in guests or last-minute treats.
—Gusty Crum, Dover, Ohio

  1 package (10 ounces) frozen sweetened raspberries, thawed
  1 tablespoon cornstarch
  1 tablespoon cold water
  1/4 cup sugar
  1/2 cup red currant jelly
  1/4 teaspoon orange extract
Vanilla ice cream

In a blender, puree raspberries. Strain and discard seeds, reserving juice.

In a small saucepan, combine cornstarch and cold water until smooth; stir in raspberry juice and sugar. Bring to a boil over medium heat; cook and stir for 2 minutes or until thickened. Whisk in jelly and extract. Chill. Serve over ice cream. **Yield:** 1-2/3 cups.

Chocolate Pizza Heart

(Pictured below)

Prep: 15 min. + chilling

I came across this recipe in an old cookbook and changed a few ingredients to suit my family's taste. They really enjoy this candy for Valentine's Day or any time at all.
—Becky Thesman, Enid, Oklahoma

1-1/2 cups milk chocolate chips
    1 cup butterscotch chips
  3/4 cup miniature marshmallows
  3/4 cup chopped salted peanuts
  3/4 cup crushed potato chips
    2 tablespoons flaked coconut
    7 maraschino cherries, halved
  1/4 cup milk chocolate M&M's
    2 tablespoons vanilla *or* white chips
  1/2 teaspoon shortening

On waxed paper, draw a 10-in. heart; place on a baking sheet. Set aside.

In a large microwave-safe bowl, melt the milk chocolate chips and butterscotch chips; stir until smooth. Stir in the miniature marshmallows, peanuts and potato chips. Immediately spread on prepared pan into heart shape. Sprinkle with the coconut; top with the cherries and M&M's.

In a small microwave-safe bowl, melt vanilla chips and shortening; stir until smooth. Drizzle over top. Refrigerate until firm, about 1-1/2 hours. Remove the waxed paper. Let stand for 10 minutes at room temperature before cutting. **Yield:** 1-3/4 lbs.

Pear Custard Pie

Pear Custard Pie

(Pictured above)

Prep: 10 min. **Bake:** 45 min. + chilling

My youngest daughter baked a pear pie for us once, and I liked it so much that I've made it several times since. The rich custard is wonderful with the mellow fruit.
—Barbara Rea, Glenshaw, Pennsylvania

    1 sheet refrigerated pie pastry
    3 medium ripe pears, peeled and thinly sliced
    1 cup sugar
  1/4 cup all-purpose flour
    2 eggs, lightly beaten
    1 cup heavy whipping cream
    1 teaspoon vanilla extract

Unroll pastry into a 9-in. pie plate; flute edges. Place pears in pastry. In a small bowl, combine sugar and flour. Stir in the eggs, cream and vanilla. Pour over pears. Bake at 375° for 45-50 minutes or until a knife inserted near the center comes out clean.

Cool on a wire rack. Cover and refrigerate for at least 2 hours. **Yield:** 6 servings.

Chocolate Pizza Heart

Chocolaty Choices

YOU COULD form Chocolate Pizza Heart (recipe above left) into a different shape to suit nearly any occasion. For example, create a shamrock for St. Patrick's Day, a football for your Super Bowl party, a candy cane for Christmas...the possibilities are endless!

Special Feast for Easter

WANT to delight every "bunny" at your Easter Sunday table? Rely on this elegant holiday dinner featuring a succulent main course of ham and all the trimmings. You'll even enjoy a warm appetizer, plus candy eggs guaranteed to get "hunted" down fast!

Glazed Snap Peas

(Pictured below)

Prep/Total Time: 20 min.

I like to make vegetables a part of every meal in some way, and this quick side dish recipe is perfect for those nonstop days when time is at a premium. I love the natural sweet taste from the snap peas and the sprinkling of bacon bits.
—Ida Tuey, Kokomo, Indiana

✓ This recipe includes Nutrition Facts and Diabetic Exchanges.

> 2 packages (24 ounces *each*) frozen sugar snap peas
> 1/4 cup honey
> 2 tablespoons butter
> 1 teaspoon salt
> 1/4 teaspoon crushed red pepper flakes
> 1/4 cup real bacon bits

Cook peas according to package directions; drain. Stir in the honey, butter, salt and pepper flakes. Sprinkle with bacon. **Yield:** 10 servings.

Nutrition Facts: 3/4 cup equals 116 calories, 3 g fat (2 g saturated fat), 8 mg cholesterol, 342 mg sodium, 19 g carbohydrate, 5 g fiber, 5 g protein. **Diabetic Exchanges:** 2 vegetable, 1/2 starch, 1/2 fat.

Herb-Swirled Rolls

Glazed Snap Peas

Herb-Swirled Rolls

(Pictured above)

Prep: 20 min. + rising **Bake:** 15 min. + cooling

Rolls are a welcome addition to any dinner, but these really stand out. The pretty swirl shape, sesame seeds and herbs are wonderful. They also freeze well...or can be prepared in advance and heated just before mealtime. —Lois Gallup Edwards Woodland, California

✓ This recipe includes Nutrition Facts and Diabetic Exchanges.

> 1 loaf (1 pound) frozen bread dough, thawed
> 3 tablespoons butter, melted
> 2 tablespoons minced chives
> 2 tablespoons dried parsley flakes
> 1/2 teaspoon dill weed *or* dried thyme
> 1/4 teaspoon salt
> 1/8 teaspoon pepper
> 1 egg
> 2 tablespoons water
> Sesame *and/or* poppy seeds

On a floured surface, roll dough into a 14-in. x 12-in. rectangle; brush with butter. Sprinkle with chives, parsley, dill, salt and pepper. Roll up jelly-roll style, starting with a long side; pinch seam to seal. Cut into 12 slices.

Place cut side down in greased muffin cups. Cover and let rise until doubled, about 45 minutes. Combine the

egg and water; brush over the tops. Sprinkle with seeds. Bake at 375° for 12-15 minutes or until golden brown. Remove rolls from the pan to a wire rack to cool. **Yield:** 1 dozen.

Nutrition Facts: 1 roll equals 133 calories, 4 g fat (2 g saturated fat), 13 mg cholesterol, 284 mg sodium, 18 g carbohydrate, 2 g fiber, 4 g protein. **Diabetic Exchanges:** 1 starch, 1/2 fat.

Ranch Potato Cubes

Prep: 10 min. **Bake:** 65 min.

I love to cook for my family and for our church. I've never taken these potatoes anywhere without coming home with a cleaned-out dish. —Mae Craft, Clarksville, Arkansas

      7 medium potatoes, cut into 1/2-inch cubes
  1/4 cup butter, cubed
      1 cup (8 ounces) sour cream
      1 envelope ranch salad dressing mix
      1 cup (4 ounces) shredded cheddar cheese

Place potatoes in a greased 11-in. x 7-in. baking dish; dot with butter. Cover and bake at 325° for 60-65 minutes or until tender.

Combine sour cream and dressing mix; spoon over potatoes. Sprinkle with cheese. Bake, uncovered, for 5-10 minutes or until cheese is melted. **Yield:** 8 servings.

Ham with Apple Raisin Sauce

(Pictured above and on page 20)

Prep: 10 min. **Bake:** 1-3/4 hours + standing

Ever since I ran across this recipe several years ago, I've been serving it for special dinners. I really appreciate the ease of preparation, especially on busy holidays when I have so many other things to take care of. Plus, cleanup is minimal because everything is done in the bag.
                                          —Sandy Olberding, Spencer, Iowa

      1 tablespoon all-purpose flour
      1 large oven roasting bag
      4 medium tart apples, peeled and chopped
      2 cups apple juice
      1 cup raisins
  1/2 cup packed brown sugar
      1 teaspoon ground cinnamon
      1 boneless fully cooked ham (about 6 pounds)

Shake flour in the oven roasting bag. Place in an ungreased 13-in. x 9-in. baking pan. Place the apples, apple juice, raisins, brown sugar and cinnamon in the bag; mix well. Place ham in bag. Close bag. Cut six 1/2-in. slits in top of bag.

Bake at 325° for 1-3/4 to 2 hours or until a meat thermometer reads 140°. Let ham stand for 10 minutes before slicing. Serve with sauce. **Yield:** 16 servings.

Lemon Ladyfinger Dessert

(Pictured above)

Prep: 20 min. + chilling

Whipped up by the home economists in our Test Kitchen, this rich and creamy treat will top off your Easter dinner beautifully. What's more, five ingredients and 20 minutes of preparation time are all you need.

> 2 packages (3 ounces *each*) ladyfingers, split
> 3 cups heavy whipping cream
> 1 package (8 ounces) cream cheese, softened
> 1/2 cup lemon curd
> 2/3 cup confectioners' sugar

Set aside five ladyfingers; line the sides and bottom of a lightly greased 9-in. springform pan with remaining ladyfingers. In a large bowl, beat cream until stiff peaks form; set aside.

In another large bowl, beat cream cheese and lemon curd until smooth; add the sugar. Beat on medium for 1 minute. Fold in the whipped cream. Spread half of the cream cheese mixture into prepared pan. Arrange reserved ladyfingers in a spoke pattern over top. Spread with remaining cream cheese mixture. Cover and chill overnight. **Yield:** 12 servings.

Confetti Succotash

Prep/Total Time: 20 min.

This vegetable side dish featuring corn, two kinds of peppers, lima beans and green onion perks up meals with its bright colors and fresh taste. Try it on holidays or any day.
—Nicole Willis, Las Vegas, Nevada

☑ **This recipe includes Nutrition Facts and Diabetic Exchanges.**

> 1/4 cup chopped sweet red pepper
> 1/4 cup chopped green pepper
> 2 tablespoons thinly sliced green onion
> 1 tablespoon butter
> 2 cups frozen corn, thawed
> 1 cup frozen lima beans, thawed
> 1/4 cup half-and-half cream
> 2 teaspoons minced fresh marjoram *or*
> 1/2 teaspoon dried marjoram
> 1/4 teaspoon salt
> 1/8 teaspoon pepper

In a large skillet, saute the peppers and green onion in butter until the vegetables are crisp-tender. Add the remaining ingredients. Bring to a gentle boil. Reduce heat; cover and simmer for 5-6 minutes or until vegetables are tender, stirring occasionally. **Yield:** 4 servings.

Nutrition Facts: 3/4 cup equals 171 calories, 5 g fat (3 g saturated fat), 15 mg cholesterol, 192 mg sodium, 28 g carbohydrate, 5 g fiber, 6 g protein. **Diabetic Exchanges:** 2 starch, 1 very lean meat.

Peanut Butter Easter Eggs

(Pictured below)

Prep: 35 min. + chilling

It's hard to eat just one of these peanut-buttery goodies. Don't forget to get the kids involved when you're making this festive recipe—it'll be worth the sticky fingers!
—Mary Joyce Johnson, Upper Darby, Pennsylvania

1/2 cup butter, softened
2-1/3 cups confectioners' sugar
1 cup graham cracker crumbs
1/2 cup creamy peanut butter
1/2 teaspoon vanilla extract
1-1/2 cups dark chocolate chips
2 tablespoons shortening
Pastel sprinkles

In a large bowl, cream the butter; gradually add the confectioners' sugar, graham cracker crumbs, peanut butter and vanilla. Shape into 16 eggs; place on waxed paper-lined baking sheets. Refrigerate for 30 minutes or until firm.

In a microwave, melt the chocolate chips and shortening; stir until smooth. Dip eggs in chocolate; allow excess to drip off. Decorate with sprinkles; return eggs to waxed paper. Chill until set. Store in an airtight container in the refrigerator. **Yield:** 16 eggs.

Peanut Butter Easter Eggs

Artichoke Spinach Dip in a Bread Bowl

Artichoke Spinach Dip In a Bread Bowl

(Pictured above)

Prep: 25 min. **Bake:** 20 min.

Baking this creamy dip in the bread shell makes it especially attractive and fun. Plus, guests can never believe how full of veggies it is. —Ella Homel, Chicago, Illinois

3 jars (7-1/2 ounces *each*) marinated quartered artichoke hearts, drained and chopped
1 cup grated Parmesan cheese
3/4 cup mayonnaise
3 green onions, sliced
1 can (4 ounces) chopped green chilies, drained
1 package (10 ounces) frozen chopped spinach, thawed and squeezed dry
1 cup (4 ounces) shredded Swiss cheese
1 round loaf (1 pound) rye *or* pumpernickel bread

In a large bowl, combine the first seven ingredients. Cut a thin slice off top of bread. Hollow out bottom half, leaving a 1/2-in. shell. Cut removed bread into 1-in. cubes. Place on an ungreased baking sheet. Broil 6 in. from heat for 2-3 minutes or until golden, stirring once.

Place bread shell on an ungreased baking sheet. Spoon dip into bread shell. Bake, uncovered, at 350° for 20-25 minutes or until heated through. Serve with bread cubes. **Yield:** 4 cups.

Editor's Note: Reduced-fat or fat-free mayonnaise is not recommended for this recipe. If any of the dip does not fit in bread shell, bake, uncovered, in a greased small baking dish until heated through.

Steak Dinner for Father's Day

TREAT DAD on his special day of the year with this hearty meat-and-potatoes meal fit for the man of the house. With jazzed-up green beans and an irresistible dessert of Triple Chocolate Cake, too, this is one dinner he won't soon forget!

Triple Chocolate Cake

(Pictured below)

Prep: 15 min. **Bake:** 45 min. + cooling

Here's a wonderful way to perk up a boxed white cake mix. Sour cream, baking cocoa, chocolate chips and chocolate frosting make this bundt cake a real showstopper.
—Melissa Just, Minneapolis, Minnesota

    1 package (18-1/4 ounces) white cake mix
1/3 cup sugar
    4 eggs
    1 cup (8 ounces) sour cream
2/3 cup canola oil
    2 tablespoons baking cocoa
1/2 cup miniature semisweet chocolate chips
    1 cup chocolate frosting
    2 tablespoons milk

In a large bowl, combine the cake mix, sugar, eggs, sour cream and oil. Beat on low for 1 minute; beat on medium for 2 minutes. Pour half of the batter into a large bowl. Stir in cocoa until blended. Fold chocolate chips into white cake batter.

Spoon batters alternately into a greased and floured 10-in. fluted tube pan. Bake at 350° for 45-50 minutes

or until a toothpick inserted near the center comes out clean. Cool for 15 minutes before removing from pan to a wire rack to cool completely.

In a small bowl, combine frosting and milk. Spoon over top of cooled cake. **Yield:** 12 servings.

Green Beans with Pecans

(Pictured at right)

Prep: 20 min. **Cook:** 15 min.

I collect cookbooks from all over the world and love to try new recipes for my husband and guests. Pecans, a splash of orange and maple syrup make this dish exceptional.
—Sharon Delaney-Chronis, South Milwaukee, Wisconsin

    1 tablespoon butter
    1 cup chopped pecans
    2 tablespoons maple syrup
1/8 teaspoon salt
BEANS:
    1/4 cup finely chopped shallots
    2 tablespoons butter
    2 teaspoons all-purpose flour
    1/2 teaspoon grated orange peel
Dash cayenne pepper
1-1/2 pounds fresh green beans, trimmed
    2/3 cup reduced-sodium chicken broth
    1/3 cup orange juice
    1 teaspoon fresh sage *or* 1/4 teaspoon dried sage leaves
    1/4 teaspoon salt
    1/8 teaspoon pepper

In a small heavy skillet, melt butter. Add pecans; cook over medium heat until toasted, about 4 minutes. Stir in syrup and salt. Cook and stir for 2-3 minutes or until pecans are glossy. Spread on foil to cool.

Meanwhile, in a large skillet, saute shallots in butter until tender; stir in the flour, orange peel and cayenne. Add the remaining ingredients; cover and cook for 5 minutes. Uncover; cook and stir 4-5 minutes longer or until beans are crisp-tender. Transfer to a serving bowl. Sprinkle with pecans. **Yield:** 8 servings.

Triple Chocolate Cake

In the Oven

TUBE CAKES (angel food cakes) and bundt cakes, including decadent Triple Chocolate Cake (recipe above left), should always be baked with the rack placed in the lowest position in the oven. This allows the most even baking for a large pan.

Green Beans with Pecans
Basil Red Potatoes
Steaks with Mushroom Sauce

Steaks with Mushroom Sauce

(Pictured above)

Prep/Total Time: 25 min.

These grilled sirloin steaks become extra-special with the creamy mushroom sauce. It's delicious over chicken and pork, too. —LaDonna Reed, Ponca City, Oklahoma

    4 boneless beef sirloin steaks (6 ounces *each*)
1/4 teaspoon salt
1/4 teaspoon pepper
SAUCE:
    1 jar (4-1/2 ounces) sliced mushrooms, drained
    1 teaspoon minced garlic
    1 teaspoon canola oil
1/2 cup French onion dip
    2 tablespoons half-and-half cream
1/2 teaspoon minced chives
1/4 teaspoon pepper

Sprinkle steaks with salt and pepper. Grill steaks, covered, over medium heat or broil 4 in. from heat for 5-7 minutes on each side or until meat reaches desired doneness (for medium-rare, a meat thermometer should read 145°; medium, 160°; well-done, 170°).

In a large skillet, saute mushrooms and garlic in oil for 3 minutes. Stir in onion dip, cream, chives and pepper. Bring to a gentle boil. Reduce heat; simmer, uncovered, for 2-3 minutes or until heated through. Serve with steaks. **Yield:** 4 servings.

Basil Red Potatoes

(Pictured above)

Prep/Total Time: 25 min.

Tender red potatoes are treated to a light coating of butter, wine, chicken flavoring and basil for this standout side. —Bernadette Bennett, Waco, Texas

    7 cups water
1-1/2 pounds red potatoes, cut into 1-inch cubes
1-1/2 teaspoons chicken bouillon granules
    3 tablespoons butter
    3 tablespoons dry red wine *or* beef broth
4-1/2 teaspoons minced fresh basil *or*
    1-1/2 teaspoons dried basil
Dash garlic salt

In a large saucepan, combine the water, potatoes and bouillon. Bring to a boil. Reduce heat; cover and cook for 7-10 minutes or until tender. Drain. Stir in the remaining ingredients. **Yield:** 4 servings.

Fourth of July Fireworks

THOSE BURSTS of color in the nighttime sky won't be the only things getting oohs and aahs on Independence Day. So will your menu, thanks to the festive summer spread here!

Fire up the grill for Teriyaki & Ginger Pork Tenderloins and Tarragon Corn on the Cob, then round out the meal with Tomato-Green Bean Salad and luscious Zinfandel Strawberry Trifle. They're all you need to make your patriotic party sparkle!

Zinfandel Strawberry Trifle

Tarragon Corn on the Cob

(Pictured below)

Prep: 10 min. **Grill:** 25 min.

To me, nothing says summer like grilled cobs of sweet corn, and these herbed ears show off the season's best.
—Brandy Jenkins, Greenwood, Mississippi

  4 **large ears sweet corn, husks removed**
  4 **tarragon sprigs**
1/3 **cup butter, melted**
  4 **teaspoons reduced-sodium soy sauce**
  2 **teaspoons minced fresh tarragon** *or*
    1/2 teaspoon dried tarragon

Place each ear of corn with a tarragon sprig on a 14-in. x 12-in. piece of heavy-duty foil. Fold foil over corn and seal tightly. Grill corn, covered, over medium heat for 25-30 minutes or until tender, turning occasionally.

In a small bowl, combine the butter, soy sauce and minced tarragon. Open foil carefully to allow steam to escape; brush corn with butter mixture. **Yield:** 4 servings.

Zinfandel Strawberry Trifle

(Pictured above)

Prep/Total Time: 25 min.

This mouth-watering dessert recipe was given to me by a friend. It's so simple to make but looks and tastes really special. To create a red-white-and-blue effect for a patriotic celebration, just include some blueberries with the strawberries.
—Nicole Clayton, Prescott, Arizona

1-1/2 **cups Zinfandel wine** *or* **grape juice**
  1/2 **cup sugar,** *divided*
    1 **quart fresh strawberries, sliced**
    1 **teaspoon vanilla extract**
    2 **loaves (10-3/4 ounces** *each***) frozen pound cake, thawed**
    2 **cups heavy whipping cream**
Additional fresh strawberries

In a large saucepan, combine wine and 1/3 cup sugar. Bring to a boil; cook until liquid is reduced to about 1/2 cup. Set saucepan in ice water and stir the mixture for 3 minutes. Stir in strawberries and vanilla.

Meanwhile, cut one cake in half widthwise (save the other half for another use). Cube the remaining cake; set aside.

In a small bowl, beat cream until it begins to thicken. Add remaining sugar; beat until soft peaks form. In a 3-qt. trifle bowl or glass serving bowl, layer a third of the cake cubes, strawberry mixture and whipped topping. Repeat twice. Chill until serving. Garnish with additional strawberries. **Yield:** 15 servings.

Tarragon Corn on the Cob

Teriyaki & Ginger Pork Tenderloins

(Pictured above)

Prep: 10 min. + marinating **Grill:** 20 min.

The home economists in our Test Kitchen hit on this recipe for pork on the grill. Teriyaki sauce and fresh ginger give the tender meat a distinctive Asian flavor you're sure to love. Start marinating the tenderloins earlier in the day, and by mealtime they'll be ready for the barbie!

    1/2 cup reduced-sodium teriyaki sauce
    1/3 cup olive oil
      4 teaspoons brown sugar
      2 pork tenderloins (1 pound *each*)
      2 teaspoons minced fresh gingerroot
    3/4 teaspoon pepper

In a small bowl, whisk the teriyaki sauce, oil and brown sugar. Pour 1/2 cup marinade into a large resealable plastic bag; add the pork, ginger and pepper. Seal bag and turn to coat; refrigerate for 4 hours. Cover and refrigerate remaining marinade.

    Coat grill rack with cooking spray before starting the grill. Prepare grill for indirect heat. Drain and discard marinade. Grill pork, covered, over indirect medium-hot heat for 25-35 minutes or until a meat thermometer reads 160°. Let stand for 10 minutes before slicing. Serve with reserved marinade. **Yield:** 5 servings.

Tomato-Green Bean Salad

(Pictured above)

Prep/Total Time: 20 min.

Feta cheese adds a salty kick to this fuss-free salad. I like to assemble it a day in advance so the flavors can meld.
          —Estelle Lauletta, Boston, Massachusetts

    1/2 pound fresh green beans, trimmed
  1-1/2 cups cherry tomatoes, halved
    3/4 cup pitted ripe olives, halved
    1/4 cup Italian salad dressing
    2/3 cup crumbled feta cheese

Place beans in a large saucepan and cover with water. Bring to a boil. Cook, uncovered, for 8-10 minutes or until crisp-tender. Drain and immediately place beans in ice water. Drain and pat dry.

    In a salad bowl, combine the beans, tomatoes and olives. Drizzle with salad dressing; toss to coat. Chill until serving. Just before serving, sprinkle with feta cheese. **Yield:** 4 servings.

Halloween Tricks and Treats

LITTLE GHOSTS, goblins and black cats are welcome visitors on October 31, so why not give them a surprise that's as frightful as it is delightful? The creepy goodies here are completely edible and full of fun, making them perfect for the spooky occasion.

Pretzel Pumpkin Grahams

(Pictured below)

Prep: 30 min. + standing

This sweet-and-salty snack recipe from our Test Kitchen staff is easy enough for kids to help with. Miniature pretzels form the cute pumpkin shapes.

    12 whole chocolate graham crackers
    1/2 pound white candy coating, coarsely
        chopped
    24 miniature pretzels
Orange colored sugar or sprinkles
    6 green gumdrops, cut into four lengthwise
        slices

Cut graham crackers in half, making squares. In a microwave, melt white candy coating; stir until smooth. Dip one pretzel in candy coating; let excess drip off.

Place on a graham cracker square. If desired, fill pretzel holes with candy coating. Decorate with sugar or sprinkles. For stem, dip the back of one gumdrop

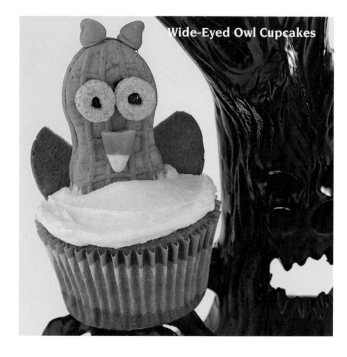

Wide-Eyed Owl Cupcakes

piece into coating; place above the pumpkin. Repeat. Let stand until set, about 30 minutes. **Yield:** 2 dozen.

Wide-Eyed Owl Cupcakes

(Pictured above)

Prep: 1 hour **Bake:** 20 min. + cooling

"Whooo" wouldn't love these whimsical goodies? Our home economists created spooky birds using purchased sandwich cookies, candies, cereal and chips.

    1 package (18-1/4 ounces) cake mix of your
        choice
    1 can (16 ounces) vanilla frosting
    24 peanut butter cream-filled sandwich cookies
    1/2 cup Froot Loops
    1/4 cup chocolate frosting
Assorted candies: candy corn, butterscotch *or*
    chocolate chips
    48 rye chips

Prepare and bake cake batter according to package directions for cupcakes; cool completely. Frost cupcakes with vanilla frosting.

On each sandwich cookie, attach Froot Loops with chocolate frosting for eyes. Cut off yellow end from candy corn. With chocolate frosting, attach candy corn for beaks and butterscotch chips for ears.

Cut a slit in each cupcake and carefully insert cookie owls. For wings, press rye chips into vanilla frosting. **Yield:** 2 dozen.

Pretzel Pumpkin Grahams

Spooky Spider Cupcakes

(Pictured below)

Prep: 50 min. **Bake:** 20 min. + cooling

These not-so-scary spider cakes are so yummy and a cinch to decorate. You can really let your imagination go wild!
—Edie Despain, Logan, Utah

  1 package (18-1/4 ounces) chocolate cake mix
  1 can (16 ounces) vanilla frosting
Orange paste food coloring
 24 cream-filled chocolate sandwich cookies
Red *or* black shoestring licorice
 48 milk chocolate M&M's

Prepare and bake cake batter according to package directions for cupcakes; cool completely.

In a small bowl, tint the frosting orange; set aside 1 tablespoon. Frost cupcakes with remaining frosting. Place one cookie on each cupcake.

For the spider legs, cut shoestring licorice into 2-in. pieces; press eight pieces into each cupcake. Attach two M&M's to each cookie for the eyes using reserved frosting. **Yield:** 2 dozen.

Creepy Crawly Cupcakes

(Pictured below)

Prep: 30 min. **Bake:** 20 min. + cooling

Even adults will dig into these fun treats. Topped with crushed sandwich cookies and gummy candies, they look like worms crawling out of dirt. I use a convenient boxed mix to make the cupcakes virtually effortless.
—Joyce Moynihan, Lakeville, Minnesota

  1 package (18-1/4 ounces) chocolate cake mix
  1 can (16 ounces) chocolate frosting
 20 cream-filled chocolate sandwich cookies, crushed
 24 gummy worms, halved

Prepare and bake the cake batter according to package directions for cupcakes. Cool completely.

Set aside 1 tablespoon frosting. Frost the cupcakes with the remaining frosting; dip each into crushed sandwich cookies.

Place a dab of the reserved frosting on the cut end of each gummy worm half; place two on each cupcake. **Yield:** 2 dozen.

Spooky Spider Cupcakes
Creepy Crawly Cupcakes

Jack-o'-Lantern Oranges

Black Cat Cupcakes

(Pictured below)

Prep: 1 hour **Bake:** 20 min. + cooling

These "purrrfectly" cute cakes from our home economists use common pantry items. Don't have a star pastry tip? Just spread on the frosting with a knife instead.

> 1 package (18-1/4 ounces) cake mix of your choice
> 1 can (16 ounces) chocolate frosting
> 48 nacho tortilla chips, broken
> 2 cups pretzel sticks
> Assorted candies: yellow gumdrops, miniature marshmallows, pink Nerds candies and red Air Heads candies

Prepare and bake cake batter according to package directions for cupcakes; cool completely. Using a star tip, pipe frosting on cupcakes.

Use pointed tips of tortilla chips for cat ears and pretzel sticks for whiskers. Slice gumdrops. For each eye, press a gumdrop slice onto a marshmallow. Add Nerds candies for noses. Cut Air Heads candies into mouth shapes; position on cupcakes. **Yield:** 2 dozen.

Jack-o'-Lantern Oranges

(Pictured above)

Prep: 1 hour

From our Test Kitchen staff, this recipe is a great way to get children to eat nutritious fruit during the candy-laden Halloween season. Youngsters can even help cut up the apples and grapes with plastic knives and decide how they want their "pumpkin" orange to look.

> 8 small navel oranges
> 1 small apple, chopped
> 1/2 cup halved seedless red grapes
> Slivered almonds and whole cloves

Choose which side of each orange will be the jack-o'-lantern's face; cut a thin slice from the bottom of each so that it rests flat. Cut another small slice from the top. Spoon out pulp. Chop pulp and combine with apple and grapes; set aside.

Cut faces as desired; decorate with almonds and cloves. Spoon fruit mixture into jack-o'-lanterns. **Yield:** 8 servings.

Black Cat Cupcakes

Quick Ghost Cookies

(Pictured above)
Prep/Total Time: 30 min.

I love dressing up store-bought peanut butter cookies to create these cute goblins for Halloween. They're a hit with everyone, and all you need are three ingredients.
—Denise Smith, Lusk, Wyoming

> 1 pound white candy coating, coarsely chopped
> 1 package (1 pound) Nutter Butter peanut butter cookies
Miniature semisweet chocolate chips

In a microwave-safe bowl, melt candy coating, stirring occasionally. Dip cookies into coating, covering completely. Place on waxed paper.

Brush the ends with a pastry brush dipped in coating where fingers touched the cookies. While coating is still warm, place two chips on each cookie for eyes. Let stand until set. Store in an airtight container. **Yield:** about 3 dozen.

Pumpkin Mousse

Prep/Total Time: 10 min.

My family absolutely loves this no-cook, taste-tempting recipe—it's become one of our favorite desserts during the autumn season. The combination of smooth mousse and crunchy graham cracker tart shell is heavenly! Top each individual treat with whipped cream and cinnamon.
—Lisa McCloskey, Dwight, Illinois

> 1 carton (4 ounces) whipped cream cheese with cinnamon and brown sugar
> 1 cup pumpkin pie filling
> 1/2 cup whipped topping
> 6 individual graham cracker tart shells
Additional whipped topping and ground cinnamon

In a small bowl, combine the cream cheese and pumpkin pie filling until blended. Fold in whipped topping. Fill tart shells.

Garnish each with additional whipped topping and sprinkle with cinnamon. Store in the refrigerator. **Yield:** 6 servings.

Thanksgiving Abundance

A CORNUCOPIA of holiday cooking is yours thanks to these special dishes. From the all-important roast bird to the gotta-save-room fruit pies, these mouth-watering favorites will have your family running to your Turkey-Day table...and leaving with smiles!

Sweet and Savory Stuffing

(Pictured below)

Prep: 20 min. **Bake:** 30 min.

This scrumptious stuffing chock-full of bacon, apple and sage is so good, you won't want to limit it to holidays!
—Sharon Ferrante, Mifflintown, Pennsylvania

        1/2 pound bacon strips, diced
        1/2 cup chopped sweet onion
          5 cups unseasoned stuffing cubes
          1 large tart apple, finely chopped
          2 tablespoons minced fresh parsley
          1 teaspoon rubbed sage
        1/2 teaspoon salt
        1/2 teaspoon pepper
    1-1/4 to 1-3/4 cups chicken broth

In a large skillet, cook bacon and onion over medium heat until bacon is crisp. Transfer to a large bowl. Add the stuffing cubes, apple, parsley, sage, salt and pepper. Stir in just enough broth to reach desired moistness.

Transfer to a greased 8-in. square baking dish. Bake, uncovered, at 350° for 30-35 minutes or until golden brown. **Yield:** 7 cups.

Apple-Berry Crumb Pie

Apple-Berry Crumb Pie

(Pictured above)

Prep: 20 min. **Bake:** 40 min. + cooling

Busy cooks on Thanksgiving will love this delectable yet easy apple pie recipe. You don't have to roll out a crust or cut up any apples. —Laurie Jonas, Portage, Wisconsin

    1-1/2 cups quick-cooking oats
        1 cup all-purpose flour
      1/2 cup packed brown sugar
       10 tablespoons butter, melted
        1 can (21 ounces) apple pie filling
      3/4 cup dried cranberries
    1-1/2 teaspoons lemon juice
      1/2 teaspoon ground cinnamon
    Vanilla ice cream, optional

In a large bowl, combine the oats, flour, brown sugar and butter; set aside 3/4 cup for topping. Press remaining mixture onto the bottom and up the sides of a greased 9-in. pie plate. Bake at 375° for 13-17 minutes or until lightly browned.

In another bowl, combine the pie filling, cranberries, lemon juice and cinnamon. Spoon into crust. Sprinkle with reserved oat mixture. Bake for 25-30 minutes or until topping is lightly browned. Cool on a wire rack. Serve with ice cream if desired. **Yield:** 8 servings.

Sweet and Savory Stuffing

Herb-Roasted Turkey

(Pictured above)

Prep: 20 min. **Bake:** 2 hours + standing

Prepared with ordinary ingredients to go in the oven in just 20 minutes, this moist bird tastes truly extraordinary!
—*Groucho_CT_, tasteofhome.com Community*

- 1 tablespoon dried sage leaves
- 1 teaspoon dried thyme
- 1 teaspoon dried rosemary, crushed
- 1 teaspoon seasoned salt
- 1/2 teaspoon pepper
- 1 turkey (14 to 16 pounds)
- 2 tablespoons canola oil
- 1 tablespoon all-purpose flour
- 1 turkey-size oven roasting bag
- 2 celery ribs, sliced
- 1 medium onion, sliced

In a small bowl, combine the first five ingredients. Pat the turkey dry; brush with oil. Sprinkle the herb mixture over the skin of turkey. Skewer turkey openings; tie drumsticks together.

Place flour in oven bag and shake to coat. Place the bag in a roasting pan; add celery and onion. Place turkey, breast side up, over vegetables. Cut six 1/2-in. slits in top of bag; close bag with tie provided.

Bake at 350° for 2 to 2-1/2 hours or until a meat thermometer reads 180°. Remove turkey to a serving platter and keep warm. Let stand for 15 minutes before carving. If desired, thicken pan drippings for gravy. **Yield:** 14 servings.

Mushroom-Rosemary Turkey Gravy

(Pictured above)

Prep/Total Time: 15 min.

This smooth, rich gravy will beautifully complement not only roast turkey and potatoes, but also pork and beef.
—*Cathy Tang, Redmond, Washington*

☑ This recipe includes Nutrition Facts.

Roasted turkey drippings
Chicken broth *or* water
- 1/2 pound sliced fresh mushrooms
- 1/2 teaspoon onion powder
- 1/4 teaspoon dried rosemary, crushed
- 1/4 cup all-purpose flour
- 1/8 teaspoon salt
- 1/8 teaspoon pepper
- 1/8 teaspoon browning sauce, optional

Pour turkey drippings into a measuring cup. Skim fat, reserving 1/4 cup; set aside. Add enough broth or water to the drippings to measure 3 cups.

In a large saucepan, saute mushrooms in reserved fat until tender. Add the onion powder and rosemary; cook 1 minute longer. Stir in the flour, salt and pepper until blended.

Gradually stir in the drippings mixture. Bring to a boil; cook and stir for 2 minutes or until thickened. Stir in browning sauce if desired. **Yield:** 3 cups.

Nutrition Facts: 2 tablespoons equals 30 calories, 2 g fat (1 g saturated fat), 2 mg cholesterol, 46 mg sodium, 2 g carbohydrate, trace fiber, 1 g protein.

Crunchy Walnut Salad

(Pictured above)

Prep/Total Time: 15 min.

This distinctive salad is crunchy, sweet, tart...delicious! I toss one together at least twice a week, but it's elegant enough for meals on holidays, too. Chopped apples, walnuts, dried cherries and Gorgonzola cheese give it special appeal.
—Barbara Discenza, Auburn, Georgia

  4 cups torn romaine
2/3 cup chopped Granny Smith apple (about 1 medium)
2/3 cup walnut halves
1/2 cup dried cherries
1/3 cup prepared raspberry vinaigrette
1/2 cup crumbled Gorgonzola cheese

In a large salad bowl, combine the romaine, apple, walnuts and cherries. Drizzle with vinaigrette. Sprinkle with cheese. **Yield:** 5 servings.

Editor's Note: As a fun variation, use dried cranberries and balsamic vinaigrette in the salad.

Fruit Compote with Brie

Prep/Total Time: 15 min.

For a standout appetizer, this is a wonderful choice. I top the round of Brie cheese, softened in the oven, with a homemade compote of golden raisins, cherries and cherry preserves. If there's any compote left over, I stir it into plain yogurt or serve it over slices of cheesecake.
—Clara Coulston, Washington Court House, Ohio

  1 round (8 ounces) Brie cheese
2/3 cup golden raisins and cherries
1/3 cup unsweetened apple juice
  1 teaspoon vanilla extract
  1 tablespoon cherry preserves
Assorted crackers

Place the Brie cheese on an ungreased oven-proof serving plate. Bake at 400° for 8-10 minutes or until cheese is softened.

Meanwhile, in a small saucepan, combine the golden raisins and cherries, apple juice and vanilla; bring to a boil. Remove from the heat; stir in the cherry preserves. Spoon over Brie cheese. Serve with assorted crackers. **Yield:** 8 servings.

Pecan Pumpkin Pie

(Pictured below)

Prep: 10 min. **Bake:** 55 min. + chilling

Here, a rich, crispy pecan topping lends a mouth-watering twist to creamy pumpkin. It's like getting two favorite pies in one! —Deborah Whitley, Nashville, Tennessee

Pastry for single-crust pie (9 inches)
 2 eggs
 1 can (15 ounces) solid-pack pumpkin
 1/2 cup maple syrup
 1/4 cup sugar
 1/4 cup heavy whipping cream
 1 teaspoon ground cinnamon
 1/2 teaspoon ground nutmeg
TOPPING:
 2 eggs, lightly beaten
 1 cup chopped pecans
 1/2 cup sugar
 1/2 cup maple syrup
Whipped topping, optional

Line a 9-in. pie plate with pastry; trim and flute edges. In a large bowl, beat the eggs, pumpkin, syrup, sugar, cream, cinnamon and nutmeg until smooth; pour into pastry. For topping, combine the eggs, pecans, sugar and syrup; spoon over top.

Bake at 425° for 15 minutes. Reduce heat to 350°. Bake 40-45 minutes longer or until crust is golden brown and top of pie is set. Cool on a wire rack for 1 hour. Refrigerate overnight or until set. Serve with whipped topping if desired. **Yield:** 8 servings.

Spiced Cider Punch

Pecan Pumpkin Pie

Spiced Cider Punch

(Pictured above)

Prep: 15 min. + chilling

I've shared this chilled beverage recipe with many friends. It never wears out its welcome and is so easy to make. It's also good warm. —Charles Piatt, Little Rock, Arkansas

 1 cup sugar
 2 quarts apple cider *or* juice, *divided*
 1 teaspoon ground cinnamon
 1 teaspoon ground allspice
 1 can (12 ounces) frozen orange juice
  concentrate, thawed
 1 quart ginger ale, chilled

In a Dutch oven, combine the sugar, 1 cup cider, cinnamon and allspice. Cook and stir over medium heat until sugar is dissolved. Remove from the heat; add the orange juice concentrate and remaining cider. Cool. Cover and refrigerate until chilled.

Just before serving, transfer to a punch bowl; stir in ginger ale. **Yield:** 13 servings (about 3 quarts).

Pie Possibilities

When I have a pumpkin pie or pumpkin cheesecake recipe that calls for vanilla extract, I replace half of it with orange extract. It adds a unique flavor. —Nancy Zimmerman, Cape May Court House, New Jersey

When making pumpkin pie, I replace half of the evaporated milk called for in the recipe with commercial eggnog. Yum! —Sam Groom, Fort Collins, Colorado

Christmas Day Dinner

DURING the holiday season, there are so many reasons to celebrate. So don't spend time worrying about your menu for December 25th—just look here!

You'll find a succulent prime rib entree, fantastic sides and two luscious cakes—plus a can't-miss appetizer and frosty Grasshopper Shakes. They're all short on fuss but sure to make spirits bright.

Eggnog Tube Cake

(Pictured below)

Prep: 15 min. **Bake:** 40 min. + cooling

My children like the eggnog flavor of this lovely cake…and I like it even more because the recipe is easy to prepare!
—Mary Ellen Severance, Biggs, California

    1 package (18-1/4 ounces) white cake mix
    1 package (3.9 ounces) instant vanilla pudding
      mix
    4 eggs
    1 cup eggnog
    1/4 cup canola oil
    2 teaspoons rum extract
    1-1/2 teaspoons ground nutmeg

Eggnog Tube Cake

GLAZE:
    1 cup confectioners' sugar
    1/4 teaspoon rum extract
    3 to 4 teaspoons eggnog

In a large bowl, combine the cake mix, pudding mix, eggs, eggnog, oil, extract and nutmeg. Beat on medium speed for 2 minutes.

Pour the cake batter into a well-greased 10-in. fluted tube pan. Bake at 350° for 38-41 minutes or until a toothpick inserted near the center comes out clean. Cool on a wire rack for 10 minutes before inverting onto a serving platter.

In a small bowl, combine the confectioners' sugar, extract and enough eggnog to achieve a drizzling consistency. Drizzle the glaze over the cooled cake. **Yield:** 12 servings.

Editor's Note: This recipe was tested with commercially prepared eggnog.

Prime Rib with Horseradish Cream

(Pictured on page 41)

Prep: 30 min. **Bake:** 3 hours + standing

This impressive main course always makes for a wonderful, special dinner. Mouths water over the slices of juicy prime rib and the topping of tongue-tingling cream sauce.
—Margaret Ann Dady, Grand Island, Nebraska

    1 bone-in beef rib roast (6 to 8 pounds)
    3 garlic cloves, sliced
    1 teaspoon pepper
HORSERADISH CREAM:
    1 cup heavy whipping cream
    2 tablespoons prepared horseradish
    2 teaspoons red wine vinegar
    1 teaspoon ground mustard
    1/4 teaspoon sugar
    1/8 teaspoon salt
Dash pepper

Place roast fat side up in a shallow roasting pan. Cut slits into roast; insert garlic slices. Sprinkle with pepper. Bake, uncovered, at 450° for 15 minutes. Reduce heat to 325°; bake 2-3/4 to 3-1/4 hours longer or until meat reaches desired doneness (for medium-rare, a meat thermometer should read 145°; medium, 160°; well-done, 170°).

Meanwhile, in a small bowl, beat the whipping cream until soft peaks form. Fold in the horseradish, vinegar, mustard, sugar, salt and pepper. Cover and refrigerate for 1 hour.

Remove roast to a serving platter and keep warm; let stand for 15 minutes. Serve with the cream. **Yield:** 12 servings (1-1/2 cups cream).

Gruyere Mashed Potatoes
Lemon-Pepper Brussels Sprouts
Prime Rib with Horseradish Cream

Lemon-Pepper Brussels Sprouts

(Pictured above)
Prep/Total Time: 25 min.

In this simple recipe, lemon-pepper seasoning and lemon juice turn brussels sprouts into a delightful side dish.
—Katherine Stallwood, Richland, Washington

☑ This recipe includes Nutrition Facts and Diabetic Exchanges.

   2 **pounds fresh *or* frozen brussels sprouts,**
     thawed and halved
   1 **tablespoon butter**
   1 **tablespoon canola oil**
   3 **green onions, sliced**
   1 **teaspoon lemon juice**
1/2 **teaspoon lemon-pepper seasoning**
1/4 **teaspoon salt**

In a large skillet over medium heat, cook the brussels sprouts in butter and oil for 10-12 minutes or until tender. Add the green onions, lemon juice, lemon-pepper and salt; cook 1 minute longer. **Yield:** 5 servings.

  Nutrition Facts: 3/4 cup equals 126 calories, 6 g fat (2 g saturated fat), 6 mg cholesterol, 227 mg sodium, 17 g carbohydrate, 7 g fiber, 6 g protein. **Diabetic Exchanges:** 2 vegetable, 1 fat.

Gruyere Mashed Potatoes

(Pictured above)
Prep/Total Time: 25 min.

This Christmas season, use this recipe to take ordinary mashed potatoes to a whole new level! The spuds are enhanced with sour cream, green onions, garlic, Gruyere cheese and chives for a wonderful accompaniment to most any meat. If you don't have chives, just use extra green onion.   *—Salsarose, tasteofhome.com Community*

   2 **pounds potatoes, peeled and cubed**
1/2 **cup sour cream**
1/3 **cup milk**
1/4 **cup butter, cubed**
1/4 **cup shredded Gruyere *or* Swiss cheese**
1/4 **cup chopped green onions**
1/4 **cup minced chives**
   1 **teaspoon minced garlic**
1/2 **teaspoon garlic salt**
1/4 **teaspoon pepper**

Place potatoes in a Dutch oven and cover with water. Bring to a boil. Reduce heat; cover and cook for 10-15 minutes or until tender. Drain.

  In a large bowl, mash potatoes with remaining ingredients. **Yield:** 8 servings.

Gingerbread with Compote

(Pictured above)

Prep: 20 min. **Bake:** 30 min. + cooling

Warm fruit and spices make an easy and festive way to dress up a boxed gingerbread mix for Christmas. Add a dollop of whipped topping for the perfect finishing touch.
—Maria Regakis, Somerville, Massachusetts

> 1 package (14-1/2 ounces) gingerbread cake mix
> 2 cans (one 20 ounces, one 8 ounces) unsweetened pineapple tidbits, drained
> 2 cups fresh *or* frozen cranberries
> 1 cup packed brown sugar
> 1 teaspoon ground cinnamon
> 1/4 teaspoon ground nutmeg

Whipped topping

Prepare and bake gingerbread cake mix according to the package directions. Cool completely on a wire rack; cut into squares.

In a small saucepan, combine the pineapple, cranberries, brown sugar, cinnamon and nutmeg. Bring to a boil. Reduce heat; simmer, uncovered, for 8-10 minutes or until cranberries pop, stirring frequently. Cool slightly. Serve with gingerbread. Garnish with whipped topping. **Yield:** 9 servings.

Spiced Pears

Prep/Total Time: 30 min.

With cranberry sauce and oranges, this nicely spiced medley is a refreshing change of pace from the veggie sides on a holiday table. Plus, it's ready in just 30 minutes.
—Ruby Williams, Bogalusa, Louisana

☑ This recipe includes Nutrition Facts.

> 1 can (14 ounces) whole-berry cranberry sauce
> 1/3 cup sugar
> 1 tablespoon lemon juice
> 1/4 teaspoon ground cinnamon
> 1/4 teaspoon ground ginger
> 6 medium pears, peeled and sliced
> 2 medium navel oranges, peeled and sectioned

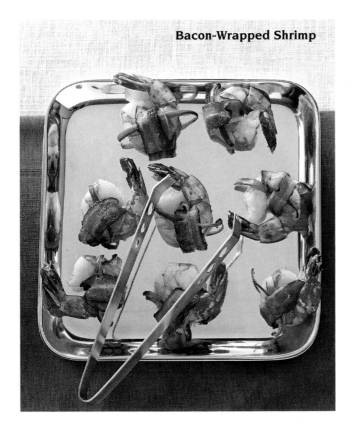

Bacon-Wrapped Shrimp

cure the ends with toothpicks. Place the shrimp on a broiler pan coated with cooking spray.

Broil 4 in. from the heat for 2-3 minutes on each side or until shrimp turn pink, basting frequently with remaining dressing. **Yield:** 2-1/2 dozen.

Nutrition Facts: 1 appetizer equals 34 calories, 2 g fat (1 g saturated fat), 26 mg cholesterol, 113 mg sodium, trace carbohydrate, trace fiber, 4 g protein. **Diabetic Exchange:** 1 lean meat.

Editor's Note: When cutting hot peppers, disposable gloves are recommended. Avoid touching your face.

Grasshopper Shakes

(Pictured below)

Prep/Total Time: 10 min.

Minty, chocolaty and cool, this spiked dessert drink is a wonderful way to toast family and friends at Christmastime gatherings. A little shaved chocolate on top of each pretty green beverage makes a festive garnish.
— *Wabeno_WI, tasteofhome.com Community*

    2 quarts vanilla ice cream
    1 carton (8 ounces) frozen whipped topping, thawed
  3/4 cup green creme de menthe
  3/4 cup creme de cacao

In a blender, cover and process the ingredients in batches until blended. Stir if necessary. Pour into chilled glasses; serve immediately. **Yield:** 10 servings (2-1/2 quarts).

In a large saucepan, combine the cranberry sauce, sugar, lemon juice, cinnamon and ginger. Bring to a boil over medium heat. Stir in pears and oranges; simmer, uncovered, for 15-20 minutes or until pears are tender. **Yield:** 8 servings.

Nutrition Facts: 3/4 cup equals 203 calories, trace fat (trace saturated fat), 0 cholesterol, 14 mg sodium, 53 g carbohydrate, 5 g fiber, 1 g protein.

Bacon-Wrapped Shrimp

(Pictured above)

Prep: 20 min. + marinating **Broil:** 10 min.

I tweaked the original recipe for this appetizer a bit to please my family, and it's been popular ever since. If you'd prefer less heat, simply leave out the sliced jalapenos.
— *Debbie Cheek, State Road, North Carolina*

☑ This recipe includes Nutrition Facts and Diabetic Exchange.

  1/2 cup creamy Caesar salad dressing, *divided*
    1 pound uncooked medium shrimp, peeled and deveined
   15 bacon strips, cut in half
    2 jalapeno peppers, seeded and thinly sliced

Pour 6 tablespoons salad dressing into a large resealable plastic bag; add the shrimp. Seal bag and turn to coat; refrigerate for 15 minutes.

Meanwhile, in a skillet or microwave, cook bacon until cooked but not crisp. Drain on paper towels.

Drain and discard the marinade; place a jalapeno slice on each shrimp. Wrap bacon around the shrimp; se-

Grasshopper Shakes

Homemade Gifts of Good Cheer

THIS CHRISTMAS SEASON, save some "dough" and spoil family and friends at the same time with these goodies from the kitchen. Everyone will love delights such as cute Rudolph Treats, moist Cranberry Pumpkin Bread and rich Microwave Marshmallow Fudge.

Cinnamon Candy Cane Cookies

(Pictured below)

Prep: 25 min. **Bake:** 10 min./batch

With these fun cinnamon goodies from our Test Kitchen staff, you won't believe how much bang you get for your buck. At only 6¢ per cookie, they're priced just right!

☑ This recipe includes Nutrition Facts and Diabetic Exchanges.

    1 cup butter, softened
    1 cup confectioners' sugar
    1 egg
    1 teaspoon vanilla extract
2-1/2 cups all-purpose flour
  3/4 teaspoon salt
  1/2 cup red-hot candies, crushed
  1/2 teaspoon ground cinnamon
Red food coloring, optional
    2 tablespoons coarse sugar

In a large bowl, cream butter and confectioners' sugar until light and fluffy. Beat in egg and vanilla. Combine flour and salt; gradually add to creamed mixture and mix well. Divide dough in half. Mix candies and cinnamon into one half; tint with food coloring if desired.

Shape 1-1/2 teaspoons plain dough into a 4-1/2-in. rope. Shape 1-1/2 teaspoons red dough into a 4-1/2-in. rope. On an ungreased baking sheet, place ropes side by side; press together lightly and twist. Curve top of cookie down to form handle of cane. Repeat with the remaining plain and red dough, placing 2 in. apart on baking sheets. Sprinkle with coarse sugar.

Bake at 375° for 7-10 minutes or until cookies are lightly browned. Cool for 1 minute before removing to wire racks to cool completely. Store in an airtight container. **Yield:** 4 dozen.

Nutrition Facts: 1 cookie equals 80 calories, 4 g fat (2 g saturated fat), 14 mg cholesterol, 65 mg sodium, 10 g carbohydrate, trace fiber, 1 g protein. **Diabetic Exchanges:** 1 fat, 1/2 starch.

Rudolph Treats

Cinnamon Candy Cane Cookies

Rudolph Treats

(Pictured above)

Prep/Total Time: 15 min.

These adorable reindeer are easy enough to make for your family, your friends and just about everyone else you know! The recipe requires only five ingredients and takes a mere 15 minutes to prepare. Kids love to help, too. —Abigail Vandersaul
Saint Paul, Missouri

☑ This recipe includes Nutrition Facts and Diabetic Exchanges.

12 miniature pretzels, halved
12 fun-size Almond Joy candy bars
12 miniature marshmallows, halved
Black decorating gel
12 red M&M's miniature baking bits

Insert an end from two pretzel halves into each candy bar to form antlers. Gently press the cut side of two marshmallow halves onto each candy bar for eyes; dot with decorating gel.

For nose, attach an M&M baking bit to the top of each candy with decorating gel. Store in an airtight container. **Yield:** 1 dozen.

Nutrition Facts: 1 treat equals 104 calories, 5 g fat (4 g saturated fat), 1 mg cholesterol, 52 mg sodium, 14 g carbohydrate, 1 g fiber, 1 g protein. **Diabetic Exchanges:** 1 starch, 1 fat.

Cinnamon Hot Chocolate Mix

(Pictured below)

Prep/Total Time: 10 min.

When our children left for college, they each insisted on taking a large container of this cinnamony cocoa mix with them to the dorm. —Linda Nilsen, Anoka, Minnesota

1-3/4 cups nonfat dry milk powder
1 cup confectioners' sugar
1/2 cup powdered nondairy creamer
1/2 cup baking cocoa
1/2 teaspoon ground cinnamon
1 cup miniature marshmallows
ADDITIONAL INGREDIENTS:
3/4 cup hot milk

Cinnamon Hot Chocolate Mix

Microwave Marshmallow Fudge

In a large bowl, combine the milk powder, confectioners' sugar, creamer, cocoa and cinnamon. Add the marshmallows; mix well. Store in an airtight container in a cool dry place for up to 3 months. **Yield:** 18-19 batches (about 3-1/2 cups total).

To prepare hot chocolate: Dissolve about 3 tablespoons hot chocolate mix in hot milk. **Yield:** 1 serving per batch.

Microwave Marshmallow Fudge

(Pictured above)

Prep: 15 min. + chilling

A batch of this smooth fudge can be whipped up in minutes, so it's perfect when time is short. If you like, use different flavors of frosting and chips for variety.
—Sue Ross, Casa Grande, Arizona

1 teaspoon butter
1 can (16 ounces) chocolate frosting
2 cups (12 ounces) semisweet chocolate chips
1/2 cup chopped walnuts
1/2 cup miniature marshmallows

Line a 9-in. square pan with foil and grease the foil with butter; set aside. In a microwave, melt frosting and chocolate chips; stir until smooth. Stir in walnuts; cool for 10 minutes. Stir in marshmallows. Transfer to prepared pan. Cover and refrigerate until firm.

Using the foil, lift the fudge out of pan. Discard foil; cut into 1-in. squares. Store in an airtight container in the refrigerator. **Yield:** about 2 pounds.

Cranberry Pumpkin Bread

Pecan Caramel Candies

(Pictured below)

Prep: 30 min. **Bake:** 5 min. + cooling

These rich candies are so simple but look and taste like you did a lot of work. Make as many—or as few—as you want. They're great as an option alongside other desserts for guests who want only a bite of something sweet.
—Julie Wemhoff, Angola, Indiana

63 miniature pretzels
63 Rolo candies
63 pecan halves

Line baking sheets with foil. Place pretzels on foil; top each pretzel with a candy.
   Bake at 250° for 4 minutes or until candies are softened (candies will retain their shape). Immediately place a pecan half on each candy and press down so candy fills pretzel. Cool slightly. Refrigerate for 10 minutes or until set. **Yield:** 63 candies (about 1-1/4 pounds).

Chocolate Pretzel Rings

(Pictured below)

Prep/Total Time: 30 min.

With that ever-popular taste combination of sweet and salty, these fun rings go over big with children and adults alike. People always find it hard to eat just one!
—Kim Scurio, Carol Stream, Illinois

48 to 50 pretzel rings *or* miniature pretzels
48 to 50 milk chocolate *or* striped chocolate kisses
1/4 cup milk chocolate M&M's

Cranberry Pumpkin Bread

(Pictured above)

Prep: 15 min. **Bake:** 50 min. + cooling

Everyone calls this "Christmas Bread"—but they insist that I bake it more often than Christmas! We like slices warm with butter or served cool with cream cheese.
—Marilou Robinson, Portland, Oregon

3 cups all-purpose flour
1 teaspoon salt
1 teaspoon baking soda
1 teaspoon baking powder
1 teaspoon ground cinnamon
1/2 teaspoon *each* ground ginger, nutmeg and cloves
3 eggs
2 cups canned pumpkin
1 cup canola oil
2/3 cup sugar
2/3 cup packed brown sugar
3 teaspoons vanilla extract
1 cup dried cranberries
1 cup chopped pecans, toasted

In a large bowl, combine the flour, salt, baking soda, baking powder and spices. In another bowl, combine the eggs, pumpkin, oil, sugars and vanilla; stir into dry ingredients just until moistened. Fold in cranberries and pecans.
   Pour into two greased 8-in. x 4-in. loaf pans. Bake at 350° for 50-55 minutes or until a toothpick inserted near the center comes out clean. Cool for 10 minutes before removing from the pans to wire racks. **Yield:** 2 loaves (12 slices each).

Chocolate Pretzel Rings
Pecan Caramel Candies

Holiday Sugar Cookies

DECORATING:
   1/3 cup light corn syrup
Assorted sprinkles
Shoestring licorice
   1/3 cup flaked coconut
   28 miniature semisweet chocolate chips
   14 red M&M's miniature baking bits
   28 miniature marshmallows, halved

In a large bowl, cream butter and confectioners' sugar until light and fluffy. Beat in egg and extracts. Combine the flour, baking soda and cream of tartar; gradually add to creamed mixture and mix well. Divide dough in half. Cover and chill in the freezer for 25 minutes or until easy to handle.

For lights: On a lightly floured surface, roll one portion of dough to 1/8-in. thickness. Cut with a floured 3-1/2-in. light-shaped cookie cutter. Place 2 in. apart on ungreased baking sheets. Using a plastic straw, make a hole 1/2 in. from the top of each cookie.

Bake at 350° for 6-8 minutes or until edges are lightly browned. Use a plastic straw to reopen holes in cookies. Remove to wire racks to cool completely.

For Santas: Roll remaining dough directly on an ungreased baking sheet into an 11-in. x 8-in. rectangle. Cut lengthwise into two strips, but do not separate. Cut each strip into seven triangles (do not separate).

Bake at 350° for 10-13 minutes or until edges are lightly browned. Cool for 2 minutes; cut around cookies to separate. Remove to a wire rack to cool completely.

To decorate: Microwave corn syrup for 6-8 seconds or until thinned. Working with a few cookies at a time, brush corn syrup over the surface.

For lights, decorate with sprinkles as desired. Thread licorice through holes.

For Santas, press coconut onto faces for beards. Attach chocolate chips for eyes and baking bits for noses. For hats, coat top of cookie with sprinkles; attach marshmallow halves for pom-poms. **Yield:** 4 dozen cookies.

Place the pretzels on greased baking sheets; place a chocolate kiss in the center of each ring. Bake at 275° for 2-3 minutes or until chocolate is softened. Remove from the oven.

Place an M&M candy on each, pressing down slightly so chocolate fills the ring. Refrigerate for 5-10 minutes or until chocolate is firm. Store in an airtight container at room temperature. **Yield:** about 4 dozen.

Holiday Sugar Cookies

(Pictured above)

Prep: 30 min. + chilling
Bake: 10 min./batch + cooling

From our Test Kitchen staff, this convenient recipe lets you make two kinds of Christmas cookies from just one batch of dough. The cute Santas and colorful string of lights are sure to steal the show on your holiday tray.

   1 cup butter, softened
1-1/2 cups confectioners' sugar
   1 egg
   1 teaspoon vanilla extract
   1/2 teaspoon almond extract
2-1/2 cups all-purpose flour
   1 teaspoon baking soda
   1 teaspoon cream of tartar

Hints for Holiday Sugar Cookies

■ A plastic straw is perfect for making the hole in each light bulb cookie. After baking them, use the same straw to reopen each hole.

■ Our Test Kitchen staff measured their dough to get the right dimensions, then cut the triangles freehand so their Santa treats would each be unique.

Apricot Cookie Strips

Apricot Cookie Strips

(Pictured above)

Prep: 25 min. **Bake:** 20 min./batch + standing

This delightfully different cookie is yummy enough to please kids, yet sophisticated enough for adults at dinner parties. —Caroline Wamelink, Cleveland Heights, Ohio

✓ This recipe includes Nutrition Facts and Diabetic Exchanges.

    3/4 cup butter, softened
    3/4 cup sugar
      1 egg
    1/4 teaspoon almond extract
      2 cups all-purpose flour
    1/2 teaspoon cream of tartar
    1/2 teaspoon baking soda
    1/2 teaspoon salt
    1/8 teaspoon ground nutmeg
    1/2 cup apricot preserves
    1/2 cup vanilla or white chips
      1 teaspoon shortening

In a large bowl, cream butter and sugar until light and fluffy. Beat in egg and extract. Combine the flour, cream of tartar, baking soda, salt and nutmeg; gradually add to creamed mixture. Divide dough in half. Shape each half into a 12-in. x 2-1/2-in. rectangle on an ungreased baking sheet.

Using the end of a wooden spoon handle, make a 1/4-in.-deep indentation lengthwise down the center of each log. Bake at 350° for 10 minutes.

Spoon preserves into indentation. Bake 10-12 minutes longer or until lightly browned. Cool for 2 minutes. Remove to a cutting board; cut into 3/4-in. slices. Place on a wire rack.

In a microwave, melt vanilla chips and shortening; stir until smooth. Drizzle over warm cookies. Let stand until set. **Yield:** about 2-1/2 dozen.

Nutrition Facts: 1 cookie equals 108 calories, 5 g fat (3 g saturated fat), 17 mg cholesterol, 88 mg sodium, 15 g carbohydrate, trace fiber, 1 g protein. **Diabetic Exchanges:** 1 starch, 1 fat.

Gingerbread Sandwich Trees

(Pictured below)

Prep: 25 min. + chilling
Bake: 10 min./batch + cooling

Fun and festive, these little Christmas tree cookies are a huge hit with everyone. They're almost too cute to eat!
—Steve Foy, Kirkwood, Missouri

✓ This recipe includes Nutrition Facts.

    3/4 cup butter, softened
      1 cup packed brown sugar
      1 egg
    3/4 cup molasses
      4 cups all-purpose flour
      3 teaspoons pumpkin pie spice
  1-1/2 teaspoons baking soda
  1-1/4 teaspoons ground ginger
    1/4 teaspoon salt
  M&M's miniature baking bits
    3/4 cup vanilla frosting
    1/4 cup confectioners' sugar
  Green food coloring, optional

In a large bowl, cream butter and brown sugar until light and fluffy. Add egg and molasses. Combine the flour, pumpkin pie spice, baking soda, ginger and salt; gradually add to creamed mixture and mix well. Cover and refrigerate for 2 hours or until easy to handle.

On a lightly floured surface, roll dough to 1/8-in. thickness. Cut with a floured 3-in. tree-shaped cookie cutter. Place 2 in. apart on ungreased baking sheets. Gently press baking bits into half of the cookies.

Bake at 325° for 8-10 minutes or until edges are firm. Remove to wire racks to cool completely.

In a small bowl, combine frosting and confectioners' sugar until smooth; tint green if desired. Spread over the bottoms of plain cookies; top with decorated cookies. Store in the refrigerator. **Yield:** 2 dozen.

Nutrition Facts: 1 cookie (calculated without M&M's

Gingerbread Sandwich Trees

miniature baking bits) equals 236 calories, 8 g fat (4 g saturated fat), 24 mg cholesterol, 174 mg sodium, 39 g carbohydrate, 1 g fiber, 2 g protein.

Chocolate-Mint Truffle Cookies

(Pictured above)

Prep: 25 min.
Bake: 10 min./batch + cooling

Wow guests at Yuletide gatherings with these truffle-like cookies from our Test Kitchen cooks. You can vary the toppings to suit different occasions, too.

☑ This recipe includes Nutrition Facts and Diabetic Exchanges.

1/4 cup butter, cubed
  1 cup (6 ounces) semisweet chocolate chips, *divided*
  1 egg
1/3 cup sugar
1/3 cup packed brown sugar
1/2 teaspoon vanilla extract
1/8 teaspoon peppermint extract
  1 cup all-purpose flour
1/3 cup baking cocoa
1/4 teaspoon baking powder
1/8 teaspoon salt
  1 package (4.6 ounces) mint Andes candies, chopped, *divided*
  2 teaspoons shortening, *divided*
1/2 cup vanilla *or* white chips
Optional toppings: chopped nuts, sprinkles and crushed candy canes

In a small saucepan over low heat, melt butter and 1/2 cup chocolate chips. Remove from the heat; stir until smooth. Cool slightly. Stir in the egg, sugars and extracts. Combine the flour, cocoa, baking powder and salt; stir into chocolate mixture. Fold in 3/4 cup Andes candies.

Roll rounded tablespoonfuls of the dough into balls. Place 2 in. apart on ungreased baking sheets. Bake at 350° for 8-10 minutes or until the tops appear slightly dry. Cool for 1 minute before removing to wire racks to cool completely.

In a microwave, melt 1 teaspoon shortening and remaining chocolate chips and Andes candies; stir until smooth. Melt vanilla chips and remaining shortening in a microwave; stir until smooth.

Dip half of the cookies in melted chocolate mixture; dip remaining cookies in melted vanilla mixture. Immediately sprinkle with toppings of your choice. Let stand until set. **Yield:** about 2-1/2 dozen.

Nutrition Facts: 1 cookie equals 112 calories, 6 g fat (4 g saturated fat), 11 mg cholesterol, 30 mg sodium, 15 g carbohydrate, 1 g fiber, 1 g protein. **Diabetic Exchanges:** 1 starch, 1 fat.

Chapter 3

HALF AN HOUR—there isn't much you can accomplish during your busy day in that small amount of time. But there is one thing you *can* do: Serve your family a delicious, wholesome, home-cooked dinner!

It may seem too good to be true...but you'll see for yourself when you glance through this extra-big chapter. It showcases 26 meals that each can be prepared from start to finish in just 30 minutes or less.

Enjoy an entree, plus a side dish or dessert with each meal. Thanks to fast, family-pleasing menus such as fun Pepper Pork Fajitas and Caramel Yogurt Sundaes, you'll have dinner done— in only half an hour!

THINKING THIRTY. Applesauce Barbecued Chicken and Beer-Flavored Potatoes (both recipes on p. 57).

Warm and Welcoming Fare

COME HOME to a fast, flavorful sit-down meal at the end of a wintry day—or any day! Just pull out your skillet and cook these tender Pear Pork Chops from Athena Russell of Florence, South Carolina.

Bacon adds a nice, smoky flavor to the healthful frozen veggie mix our Test Kitchen created to pair with the chops. Dressed up with a little parsley and garlic, colorful Bacon Vegetable Medley makes a versatile and special side dish.

Pear Pork Chops

Prep/Total Time: 25 min.

- 1/4 cup all-purpose flour
- 1 tablespoon dried thyme
- 1/4 teaspoon salt
- 1/4 teaspoon pepper
- 4 boneless pork loin chops (1/2 inch thick and 5 ounces *each*)
- 2 tablespoons olive oil
- 2 tablespoons butter
- 1 medium pear, cut into wedges

In a large resealable plastic bag, combine the flour, thyme, salt and pepper. Add pork, a few pieces at a time, and shake to coat.

In a large skillet, cook chops in oil and butter over medium heat for 6-8 minutes on each side or until meat juices run clear. Remove to a serving plate and keep warm. In the same skillet, saute pear until tender. Serve with pork. **Yield:** 4 servings.

Bacon Vegetable Medley

Prep/Total Time: 20 min.

☑ This recipe includes Nutrition Facts and Diabetic Exchanges.

- 4 cups frozen mixed vegetables
- 2 tablespoons water
- 4 bacon strips, cooked and crumbled
- 1 tablespoon olive oil
- 1/2 teaspoon dried parsley flakes
- 1/4 teaspoon garlic powder
- 1/4 teaspoon pepper
- 1/8 teaspoon salt

Place vegetables and water in a 1-qt. microwave-safe dish. Cover and microwave on high for 13-15 minutes or until crisp-tender, stirring once; drain. Stir in the remaining ingredients. **Yield:** 4 servings.

Editor's Note: This recipe was tested in a 1,100-watt microwave.

Nutrition Facts: 3/4 cup equals 172 calories, 6 g fat (1 g saturated fat), 7 mg cholesterol, 284 mg sodium, 24 g carbohydrate, 8 g fiber, 8 g protein. **Diabetic Exchanges:** 2 vegetable, 1 starch, 1 fat.

Bacon Vegetable Medley
Pear Pork Chops

Southwest Tortilla Pizzas
Easy Spanish Rice

Spicy Spread For Supper

LOOKING to give dinnertime a kick? Fix this fast menu bursting with Tex-Mex flavor. For a heat level that suits your family, simply choose the appropriate picante sauce and salsa: mild, medium or hot.

From Martha Pollock of Oregonia, Ohio, Southwest Tortilla Pizzas will make you want to crank up the mariachi music! These meatless pies are filling thanks to plenty of refried beans and cheese.

Easy Spanish Rice makes the ideal side. "I created it while trying to replace a microwave rice dish," says Susan LeBrun of Sulphur, Louisiana. "I like that this version has fewer calories and less sodium."

Southwest Tortilla Pizzas

Prep/Total Time: 25 min.

1 can (16 ounces) refried beans
1 can (4 ounces) chopped green chilies, drained
1/4 teaspoon garlic powder
1/4 teaspoon ground cumin
1/4 teaspoon chili powder
8 flour tortillas (6 inches)
3/4 cup salsa
1/2 cup chopped green pepper
1/2 cup chopped sweet onion
3/4 cup shredded cheddar cheese

In a small bowl, combine the first five ingredients. Place four tortillas on an ungreased baking sheet; spread with bean mixture to within 1/2 in. of the edges. Top with remaining tortillas. Spoon salsa over tops. Sprinkle with pepper, onion and cheese.

Bake at 400° for 10-15 minutes or until cheese is melted. **Yield:** 4 servings.

Easy Spanish Rice

Prep/Total Time: 15 min.

2 cups water
2 cups instant brown rice
1 envelope enchilada sauce mix
1 cup picante sauce

In a large saucepan, bring water to a boil; stir in rice and sauce mix. Return to a boil. Reduce heat; cover and simmer for 5 minutes. Remove from the heat; stir in picante sauce. Let stand for 5 minutes before serving. **Yield:** 4 servings.

Awesome Asian Menu

BORED with the same old foods on weeknights? Try something new for dinner tonight. This quick menu with Asian flair is guaranteed to shake the doldrums out of any evening.

In fact, your family will feel like they're dining on specialties at an Asian restaurant instead of on a home-cooked meal at your kitchen table! And they'll never guess that this impressive meal required a mere 25 minutes to prepare.

Start out your deliciously different supper with Asian Sesame Cod from Trisha Kruse. The wonderfully flavored seafood entree will have everyone at the table raving.

"I always get compliments when I serve this main course," Trisha writes from Eagle, Idaho. "And I love the fact that it's on the healthier side—low in fat, calories and sodium."

Pair the fish with super-easy Vegetable Stir-Fry from Kelly Graham of St. Thomas, Ontario. After you chop the veggies, the side dish comes together in less than 10 minutes...and is so aromatic that mouths will be watering from rooms away.

Add some store-bought sesame or fortune cookies and cups of hot tea, and you'll finish off your taste-of-the-Orient feast in perfect fashion!

Vegetable Stir-Fry

Prep/Total Time: 20 min.

☑ This recipe includes Nutrition Facts and Diabetic Exchanges.

      4 teaspoons cornstarch
      1 cup chicken broth
    3/4 teaspoon soy sauce
  1-1/4 cups julienned celery
  1-1/4 cups julienned green pepper
  1-1/4 cups julienned carrot
    2/3 cup sliced fresh mushrooms
    1/3 cup chopped onion
      2 tablespoons canola oil

In a small bowl, combine the cornstarch, chicken broth and soy sauce until smooth; set aside.

In a large skillet or wok, stir-fry the vegetables in oil for 4-7 minutes or until crisp-tender. Stir in the soy sauce mixture. Bring to a boil; cook and stir for 2 minutes or until thickened. **Yield:** 4 servings.

Nutrition Facts: 3/4 cup equals 110 calories, 7 g fat (1 g saturated fat), 1 mg cholesterol, 361 mg sodium, 11 g carbohydrate, 3 g fiber, 2 g protein. **Diabetic Exchanges:** 2 vegetable, 1-1/2 fat.

Asian Sesame Cod

Prep/Total Time: 25 min.

☑ This recipe includes Nutrition Facts and Diabetic Exchanges.

      1 pound cod fillets
    1/4 cup white wine *or* chicken broth
      3 green onions, thinly sliced
      1 tablespoon brown sugar
      1 tablespoon minced fresh gingerroot
      1 tablespoon rice vinegar
      1 tablespoon soy sauce
      1 tablespoon sesame oil
  1-1/2 teaspoons minced garlic
    1/2 teaspoon lemon-pepper seasoning
      1 tablespoon sesame seeds, toasted

Place the cod fillets in a greased 8-in. square baking dish. In a small bowl, combine the wine, green onions, brown sugar, ginger, rice vinegar, soy sauce, oil, garlic and lemon-pepper. Spoon over the fish fillets; sprinkle with sesame seeds.

Bake, uncovered, at 400° for 15-20 minutes or until fish flakes easily with a fork. **Yield:** 4 servings.

Nutrition Facts: 1 serving equals 158 calories, 5 g fat (1 g saturated fat), 43 mg cholesterol, 354 mg sodium, 6 g carbohydrate, trace fiber, 19 g protein. **Diabetic Exchanges:** 3 very lean meat, 1 fat, 1/2 starch.

Vegetable Stir-Fry
Asian Sesame Cod

Fried Chicken Dinner—Fast!

ANY NIGHT is the perfect night for a fried chicken dinner with mashed potatoes and gravy. But this is not take-out chicken—this is Shirley Little's quick-and-simple recipe for Fried Chicken Tenders. The Alvord, Texas cook uses tasty sesame crackers in the crust. Whip up the gravy, and you've got the majority of the work done!

For the perfect side, try Garlic Mashed Potatoes. "It's a good way to spice up instant potatoes," says Carolyn Coop of Stuarts Draft, Virginia. "I fix this when I want something that tastes homemade but am running out of time to get dinner on the table."

Fried Chicken Tenders

Prep/Total Time: 25 min.

2 eggs
1 tablespoon water
1 pound boneless skinless chicken breasts, cut into 1-inch strips
1 package (8 ounces) sesame crackers, crushed (about 4 cups)
1/4 to 1/2 cup canola oil
1 envelope instant chicken gravy mix, optional

In a shallow bowl, combine eggs and water. Dip chicken in egg mixture, then coat with cracker crumbs. In an electric skillet, heat oil to 375°. Fry chicken strips, a few at a time, for 5-6 minutes or until golden brown. Drain on paper towels.

Meanwhile, prepare gravy according to package directions if desired. Serve with chicken. **Yield:** 4 servings.

Garlic Mashed Potatoes

Prep/Total Time: 15 min.

2 cups water
3 tablespoons butter, cubed
1/2 to 1 teaspoon garlic powder
1/2 teaspoon salt
1/4 teaspoon pepper
3/4 cup milk
2 cups mashed potato flakes

In a large saucepan, combine water, butter, garlic powder, salt and pepper. Bring to a boil. Remove from the heat; add milk. Stir in flakes with a fork. **Yield:** 4 servings.

Flavor They'll Rave Over

A VEGGIE COMBO with chili powder, nuts, vinegar and maple syrup? It may sound strange, but the irresistible flavor of Glazed Brussels Sprouts from Joan Braun of Lakewood, Wisconsin will have your family asking for more. It's a terrific side dish for Saucy Beef Patties, the zesty main course shared by Bernice Morris of Marshfield, Missouri. Try it and see!

Saucy Beef Patties

Prep/Total Time: 30 min.

✓ This recipe includes Nutrition Facts and Diabetic Exchanges.

```
   1 egg, lightly beaten
 1/2 cup soft bread crumbs
 1/2 teaspoon salt
 1/4 teaspoon pepper
   1 pound ground beef
   1 can (8 ounces) tomato sauce
   2 tablespoons chopped green onion
   2 tablespoons brown sugar
   1 teaspoon Worcestershire sauce
   1 teaspoon prepared yellow mustard
```

In a large bowl, combine the egg, bread crumbs, salt and pepper. Crumble beef over mixture and mix well. Shape into four patties. In a large skillet, brown patties on each side. Remove and set aside; drain drippings.

In the same skillet, combine the remaining ingredients. Return patties to the skillet. Bring to a boil. Reduce heat; simmer, uncovered, for 10 minutes or until a meat thermometer reads 160°. **Yield:** 4 servings.

Nutrition Facts: 1 beef patty with 1/4 cup sauce equals 253 calories, 12 g fat (5 g saturated fat), 108 mg cholesterol, 717 mg sodium, 13 g carbohydrate, 1 g fiber, 23 g protein. **Diabetic Exchanges:** 3 lean meat, 1 starch, 1 fat.

Glazed Brussels Sprouts

Prep/Total Time: 25 min.

```
   1 pound fresh brussels sprouts, halved
 1/2 cup fresh baby carrots, halved
   1 cup pecan halves
 1/4 teaspoon chili powder
   3 tablespoons butter
 1/4 cup maple syrup
   2 teaspoons cider vinegar
 1/2 teaspoon salt
```

Place brussels sprouts and carrots in a large saucepan; cover with water. Bring to a boil. Reduce heat; cover and simmer for 8 minutes or until crisp-tender. Meanwhile, in a large skillet, saute pecans and chili powder in butter for 2 minutes. Drain vegetables; add to pecan mixture. Stir in syrup, vinegar and salt. Cook and stir for 3-5 minutes or until brussels sprouts are tender. Serve with a slotted spoon. **Yield:** 5 servings.

Barbecue Appeal Indoors

FEED your family with a stick-to-your-ribs meal that's sure to fill 'em up quick! You'll need only a few ingredients for the main course—sweet and peppery Applesauce Barbecue Chicken from Darla Andrews of Farmers Branch, Texas.

"A side of Beer-Flavored Potatoes always goes over big," relates Lucile Cline from her kitchen in Wichita, Kansas. Chopped green pepper and onion add a great extra layer of taste and texture.

Applesauce Barbecue Chicken

Prep/Total Time: 20 min.

☑ This recipe includes Nutrition Facts and Diabetic Exchanges.

    4 boneless skinless chicken breast halves
      (6 ounces *each*)
1/2 teaspoon pepper
    1 tablespoon olive oil
2/3 cup chunky applesauce
2/3 cup spicy barbecue sauce
    2 tablespoons brown sugar
    1 teaspoon chili powder

Sprinkle chicken with pepper. In a large skillet, brown chicken in oil on both sides.

In a small bowl, combine the remaining ingredients; pour over the chicken. Cover and cook 7-10 minutes longer or until a meat thermometer reads 170°. **Yield:** 4 servings.

Nutrition Facts: 1 chicken breast half with 1/3 cup sauce equals 308 calories, 8 g fat (2 g saturated fat), 94 mg cholesterol, 473 mg sodium, 22 g carbohydrate, 1 g fiber, 35 g protein. **Diabetic Exchanges:** 5 very lean meat, 1-1/2 starch, 1/2 fat.

Beer-Flavored Potatoes

Prep/Total Time: 30 min.

    4 medium potatoes (about 1-1/4 pounds), cut
      into 1/2-inch wedges
    2 tablespoons olive oil
1/4 teaspoon salt
1/4 teaspoon pepper
    1 medium green pepper, cut into 1/2-inch
      pieces
1/2 cup chopped onion
1/4 cup beer *or* nonalcoholic beer
1/4 cup beef broth
    1 tablespoon brown sugar

In a large skillet over medium heat, cook potatoes in oil for 15 minutes, turning occasionally. Sprinkle with salt and pepper. Stir in green pepper and onion; cook 5 minutes longer, stirring occasionally.

In a small bowl, combine the beer, broth and brown sugar. Stir into vegetables. Bring to boil. Reduce heat; cook 2 minutes longer. **Yield:** 4 servings.

Beer-Flavored Potatoes
Applesauce Barbecue Chicken

Orange-Glazed Broccoli
Crispy Herb-Coated Pork Chops

Pork Chop Perfection

WONDERING WHAT to serve for dinner tonight? With this go-to menu at your fingertips, you'll have it all figured out in no time!

From Ann Jovanovic of Chicago, Illinois, Crispy Herb-Coated Pork Chops will please everyone at the table. "I created this one night when I ran out of my usual coating mix for pork chops," says Ann.

For a great green veggie, try sweet Orange-Glazed Broccoli. "The recipe's based on one my neighbor gave me, years ago," says Barbara Langan of Croton-On-Hudson, New York. "We all love it."

Crispy Herb-Coated Pork Chops

Prep/Total Time: 25 min.

1/3 cup butter, cubed
2/3 cup butter and herb-flavored mashed potato flakes
2/3 cup grated Parmesan cheese
3/4 teaspoon garlic powder
4 bone-in center-cut pork loin chops (6 ounces *each* and 1 inch thick)
2 tablespoons canola oil

In a shallow bowl, melt butter. In a large resealable plastic bag, combine the potato flakes, cheese and gar-lic powder. Dip the chops, one at a time, in butter, then place in bag; seal and shake to coat.

In a large skillet, cook chops in oil over medium heat for 7-8 minutes on each side or until meat juices run clear. **Yield:** 4 servings.

Orange-Glazed Broccoli

Prep/Total Time: 20 min.

☑ This recipe includes Nutrition Facts and Diabetic Exchanges.

5 cups frozen broccoli florets
2 tablespoons water
1 tablespoon butter
2 green onions, sliced
1/2 cup orange juice
1 tablespoon brown sugar
1-1/2 teaspoons cornstarch
1/2 teaspoon salt
1 teaspoon grated orange peel

Place broccoli and water in a microwave-safe bowl. Cover and microwave on high for 6-8 minutes or until broccoli is tender; drain.

Meanwhile, in a small saucepan, melt butter. Cook onions in butter for 1 minute. In a small bowl, combine the orange juice, brown sugar, cornstarch and salt until smooth. Stir into saucepan. Bring to a boil; cook and stir for 2 minutes or until thickened. Stir in orange peel; toss broccoli with sauce. **Yield:** 4 servings.

Editor's Note: This recipe was tested in a 1,100-watt microwave.

Nutrition Facts: 3/4 cup equals 81 calories, 3 g fat (2 g saturated fat), 8 mg cholesterol, 336 mg sodium, 12 g carbohydrate, 2 g fiber, 2 g protein. **Diabetic Exchanges:** 1 vegetable, 1/2 starch, 1/2 fat.

A Line on a Fish Dinner

LOOKING for a way to get more heart-healthy fish into your family's diet? You'll win them over hook, line and sinker with Tilapia Florentine from Melanie Bachman of Ulysses, Pennsylvania. Featuring spinach and a splash of lime, it's sure to become a favorite.

Pair that entree with pretty Pineapple-Glazed Carrots from Anna Stodolak of Volant, Pennsylvania. They're table-ready in just 10 minutes!

Tilapia Florentine

Prep/Total Time: 30 min.

- 1 package (6 ounces) fresh baby spinach
- 6 teaspoons canola oil, *divided*
- 4 tilapia fillets (4 ounces *each*)
- 2 tablespoons lime juice
- 2 teaspoons garlic-herb seasoning blend
- 1 egg, lightly beaten
- 1/2 cup part-skim ricotta cheese
- 1/4 cup grated Parmesan cheese

In a nonstick skillet, cook spinach in 4 teaspoons oil until wilted; drain.

Meanwhile, place tilapia in a greased 13-in. x 9-in. baking dish. Drizzle with lime juice and remaining oil. Sprinkle with seasoning blend. In a small bowl, combine the egg, ricotta cheese and spinach; spoon over fillets. Sprinkle with Parmesan cheese.

Bake at 375° for 15-20 minutes or until fish flakes easily with a fork. **Yield:** 4 servings.

Pineapple-Glazed Carrots

Prep/Total Time: 10 min.

☑ **This recipe includes Nutrition Facts and Diabetic Exchanges.**

- 1 package (16 ounces) fresh baby carrots
- 2 tablespoons water
- 1/4 cup pineapple preserves
- 2 tablespoons sugar
- 2 tablespoons butter
- 1/4 teaspoon salt
- 1 tablespoon minced fresh parsley

Place carrots and water in a microwave-safe bowl. Cover and microwave on high for 4-6 minutes or until crisp-tender; drain and keep warm.

In another microwave-safe bowl, combine preserves, sugar, butter and salt; cook on high for 1-2 minutes or until preserves are melted. Pour over carrots; toss to coat. Sprinkle with parsley. **Yield:** 4 servings.

Editor's Note: This recipe was tested in a 1,100-watt microwave.

Nutrition Facts: 3/4 cup equals 164 calories, 6 g fat (4 g saturated fat), 15 mg cholesterol, 277 mg sodium, 29 g carbohydrate, 2 g fiber, 1 g protein. **Diabetic Exchanges:** 2 vegetable, 1 starch, 1 fat.

**Pineapple-Glazed Carrots
Tilapia Florentine**

Soup for a Super Meal

1 tablespoon soy sauce
1 tablespoon molasses

In a large skillet, cook beef and onion over medium heat until meat is no longer pink; drain. Stir in the remaining ingredients. Bring to a boil. Reduce heat; cover and simmer for 10 minutes or until hot and bubbly. **Yield:** 4 servings.

AT THE END of a long day, you want to serve your family something fast yet substantial. Hot and hearty Beef Vegetable Soup from D. M. Hillock of Hartford, Michigan really fills the bill.

To round out your satisfying supper, bake a batch of savory Walnut Cheese Crescents, shared by Irene McDade of Cumberland, Rhode Island.

Beef Vegetable Soup
Prep/Total Time: 25 min.

1 pound ground beef
1/2 cup chopped onion
1 can (15 ounces) tomato sauce
1-1/2 cups frozen mixed vegetables, thawed
1-1/4 cups frozen corn, thawed
1-1/4 cups beef broth

Walnut Cheese Crescents
Prep/Total Time: 25 min.

1 tablespoon butter, melted
1/4 teaspoon onion powder
1/8 teaspoon dill weed
1/8 teaspoon paprika
1 tube (8 ounces) refrigerated crescent rolls
1/2 cup finely chopped walnuts
1/4 cup grated Parmesan cheese

In a small bowl, combine the butter, onion powder, dill and paprika; set aside. Unroll and separate crescent dough into eight triangles. Brush with the butter mixture; sprinkle with walnuts and Parmesan cheese to within 1/8 in. of edges.

Roll up from the wide end and place point side down 2 in. apart on an ungreased baking sheet. Curve ends to form crescents. Bake at 375° for 8-10 minutes or until golden brown. Serve warm. **Yield:** 8 servings.

Summer's Breezy Best

ON THOSE hot summer days when you want something light and refreshing but fuss-free, consider whipping up the rapid recipes here. You'll have a complete, crowd-pleasing meal ready to serve your family in just 25 minutes!

Loaded with colorful, garden-fresh ingredients, Mary Meek's hearty Cobb Salad with Chili-Lime Dressing has something for everyone. "I made this dish for a party, and it was a huge hit," she relates from Toledo, Ohio.

Hot sauce gives the salad a little kick, while cilantro and avocado cool things off. "This recipe is also a great way to use up any leftover cooked chicken you may have in the fridge," Mary notes.

From Linda Finchman of Spencer, West Virginia, five-ingredient Parmesan Breadsticks make a goof-proof accompaniment to the main-dish salad. Convenient refrigerated breadsticks are jazzed up with cumin and paprika. Serve them warm from the oven, then watch them disappear in a flash!

Cobb Salad with Chili-Lime Dressing

Prep/Total Time: 25 min.

- 1 can (4 ounces) chopped green chilies, undrained
- 2/3 cup sour cream
- 1/4 cup fresh cilantro leaves, coarsely chopped
- 2 tablespoons lime juice
- 1/2 teaspoon pepper
- 1/4 to 1/2 teaspoon hot pepper sauce
- 1/4 teaspoon salt
- 1 package (10 ounces) hearts of romaine salad mix
- 1 can (16 ounces) kidney beans, rinsed and drained
- 1 cup (4 ounces) shredded Monterey Jack cheese
- 1 cup chopped tomatoes
- 1 package (7-1/2 ounces) frozen diced cooked chicken breast, thawed
- 1 medium ripe avocado, peeled and cubed
- 1/2 cup chopped red onion
- 1/3 cup real bacon bits

Place the first seven ingredients in a food processor; cover and process until blended. Chill the salad dressing until serving.

In a large bowl, layer the romaine salad mix, kidney beans, Monterey Jack cheese, tomatoes, chicken, avocado, red onion and bacon bits. Drizzle with prepared salad dressing. **Yield:** 8 servings.

Parmesan Breadsticks

Prep/Total Time: 15 min.

☑ This recipe includes Nutrition Facts and Diabetic Exchanges.

- 1/2 cup grated Parmesan cheese
- 1/4 teaspoon paprika
- 1/8 teaspoon ground cumin
- 3 tablespoons butter, melted
- 1 tube (11 ounces) refrigerated breadsticks

In a shallow bowl, combine the Parmesan cheese, paprika and cumin. Place the butter in another shallow bowl. Separate the breadstick dough into individual breadsticks. Dip in the butter, then in the cheese mixture. Twist two to three times and place on an ungreased baking sheet.

Bake at 375° for 10-12 minutes or until breadsticks are golden brown. Serve immediately. **Yield:** 1 dozen.

Editor's Note: This recipe was tested with Pillsbury refrigerated breadsticks.

Nutrition Facts: 1 breadstick equals 110 calories, 5 g fat (3 g saturated fat), 10 mg cholesterol, 256 mg sodium, 13 g carbohydrate, trace fiber, 3 g protein. **Diabetic Exchanges:** 1 starch, 1/2 fat.

Parmesan Breadsticks
Cobb Salad with Chili-Lime Dressing

Saucy and Special Supper

YES, YOU CAN serve quick-and-easy recipes and still treat your family and friends to fancy, restaurant-quality fare. This impressive 20-minute dinner proves it's true!

From Priscilla Gilbert of Indian Harbour Beach, Florida, Pork Chops with Blackberry Sauce will make an ordinary weeknight supper seem like an event. The tongue-tingling topping goes together in a snap on the stovetop...and really dresses up the tender broiled chops.

For the ideal accompaniment, look no further than Herb Vegetable Medley. Shared by Taryn Kuebelbeck of Plymouth, Minnesota, the nicely seasoned beans and carrots make a colorful, tasty plate-filler.

You'll want to keep these herb-flecked veggies in mind for other menus as well. That's because they go well not only with pork, but also with grilled chicken, fish fillets—nearly any entree at all.

Herb Vegetable Medley
Pork Chops with Blackberry Sauce

Pork Chops with Blackberry Sauce
Prep/Total Time: 20 min.

✓ This recipe includes Nutrition Facts and Diabetic Exchanges.

> 4 bone-in pork loin chops (7 ounces *each*)
> 1/4 cup seedless blackberry spreadable fruit
> 3 tablespoons ketchup
> 1/4 teaspoon minced garlic
> 1/4 teaspoon prepared mustard
> 1/4 teaspoon cornstarch
> 1 tablespoon A.1. steak sauce

Broil chops 3-4 in. from the heat for 4-6 minutes on each side or until a meat thermometer reads 160°.

Meanwhile, in a small saucepan, combine the spreadable fruit, ketchup, garlic and mustard. Bring to a boil. Combine cornstarch and steak sauce until smooth. Gradually stir into pan. Bring to a boil; cook and stir for 2 minutes or until thickened. Serve with chops. **Yield:** 4 servings.

Nutrition Facts: 1 chop with 2 tablespoons sauce equals 261 calories, 8 g fat (3 g saturated fat), 86 mg cholesterol, 279 mg sodium, 14 g carbohydrate, trace fiber, 30 g protein. **Diabetic Exchanges:** 4 lean meat, 1 starch.

Herb Vegetable Medley
Prep/Total Time: 20 min.

✓ This recipe includes Nutrition Facts and Diabetic Exchange.

> 1 package (16 ounces) frozen waxed beans, green beans and carrots
> 2 tablespoons water
> 1/4 to 1/2 teaspoon dried thyme
> 1/4 to 1/2 teaspoon dried basil
> 1/4 teaspoon salt
> 1/4 teaspoon pepper
> 2 teaspoons olive oil
> 1/2 teaspoon white wine vinegar

Place vegetables and water in a microwave-safe bowl. Cover and microwave on high for 9-11 minutes or until vegetables are tender.

Meanwhile, combine thyme, basil, salt and pepper. Drain vegetables; drizzle with oil and vinegar. Sprinkle with seasoning mixture; toss to coat. **Yield:** 4 servings.

Nutrition Facts: 3/4 cup equals 58 calories, 2 g fat (trace saturated fat), 0 cholesterol, 151 mg sodium, 9 g carbohydrate, 3 g fiber, 2 g protein. **Diabetic Exchange:** 2 vegetable.

Why White Wine?

Although its flavor is pungent, white wine vinegar is milder than distilled white vinegar. Distilled white vinegar has a strong sharp flavor and is most often used for pickling foods and as a cleaning agent. For savory dishes, most people prefer white wine vinegar.

Toasted Artichoke Sandwiches
Cajun Potato Wedges

Casual Combo Anytime

WHETHER you want something hot and hearty for a weekend lunch or need an effortless supper on a busy weekday, you'll have your meal well in hand with this casual, carefree menu.

Everyone is sure to love Toasted Artichoke Sandwiches from Teri Lange of Schaumburg, Illinois...and even more so with a side of Cajun Potato Wedges from Merle Dyck of Elkford, British Columbia.

Cajun Potato Wedges

Prep/Total Time: 30 min.

☑ This recipe includes Nutrition Facts and Diabetic Exchange.

 3 medium potatoes (1-1/2 pounds)
 1 tablespoon olive oil
 2 to 3 teaspoons Cajun seasoning

Cut each potato lengthwise into eight wedges; place in a greased 15-in. x 10-in. x 1-in. baking pan. Drizzle with oil. Sprinkle with Cajun seasoning; toss to coat.

Bake at 450° for 20-25 minutes or until the potato wedges are tender, turning once. **Yield:** 4 servings.

Nutrition Facts: 6 potato wedges equals 156 calories, 4 g fat (1 g saturated fat), 0 cholesterol, 341 mg sodium, 29 g carbohydrate, 3 g fiber, 3 g protein. **Diabetic Exchange:** 2 starch.

Toasted Artichoke Sandwiches

Prep/Total Time: 20 min.

 1 can (14 ounces) water-packed artichoke hearts, rinsed, drained and chopped
 1 medium sweet red pepper, julienned
 1 medium onion, halved and thinly sliced
 1 tablespoon canola oil
 3/4 cup shredded Parmesan cheese
 1/3 cup mayonnaise
 1/3 cup sun-dried tomatoes (not packed in oil)
 8 slices Italian bread (1/2 inch thick)
 8 spinach leaves
 1/4 cup butter, softened

In a large skillet, saute the artichokes, pepper and onion in oil until tender; stir in cheese. Remove from the heat.

In a food processor, combine mayonnaise and tomatoes; cover and process until finely chopped.

Spread four bread slices with half of the mayonnaise mixture; layer with a spinach leaf, artichoke mixture and remaining spinach. Spread the remaining bread with the mayonnaise mixture; place on top. Butter the outsides of sandwiches.

On a griddle, toast sandwiches for 2-3 minutes on each side or until bread is lightly browned. **Yield:** 4 servings.

From the Sea In a Snap

SEAFOOD AND PASTA are a natural combination, but toss in fresh broccoli and white wine, and *voila*—you have an unforgettable entree! After savoring Shrimp & Broccoli with Pasta from Betty Anderson of Cokato, Minnesota, treat everyone to ice cream with Orange Rhubarb Sauce. Pat Burnley of Lancaster, Pennsylvania shares the yummy recipe.

Orange Rhubarb Sauce

Prep/Total Time: 30 min.

☑ This recipe includes Nutrition Facts.

> 2 cups chopped fresh *or* frozen rhubarb
> 1 cup sugar
> 1/2 cup water
> 1 tablespoon quick-cooking tapioca
> 2 medium navel oranges, peeled and sectioned
> 1 can (11 ounces) mandarin oranges, drained
> Vanilla ice cream *and/or* pound cake

In a large saucepan, combine the rhubarb, sugar, water and tapioca; let stand for 15 minutes. Cook and stir over medium-high heat until mixture comes to a boil. Reduce heat; simmer, uncovered, for 7 minutes or until rhubarb is tender. Stir in oranges; heat through. Serve over ice cream and/or pound cake. **Yield:** about 2 cups.

Nutrition Facts: 1/4 cup (calculated without ice cream and pound cake) equals 149 calories, trace fat (trace saturated fat), 0 cholesterol, 4 mg sodium, 38 g carbohydrate, 2 g fiber, 1 g protein.

Shrimp & Broccoli with Pasta

Prep/Total Time: 25 min.

> 8 ounces uncooked angel hair pasta
> 1-1/2 pounds uncooked large shrimp, peeled and deveined
> 5 teaspoons canola oil, *divided*
> 1 bunch broccoli, cut into florets
> 4 garlic cloves, thinly sliced
> 6 tablespoons butter, cubed
> 6 tablespoons white wine *or* chicken broth
> 2 tablespoons grated Parmesan cheese
> 1/2 teaspoon salt
> 1/4 teaspoon pepper

Cook pasta according to package directions. Meanwhile, in a large skillet or wok, stir-fry shrimp in 3 teaspoons oil for 1-2 minutes or until shrimp turn pink. Remove with a slotted spoon and keep warm.

Stir-fry broccoli in remaining oil for 3 minutes. Add garlic; stir-fry 2 minutes longer or until vegetables are crisp-tender.

Add the butter, wine, cheese, salt and pepper. Drain pasta; add to skillet. Stir in shrimp; heat through. **Yield:** 6 servings.

Orange Rhubarb Sauce

Home Cooking On a Budget

HERE'S a family-pleasing meal that's as easy on your pocketbook as it is on your schedule! At just about a dollar a plate, this mouth-watering menu is hard to beat on a busy weeknight.

From Joe Vince of Port Huron, Michigan, juicy Italian Pork Chops are simmered in a scrumptious sauce. And Green Peas with Onion from Lorraine Stromberg of Taylor, Texas offers a hint of garlic for a tasty side.

Italian Pork Chops

Prep/Total Time: 30 min.

    4 boneless pork loin chops (1 inch thick and
        6 ounces each)
1/4 teaspoon pepper
    4 teaspoons butter
1/3 cup white wine *or* chicken broth
1/3 cup prepared Italian salad dressing

Sprinkle pork chops with pepper. In a large skillet, brown chops in butter over medium heat. Add wine and salad dressing. Cover and cook for 10-12 minutes or until a meat thermometer reads 160°.

Remove pork chops and keep warm. Bring cooking juices to a boil; cook until reduced to 1/2 cup. Serve with pork. **Yield:** 4 servings.

Green Peas with Onion

Prep/Total Time: 20 min.

✓ This recipe includes Nutrition Facts and Diabetic Exchanges.

    1 medium onion, sliced
    1 teaspoon minced garlic
    2 tablespoons butter
    1 package (16 ounces) frozen peas
    3 tablespoons water
1/2 teaspoon salt
1/4 teaspoon pepper

In a large skillet, saute onion and garlic in butter until tender. Add peas and water. Bring to a boil. Reduce heat; cover and simmer for 4-5 minutes or until peas are tender. Season with salt and pepper. **Yield:** 5 servings.

Nutrition Facts: 3/4 cup equals 123 calories, 5 g fat (3 g saturated fat), 12 mg cholesterol, 371 mg sodium, 15 g carbohydrate, 5 g fiber, 5 g protein. **Diabetic Exchanges:** 1 starch, 1 fat.

Italian Pork Chops
Green Peas with Onion

Fresh Catch For Dinner

WANT a quick yet nutritious supper? Look no further! Begin with Tara Ernspiker's simple take on baked salmon. In Falling Waters, West Virginia, she needs just three extra ingredients and a few moments of time to make this delightful main dish.

While you're baking and basting the fish, toss together gorgeous Summer Strawberry Salad from Diane Sahley of Lakewood, Ohio. It's a refreshing and colorful side dish for a speedy meal.

Glazed Salmon

Prep/Total Time: 25 min.

   1/3 cup packed brown sugar
   1/4 cup unsweetened pineapple juice
   2 tablespoons soy sauce
   4 salmon fillets (6 ounces *each*)

Line a 15-in. x 10-in. x 1-in. baking pan with foil; grease the foil. Set aside. In a small bowl, combine the brown sugar, pineapple juice and soy sauce. Place salmon skin side down on prepared pan. Spoon sauce mixture over the fish.

Bake, uncovered, at 350° for 20-25 minutes or until fish flakes easily with a fork, basting frequently with pan juices. **Yield:** 4 servings.

Summer Strawberry Salad

Prep/Total Time: 15 min.

   4 cups hearts of romaine salad mix
   3/4 cup sliced fresh strawberries
   1/2 cup unsweetened pineapple tidbits, drained
   1/4 cup mandarin oranges, drained
   1/4 cup fresh blueberries
   1/4 cup chopped pecans
   1/4 cup poppy seed salad dressing

Arrange salad mix among four salad plates. Top with the strawberries, pineapple, oranges and blueberries. Sprinkle with pecans. Drizzle with dressing. **Yield:** 4 servings.

Summer Strawberry Salad
Glazed Salmon

Caramel Yogurt Sundaes
Pepper Pork Fajitas

Southwestern Sensation

READY to add some excitement to suppertime? Get sizzling with the bold flavors of Pepper Pork Fajitas from Lise Thomson of Magrath, Alberta. Then balance that entree's heat with a cool treat—Caramel Yogurt Sundaes from Marlene Kroll of Chicago, Illinois. "They're spoon-licking good!" says Marlene.

Pepper Pork Fajitas

Prep/Total Time: 20 min.

2 tablespoons cornstarch
1 pound boneless pork loin, cut into 1/4-inch slices
1/2 *each* medium green, sweet yellow, red and orange pepper, julienned
1/2 cup sliced onion
1 tablespoon canola oil
1/2 cup salsa
4 flour tortillas (8 inches), warmed
1/2 cup shredded cheddar cheese
1/4 cup sour cream

Place cornstarch in a large resealable plastic bag. Add pork, a few pieces at a time, and shake to coat. In a large skillet, cook the pork, peppers and onion in oil over medium heat until pork is no longer pink and vegetables are tender. Stir in salsa; heat through.

Place about 3/4 cup filling down the center of each tortilla; top with shredded cheese and sour cream. Fold in sides of tortillas. **Yield:** 4 servings.

Caramel Yogurt Sundaes

Prep/Total Time: 15 min.

1/2 cup butter, cubed
1 cup packed brown sugar
1/2 cup heavy whipping cream
3 teaspoons vanilla extract
Frozen vanilla yogurt

In a small saucepan, melt butter; stir in brown sugar. Cook and stir over medium heat for 3-4 minutes or until sugar is dissolved. Stir in cream. Cook and stir until mixture comes to a boil. Remove from the heat; stir in vanilla. Serve warm over yogurt. **Yield:** 1-1/2 cups.

Super Slaw And Sandwich

A CLASSIC COMBO gets a quick—and delicious—twist thanks to the mouth-watering menu here. And you can fix it in no time flat!

From Bridget Evans of Forreston, Illinois, open-face Garlic Roast Beef Sandwiches make a hot and hearty main course. And Easy Caesar Coleslaw from Maryrose DeGroot of State College, Pennsylvania completes the winning combination.

"I adapted it from a more time-consuming recipe," Maryrose says. "It's easy to double or triple, too."

Easy Caesar Coleslaw

Prep/Total Time: 10 min.

1 package (16 ounces) coleslaw mix
1 cup grape tomatoes
1/4 cup shredded Parmesan cheese
3/4 cup creamy Caesar salad dressing
1 green onion, sliced

In a salad bowl, combine the coleslaw mix, tomatoes and Parmesan cheese. Add the salad dressing; toss to coat. Chill until serving. Sprinkle with green onion. **Yield:** 6 servings.

Garlic Roast Beef Sandwiches

Prep/Total Time: 25 min.

1 loaf (10 ounces) frozen garlic bread
1/2 pound sliced fresh mushrooms
2/3 cup sliced onion
1 teaspoon minced garlic
4 teaspoons butter
1 teaspoon Worcestershire sauce
1 pound shaved deli roast beef
6 slices Colby cheese

Bake garlic bread according to the package directions. Meanwhile, in a large skillet, saute the mushrooms, onion and garlic in butter until vegetables are tender. Stir in Worcestershire sauce.

Layer each half of garlic bread with roast beef, mushroom mixture and cheese. Return to oven; bake 1-2 minutes longer or until cheese is melted. Slice and serve immediately. **Yield:** 6 servings.

Easy Caesar Coleslaw
Garlic Roast Beef Sandwiches

Spicy Sausage Patties
Gourmet Scrambled Eggs

Memorable Morning Meal

EVERYONE loves a good breakfast, and this one jazzes up basic morning fare. Start your day off right with Diana Bird's recipe for restaurant-quality eggs.

"A visiting friend fixed these for us," writes Diana from Jeffersonton, Virginia. "They're now a favorite."

For the perfect partner, try the subtly spiced sausage from Athena Russell of Florence, South Carolina. It's sure to wake up your taste buds!

Spicy Sausage Patties

Prep/Total Time: 20 min.

1/2 teaspoon salt
1/2 teaspoon dried sage leaves
1/4 teaspoon ground coriander
1/4 teaspoon pepper
1/8 to 1/4 teaspoon crushed red pepper flakes
3/4 pound ground pork

In a large bowl, combine the first five ingredients. Crumble pork over mixture and mix well. Shape into four 3-in. patties.

In a large skillet, cook patties over medium heat for 5-6 minutes on each side or until meat is no longer pink. Drain on paper towels. **Yield:** 4 servings.

Gourmet Scrambled Eggs

Prep/Total Time: 25 min.

8 eggs
1/4 cup shredded Parmesan cheese
1/4 cup mayonnaise
1 tablespoon snipped chives
1 tablespoon minced fresh basil
1 tablespoon butter

In a small bowl, whisk the eggs, Parmesan cheese, mayonnaise, chives and basil.

In a large skillet, heat butter over medium heat. Add egg mixture; cook and stir until completely set. **Yield:** 4 servings.

A Taste of The Orient

HAS DINNERTIME in your household become a ho-hum occasion? Then it may be time to "set sail" for some exotic flavors!

This deliciously different menu combines two extremely basic recipes for a meal that simply bursts with fresh taste. And it can be prepared from start to finish in just 20 minutes.

A blend of Thai chili and barbecue sauces gives the salmon entree from Pamela Brick of Chicago, Illinois a sweet, spicy kick. The fish cooks on an indoor grill for easy prep...but everyone at the table will feel like they're dining on a complicated specialty from a Thai restaurant!

Smoked almonds add extra appeal to the nicely seasoned side dish. Rachel Magoncia-O'Leary of Creswell, Oregon shares the crunchy treatment for tender sauteed zucchini.

To complete your out-of-the ordinary dinner, add a frosty pitcher of iced tea and slices of lemon on the side—you're sure to hear rave reviews.

Thai Barbecued Salmon

Prep/Total Time: 15 min.

2/3 cup barbecue sauce
1/3 cup Thai chili sauce
1/4 cup minced fresh cilantro
4 salmon fillets (1 inch thick and 4 ounces *each*)

In a small bowl, combine the barbecue sauce, chili sauce and cilantro. Set aside 1/4 cup for serving.

Cook salmon on an indoor grill coated with cooking spray for 4-5 minutes or until fish flakes easily with a fork, basting frequently with sauce mixture. Serve salmon with reserved sauce. **Yield:** 4 servings.

Almond-Topped Zucchini

Prep/Total Time: 20 min.

3 medium zucchini, thinly sliced
1 teaspoon minced garlic
1 tablespoon olive oil
1 tablespoon butter
1/4 teaspoon salt
1/8 teaspoon pepper
1/4 cup smoked almonds, chopped

In a large skillet, saute zucchini and garlic in oil and butter until tender. Stir in salt and pepper; sprinkle with almonds. **Yield:** 4 servings.

Thai Barbecued Salmon
Almond-Topped Zucchini

Roasted Potatoes with Thyme and Gorgonzola
Garlic-Butter Steak

Steak and Potatoes Pronto

WHEN it's just the two you at the table, make it an extra-special occasion with the downsized dinner featured here. Each rapid recipe yields only a few servings, so you can enjoy fantastic fare that doesn't result in lots of leftovers.

From Lillian Julow of Gainesville, Florida, Garlic-Butter Steak gives you a restaurant-quality main dish. Complete your memorable meal by adding Roasted Potatoes with Thyme and Gorgonzola, shared by Virginia Strum of San Francisco, California.

Garlic-Butter Steak

Prep/Total Time: 20 min.

  1 beef flat iron steak *or* top sirloin steak
    (3/4 pound)
1/8 teaspoon salt
1/8 teaspoon pepper
  2 tablespoons butter, softened, *divided*
  1 teaspoon minced fresh parsley
  1 small garlic clove, minced
1/4 teaspoon soy sauce

Sprinkle steak with salt and pepper. In a large skillet, cook steak in 1 tablespoon butter over medium-high heat for 4-5 minutes on each side or until meat reaches desired doneness (for medium-rare, a meat thermometer should read 145°; medium, 160°; well-done, 170°). Let stand for 5 minutes before slicing.

In a small bowl, combine parsley, garlic, soy sauce and remaining butter. Serve with steak. **Yield:** 2 servings.

Roasted Potatoes With Thyme and Gorgonzola

Prep/Total Time: 30 min.

☑ This recipe includes Nutrition Facts and Diabetic Exchanges.

  1/2 pound small red potatoes, halved
1-1/2 teaspoons olive oil
1-1/2 teaspoons minced fresh thyme *or*
      1/2 teaspoon dried thyme
  1/8 teaspoon salt
  1/8 teaspoon pepper
    3 tablespoons crumbled Gorgonzola cheese

In a large bowl, combine the first five ingredients. Arrange in a greased 15-in. x 10-in. x 1-in. baking pan. Bake, uncovered, at 425° for 20-25 minutes or until potatoes are tender, stirring once. Sprinkle with cheese. **Yield:** 2 servings.

Nutrition Facts: 2/3 cup equals 150 calories, 7 g fat (3 g saturated fat), 9 mg cholesterol, 297 mg sodium, 19 g carbohydrate, 2 g fiber, 4 g protein. **Diabetic Exchanges:** 1 starch, 1 fat.

Italian Roasted Vegetables
Cheese-Topped Lemon Chicken Breasts

Can't-Miss Chicken Dinner

FAMILY COOKS know it's true—chicken is a sure bet when it comes to pleasing the whole family. From Renee Mitchell of McChord AFB, Washington, Cheese-Topped Lemon Chicken Breasts come to the table moist, tender and delicious.

Our Test Kitchen cooks created Italian Roasted Vegetables, a great complement for the chicken and a wholesome side everyone will savor.

Cheese-Topped Lemon Chicken Breasts

Prep/Total Time: 20 min.

4 boneless skinless chicken breast halves (4 ounces *each*)
1/4 teaspoon salt
1/4 teaspoon pepper
3 tablespoons butter
1/4 cup lemon juice
2 tablespoons soy sauce
3/4 cup shredded Colby cheese

Sprinkle chicken with salt and pepper. In a large skillet, brown chicken in butter on both sides over medium heat. Stir in lemon juice and soy sauce. Bring to a boil. Reduce heat; cover and cook for 4-5 minutes or until meat juices run clear.

Remove from the heat. Sprinkle each chicken breast with cheese. Cover and let stand for 2-3 minutes or until cheese is melted. **Yield:** 4 servings.

Italian Roasted Vegetables

Prep/Total Time: 25 min.

☑ This recipe includes Nutrition Facts and Diabetic Exchanges.

2 medium yellow summer squash, sliced
1 medium sweet red pepper, cut into 1-inch pieces
1/4 pound fresh green beans, trimmed
1/4 cup sun-dried tomato salad dressing
1/4 teaspoon salt
1/4 teaspoon dried basil
1/8 teaspoon pepper

In a large bowl, combine all ingredients. Transfer to an ungreased 15-in. x 10-in. x 1-in. baking pan.

Bake, uncovered, at 425° for 15-20 minutes or until vegetables are tender, stirring once. Serve immediately. **Yield:** 4 servings.

Nutrition Facts: 3/4 cup equals 61 calories, 3 g fat (trace saturated fat), 0 cholesterol, 322 mg sodium, 9 g carbohydrate, 3 g fiber, 2 g protein. **Diabetic Exchanges:** 2 vegetable, 1/2 fat.

Fast Fare for Lunch or Later

Hot Dog Potato Soup

THINK you don't have time for lunch? You'll think again when you try these rapid recipes. They're terrific not only at noon, but also as a speedy supper.

Your family will be dipping in no time when you assemble French Dip Sandwiches from Carole Lanthier of Courtice, Ontario. Serve them with refreshing Poppy Seed Mixed Salad from Rhonda Browne of Plymouth, Michigan and Hot Dog Potato Soup from Jeannie Klugh of Lancaster, Pennsylvania.

French Dip Sandwiches

Prep/Total Time: 15 min.

1 pound sliced deli roast beef
1 can (10-1/2 ounces) condensed beef broth, undiluted
1/2 cup steak sauce, *divided*
1 tablespoon Dijon mustard
4 French rolls, split

In a 1-1/2-qt. microwave-safe bowl, combine beef, broth and 1/4 cup steak sauce. Cover and microwave on high for 2-3 minutes or until heated through.

Meanwhile, combine mustard and remaining steak sauce; spread over roll bottoms. Using a slotted spoon, place beef on rolls; replace tops. Serve with broth mixture for dipping. **Yield:** 4 servings.

Editor's Note: This recipe was tested in a 1,100-watt microwave.

Hot Dog Potato Soup

Prep/Total Time: 15 min.

2 cans (18.8 ounces *each*) ready-to-serve chunky baked potato with cheddar and bacon bits soup
4 hot dogs, halved lengthwise and sliced
1 cup (4 ounces) shredded cheddar-Monterey Jack cheese
1 cup frozen corn
1 cup milk

In a large microwave-safe bowl, combine all the ingredients. Cover and microwave on high for 8-10 minutes or until heated through, stirring every 2 minutes. **Yield:** 5 servings.

Editor's Note: This recipe was tested in a 1,100-watt microwave.

Poppy Seed Mixed Salad

Prep/Total Time: 5 min.

1-1/2 cups torn mixed salad greens
3 tablespoons trail mix
1 slice red onion, separated into rings
2 teaspoons grated Parmesan cheese, *divided*
2 tablespoons prepared poppy seed salad dressing

In a small serving bowl, combine the salad greens, trail mix, onion and 1 teaspoon cheese. Drizzle with salad dressing; toss to coat. Sprinkle with remaining cheese. **Yield:** 2 servings.

French Dip Sandwiches
Poppy Seed Mixed Salad

Supper Sized Just Right

SAVOR a complete, satisfying meal even when it's just the two of you at the table. All you need is the pared-down menu here!

Start with nicely flavored Lemon-Pepper Chicken from Phyl Broich-Wessling of Garner, Iowa, then fill each plate with a side of Microwave Veggie Pilaf from Mary Houle of Stephenson, Michigan. Chances are, after trying this meal, you'll fix it again and again!

Lemon-Pepper Chicken

Prep/Total Time: 25 min.

2 boneless skinless chicken breast halves (4 ounces *each*)
2 tablespoons butter, *divided*
2 tablespoons thinly sliced green onion
4-1/2 teaspoons lemon juice
1 tablespoon sherry *or* chicken broth
1 tablespoon Worcestershire sauce
1/8 teaspoon ground mustard
1/8 teaspoon lemon-pepper seasoning

Flatten the chicken to 1/2-in. thickness. In a large skillet, cook chicken in 1 tablespoon butter over medium heat for 5-7 minutes on each side or until juices run clear. Remove and keep warm.

In the same skillet, combine the green onion, lemon juice, sherry, Worcestershire sauce, mustard, lemon-pepper and remaining butter. Cook and stir over medium heat for 3-4 minutes or until heated through. Serve with chicken. **Yield:** 2 servings.

Microwave Veggie Pilaf

Prep/Total Time: 20 min.

1 cup uncooked instant rice
1 cup water
1/3 cup finely chopped onion
1/3 cup finely chopped green pepper
1/3 cup shredded carrot
1/3 cup finely chopped celery
3 tablespoons butter
1 tablespoon beef bouillon granules
1/4 teaspoon ground cumin
1/8 teaspoon ground coriander
Dash pepper

In an ungreased 1-1/2-qt. microwave-safe dish, combine all ingredients. Cover and microwave on high for 6-8 minutes or until rice is tender, stirring once. Let stand, covered, for 5 minutes; fluff with a fork before serving. **Yield:** 2 servings.

Editor's Note: This recipe was tested in a 1,100-watt microwave.

Microwave Veggie Pilaf
Lemon-Pepper Chicken

Chinese Food With a Twist

HAVE A TASTE for the flavors featured at your local Chinese restaurant? There's no need to get take-out thanks to these rapid recipes, each shared by a busy cook like you.

A fan of all-American classics as well as Asian cuisine, Mike Tchou of Pepper Pike, Ohio combined the best of both worlds in Moo Shu Sloppy Joes. Soy, barbecue and hoisin sauces blend to create a surprising taste sensation. And you'll need just 30 minutes to prepare these unique roll-ups.

Colorful Sesame Carrots will be on the table in even less time—a mere 10 minutes! Dressed up with onion, sesame seeds, ginger and molasses, this veggie dish will make your stovetop supper complete. Marlene Muckenhirn of Delano, Minnesota shares the idea for this simple accompaniment.

Budget-conscious cooks are sure to appreciate these recipes even more. The main course costs just $2.47 per serving, while the side dish costs only $1.45 per serving—a lot less expensive than take-out!

Moo Shu Sloppy Joes
Sesame Carrots

Moo Shu Sloppy Joes
Prep/Total Time: 30 min.

- 2 teaspoons cornstarch
- 1/2 cup cold water
- 1/4 cup barbecue sauce
- 1/4 cup hoisin sauce
- 2 tablespoons reduced-sodium soy sauce
- 2 teaspoons minced fresh gingerroot
- 1 teaspoon minced garlic
- 1/4 teaspoon salt
- 1 small onion, sliced
- 1 small sweet red pepper, sliced
- 2 teaspoons canola oil
- 1 pound lean ground beef
- 3 cups coleslaw mix
- 8 flour tortillas (6 inches), warmed

In a small bowl, combine the cornstarch, water, barbecue sauce, hoisin sauce, soy sauce, ginger, garlic and salt until blended; set aside.

In a large skillet, saute the onion and red pepper in oil until crisp-tender; remove and set aside. In the same skillet, cook the ground beef over medium heat until meat is no longer pink; drain.

Stir the cornstarch mixture and add to the skillet. Bring to a boil; cook and stir for 1-2 minutes or until thickened. Add the coleslaw mix; stir to coat. Spoon the ground beef mixture into the center of each tortilla; top with the onion mixture. Roll up tightly. **Yield:** 4 servings.

Sesame Carrots
Prep/Total Time: 10 min.

- 1 package (16 ounces) frozen sliced carrots
- 3 tablespoons dried minced onion
- 2 tablespoons sesame seeds
- 1/2 teaspoon salt
- 1/2 teaspoon ground ginger
- 1/8 teaspoon pepper
- 3 tablespoons butter
- 2 teaspoons molasses *or* sugar

In a large skillet, saute the carrots, onion, sesame seeds, salt, ginger and pepper in butter for 4-5 minutes or until tender. Stir in molasses. **Yield:** 4 servings.

Just Ginger

FRESH GINGERROOT is available in your supermarket's produce section. Look for fresh gingerroot that has smooth, wrinkle-free skin and a spicy fragrance. Fresh, unpeeled gingerroot should be wrapped in a paper towel, placed in a plastic bag and refrigerated for up to 3 weeks. It can also be tightly wrapped and frozen for up to 2 months.

Green Beans with Savory
Pineapple Cranberry Ham

Ham Fit for The Holidays

WHEN the holiday season arrives, time is at a premium. So when an extra-special menu is called for, don't spend hours in the kitchen. Rely on this elegant ham dinner that's special enough for company.

Pineapple-Cranberry Ham from Rita Brower of Exeter, California features ham steaks topped with a sweet and tangy relish, adding lots of flavor and color. And Green Beans with Savory, created by our Test Kitchen staff, tingles taste buds with almonds, a splash of lemon and a hint of cayenne.

Pineapple Cranberry Ham

Prep/Total Time: 25 min.

  4 boneless fully cooked ham steaks
    (6 ounces *each*)
1-1/2 teaspoons canola oil
  1/2 cup jellied cranberry sauce

  1/2 cup undrained crushed pineapple
    3 tablespoons brown sugar
  1/8 teaspoon ground cloves

Cut each ham steak in half. In a large skillet over medium heat, cook ham in oil in batches for 3-5 minutes on each side or until heated through. Set aside; keep warm.

Meanwhile, in a small saucepan, mash the cranberry sauce; stir in the remaining ingredients. Bring to a boil; cook and stir for 3-5 minutes or until slightly thickened. Serve with ham. **Yield:** 4 servings.

Green Beans with Savory

Prep/Total Time: 20 min.

  5 cups frozen French-style green beans
1/4 cup sliced almonds
  2 tablespoons butter
  1 teaspoon fresh savory *or* 1/4 teaspoon dried
    savory
  1 teaspoon lemon juice
1/4 teaspoon salt
1/8 to 1/4 teaspoon cayenne pepper

Cook the green beans according to package directions. Meanwhile, in a small skillet, saute almonds in butter until toasted. Remove from the heat; stir in the remaining ingredients. Drain beans; add almond mixture and toss gently to coat. Serve immediately. **Yield:** 4 servings.

All-in-One Dish Plus Dessert

WHAT IF you could get your main course and side together in one convenient, delicious dinner dish? You can, thanks to Angel Hair Pasta with Chicken from Margaret Wilson of Sun City, California.

She combined moist chicken chunks, tender angel hair pasta, carrots and broccoli in a stovetop supper you and your family are sure to love. And it all takes just 20 minutes to prepare!

Top off the meal with Creamy Chocolate Mousse from Shirley Little of Alvord, Texas. "I like to serve it with a Pirouette or sugar cookie on the side of each glass. It looks pretty and adds a fun crunch."

Angel Hair Pasta with Chicken

Prep/Total Time: 20 min.

    8 ounces uncooked angel hair pasta
    1 pound boneless skinless chicken breasts, cut
      into 1-inch pieces
    2 tablespoons olive oil, *divided*
    2 medium carrots, sliced diagonally
1-1/2 cups fresh broccoli florets
    2 to 3 teaspoons minced garlic
1-1/3 cups chicken broth
  1/2 cup grated Parmesan cheese
    2 teaspoons dried basil
  1/2 teaspoon salt
Additional grated Parmesan cheese

Creamy Chocolate Mousse

Angel Hair Pasta with Chicken

Cook pasta according to package directions. Meanwhile, in a large skillet, saute chicken in 1 tablespoon oil for 4-5 minutes or until chicken is no longer pink; drain. Remove and keep warm.

In the same skillet over medium heat, cook carrots in remaining oil for 3 minutes, stirring occasionally. Add broccoli and garlic; cook 2 minutes longer. Stir in the chicken, broth, cheese, basil and salt. Bring to a boil. Reduce heat; simmer, uncovered, for 4-6 minutes or until vegetables are tender.

Drain pasta. Serve chicken mixture with pasta. Sprinkle with additional cheese. **Yield:** 4 servings.

Creamy Chocolate Mousse

Prep/Total Time: 10 min.

    2 cups cold milk
    1 package (5.9 ounces) instant chocolate
      pudding mix
    1 carton (8 ounces) frozen whipped topping,
      thawed
  1/2 cup sour cream
Additional whipped topping, optional

In a large bowl, whisk milk and pudding mix for 2 minutes. Let stand for 2 minutes or until soft-set. Fold in whipped topping and sour cream. Pour into individual dessert dishes. Dollop with whipped topping if desired. **Yield:** 6 servings.

Chapter 4

MOMS KNOW—getting children to eat wholesome, nourishing food can sometimes be a challenge. That's where this kid-focused chapter comes in!

From hot and hearty dinners such as Crispy Chicken Fingers and Pepperoni Pizza Skillet to Chocolate Chip Dip and other after-school snacks, the youth-inspired favorites featured here just can't miss.

You'll even find great breakfast options such as PBJ-Stuffed French Toast, as well as Oatmeal Surprise Cookies, Chocolate Candy Clusters and other take-along treats for the classroom.

Whichever foods you choose to make, you'll see smiling faces all around the table!

POPULAR WITH TOTS. Cheeseburger Cups (p. 87).

Southwest Chicken and Rice

Creamy Beef Enchiladas

(Pictured below)

Prep: 25 min. **Bake:** 20 min.

These American-style enchiladas are rich, creamy and loaded with cheese. Kids like the texture and the fact that there's only a touch of south-of-the-border heat. Add a side of tortilla chips for a satisfying Mexican meal.
—Belinda Moran, Woodbury, Tennessee

- 2 pounds lean ground beef
- 1 cup chopped onion
- 1 can (10-3/4 ounces) condensed cream of mushroom soup, undiluted
- 1 cup (8 ounces) sour cream
- 1 can (4 ounces) chopped green chilies
- 3 cups (12 ounces) shredded cheddar cheese, *divided*
- 3 cans (10 ounces *each*) enchilada sauce, *divided*
- 12 flour tortillas (8 inch), warmed

In a Dutch oven, cook the ground beef and onion over medium heat until meat is no longer pink; drain. Add soup, sour cream, green chilies, 1 cup cheddar cheese and 1/2 cup enchilada sauce; heat through.

Spread 1/4 cup enchilada sauce into each of two ungreased 13-in. x 9-in. baking dishes. Place 1/2 cup beef mixture down the center of each tortilla. Roll up and place seam side down in each prepared baking dish.

Pour the remaining enchilada sauce over the top; sprinkle with the remaining cheese. Bake, uncovered, at 350° for 20-25 minutes or until heated through. **Yield:** 12 servings.

Southwest Chicken and Rice

(Pictured above)

Prep/Total Time: 10 min.

With whole grain brown rice and diced tomatoes, this super-fast Southwestern dinner is such an easy way to get your family to eat more fiber. They won't even realize it—all anyone will notice is the great taste!
—Penny Hawkins, Mebane, North Carolina

- 2 packages (8-1/2 ounces *each*) ready-to-serve Santa Fe whole grain rice medley
- 2 packages (6 ounces *each*) ready-to-use Southwestern chicken strips, cut into chunks
- 1 can (10 ounces) diced tomatoes and green chilies, drained
- 1/2 cup shredded Monterey Jack cheese

Heat the rice according to the package directions. In a 2-qt. microwave-safe dish, combine the chicken and tomatoes; stir in rice. Cover and microwave on high for 2-3 minutes.

Sprinkle with cheese; cook 1 minute longer or until cheese is melted. **Yield:** 4 servings.

Editor's Note: This recipe was tested in a 1,100-watt microwave.

Creamy Beef Enchiladas

Chocolate Candy Clusters

Macaroni & Cheese Pizza

(Pictured below)

Prep: 25 min. **Bake:** 10 min.

It's no surprise children love this recipe—they get two kid-favorite foods in one. Mac 'n' cheese forms the crust, which is topped with pizza ingredients such as sausage and mushrooms. For simpler prep, use purchased pizza sauce instead of the tomato sauce, oregano and basil.
—*Jenny Staniec, Oak Grove, Minnesota*

    1 carton (7-1/4 ounces) macaroni and cheese
      dinner mix
    2 eggs, beaten
1/2 pound bulk Italian sausage
1/4 cup chopped onion
    1 can (8 ounces) tomato sauce
    1 teaspoon dried basil
    1 teaspoon dried oregano
    1 can (4 ounces) mushroom stems and pieces,
      drained
    1 cup (4 ounces) shredded part-skim
      mozzarella cheese

Prepare macaroni dinner mix according to package directions; stir in eggs. Spread onto a greased 12-in. pizza pan. Bake at 375° for 10 minutes.

Meanwhile, in a large skillet, cook sausage and onion over medium heat until meat is no longer pink; drain.

In a small bowl, combine the tomato sauce, basil and oregano. Spread over macaroni mixture. Layer with sausage mixture, mushrooms and mozzarella cheese. Bake 10 minutes longer or until the cheese is melted. **Yield:** 8 servings.

Chocolate Candy Clusters

(Pictured above)

Prep/Total Time: 30 min.

This sweet-salty combination is always a hit, whether I give the clusters as a gift, bring them to parties or serve them on my Christmas treat tray. Plus, with only five ingredients, they couldn't be much easier to make! For a change of pace, try using peanuts instead of the walnuts.
—*Taylor Carroll, Parkesburg, Pennsylvania*

✓ This recipe includes Nutrition Facts and Diabetic Exchanges.

    8 squares (1 ounce *each*) white baking
      chocolate, chopped
    1 cup milk chocolate chips
    1 cup semisweet chocolate chips
1-1/2 cups chopped walnuts
1-1/2 cups miniature pretzels, broken

In a microwave-safe bowl, melt the white chocolate and chocolate chips; stir until smooth. Stir in the walnuts and pretzel pieces.

Drop the chocolate mixture by rounded tablespoonfuls onto waxed paper-lined baking sheets. Refrigerate until firm. Store the candy in an airtight container. **Yield:** about 3 dozen.

Nutrition Facts: 1 cluster equals 132 calories, 9 g fat (3 g saturated fat), 3 mg cholesterol, 41 mg sodium, 12 g carbohydrate, 1 g fiber, 3 g protein. **Diabetic Exchanges:** 1 starch, 1 fat.

Macaroni & Cheese Pizza

Macaroni & Cheese Bake

(Pictured below)

Prep: 20 min. **Bake:** 35 min.

I've been experimenting in the kitchen with macaroni and cheese forever. This bubbly baked version featuring three kinds of cheese is the one my husband likes best.
—Margaret Spear, Morris, Illinois

2-1/2 cups uncooked elbow macaroni
1/4 cup butter, cubed
1 can (12 ounces) evaporated milk
3 eggs, lightly beaten
5 slices process American cheese, chopped
1 cup (8 ounces) sour cream
3/4 cup process cheese sauce
3/4 teaspoon onion powder
1/2 teaspoon seasoned salt
1/8 teaspoon pepper
2-1/2 cups (10 ounces) shredded cheddar cheese, *divided*

Cook macaroni according to package directions. Meanwhile, in a large saucepan, melt butter. Stir in the milk, eggs, process cheese, sour cream, cheese sauce and seasonings. Cook and stir over medium heat for 3-4 minutes or until cheeses are melted. Drain macaroni; toss with 2 cups cheddar cheese.

Transfer to a greased 13-in. x 9-in. baking dish. Add the sauce mixture and mix well. Sprinkle with the remaining cheddar cheese. Bake, uncovered, at 350° for 35-40 minutes or until golden brown and bubbly. **Yield:** 8 servings.

Macaroni & Cheese Bake

PBJ-Stuffed French Toast

PBJ-Stuffed French Toast

(Pictured above)

Prep/Total Time: 10 min.

I used some of my favorite foods to create this yummy breakfast…and now it's become a "go-to" recipe when friends drop in. —Ruth Ann Bott, Lake Wales, Florida

3 tablespoons cream cheese, softened
2 tablespoons creamy peanut butter
4 slices Italian bread (3/4 inch thick)
2 tablespoons red raspberry preserves
2 eggs, lightly beaten
1 tablespoon evaporated milk
Maple pancake syrup, optional

In a small bowl, combine cream cheese and peanut butter. Spread on two slices of bread; top with preserves and remaining bread. In a shallow bowl, whisk eggs and milk. Dip both sides of sandwiches into egg mixture.

In a greased large nonstick skillet, toast sandwiches for 2-3 minutes on each side or until golden brown. Serve with syrup if desired. **Yield:** 2 servings.

Toast Twists

FEEL FREE to change up the recipe for PBJ-Stuffed French Toast (above) to suit your family's tastes. For example, you could substitute a different kind of preserves for the red raspberry variety. Or, finish off the toast with a sprinkling of confectioners' sugar.

Monkey Muffins

(Pictured below)

Prep: 20 min. **Bake:** 15 min./batch

These bite-sized muffins are sure to be winners with your family and friends—and anyone who loves the combination of bananas, peanut butter and chocolate. Keep this recipe in mind whenever you have overripe bananas.
—*Amie Longstaff, Painesville Township, Ohio*

✓ This recipe includes Nutrition Facts and Diabetic Exchanges.

> 1/2 cup butter, softened
> 1 cup plus 1 tablespoon sugar, *divided*
> 2 eggs
> 1 cup mashed ripe bananas
> 2/3 cup peanut butter
> 1 tablespoon milk
> 1 teaspoon vanilla extract
> 2 cups all-purpose flour
> 1 teaspoon baking soda
> 1/2 teaspoon salt
> 3/4 cup miniature semisweet chocolate chips

In a large bowl, cream the butter and 1 cup sugar until light and fluffy. Add eggs, one at a time, beating well after each addition. Beat in the bananas, peanut butter, milk and vanilla. Combine the flour, baking soda and salt; add to the creamed mixture just until moistened. Fold in chips.

Fill greased or paper-lined miniature muffin cups three-fourths full. Sprinkle with remaining sugar. Bake at 350° for 14-16 minutes or until a toothpick comes out clean. Cool for 5 minutes before removing from pans to wire racks. **Yield:** 6 dozen.

Nutrition Facts: 2 muffins equals 126 calories, 6 g fat (3 g saturated fat), 18 mg cholesterol, 112 mg sodium, 16 g carbohydrate, 1 g fiber, 3 g protein. **Diabetic Exchanges:** 1 starch, 1 fat.

Monkey Muffins

Chili Spaghetti with Hot Dogs

Chili Spaghetti with Hot Dogs

(Pictured above)

Prep/Total Time: 30 min.

I've been making this for over 35 years! It's one of the dinners my husband requests most. The recipe works just as well with lower-fat franks and reduced-fat cheddar cheese.
—*Karen Tausend, Bridgeport, Michigan*

> 8 ounces uncooked spaghetti
> 1 package (1 pound) hot dogs, halved lengthwise and sliced
> 1/2 cup chopped onion
> 1/2 cup chopped celery
> 2 tablespoons canola oil
> 1 can (15 ounces) tomato sauce
> 1 tablespoon prepared mustard
> 1 teaspoon chili powder
> 1/2 teaspoon Worcestershire sauce
> 1/4 teaspoon salt
> 1/4 teaspoon pepper
> 1 cup (4 ounces) shredded cheddar cheese

Cook spaghetti according to package directions. Meanwhile, in a large skillet, saute the hot dogs, onion and celery in oil until tender. Stir in the tomato sauce, mustard, chili powder, Worcestershire sauce, salt and pepper. Cook, uncovered, for 5-8 minutes or until heated through, stirring occasionally.

Drain spaghetti; toss with hot dog mixture. Sprinkle with cheese. **Yield:** 6 servings.

Banana Chip Pancakes

Banana Chip Pancakes

(Pictured above)

Prep/Total Time: 30 min.

Special enough for a birthday-morning breakfast or holiday brunch, these fluffy pancakes can be changed up to your heart's content. One of my children prefers the plain banana pancakes, another wants just the chocolate and peanut butter chips, and a third goes for the works.
—Christeen Kelley, Newark, California

    2 cups biscuit/baking mix
    1 egg
    1 cup milk
    1 cup mashed ripe bananas
    3/4 cup swirled milk chocolate and peanut
        butter chips
Maple syrup and additional swirled milk chocolate
    and peanut butter chips, optional

Place biscuit mix in a large bowl. Combine the egg, milk and bananas; stir into biscuit mix just until moistened. Stir in swirled chocolate and peanut butter chips.

    Pour pancake batter by 1/4 cupfuls onto a greased hot griddle; turn when bubbles form on top. Cook un-til the second side is golden brown. Serve with maple syrup and additional swirled chocolate and peanut butter chips if desired. **Yield:** 12 pancakes.

Yummy Chocolate Dip

Prep/Total Time: 10 min.

Turn just about any fresh fruit into an irresistible and tantalizing snack or dessert with this dreamy, creamy chocolate dip. Four ingredients and 10 minutes are all it takes! If you like, try other dippers such as graham crackers.
—Stacey Shew, Cologne, Minnesota

    3/4 cup semisweet chocolate chips
    1 carton (8 ounces) whipped topping, *divided*
    1/2 teaspoon ground cinnamon
    1/2 teaspoon rum *or* vanilla extract
Assorted fresh fruit

In a microwave, melt chocolate chips; stir until smooth. Stir in 1/2 cup whipped topping, cinnamon and extract; cool for 5 minutes.

    Fold in remaining whipped topping. Serve with fresh fruit. Refrigerate leftovers. **Yield:** 2 cups.

Ham & Cheese Pizza Snacks

(Pictured below)

Prep/Total Time: 15 min.

I remember munching these yummy bagels as a child. They're also great as casual party appetizers...or even a quick supper. —Kimberly Leman, Fairbury, Illinois

　　1 cup (4 ounces) shredded Colby cheese
　1/2 cup diced deli ham
　1/2 cup mayonnaise
　　4 bacon strips, cooked and crumbled
　　6 miniature bagels, split

In a small bowl, combine the first four ingredients. Spread over the bagel halves. Place on an ungreased baking sheet.

　Broil 4-6 in. from the heat for 2-4 minutes or until lightly browned and bubbly. **Yield:** 1 dozen.

S'more Bars

(Pictured at right)

Prep: 20 min. **Bake:** 25 min. + cooling

Once school starts in the fall, it can be hard for children to let go of summertime fun. But you'll bring back sweet campfire memories—and smiles—when you serve these rich and gooey bars, whether as a dessert or snack.
　　　　　　　　　—Lisa DiPrima, Wilton, New Hampshire

☑ This recipe includes Nutrition Facts and Diabetic Exchanges.

Ham & Cheese Pizza Snacks

S'more Bars

　1/2 cup butter, softened
　3/4 cup sugar
　　1 egg
　　1 teaspoon vanilla extract
1-1/3 cups all-purpose flour
　3/4 cup graham cracker crumbs
　　1 teaspoon baking powder
　1/8 teaspoon salt
　　5 milk chocolate candy bars (1.55 ounces *each*)
　　1 cup marshmallow creme

In a large bowl, cream butter and sugar until light and fluffy. Add egg and vanilla; beat well. Combine the flour, cracker crumbs, baking powder and salt; gradually add to creamed mixture. Set aside 1/2 cup for topping.

　Press remaining mixture into a greased 9-in. square baking pan. Place candy bars over crust; spread with marshmallow creme. Crumble remaining graham cracker mixture over top.

　Bake at 350° for 25-30 minutes or until golden brown. Cool on a wire rack. Cut into bars. Store in an airtight container. **Yield:** 1-1/2 dozen.

　Nutrition Facts: 1 bar equals 213 calories, 9 g fat (5 g saturated fat), 28 mg cholesterol, 114 mg sodium, 30 g carbohydrate, 1 g fiber, 3 g protein. **Diabetic Exchanges:** 2 starch, 1 fat.

Sticky Solution

To easily remove marshmallow creme from a jar, I simply place the jar in a pan of very hot water. I repeat this once or twice, then spoon out the creme with a wooden spoon. It works like a charm.
　　　　　　　　　—Mary French, Port Orange, Florida

Chocolate Chip Dip

(Pictured below)

Prep/Total Time: 15 min.

Is there any kid (or kid at heart) who wouldn't love this creamy dip for graham crackers? It beats dunking them in milk, hands down! Try it with apple wedges, too.
—*Heather Koenig, Prairie du Chien, Wisconsin*

> 1 package (8 ounces) cream cheese, softened
> 1/2 cup butter, softened
> 3/4 cup confectioners' sugar
> 2 tablespoons brown sugar
> 1 teaspoon vanilla extract
> 1 cup (6 ounces) miniature semisweet
>   chocolate chips
> Graham cracker sticks

In a small bowl, beat cream cheese and butter until light and fluffy. Add the sugars and vanilla; beat until smooth. Stir in chocolate chips. Serve with graham cracker sticks. **Yield:** 2 cups.

Peanut Butter & Jelly Waffles

Chocolate Chip Dip

Peanut Butter & Jelly Waffles

(Pictured above)

Prep/Total Time: 25 min.

Don't count out the grown-ups when it comes to fans of these golden-brown, made-from-scratch waffles. Delectably flavored with peanut butter, jelly and a sprinkling of cinnamon, they're guaranteed pleasers for all ages.
—*Helena Georgette Mann, Sacramento, California*

> 1-1/4 cups all-purpose flour
> 3 tablespoons sugar
> 1 tablespoon baking powder
> 1/4 teaspoon baking soda
> 1/4 teaspoon ground cinnamon
> 2 eggs, *separated*
> 1-1/4 cups milk
> 1/3 cup peanut butter
> 3 tablespoons butter, melted
> Jelly of your choice

In a large bowl, combine the flour, sugar, baking powder, baking soda and cinnamon. In another bowl, whisk the egg yolks, milk, peanut butter and butter; stir mixture into dry ingredients just until moistened.

In a small bowl, beat the egg whites until stiff peaks form; fold into the waffle batter. Bake in a preheated waffle iron according to the manufacturer's directions until golden brown. Serve waffles with the jelly of your choice. **Yield:** 10 waffles.

Cheeseburger Cups

(Pictured below and on page 78)
Prep/Total Time: 30 min.

A terrific recipe for moms who have young children and nonstop schedules, these simple, inexpensive dinner bites are made with handy ingredients and take just a short time to fix. Best of all, youngsters go crazy for the ground beef, biscuit "cups" and popular cheeseburger toppings.
—*Jeri Millhouse, Ashland, Ohio*

    1 pound ground beef
  1/2 cup ketchup
    2 tablespoons brown sugar
    1 tablespoon prepared mustard
1-1/2 teaspoons Worcestershire sauce
    1 tube (12 ounces) refrigerated buttermilk
      biscuits
  1/2 cup cubed process cheese (Velveeta)

In a large skillet, cook beef over medium heat until no longer pink; drain. Stir in the ketchup, brown sugar, mustard and Worcestershire sauce. Remove from the heat; set aside.

Press each buttermilk biscuit onto the bottom and up the sides of a greased muffin cup. Spoon the ground beef mixture into the cups; top with the cheese cubes. Bake at 400° for 14-16 minutes or until golden brown. **Yield:** 5 servings.

Crispy Chicken Fingers

Cheeseburger Cups

Crispy Chicken Fingers

(Pictured above)
Prep: 20 min. **Cook:** 5 min./batch

My kids can't get enough of these tender, moist, fun-to-dip chicken strips. For our own dinners, my husband and I cut up the prepared chicken, then add it to a lettuce salad with eggs, tomatoes and cheese. Everybody's happy!
—*Rachel Fizel, Woodbury, Minnesota*

    1 cup all-purpose flour
    1 cup dry bread crumbs
    2 tablespoons grated Parmesan cheese
    1 teaspoon salt
  3/4 teaspoon garlic powder
  1/2 teaspoon baking powder
    1 egg
    1 cup buttermilk
1-3/4 pounds boneless skinless chicken breasts,
      cut into strips
Oil for deep-fat frying

In a large resealable plastic bag, combine the first six ingredients. In a shallow bowl, whisk the egg and buttermilk. Dip a few pieces of chicken at a time in the buttermilk mixture, then place in the plastic bag; seal and shake to coat.

In an electric skillet, heat oil to 375°. Fry chicken, a few strips at a time, for 2-3 minutes on each side or until a meat thermometer reads 170°. Drain on paper towels. **Yield:** 7 servings.

Oatmeal Surprise Cookies

(4 g saturated fat), 25 mg cholesterol, 80 mg sodium, 21 g carbohydrate, 1 g fiber, 2 g protein. **Diabetic Exchanges:** 1-1/2 starch, 1 fat.

Butter Pecan French Toast

(Pictured below)

Prep/Total Time: 25 min.

Flavored coffee creamer is the secret ingredient in this oh-so-fast-and-easy breakfast treat your whole family will gobble up. I sometimes substitute French vanilla or caramel coffee creamer for the Southern butter pecan variety, and add a little nutmeg and cinnamon to the eggs.
—Cathy Hall, Phoenix, Arizona

    1 teaspoon plus 1 tablespoon butter, *divided*
  1/2 cup chopped pecans
    2 eggs
  1/2 cup refrigerated Southern butter pecan
      nondairy creamer
    6 slices French bread (1 inch thick)
  1/4 cup confectioners' sugar
  1/4 teaspoon ground cinnamon
Maple syrup, optional

In a small skillet, melt 1 teaspoon butter over medium heat. Add the pecans; cook and stir for 3 minutes or until toasted.

In a shallow bowl, whisk the eggs and coffee creamer. Dip both sides of each slice of bread in egg mixture. In a large skillet, melt remaining butter over medium heat. Cook bread for 2-3 minutes on each side or until golden brown. Sprinkle with pecans, confectioners' sugar and cinnamon. Serve with maple syrup if desired. **Yield:** 3 servings.

Oatmeal Surprise Cookies

(Pictured above)

Prep: 20 min. **Bake:** 15 min./batch

Chocolate-covered raisins and pumpkin pie spice turn these oatmeal cookies into prize-worthy gourmet goodies. Children of all ages will down 'em by the dozen.
—Rebecca Clark, Warrior, Alabama

✓ **This recipe includes Nutrition Facts and Diabetic Exchanges.**

     1 cup butter, softened
  3/4 cup packed brown sugar
  1/2 cup sugar
     2 eggs
1-1/2 cups all-purpose flour
     1 teaspoon baking soda
     1 teaspoon pumpkin pie spice
2-3/4 cups quick-cooking oats
1-1/2 cups chocolate-covered raisins

In a large bowl, cream butter and sugars until light and fluffy. Beat in eggs. Combine the flour, baking soda and pumpkin pie spice; gradually add to creamed mixture and mix well. Stir in oats and raisins.

Drop by tablespoonfuls 2 in. apart onto greased baking sheets. Flatten slightly. Bake at 350° for 13-15 minutes or until golden brown. Cool for 5 minutes before removing to wire racks. Store in an airtight container. **Yield:** 3 dozen.

Nutrition Facts: 1 cookie equals 149 calories, 7 g fat

Butter Pecan French Toast

Macaroni Taco Bake

Pepperoni Pizza Skillet

(Pictured below)

Prep/Total Time: 30 min.

For those hectic school nights, no household can have too many hearty, 30-minute meals the entire family likes. This beefy pasta supper gets requested again and again.
—Anna Miller, Quaker City, Ohio

    5 cups uncooked wide egg noodles
1-1/2 pounds ground beef
  1/2 cup chopped onion
  1/2 cup chopped green pepper
1-1/2 cups chopped pepperoni
    1 jar (14 ounces) pizza sauce
    1 can (10-3/4 ounces) condensed cream of
      mushroom soup, undiluted
    1 can (4-1/2 ounces) sliced mushrooms,
      drained
  1/2 cup grated Parmesan cheese
  1/4 teaspoon garlic powder
  1/4 teaspoon dried oregano
  1/2 cup shredded part-skim mozzarella cheese

Cook noodles according to package directions. Meanwhile, in a large skillet, cook the beef, onion and pepper over medium heat until meat is no longer pink; drain. Stir in the pepperoni, pizza sauce, soup, mushrooms, Parmesan cheese, garlic powder and oregano.

Drain noodles; stir into skillet and heat through. Sprinkle with mozzarella cheese. **Yield:** 8 servings.

Macaroni Taco Bake

(Pictured above)

Prep: 30 min. **Bake:** 15 min.

Mac and cheese with mild taco flavor and crunchy tortilla chips...no wonder kids love this casserole! And moms love the fact that it's ready to bake in just half an hour.
—Betsy King, Duluth, Minnesota

    2 packages (7-1/4 ounces *each*) macaroni and
      cheese dinner mix
    1 pound ground beef
    1 cup chunky salsa
    2 cups crushed tortilla chips
    1 can (2-1/4 ounces) sliced ripe olives, drained
    2 cups (8 ounces) shredded taco cheese
Sour cream, optional

Prepare the macaroni and cheese according to the package directions. Meanwhile, in a large skillet, cook the ground beef until no longer pink; drain. Stir in the salsa; set aside.

Spread macaroni into a greased 13-in. x 9-in. baking dish. Layer with beef mixture, chips and olives; sprinkle with cheese. Bake, uncovered, at 350° for 15-20 minutes or until heated through. Serve with sour cream if desired. **Yield:** 8 servings.

Pepperoni Pizza Skillet

Chapter 5

ON THOSE LONG DAYS when you feel like you've been going nonstop, take a break by taking five—five *ingredients*, that is.

Simply grab the handful of items needed to fix any of these short-but-sweet recipes for supper. Cooking will be so fuss-free, you'll feel more like you're relaxing than making dinner!

Each delectable dish calls for just five ingredients or less (not including the staples of water, salt and pepper)...so you won't have to gather dozens of items before you can even start preparing your meal.

Serve favorites such as Chip-Crusted Chicken, Pesto Corn and more. No one will suspect how simple they actually are!

STRIVE FOR FIVE. Honey-Glazed Lamb Chops and Southwestern Corn Salad (both recipes on p. 94).

Harvest Salads with Pear Vinaigrette

Harvest Salads with Pear Vinaigrette

(Pictured above)

Prep/Total Time: 15 min.

You'll love the subtly tart dressing and refreshing taste of this simple but elegant salad. Bagged greens are topped with fresh pears, cheese and almonds, then drizzled with a jazzed-up dressing. It's a fantastic combination! If you don't have Gouda cheese, try Swiss instead.
—Cheryl Perry, Hertford, North Carolina

> 3 medium pears
> 1/3 cup oil and vinegar salad dressing
> 1 package (5 ounces) spring mix salad greens
> 6 ounces Gouda cheese, shaved
> 3/4 cup honey-roasted sliced almonds

Peel and core one pear; coarsely chop. Place in a small food processor; cover and process until smooth. While processing, gradually add salad dressing in a steady stream. Set aside.

Divide salad greens among six salad plates. Slice re-maining pears. Arrange pears and cheese over salads. Sprinkle with almonds; drizzle with prepared dressing. **Yield:** 6 servings.

Ramen Broccoli Soup

(Pictured below)

Prep/Total Time: 20 min.

I think cheese and garlic powder are the keys to the great taste of this warm-you-up soup. Loaded with noodles and nutritious broccoli, it really hits the spot on cold winter days and takes a mere 20 minutes to fix.
—Luella Dirks, Emelle, Alabama

☑ **This recipe includes Nutrition Facts and Diabetic Exchanges.**

> 5 cups water
> 1 package (16 ounces) frozen broccoli cuts
> 2 packages (3 ounces *each*) chicken ramen noodles
> 1/4 teaspoon garlic powder
> 3 slices process American cheese, cut into strips

In a large saucepan, bring water to a boil. Add broc-coli; return to a boil. Reduce heat; cover and simmer for 3 minutes. Return to a boil. Break noodles into small pieces; add to water. Cook 3 minutes longer, stir-ring occasionally.

Remove from the heat. Stir in contents of seasoning packets from the noodles, garlic powder and cheese, stirring until the cheese is melted. Serve immediately. **Yield:** 7 servings.
Nutrition Facts: 1 cup equals 150 calories, 6 g fat (4 g saturated fat), 6 mg cholesterol, 573 mg sodium, 20 g carbohydrate, 2 g fiber, 5 g protein. **Diabetic Exchanges:** 1 starch, 1 vegetable, 1 fat.

Ramen Broccoli Soup

Ripe Idea

TO QUICKLY ripen fresh pears for Harvest Salads with Pear Vinaigrette (recipe above), place them in a pa-per bag with a banana and fold the top of the bag. Ba-nanas emit ethylene gas, which gets trapped in the bag and promotes ripening. The pears absorb the gas and produce their own, causing them to ripen faster.

Tomato Pasta Side Dish
Spinach Steak Pinwheels

Tomato Pasta Side Dish

(Pictured above)

Prep/Total Time: 20 min.

This pleasantly seasoned pasta dish offers cooks an elegant way to round out almost any meal. And with so few ingredients, it couldn't get much easier to prepare.
—Mandi Smith, Knoxville, Tennessee

☑ This recipe includes Nutrition Facts and Diabetic Exchanges.

    8 ounces uncooked angel hair pasta
    1 medium tomato, chopped
    2 tablespoons olive oil
    1 tablespoon lemon juice
    1/2 teaspoon Cajun seasoning
    1/4 teaspoon salt
    1/4 teaspoon pepper

Cook pasta according to package directions. Meanwhile, in a small bowl, combine the tomato, oil, lemon juice, Cajun seasoning, salt and pepper. Drain pasta; transfer to a serving bowl. Add tomato mixture; toss to coat. **Yield:** 5 servings.

    Nutrition Facts: 3/4 cup equals 222 calories, 6 g fat (1 g saturated fat), 0 cholesterol, 176 mg sodium, 35 g carbohydrate, 2 g fiber, 6 g protein. **Diabetic Exchanges:** 2 starch, 1 fat.

Spinach Steak Pinwheels

(Pictured above)

Prep/Total Time: 30 min.

I get a kick out of wowing guests with this succulent entree. Even people who usually don't care for spinach like this. —Mary Ann Marino, West Pittsburg, Pennsylvania

    1 beef flank steak (1-1/2 pounds)
    1 package (10 ounces) frozen chopped
      spinach, thawed and squeezed dry
    1/4 cup grated Parmesan cheese
    1/4 cup sour cream
Dash *each* salt and pepper

Cut steak horizontally from a long side to within 1/2 in. of opposite side. Open meat so it lies flat; cover with plastic wrap. Flatten to 1/4-in. thickness. Remove plastic.

    In a small bowl, combine the spinach, cheese and sour cream; spread over steak to within 1/2 in. of edges. With the grain of the meat going from left to right, roll up jelly-roll style. Slice the beef across the grain into eight slices.

    Transfer to an ungreased baking sheet. Sprinkle with salt and pepper. Broil 4-6 in. from the heat for 5-7 minutes on each side or until meat reaches desired doneness (for medium-rare, a meat thermometer should read 145°; medium, 160°; well-done, 170°). **Yield:** 4 servings.

Honey-Glazed Lamb Chops
Southwestern Corn Salad

Southwestern Corn Salad

(Pictured above and on page 90)

Prep: 10 min. + chilling

This terrific side salad made with just five ingredients, plus salt and pepper, mellows as it chills and stays fresh for several days in the fridge. A great do-ahead dish from our Test Kitchen cooks, it's ideal for potlucks and picnics.

> 4 cans (11 ounces *each*) white *or* shoepeg corn, drained
> 8 green onions, chopped
> 3 jalapeno peppers, seeded and chopped
> 1/4 cup minced fresh cilantro
> 1/2 cup mayonnaise
> 1/2 teaspoon salt
> 1/4 teaspoon pepper

In a large bowl, combine the corn, onions, jalapenos and cilantro. Combine the mayonnaise, salt and pepper; gently stir into corn mixture. Cover and refrigerate for 4 hours. **Yield:** 9 servings.

Editor's Note: When cutting hot peppers, disposable gloves are recommended. Avoid touching your face.

Honey-Glazed Lamb Chops

(Pictured above and on page 90)

Prep/Total Time: 20 min.

What an amazing amount of flavor for such little effort! This main course is "company-special" but so fast to put together thanks to the simple honey-mustard glaze.
—Dolores Hurtt, Florence, Montana

☑ This recipe includes Nutrition Facts and Diabetic Exchanges.

> 1/3 cup honey
> 1/3 cup prepared mustard
> 1/8 teaspoon onion salt
> 1/8 teaspoon pepper
> 8 lamb loin chops (1 inch thick and 3 ounces *each*)

In a small saucepan, combine the honey, mustard, onion salt and pepper. Cook and stir over medium-low heat for 2-3 minutes or until heated through.

Brush the sauce over both sides of lamb. Broil 4-6 in. from the heat for 5-7 minutes on each side or until the meat reaches desired doneness (for medium-rare, a meat thermometer should read 145°; medium, 160°; well-done, 170°). **Yield:** 4 servings.

Nutrition Facts: 2 lamb chops equal 254 calories, 8 g fat (3 g saturated fat), 68 mg cholesterol, 345 mg sodium, 24 g carbohydrate, 1 g fiber, 22 g protein. **Diabetic Exchanges:** 3 lean meat, 1-1/2 starch.

Busy Day Bacon Muffins

(Pictured below)

Prep/Total Time: 30 min.

Tender and loaded with the mouth-watering taste of bacon, these savory muffins always disappear in a hurry. Serve them with breakfast...or later in the day with soup or salad. —*Gracie Shrader, Trenton, Georgia*

    6 **bacon strips, diced**
    2 **cups biscuit/baking mix**
    2 **tablespoons sugar**
    1 **egg**
  2/3 **cup milk**

Cook the bacon according to the package directions; drain. Meanwhile, in a large bowl, combine the biscuit mix and sugar. In a small bowl, combine the egg and milk. Stir into the dry ingredients just until moistened. Fold in bacon.

Fill greased muffin cups three-fourths full. Bake at 400° for 13-15 minutes or until a toothpick comes out clean. Serve warm. **Yield:** 9 muffins.

Busy Day Bacon Muffins

Blizzard Party Mix

Blizzard Party Mix

(Pictured above)

Prep/Total Time: 30 min.

This sweet-salty combo with a "snowy" coating of vanilla chips is sure to be popular. Try it not only for parties, but also for munching at home and giving as a gift. —*Kelley Scott, Parma, Ohio*

    2 **cups Corn Chex**
    2 **cups miniature pretzels**
    1 **cup dry roasted peanuts**
  20 **caramels, coarsely chopped**
    1 **package (10 to 12 ounces) vanilla *or* white chips**

In a large bowl, combine the first four ingredients. In a microwave-safe bowl, melt chips; stir until smooth. Pour over cereal mixture and toss to coat. Immediately spread onto waxed paper-lined baking sheet; let stand until set, about 20 minutes.

Break into pieces. Store in an airtight container. **Yield:** 4-1/2 cups.

Snack Substitute

WHEN preparing fun and festive Blizzard Party Mix (recipe above), feel free to experiment with different ingredients you have on hand. For example, if you don't have the Corn Chex cereal called for in the recipe, simply substitute Life cereal.

Easy Cheesecake Pie

(Pictured at left)

Prep/Total Time: 5 min.

Love dessert but don't want to invest a lot of time and effort? This decadent pie is so quick, you'll have it ready in a mere 5 minutes. All you need is ready-to-serve cheesecake filling, chocolate sandwich cookies and a prepared crust.
—Cathy Shortall, Easton, Maryland

1 carton (24.3 ounces) ready-to-serve
  cheesecake filling
1-1/2 cups coarsely crushed cream-filled chocolate
  sandwich cookies (about 12 cookies), *divided*
1 chocolate crumb crust (9 inches)

In a large bowl, combine the cheesecake filling and 1-1/4 cups chocolate cookie crumbs. Spoon into crust; sprinkle with remaining crumbs. Chill until serving. **Yield:** 8 servings.

Chip-Crusted Chicken

(Pictured at left)

Prep/Total Time: 30 min.

Dijon-mayonnaise blend and barbecue potato chips might sound like a strange combination, but they combine beautifully in this 30-minute chicken entree. Don't be surprised if you find yourself fixing this recipe again and again!
—Mike Tchou, Pepper Pike, Ohio

2/3 cup Dijon-mayonnaise blend
6 cups barbecue potato chips, finely crushed
6 boneless skinless chicken breast halves
  (5 ounces *each*)

Place the Dijon-mayonnaise blend in a shallow bowl. Place the potato chips in another shallow bowl. Dip the chicken breast halves in the mayonnaise blend, then coat with the potato chips.

Transfer the coated chicken breast halves to an ungreased baking sheet. Bake at 375° for 20-25 minutes or until juices run clear. **Yield:** 6 servings.

Pesto Corn

(Pictured at left)

Prep/Total Time: 10 min.

This three-ingredient side dish is one of my very favorite comfort foods—not only because it's easy to make, but also because it's delicious! The bright flavors of the pesto bring out the natural sweetness of the corn.
—Laurie Bock, Lynden, Washington

1 package (16 ounces) frozen corn, thawed
3/4 cup shredded sharp cheddar cheese
1 tablespoon prepared pesto

In a small microwave-safe dish, combine all ingredients. Cover and cook on high for 2-3 minutes or until heated through. **Yield:** 3 servings.

Maple Nut Truffles

(Pictured below)

Prep: 25 min. + chilling

Rich with cream cheese and rolled in chopped walnuts, these maple-flavored truffles are guaranteed to satisfy the chocolate lovers you know. Keep these treats in mind for Christmastime or any special occasion—they're a terrific no-bake option for your tray of cookies and candies.
—Rebekah Radewahn, Wauwatosa, Wisconsin

☑ This recipe includes Nutrition Facts and Diabetic Exchanges.

1-1/2 cups semisweet chocolate chips
4 ounces cream cheese, softened
1-1/2 cups confectioners' sugar
3/4 teaspoon maple flavoring
1 cup chopped walnuts

In a small microwave-safe bowl, melt chocolate chips. Set aside to cool.

In another bowl, beat the cream cheese and confectioners' sugar until smooth. Add the melted chocolate and maple flavoring; beat until well blended. Chill for 15 minutes or until firm enough to handle.

Shape chilled mixture into 1-in. balls; roll in walnuts. Store in an airtight container in the refrigerator. **Yield:** 2-1/2 dozen.

Nutrition Facts: 1 truffle equals 103 calories, 6 g fat (2 g saturated fat), 4 mg cholesterol, 12 mg sodium, 12 g carbohydrate, 1 g fiber, 2 g protein. **Diabetic Exchanges:** 1 starch, 1 fat.

Maple Nut Truffles

Cheese & Onion French Bread

Prep/Total Time: 20 min.

Jazz up an ordinary loaf of French bread in a hurry with this simple idea. Mayo keeps the bread moist, while the cheeses and green onion add mouth-watering taste. Just try to resist a warm-from-the-oven slice—it's impossible!
—Carolyn Schmeling, Brookfield, Wisconsin

> 2 cups (8 ounces) shredded Italian cheese blend
> 2/3 cup mayonnaise
> 1/4 cup grated Parmesan cheese
> 1/4 cup chopped green onions
> 1 loaf (1 pound) unsliced French bread, halved lengthwise

In a small bowl, combine the cheese blend, mayonnaise, Parmesan cheese and onions; spread over the cut sides of bread.

Place on an ungreased baking sheet. Bake at 375° for 12-15 minutes or until the cheese is melted. **Yield:** 16 servings.

French Onion Cheese Fondue

Effortless Egg Rolls

(Pictured below)

Prep/Total Time: 30 min.

This recipe makes homemade egg rolls surprisingly easy. With sausage and stir-fry veggies, they have restaurant taste but are ready to eat in just half an hour. Look for a good dipping sauce in the Asian aisle of your supermarket.
—Angel Randol, Apple Valley, California

> 1/2 pound bulk pork sausage
> 2-1/2 cups frozen stir-fry vegetable blend, thawed and chopped

> 1 tablespoon teriyaki sauce
> 10 egg roll wrappers
> Oil for deep-fat frying

In a large skillet, cook sausage and vegetables over medium heat until meat is no longer pink; drain. Stir in teriyaki sauce.

Place 3 tablespoons sausage mixture in the center of each egg roll wrapper. Fold bottom corner over filling. Fold sides toward center over filling. Moisten remaining corner with water; roll up tightly to seal.

In an electric skillet, heat 1 in. of oil to 375°. Fry the egg rolls in batches for 3-4 minutes on each side or until golden brown. Drain egg rolls on paper towels. **Yield:** 10 egg rolls.

French Onion Cheese Fondue

(Pictured above)

Prep/Total Time: 15 min.

With just three ingredients, this fondue is a breeze to whip up for company. Plus, leftovers are great over potatoes or pasta. *—Cathy Ostrawski, Amherst, New York*

> 1 can (10-3/4 ounces) condensed cheddar cheese soup, undiluted
> 1 carton (8 ounces) French onion dip
> 2 cups (8 ounces) shredded cheddar cheese
> 1 loaf (1 pound) French bread, cubed *or* assorted fresh vegetables

In a large saucepan, combine soup and dip. Add cheese. Cook and stir over medium-low heat until cheese is melted; keep warm. Serve with bread cubes or vegetables. **Yield:** 3 cups.

Effortless Egg Rolls

Gorgonzola Phyllo Cups

(Pictured below)

Prep/Total Time: 20 min.

These appetizing bites appear fancy but come together in virtually no time at all. With dried cranberries, apples and walnuts, the little cups are especially fun for parties during the Thanksgiving and Christmas holiday season.

—Trisha Kruse, Eagle, Idaho

☑ This recipe includes Nutrition Facts.

2 packages (1.9 ounces *each*) frozen miniature
    phyllo tart shells
1-1/3 cups crumbled Gorgonzola cheese
1/2 cup chopped tart apple
1/3 cup dried cranberries
1/3 cup chopped walnuts

Place the phyllo tart shells on a baking pan. In a small bowl, combine the remaining ingredients; spoon into tart shells.

Bake at 350° for 6-8 minutes or until lightly browned. Serve warm or at room temperature. Refrigerate leftovers. **Yield:** 2-1/2 dozen.

Nutrition Facts: 1 appetizer equals 54 calories, 3 g fat (1 g saturated fat), 4 mg cholesterol, 77 mg sodium, 4 g carbohydrate, trace fiber, 2 g protein.

Pepperoni Pinwheels

Pepperoni Pinwheels

(Pictured above)

Prep/Total Time: 25 min.

Young or old, everyone snatches up these little spiral-shape snacks. Convenient refrigerated dough, mozzarella cheese, Parmesan and pepperoni make the oven-baked pinwheels taste like miniature pizzas. For extra fun, serve them with warmed spaghetti sauce on the side for dipping.

—Dorothy Smith, El Dorado, Arkansas

1 tube (13.8 ounces) refrigerated pizza crust
1 cup (4 ounces) shredded part-skim
    mozzarella cheese
1/4 cup grated Parmesan cheese
1 cup chopped pepperoni (about 64 slices)
1/2 cup spaghetti sauce, warmed, optional

On a lightly floured surface, roll dough into a 16-in. x 10-in. rectangle. Sprinkle with the mozzarella cheese, Parmesan cheese and pepperoni.

Roll up jelly-roll style, starting with a long side. Cut roll into 2-in. slices. Place the slices cut side down in a greased 15-in. x 10-in. x 1-in. baking pan; lightly press down to flatten.

Bake at 400° for 8-10 minutes or until golden brown. Serve with warmed spaghetti sauce if desired. **Yield:** 8 appetizers.

Gorgonzola Phyllo Cups

Facts on Phyllo

THIN AND CRISPY layers of phyllo dough make this ingredient popular with many cooks. It's versatile, too—great for desserts as well as appetizers such as Gorgonzola Phyllo Cups (recipe above left). Phyllo dough sheets and appetizer-size tartlets are found in the freezer section of most supermarkets.

Blueberry Ice Cream Tart

Blueberry Ice Cream Tart

(Pictured at left)

Prep: 15 min. + freezing

Absolutely no one will guess how effortless this cool, summery dessert is to make—and it can be your little secret! The quick crust boasts just a hint of cinnamon, which wonderfully complements the berries and ice cream.
—Shirley Foltz, Dexter, Kansas

1-1/2 cups crushed vanilla wafers (about 45 wafers)
1 teaspoon ground cinnamon
1/3 cup butter, melted
1 quart vanilla ice cream, softened
1 can (21 ounces) blueberry pie filling

In a small bowl, combine wafer crumbs and cinnamon; stir in butter. Press onto the bottom of a greased 9-in. springform pan; set aside.

Place the vanilla ice cream in a large bowl; gently fold in the blueberry pie filling. Spread over the prepared crust. Cover and freeze until firm. Remove from the freezer 10 minutes before serving. Remove the sides of the pan. **Yield:** 12 servings.

Peachy Sweet Potatoes

(Pictured below)

Prep/Total Time: 20 min.

Here, juicy pieces of fresh peach and cinnamon-sugar turn ordinary sweet potatoes into a standout recipe worthy of special occasions. The microwave makes this side dish a cinch to prepare...and convenient when your oven and stovetop are needed for other items on the menu.
—Josie Bochek, Sturgeon Bay, Wisconsin

Peachy Sweet Potatoes

Gouda Melt with Baguette Slices

4 medium sweet potatoes
1 medium peach, peeled and chopped
3 tablespoons butter
2 tablespoons cinnamon-sugar
Dash salt
3 tablespoons chopped pecans, toasted

Scrub and pierce potatoes; place on a microwave-safe plate. Microwave, uncovered, on high for 10-12 minutes or until tender, turning once.

Meanwhile, in a small saucepan, combine chopped peach, butter, cinnamon-sugar and salt; bring to a boil. Cook and stir for 2-3 minutes or until the peach pieces are tender.

Cut an "X" in the top of each potato; fluff pulp with a fork. Spoon peach mixture into each potato. Sprinkle with pecans. **Yield:** 4 servings.

Editor's Note: This recipe was tested in a 1,100-watt microwave.

Gouda Melt with Baguette Slices

(Pictured above)

Prep/Total Time: 20 min.

This fun appetizer comes together in a snap and is guaranteed to wow your guests—with both its appearance and taste!
—Susan Lewis, Reading, Pennsylvania

1 French bread baguette (4 ounces), sliced
1 round (7 ounces) Gouda cheese
1 plum tomato, seeded and chopped
1 tablespoon minced fresh basil

Place baguette slices on an ungreased baking sheet. Broil 3-4 in. from the heat for 1-2 minutes on each side or until toasted. Meanwhile, carefully remove waxed coating from cheese round. Using a 3-in. biscuit cutter, press into the center of cheese, but not all the way through. Scoop out center, leaving a 1/4-in. shell; set shell aside.

Place the tomato, basil and removed cheese in a small microwave-safe bowl. Cover and microwave on high for 1 minute or until the cheese is melted. Stir until combined; pour into the shell. Serve with baguette toasts. **Yield:** 4 servings.

Chapter 6

THINK the only way to feed your family fast is to race to the drive-thru? You'll think again when you page through this super-fast chapter!

Every recipe goes together from start to finish in a mere 10 minutes—or less. In the time it takes to get restaurant take-out, you can have scrumptious homemade dishes ready for the whole family.

From warm-you-up Cordon Bleu Potato Soup and savory Mushroom Beef Tips with Rice to luscious desserts such as Easy Tiramisu and Glazed Pear Short-cakes, these surprisingly speedy dishes are guaranteed to please everyone at the table—even the busy-as-can-be cook!

FAST FORWARD. Black-Eyed Pea Salad (p. 111).

Asian Meatless Wraps

(Pictured below)

Prep/Total Time: 10 min.

I'd purchased some vegetarian chicken patties but wasn't sure exactly what to do with them. This recipe, an impromptu creation on a busy weeknight, turned out so well that my husband never knew it wasn't "real" chicken! For added sweetness, I sometimes toss in a child's snack-size container of mandarin oranges, drained.
—Heidi Heimgartner, Blooming Prairie, Minnesota

4 frozen vegetarian chicken patties
1 cup coleslaw mix
1/3 cup Asian toasted sesame salad dressing
4 flour tortillas (10 inches), warmed
1/2 cup chow mein noodles
1/4 cup sliced almonds

Microwave the vegetarian chicken patties according to package directions. Meanwhile, combine the coleslaw mix and toasted sesame salad dressing; set coleslaw mixture aside.

Cut patties in half; place two halves off center on each tortilla; top with 3 tablespoons coleslaw mixture, 2 tablespoons chow mein noodles and 1 tablespoon almonds. Fold sides and ends over the filling and roll up.
Yield: 4 servings.

Editor's Note: This recipe was tested in a 1,100-watt microwave.

Chicken Tostada Salad

Chicken Tostada Salad

(Pictured above)

Prep/Total Time: 10 min.

If I don't have any tostada shells on hand for this speedy Southwestern salad, I just heat taco shells, break them in half and lay them flat on the plates. It works just as well! —Edie DeSpain, Logan, Utah

4 cups shredded lettuce
1 medium tomato, cut into wedges
1/2 cup reduced-fat ranch salad dressing
1/4 cup sliced ripe olives
2 tablespoons taco sauce
4 tostada shells
2 packages (6 ounces *each*) ready-to-use
   Southwestern chicken strips
1/2 cup shredded Mexican cheese blend

In a large bowl, combine the first five ingredients. Divide among shells. Top with chicken; sprinkle with cheese.
Yield: 4 servings.

Tortilla Treat

HAVE an opened package of flour tortillas in the refrigerator? Why not use them to create a sweet finale for your Southwestern meal...or to fix an afternoon snack for the kids? Simply brush the tortillas with butter and sprinkle them with cinnamon-sugar, then bake them on a cookie sheet until crisp.

Asian Meatless Wraps

Easy Tiramisu

(Pictured above)

Prep/Total Time: 10 min.

What a fun use for those pudding snack cups! This quick take on a classic Italian recipe makes a wonderful dessert for a special occasion or anytime. It's easily doubled if needed. My husband is diabetic, so I use sugar-free pudding and vanilla wafers when I make this for him.
—Betty Claycomb, Adverton, Pennsylvania

☑ **This recipe includes Nutrition Facts.**

12 vanilla wafers, *divided*
 1 teaspoon instant coffee granules
 2 tablespoons hot water
 2 snack-size cups (3-1/2 ounces *each***) vanilla pudding**
 1/4 cup whipped topping
 1 teaspoon baking cocoa

Set aside two vanilla wafers; coarsely crush the remaining wafers. Divide the wafer crumbs between two dessert dishes. In a small bowl, dissolve coffee granules in hot water. Drizzle over wafer crumbs. Spoon pudding into dessert dishes. Top with whipped topping; sprinkle with cocoa. Garnish with reserved vanilla wafers. **Yield:** 2 servings.

Nutrition Facts: 1 serving equals 267 calories, 9 g fat (4 g saturated fat), 4 mg cholesterol, 219 mg sodium, 41 g carbohydrate, 1 g fiber, 3 g protein.

Chicken Pesto Clubs

Chicken Pesto Clubs

(Pictured above)

Prep/Total Time: 10 min.

If you're a fan of sandwiches, you'll definitely want to put this one on your must-try list. The colorful creation is a crisp golden brown on the outside, with a fresh-tasting filling of chicken strips, bacon, cheddar cheese, prepared pesto and more on sourdough bread. Delicious!
—Terri Crandall, Gardnerville, Nevada

4 slices ready-to-serve fully cooked bacon
4 slices sourdough bread
2 tablespoons prepared pesto
1 cup ready-to-use grilled chicken breast strips
2 slices cheddar cheese
1 medium tomato, sliced
1 cup fresh arugula *or* baby spinach
1 tablespoon olive oil

Heat bacon according to package directions. Meanwhile, spread bread slices with pesto. Layer two slices with chicken, cheese, tomato, arugula and bacon; top with remaining bread slice. Brush outsides of sandwiches with oil.

Cook sandwiches on an indoor grill for 3-4 minutes or until the bread is browned and the cheese is melted. **Yield:** 2 servings.

Makin' Bacon

We often enjoy BLT sandwiches in summer. To keep my kitchen free of bacon odor, I move my indoor grill outside. I place it on top of my closed outdoor grill, plug it in and cook the bacon in it. It's fast, too!
—Margaret Stevenson, Franklin, Michigan

Tex-Mex Seasoning Mix

(Pictured below)

Prep/Total Time: 5 min.

You can create this mix in a mere five minutes. Give it as a gift and keep some to make a Tex-Mex dip and chicken entree. —Tammy and Corinna Rose, Danville, Arkansas

- 2 tablespoons dried parsley flakes
- 4 teaspoons dried minced onion
- 4 teaspoons chili powder
- 3 teaspoons dried minced chives
- 3 teaspoons ground cumin

ADDITIONAL INGREDIENTS FOR TEX-MEX DIP:
- 1/2 cup mayonnaise
- 1/2 cup sour cream

Corn chips

ADDITIONAL INGREDIENTS FOR TEX-MEX CHICKEN:
- 7 cups uncooked wide egg noodles
- 1 package (16 ounces) process cheese (Velveeta), cubed
- 1 cup (8 ounces) sour cream
- 2 tablespoons milk
- 3 packages (6 ounces *each*) ready-to-use Southwestern chicken strips
- 1 can (15 ounces) black beans, rinsed and drained
- 1 can (10 ounces) diced tomatoes and green chilies, undrained

Ambrosia Fruit Salad

In a small bowl, combine seasonings. Store in an airtight container in a cool dry place for up to 6 months. **Yield:** about 6 tablespoons.

To prepare dip: In a small bowl, combine the mayonnaise, sour cream and 4-1/2 teaspoons seasoning mix. Serve with corn chips. **Yield:** about 1 cup.

To prepare chicken: Cook the egg noodles according to the package directions. Meanwhile, in a large saucepan, combine the process cheese, sour cream and milk. Cook and stir over medium-low heat until the cheese is melted. Add the chicken strips, black beans, diced tomatoes and 2 tablespoons seasoning mix; heat through.

Drain the egg noodles; add to sauce and toss to coat. **Yield:** 7 servings.

Ambrosia Fruit Salad

(Pictured above)

Prep/Total Time: 10 min.

This refreshing, creamy salad is a favorite around my house. I toss together plenty of fruit, using vanilla yogurt as the dressing, then add "goodies"—marshmallows and coconut—so it tastes like the rich version I grew up with. —Trisha Kruse, Eagle, Idaho

☑ This recipe includes Nutrition Facts.

- 1 can (8-1/4 ounces) fruit cocktail, drained
- 1 can (8 ounces) unsweetened pineapple chunks, drained
- 1 cup green grapes
- 1 cup seedless red grapes
- 1 cup miniature marshmallows
- 1 medium banana, sliced
- 3/4 cup reduced-fat vanilla yogurt
- 1/2 cup flaked coconut

In a large bowl, combine all ingredients for salad. **Yield:** 6 servings.

Nutrition Facts: 3/4 cup equals 191 calories, 4 g fat (3 g saturated fat), 2 mg cholesterol, 48 mg sodium, 40 g carbohydrate, 2 g fiber, 3 g protein.

Tex-Mex Seasoning Mix

Chicken Melts

Sun-Dried Tomato Dip

(Pictured below)

Prep/Total Time: 10 min.

*I like to serve this snack at tailgate parties or as an appe-
tizer for a special meal. The cream-cheese dip is so easy
to pull together, but my guests never suspect that—they
just keep coming back for more! Serve it with a variety of
crackers and fresh vegetables for the perfect dippers.*
    —Andrea Reynolds, Rocky River, Ohio

  1 package (8 ounces) cream cheese, softened
1/2 cup sour cream
1/2 cup mayonnaise
1/4 cup oil-packed sun-dried tomatoes, drained
    and patted dry
1/2 teaspoon salt
1/4 teaspoon pepper
1/4 teaspoon hot pepper sauce
  2 green onions, sliced
Assorted crackers *and/or* **fresh vegetables**

Place the first seven ingredients in a food processor; cover and process until blended. Add green onions; cover
and pulse until finely chopped.

    Serve the dip with assorted crackers and/or fresh veg-
etables. **Yield:** 2 cups.

Chicken Melts

(Pictured above)

Prep/Total Time: 10 min.

*Toasty and tasty, these hefty skillet sandwiches boast a
touch of sweetness from the cinnamon-raisin bread and
jalapeno pepper jelly. If your family would prefer brick
cheese, substitute that for the creamy Havarti.*
    —Diane Halferty, Corpus Christi, Texas

  4 slices cinnamon-raisin bread
  2 tablespoons jalapeno pepper jelly
  1 package (6 ounces) thinly sliced deli smoked
    chicken breast
  3 ounces Havarti cheese, sliced
  1 tablespoon butter, softened

Spread two bread slices with jelly. Layer with chicken
and cheese; top with remaining bread. Butter outsides
of sandwiches.

    In a large skillet over medium heat, toast sandwiches
for 2-3 minutes on each side or until cheese is melted.
Yield: 2 servings.

Processing Pointer

TO PULSE foods in your food processor or blender
means to process them using short bursts of power.
This is accomplished by quickly turning the ma-
chine on. Use this easy technique when making Sun-
Dried Tomato Dip (recipe above right).

Sun-Dried Tomato Dip

In a large microwave-safe serving bowl, microwave chili on high for 2-3 minutes or until heated through. Top with cheese, lettuce and guacamole. Serve with chips. **Yield:** 3 cups.

Editor's Note: This recipe was tested in a 1,100-watt microwave.

Cordon Bleu Potato Soup

(Pictured below)

Prep/Total Time: 10 min.

I came up with this microwave recipe when I was looking for a way to use up some leftover ingredients. The result tasted nothing like leftovers! I've whipped up this creamy, cheesy ham-and-potato soup many times since.
—Noelle Myers, Grand Forks, North Dakota

> 2 cans (10-3/4 ounces *each*) condensed cream of potato soup, undiluted
> 1 can (14-1/2 ounces) chicken broth
> 1 cup (4 ounces) shredded Swiss cheese
> 1 cup diced fully cooked ham
> 1 cup milk
> 1 can (5 ounces) chunk white chicken, drained
> 2 teaspoons Dijon mustard

In a 2-quart microwave-safe dish, combine all ingredients. Cover and microwave on high for 5-8 minutes or until the soup is heated through, stirring twice. **Yield:** 4 servings.

Editor's Note: This recipe was tested in a 1,100-watt microwave oven.

Zesty Crouton Salad

Zesty Crouton Salad

(Pictured above)

Prep/Total Time: 10 min.

It takes no time at all to prep the tomatoes, cheese, basil and garlic for this recipe. And everyone loves the resulting medley of flavors and textures. You'll want to pair the salad with everything from grilled entrees to pasta.
—Valerie Smith, Aston, Pennsylvania

> 2 cups grape tomatoes, halved
> 1-1/2 cups salad croutons
> 4 pieces string cheese, cut into 1/2-inch pieces
> 8 fresh basil leaves, thinly sliced
> 2 tablespoons red wine vinegar
> 1 tablespoon olive oil
> 1/2 teaspoon minced garlic

In a large bowl, combine all ingredients for salad. **Yield:** 5 servings.

Chili Cheese Dip

Prep/Total Time: 10 min.

Perfect for casual gatherings, this irresistible dip gets a Southwestern kick from canned chili and guacamole. Keep the recipe in mind on movie night, for the big game or when friends drop in and you need something fast.
—Martha Blonde, Lansing, Michigan

> 1 can (15 ounces) chili without beans
> 1-1/2 cups (6 ounces) shredded cheddar cheese
> 1 cup chopped lettuce
> 1 cup prepared guacamole dip
> Tortilla chips

Cordon Bleu Potato Soup

Ranch Turkey Wraps

(Pictured below)

Prep/Total Time: 10 min.

This handheld meal-in-one makes a terrific lunch or even a quick dinner on the go. Customize each wrap with different ingredients to suit your family members' tastes, and the whole gang will be happy in no time!
—Emily Hanson, Logan, Utah

```
1/4 cup cream cheese, softened
1/4 cup prepared ranch salad dressing
  4 flour tortillas (10 inch), warmed
3/4 pound sliced deli turkey
  8 slices Monterey Jack cheese
  1 medium ripe avocado, peeled and sliced
  1 medium tomato, sliced
```

In a small bowl, beat cream cheese and salad dressing until smooth. Spread over tortillas. Layer with turkey, cheese, avocado and tomato. Roll up tightly; cut in half. **Yield:** 4 servings.

Italian Tossed Salad

Prep/Total Time: 10 min.

I like to serve this fresh vegetable salad alongside Italian food or with grilled steak or chicken and a baked potato. It's such a colorful, appetizing side dish—no matter what kind of main course you pair it with, you really can't go wrong.
—Rita Addicks, Weimar, Texas

Ranch Turkey Wraps

Glazed Pear Shortcakes

✓ This recipe includes Nutrition Facts and Diabetic Exchanges.

```
2 cups fresh cauliflowerets
1 cup chopped tomatoes
1/2 cup chopped celery
1/2 cup sliced red onion
1/4 cup chopped green pepper
1/2 cup Italian salad dressing
4 cups shredded lettuce
```

In a large salad bowl, combine the cauliflower, tomatoes, celery, red onion and green pepper. Add the Italian salad dressing; toss to coat. Cover and chill salad until serving.

Just before serving, add the lettuce and toss to coat. **Yield:** 6 servings.

Nutrition Facts: 1 cup equals 100 calories, 8 g fat (1 g saturated fat), 0 cholesterol, 368 mg sodium, 7 g carbohydrate, 2 g fiber, 2 g protein. **Diabetic Exchanges:** 1 vegetable, 1 fat.

Glazed Pear Shortcakes

(Pictured above)

Prep/Total Time: 10 min.

Your family and friends will savor every last crumb of this attractive, lickety-split dessert. The sliced pound cake soaks in the apricot flavor and the warm sweetness of the pears. It's special enough to serve company.
—Fran Thomas, St. James City, Florida

```
2 medium pears, sliced
2 tablespoons butter
4 teaspoons apricot spreadable fruit
8 thin slices pound cake
4 teaspoons chopped walnuts
4 tablespoons whipped topping
```

Black-Eyed Pea Salad

In a small skillet, saute pears in butter until tender. Remove from the heat; stir in spreadable fruit. Place cake slices on four dessert dishes; top with pear mixture, walnuts and whipped topping. **Yield:** 4 servings.

Black-Eyed Pea Salad

(Pictured above and on page 102)

Prep/Total Time: 10 min.

I've had a lot of compliments on this over the years. The salad dressing keeps the avocado from turning dark, even if you have leftovers—which doesn't happen often!
—Nancy Cariker, Bakersfield, California

1 can (15-1/2 ounces) black-eyed peas, rinsed and drained
1 large tomato, diced
1 medium ripe avocado, peeled and diced
1/3 cup chopped green pepper
2 green onions, chopped
1 tablespoon minced fresh cilantro
1 jalapeno pepper, seeded and chopped
1/3 cup prepared Italian salad dressing

In a large serving bowl, combine all of the ingredients; toss to coat. Serve the salad with a slotted spoon. **Yield:** 4 servings.

Editor's Note: When cutting hot peppers, disposable gloves are recommended. Avoid touching your face.

Bart's Black Bean Soup

Bart's Black Bean Soup

(Pictured above)

Prep/Total Time: 10 min.

It's almost hard to believe that this zesty soup comes together in minutes. For a complete meal, we serve it with fresh-from-the-oven dinner rolls and a simple salad.
—*Sharon Ullyot, London, Ontario*

    1 can (15 ounces) black beans, rinsed and drained
1-1/2 cups chicken broth
    3/4 cup chunky salsa
    1/2 cup canned whole kernel corn, drained
Dash hot pepper sauce
    2 teaspoons lime juice
    1 cup (4 ounces) shredded cheddar cheese
    2 tablespoons chopped green onions

In a microwave-safe bowl, combine the first five ingredients. Cover and microwave on high for 2 minutes or until heated through. Pour into four serving bowls; drizzle each with lime juice. Sprinkle with cheese and green onions. **Yield:** 4 servings.

    Editor's Note: This recipe was tested in a 1,100-watt microwave.

Mushroom Beef Tips with Rice

Prep/Total Time: 10 min.

Here's a quick and easy version of the beef tip dinner my husband absolutely loves. Even though the recipe calls for pre-made beef tips, the finished main dish is tender and delicious—you get the flavor of Stroganoff with only five ingredients! It's wonderful for hectic weeknights.
—*Pamela Shank, Parkersburg, West Virginia*

    1 cup sliced fresh mushrooms
    2 tablespoons butter
    1 package (17 ounces) refrigerated beef tips with gravy
    1 package (8.8 ounces) ready-to-serve long grain rice
    1/2 cup sour cream

In a large skillet, saute the fresh mushrooms in butter for 2 minutes; set aside 1/4 cup. Add the beef tips to the pan; cook for 4-6 minutes or until heated through, stirring occasionally.

    Meanwhile, cook rice according to package directions. Remove beef mixture from the heat; stir in sour cream. Serve with rice; top with reserved mushrooms. **Yield:** 3 servings.

Coconut-Layered Pound Cake

Coconut-Layered Pound Cake

(Pictured above)

Prep/Total Time: 10 min.

This cake tastes just like an Almond Joy candy bar. If you like coconut, chocolate and almonds, this is the dessert for you! —Linda Nichols, Steubenville, Ohio

 1 loaf (16 ounces) frozen pound cake, thawed
 1 can (14 ounces) sweetened condensed milk
2-2/3 cups flaked coconut
 1/2 cup chopped almonds, toasted
 1 cup chocolate fudge frosting

Cut cake horizontally into four layers. In a small bowl, combine the milk, coconut and almonds. Place bottom layer on a serving plate; top with half of the coconut mixture, one cake layer and 1/2 cup frosting. Repeat layers. **Yield:** 8 servings.

Chicken and Pear Salad

Prep/Total Time: 10 min.

Turn everyday greens into a spectacular salad by adding chicken, red pepper and sliced pears. It makes a hearty lunch—or dinner with some bread and soup.
 —Sarita Johnston, San Antonio, Texas

 6 cups torn mixed salad greens
1-1/4 cups sliced cooked chicken
 1 cup chopped sweet red pepper
 1 can (15-1/4 ounces) sliced pears, drained
 1/4 teaspoon pepper
 1/2 cup ranch salad dressing

Divide salad greens among four plates. Top with chicken, red pepper and pears. Sprinkle with pepper; serve with salad dressing. **Yield:** 4 servings.

Peachy Shrimp Tacos

(Pictured below)

Prep/Total Time: 10 min.

With three always-on-the-go children, we frequently have only about 10 minutes to get dinner on the table. This no-fuss recipe has become a family favorite. You can use flour tortillas or even hard taco shells, but I like to use corn tortillas because of their slightly higher fiber content.
 —Veronica Callaghan, Glastonbury, Connecticut

✓ This recipe includes Nutrition Facts and Diabetic Exchanges.

 1 jar (8 ounces) salsa
 1 cup frozen unsweetened sliced peaches, thawed and diced
 1 pound cooked medium shrimp, peeled and deveined
 1 tablespoon minced fresh cilantro
1-1/2 cups shredded Chinese *or* napa cabbage
 6 corn tortillas (6 inches), warmed

In a large skillet, combine salsa and peaches over medium heat until warmed. Add shrimp and cilantro; cook and stir until heated through. Place 1/4 cupful cabbage down the center of each corn tortilla; top with a scant 1/2 cupful shrimp mixture. **Yield:** 6 servings.
 Nutrition Facts: 1 taco equals 165 calories, 2 g fat (trace saturated fat), 115 mg cholesterol, 308 mg sodium, 19 g carbohydrate, 2 g fiber, 17 g protein. **Diabetic Exchanges:** 2 very lean meat, 1 starch.

Peachy Shrimp Tacos

Chapter 7

YOUR WEEKDAYS just got a whole lot easier! That's because we've done much of the planning for you right here.

This handy chapter features six weeks of Monday-through-Friday entree recipes, most created by our Test Kitchen cooks. You get a complete grocery list with each week, so you'll know exactly what you need to get in only one trip to the store.

There's no fuss, no guesswork and no planning on your part... just mouth-watering favorites such as Southwest Beef Pie, Savory Onion Chicken, Shrimp Burritos and Pork Roast with Mashed Potatoes and Gravy.

Plus, most of them are table-ready in just 30 minutes or less!

HERE'S THE PLAN. Vegetable Beef Bow Tie Skillet (p. 126).

Week 1

Shopping List

Check for these staples:

- brown sugar
- butter
- cider vinegar
- cornstarch
- dill weed
- dried rosemary
- eggs
- flour
- instant rice
- Italian seasoning
- lemon juice
- milk
- minced garlic
- onions
- oregano
- paprika
- pepper
- salt
- seasoned salt
- Worcestershire sauce

Shop for these items:

- 2 cans (14-1/2 ounces) chicken broth
- 1 can (16 ounces) kidney beans
- 1 can (10-3/4 ounces) condensed nacho cheese soup
- 1 can (14-1/2 ounces) diced tomatoes
- 1 package (24 ounces) refrigerated mashed potatoes
- 1 package (8 ounces) sliced fresh mushrooms
- 1 package (8 ounces) shredded cheddar cheese
- 1 package (5 ounces) shredded Swiss cheese
- 1 large sweet red pepper
- 2 large onions
- 2 pounds ground beef
- 1 boneless whole pork loin roast (3 to 4 pounds)
- 4 salmon fillets (6 ounces each)
- 1 package (16 ounces) frozen puff pastry
- 1 package (16 ounces) frozen broccoli-cauliflower blend

Time-Saving Tips

- When preparing Pork Roast with Mashed Potatoes and Gravy on Monday, cut an extra onion so you have the 1/2 cup needed for Tuesday's Beefy Swiss Bundles. Also, cube 2-1/2 cups of the cooked pork for Thursday's Creamy Pork Potpie.
- On Tuesday, cut your prep time by using sliced mushrooms and jarred minced garlic. You'll use the extra mushrooms on Wednesday.
- Round out Wednesday's main dish, Salmon with Lemon-Mushroom Sauce, by tossing together a quick salad and baking some French bread.
- Save the rest of the frozen veggies from Thursday's Creamy Pork Potpie to use for Friday's dinner, Vegetable Beef Skillet. You could also stir in any leftover veggies or cheese you may have in the fridge.

Monday

Pork Roast with Mashed Potatoes and Gravy

(Pictured above)

Prep: 20 min. **Cook:** 3 hours

This home-style supper can be prepared on Sunday. Strain and skim the cooking juices, then cover and store it all in the refrigerator. On Monday, reheat the pork to 165° and finish the gravy in a pan.

- 1 boneless whole pork loin roast (3 to 4 pounds)
- 1 can (14-1/2 ounces) chicken broth
- 1 cup julienned sweet red pepper
- 1/2 cup chopped onion
- 1/4 cup cider vinegar
- 2 tablespoons Worcestershire sauce
- 1 tablespoon brown sugar
- 2 teaspoons Italian seasoning
- 1 teaspoon salt
- 1 teaspoon pepper
- 2 teaspoons cornstarch
- 2 teaspoons cold water
- 2 cups refrigerated mashed potatoes

Cut roast in half; transfer to a 5-qt. slow cooker. In a small bowl, combine the broth, red pepper, onion, vinegar, Worcestershire sauce, brown sugar and seasonings; pour over pork. Cover and cook on low for 3-4 hours or until a meat thermometer reads 160° and meat is tender.

Remove the pork; cut some into cubes measuring 2-1/2 cups for Creamy Pork Potpie (recipe on page 118) or save for another use. (Keep remaining pork warm.)

For gravy, strain cooking juices and skim fat; pour 1 cup into a small saucepan. Combine cornstarch and water until smooth; stir into cooking juices. Bring to a boil; cook and stir for 2 minutes or until thickened.

Meanwhile, in a small microwave-safe bowl, cook potatoes on high for 2-3 minutes or until heated through. Slice remaining pork; serve with potatoes and gravy. **Yield:** 4 servings.

Editor's Note: This recipe was tested in a 1,100-watt microwave.

Tuesday

Beefy Swiss Bundles

(Pictured below)

Prep: 20 min. **Bake:** 20 min.

Children and adults alike will devour these comforting yet easy pockets. With creamy mashed potatoes, gooey cheese and flavorful seasonings, what's not to love?

    1 pound ground beef
1-1/2 cups sliced fresh mushrooms
   1/2 cup chopped onion
1-1/2 teaspoons minced garlic
    4 teaspoons Worcestershire sauce
   3/4 teaspoon dried rosemary, crushed
   3/4 teaspoon paprika
   1/2 teaspoon salt
   1/4 teaspoon pepper
    1 sheet frozen puff pastry, thawed
   2/3 cup refrigerated mashed potatoes
    1 cup (4 ounces) shredded Swiss cheese
    1 egg
    2 tablespoons water

In a large skillet, cook the beef, mushrooms, onion and garlic over medium heat until meat is no longer pink; drain. Stir in Worcestershire sauce and seasonings. Remove from the heat; set aside.

On a lightly floured surface, roll the puff pastry into a 15-in. x 13-in. rectangle. Cut into four 7-1/2-in. x 6-1/2-in. rectangles. Place about 2 tablespoons potatoes

Beefy Swiss Bundles

Salmon with Lemon-Mushroom Sauce

over each rectangle; spread to within 1 in. of edges. Top with 3/4 cup beef mixture; sprinkle with 1/4 cup cheese.

Beat egg and water; brush some over pastry edges. Bring opposite corners of pastry over each bundle; pinch seams to seal. Transfer to a greased baking sheet; brush with remaining egg mixture. Bake at 400° for 17-20 minutes or until golden brown. **Yield:** 4 servings.

Wednesday

Salmon with Lemon-Mushroom Sauce

(Pictured above)

Prep/Total Time: 15 min.

The microwave makes this special seafood dinner super-fast. It blends the flavors of lemon, dill and fresh mushrooms with tender, flaky salmon.

    2 cups sliced fresh mushrooms
    2 tablespoons butter
    2 tablespoons lemon juice
   1/2 teaspoon dill weed
   1/4 teaspoon salt
   1/4 teaspoon pepper
    4 salmon fillets (6 ounces *each*)

Place mushrooms and butter in a small microwave-safe bowl. Cover and microwave on high for 3-4 minutes or until mushrooms are tender, stirring twice. Add the lemon juice and seasonings.

Place fillets in an 8-in. square microwave-safe dish; top with mushroom mixture. Cover and microwave on high for 4-6 minutes or until fish flakes easily with a fork. Let stand for 5 minutes before serving. **Yield:** 4 servings.

Editor's Note: This recipe was tested in a 1,100-watt microwave.

Creamy Pork Potpie

Vegetable Beef Skillet

(Pictured below)

Prep/Total Time: 30 min.

With ground beef and plenty of cheese, this 30-minute, one-pan wonder will satisfy everyone at the table. Plus, cleanup is a breeze—so you'll be on your way toward savoring the weekend in no time at all!

> 1 pound ground beef
> 1/2 cup chopped onion
> 2 cups frozen broccoli-cauliflower blend, thawed and chopped
> 1 can (16 ounces) kidney beans, rinsed and drained
> 1 can (14-1/2 ounces) diced tomatoes, undrained
> 1 can (10-3/4 ounces) condensed nacho cheese soup, undiluted
> 3/4 cup water
> 1 teaspoon dried oregano
> 1/2 teaspoon salt
> 1 cup uncooked instant rice
> 1/2 cup shredded cheddar cheese

In a large skillet, cook beef and onion over medium heat until meat is no longer pink; drain.

Stir in the vegetables, nacho cheese soup, water, oregano and salt. Bring to a boil. Stir in the rice. Remove from the heat; cover and let stand for 5 minutes or until the rice is tender. Sprinkle with the cheddar cheese. **Yield:** 6 servings.

Creamy Pork Potpie

(Pictured above)

Prep: 20 min. **Cook:** 20 min.

This hearty main dish was practically made for chilly weather, so huddle up with the family and enjoy! Save any leftovers for lunch the next day.

> 1/4 cup butter, cubed
> 1/2 cup all-purpose flour
> 1 can (14-1/2 ounces) chicken broth
> 3/4 cup milk
> 2-1/2 cups cubed cooked pork
> 2-1/2 cups frozen broccoli-cauliflower blend
> 1-1/2 cups (6 ounces) shredded cheddar cheese
> 1/2 teaspoon seasoned salt
> Dash pepper
> 1 sheet frozen puff pastry, thawed
> 1 egg, beaten

In a large saucepan, melt the butter. Stir in flour until smooth; gradually add broth and milk. Bring to a boil; cook and stir for 2 minutes or until thickened. Add the pork, vegetables, cheese, seasoned salt and pepper; heat through.

Transfer to a greased 11-in. x 7-in. baking dish. On a lightly floured surface, roll the puff pastry into an 11-in. x 7-in. rectangle. Place over the pork mixture. Brush with beaten egg.

Bake, uncovered, at 425° for 18-22 minutes or until golden brown. Let stand for 5 minutes before cutting. **Yield:** 6 servings.

Vegetable Beef Skillet

Week 2

Shopping List

Check for these staples:

- all-purpose flour
- brown sugar
- butter
- cayenne pepper
- chili powder
- cornstarch
- dried parsley flakes
- egg
- garlic powder
- honey
- instant rice
- Italian seasoning
- olive oil
- 3 small onions
- orange juice
- paprika
- pepper
- salt
- seasoned bread crumbs
- seasoned salt
- sesame seeds
- soy sauce
- sugar

Shop for these items:

1   can (15 ounces) chili with beans
1   can (14-1/2 ounces) beef broth
1   bottle (16 ounces) reduced-fat ranch salad dressing
1   package (8-1/2 ounces) corn bread/muffin mix
1   package (4 ounces) chopped walnuts
2   packages (5 ounces each) spring mix salad greens
1   medium apple
2   large green peppers
1   bunch celery
1   package (1 pound) carrots
1   package (8 ounces) shredded cheddar cheese
1   package (1 pound) hot dogs
4   boneless skinless chicken breast halves (4 ounces each)
1   pound boneless skinless chicken breast halves
1   pound ground beef
4   fresh or frozen orange roughy fillets (5 ounces each)
1   package (16 ounces) frozen mixed vegetables
1   package (16 ounces) frozen cheese and potato pierogies

Time-Saving Tips

- If you have time on Monday, chop an extra cup of onion, 1-1/2 cups of celery and the remaining green pepper for later in the week.
- A pound of cooked and crumbled ground beef could be substituted for the hot dogs in Tuesday's Chili Cheese Dog Casserole. Just omit the oil and cook the ground beef with the veggies.

Monday

Orange Chicken and Veggies with Rice

(Pictured below)

Prep: 15 min. **Cook:** 20 min.

A flavorful orange glaze coats tender pieces of chicken and fresh vegetables in this delicious dinner recipe. It's guaranteed to bring praises to the chef.

1-1/2 cups uncooked instant rice
   1 tablespoon plus 1/3 cup cornstarch, *divided*
   1 cup orange juice
   1 tablespoon soy sauce
   1 teaspoon sugar
  1/4 teaspoon salt
  1/4 teaspoon pepper
   1 pound boneless skinless chicken breasts, cut into 1-inch cubes
   3 tablespoons olive oil, *divided*
1-1/2 cups sliced fresh carrots
   1 cup chopped green pepper
  1/2 cup chopped onion

Prepare rice according to package directions. Meanwhile, in a small bowl, combine 1 tablespoon cornstarch, juice, soy sauce, sugar, salt and pepper; set aside.

Place remaining cornstarch in a large resealable plastic bag. Add chicken, a few pieces at a time, and shake to coat. In a large skillet over medium heat, cook chicken in 2 tablespoons oil for 7-9 minutes or until chicken juices run clear. Remove and keep warm.

In the same skillet, saute carrots in remaining oil for 2 minutes. Add green pepper and onion; saute 2-3 minutes longer or until vegetables are crisp-tender. Stir cornstarch mixture and add to the pan. Bring to a boil; cook and stir for 2 minutes or until thickened. Add chicken; heat through. Serve with rice. **Yield:** 4 servings.

Orange Chicken and Veggies with Rice

Chili Cheese Dog Casserole

(Pictured below)

Prep: 20 min. **Bake:** 30 min.

Grown-ups will like this comforting dish just as much as kids do. With a crispy cheese topping on a warm corn bread crust, the recipe is definitely a keeper.

- 1 package (8-1/2 ounces) corn bread/muffin mix
- 1 cup chopped green pepper
- 1/2 cup chopped onion
- 1/2 cup chopped celery
- 1 tablespoon olive oil
- 1 package (1 pound) hot dogs, halved lengthwise and cut into bite-size pieces
- 1 can (15 ounces) chili with beans
- 2 tablespoons brown sugar
- 1/2 teaspoon garlic powder
- 1/2 teaspoon chili powder
- 1 cup (4 ounces) shredded cheddar cheese, *divided*

Prepare corn bread batter according to package directions. Spread half the batter into a greased 8-in. square baking dish; set aside.

In a large skillet, saute the green pepper, onion and celery in oil until crisp-tender. Stir in hot dogs; saute 3-4 minutes longer or until lightly browned. Stir in the chili, brown sugar, garlic powder and chili powder; heat through. Stir in 3/4 cup cheese. Spoon over prepared corn bread. Spread remaining batter onto hot dog mixture. Sprinkle with remaining cheese.

Bake, uncovered, at 350° for 28-32 minutes or until a toothpick inserted near the center comes out clean. Let stand for 5 minutes before serving. **Yield:** 6 servings.

Chili Cheese Dog Casserole

Ranch Chicken Salad

Ranch Chicken Salad

(Pictured above)

Prep/Total Time: 30 min.

Serving salad for supper is anything but skimpy—when the salad is as hearty and filling as this one! It gives you tender chicken and cheddar cheese in every bite. Plus, celery and apple add a pleasing crunch.

- 2 tablespoons plus 1 teaspoon paprika
- 4 teaspoons brown sugar
- 3 teaspoons garlic powder
- 1 teaspoon seasoned salt
- 1/8 teaspoon cayenne pepper
- 4 boneless skinless chicken breast halves (4 ounces *each*)
- 2 packages (5 ounces *each*) spring mix salad greens
- 1 cup chopped celery
- 1 cup shredded carrots
- 1 medium apple, chopped
- 1/2 cup shredded cheddar cheese
- 1/2 cup reduced-fat ranch salad dressing

In a large resealable plastic bag, combine the first five ingredients. Add chicken, one piece at a time, and shake to coat. Place chicken on a greased broiler pan. Broil 6 in. from the heat for 6-8 minutes on each side or until chicken juices run clear.

Meanwhile, divide salad greens among four dinner plates. Top each with celery, carrots, apple and cheese. Cut chicken into strips; arrange over salad. Drizzle with dressing. **Yield:** 4 servings.

Thursday

Pierogi Beef Skillet

(Pictured below)

Prep/Total Time: 30 min.

Loaded with ground beef, vegetables and potatoes, this is a complete meal-in-one that'll satisfy even the biggest appetites. And thanks to convenient packaged pierogies, dinner is served in just half an hour.

- 1 pound ground beef
- 1/2 cup chopped onion
- 1/4 cup all-purpose flour
- 1 can (14-1/2 ounces) beef broth
- 1 package (16 ounces) frozen cheese and potato pierogies, thawed
- 2 cups frozen mixed vegetables, thawed and drained
- 1/2 teaspoon salt
- 1/2 teaspoon pepper
- 1/2 teaspoon Italian seasoning
- 1/2 cup shredded cheddar cheese

In a large skillet, cook ground beef and onion over medium heat until the meat is no longer pink; drain, reserving 3 tablespoons drippings. Sprinkle flour over the beef and drippings; stir until blended. Gradually add beef broth. Bring to a boil; cook and stir for 2 minutes or until thickened.

Stir in pierogies, vegetables and seasonings. Cook, uncovered, for 4-5 minutes or until heated through. Sprinkle with cheese. **Yield:** 4 servings.

Friday

Walnut-Crusted Orange Roughy

(Pictured above)

Prep/Total Time: 25 min.

A crispy, crunchy crust and moist, tender fish make this recipe a surefire winner. The dipping sauce is salty-sweet and pairs beautifully with the walnuts. If you like, substitute flounder or sole for the orange roughy.

- 4 fresh *or* frozen orange roughy fillets, thawed (5 ounces *each*)
- 1/2 teaspoon salt
- 1/4 teaspoon pepper
- 1/4 cup all-purpose flour
- 1 egg, beaten
- 1 cup finely chopped walnuts
- 3 tablespoons seasoned bread crumbs
- 1 tablespoon sesame seeds
- 1 tablespoon dried parsley flakes
- 2 tablespoons butter
- 1/4 cup honey
- 1-1/2 teaspoons soy sauce

Sprinkle orange roughy fillets with salt and pepper. Place flour and egg in separate shallow bowls. In another shallow bowl, combine the walnuts, bread crumbs, sesame seeds and parsley. Dip fish in the flour, egg, then walnut mixture.

In a large skillet over medium heat, cook fish in butter in batches for 2-3 minutes on each side or until fish flakes easily with a fork. In a small bowl, whisk honey and soy sauce; serve with fish. **Yield:** 4 servings.

Pierogi Beef Skillet

Week 3

Roasted Turkey Breast Tenderloins & Vegetables

Shopping List

Check for these staples:

- A.1. steak sauce
- all-purpose flour
- butter
- chicken broth
- cornstarch
- dill weed
- dried basil
- dried minced onion
- dried oregano
- dried parsley flakes
- dried thyme
- Louisiana-style hot sauce
- milk
- minced garlic
- olive oil
- onions
- paprika
- Parmesan cheese
- pepper
- salt
- seafood seasoning

Shop for these items:

- 1 can (10-3/4 ounces) condensed cream of celery soup
- 1 package (16 ounces) linguine
- 1 package (12-1/2 ounces) pita breads
- 1 package flour tortillas (10 in.)
- 1 package (16 ounces) fresh baby carrots
- 1 bunch celery
- 1 pound cooked medium shrimp, peeled and deveined
- 8 turkey breast tenderloins (5 ounces each)
- 1-1/4 pounds boneless beef sirloin steak
- 8 ounces cubed fully cooked ham
- 1 bunch romaine lettuce
- 1 package (8 ounces) shredded cheddar-Monterey Jack cheese
- 1 package (4 ounces) crumbled blue cheese
- 1 package (8 ounces) cream cheese
- 1 package (14 ounces) frozen pepper strips
- 1 package (19 ounces) frozen cheese tortellini

Time-Saving Tips

- You don't need to cook all eight of the tenderloins called for in Monday's recipe, but the cooked turkey comes in handy for Buffalo Turkey with Linguine on Wednesday.
- If you like, a pound of cooked boneless, skinless chicken breasts could be substituted for the turkey in Wednesday's entree.
- To buy the whole pita breads needed for Hearty Sirloin Pitas on Tuesday, look near the deli area of your supermarket.
- Our Test Kitchen staff preferred fixing Thursday's dinner with cheese tortellini, but any flavor will work. You could also use bow tie pasta.

Monday

Roasted Turkey Breast Tenderloins & Vegetables

(Pictured above)

Prep: 15 min. **Bake:** 35 min.

Classic flavors come together quickly in this well seasoned, family-pleasing turkey dinner. With plenty of carrots, celery and onions, it's a complete meal in one.

- 1 teaspoon dill weed
- 1 teaspoon dried thyme
- 1 teaspoon dried oregano
- 1 teaspoon dried minced onion
- 3/4 teaspoon salt
- 1/4 teaspoon pepper
- 1/4 cup butter, melted
- 3 cups fresh baby carrots
- 4 celery ribs, cut into 2-inch pieces
- 2 medium onions, cut into wedges
- 1 tablespoon olive oil
- 8 turkey breast tenderloins (5 ounces *each*)
- 2 teaspoons cornstarch
- 1/4 cup water

In a small bowl, combine the first six ingredients. Combine 2 teaspoons of the seasoning mixture with butter; toss with vegetables. Transfer to a roasting pan. Bake, uncovered, at 425° for 15 minutes.

Meanwhile, rub oil over turkey; sprinkle with remaining seasoning mixture. Move vegetables to edges of pan; place turkey in the center. Bake, uncovered, at 425° for 20-25 minutes or until a meat thermometer reads 170° and vegetables are tender.

Save half of the roasted turkey for Buffalo Turkey with Linguine (recipe on page 123) or save for another use. Remove the remaining turkey and vegetables to a serving platter and keep warm.

Pour the cooking juices into a small saucepan. Combine the cornstarch and water until smooth; gradually stir into pan. Bring to a boil; cook and stir for 2 minutes or until thickened. Serve with the turkey and vegetables. **Yield:** 4 servings plus 16 ounces cooked turkey breast tenderloins.

Buffalo Turkey with Linguine

Tuesday

Hearty Sirloin Pitas

(Pictured below)

Prep/Total Time: 20 min.

Blue cheese and steak sauce make these change-of-pace sandwiches taste terrific. To soften the pitas a bit, warm them in the oven or microwave.

1-1/4 pounds boneless beef sirloin steak, cut into 1/4-inch slices
1/4 teaspoon salt
1/4 teaspoon pepper
3 teaspoons olive oil, *divided*
2-1/3 cups frozen pepper strips, thawed
1/2 cup thinly sliced onion
2 teaspoons A.1. steak sauce
4 whole pita breads, warmed
1/4 cup crumbled blue cheese

Sprinkle beef with salt and pepper. In a large skillet, cook beef in batches in 2 teaspoons oil over medium heat until meat reaches desired doneness. Remove and keep warm. In the same pan, saute pepper strips and onion in remaining oil until crisp-tender. Add beef and steak sauce; heat through.

Top each pita with beef mixture; sprinkle with cheese. Fold over. **Yield:** 4 servings.

Wednesday

Buffalo Turkey with Linguine

(Pictured above)

Prep/Total Time: 25 min.

Cooking extra turkey on Monday to use for this delicious pasta dish is a great timesaver. If you're serving this to kids, simply omit the hot sauce and blue cheese.

8 ounces uncooked linguine
1 cup chopped onion
1 cup chopped celery
3/4 cup chopped carrot
1 teaspoon minced garlic
2 tablespoons butter
1 tablespoon all-purpose flour
1/2 teaspoon salt
2 cups milk
4 ounces cream cheese, softened
4 cooked Roasted Turkey Breast Tenderloins (recipe on page 122), chopped
2 to 3 tablespoons Louisiana-style hot sauce
1/4 cup crumbled blue cheese

Cook the linguine according to the package directions. Meanwhile, in a Dutch oven, saute the onion, celery, carrot and garlic in the butter until tender. Stir in the flour and salt until blended. Gradually add the milk. Bring to a boil. Cook and stir for 1-2 minutes or until slightly thickened.

Stir in the cream cheese until melted. Add the turkey and hot sauce; heat through. Drain the linguine; toss with the turkey mixture. Sprinkle with blue cheese. **Yield:** 5 servings.

Hearty Sirloin Pitas

Tortellini and Ham

Shrimp Burritos

(Pictured below)

Prep/Total Time: 20 min.

These may sound unusual, but give them a try—you and your family will be glad you did! The gooey, creamy and rich burritos take just 20 minutes to assemble and are packed full of tender shrimp and shredded cheese. Children and adults alike love diving in.

  1 can (10-3/4 ounces) condensed cream of celery soup, undiluted
  3 ounces cream cheese, softened
1/4 cup milk
1/4 teaspoon paprika
1/4 teaspoon pepper
1/8 teaspoon seafood seasoning
  1 pound cooked medium shrimp, peeled and deveined
  4 flour tortillas (10 inches), warmed
1/2 cup shredded cheddar-Monterey Jack cheese
  1 cup torn romaine, chopped

In a large skillet, combine the first six ingredients. Cook and stir over medium heat until cream cheese is melted and blended. Stir in shrimp; heat through.

Spoon 2/3 cup filling off center on each tortilla. Sprinkle each with 2 tablespoons cheese. Fold the sides and ends over the filling and roll up. Serve with the lettuce. **Yield:** 4 servings.

Tortellini and Ham

(Pictured above)

Prep/Total Time: 25 min.

A couple of convenience items—frozen cheese tortellini and frozen pepper strips—are the basis of this quick meal. It's sure to become a staple when you need something at the last minute on a weeknight.

    1 package (19 ounces) frozen cheese tortellini
    1 cup frozen pepper strips, thawed
    3 tablespoons butter
1-1/4 cups cubed fully cooked ham
    1 teaspoon minced garlic
1-1/2 teaspoons cornstarch
  1/2 cup chicken broth
    1 teaspoon dried basil
  1/2 teaspoon dried parsley flakes
  1/4 teaspoon pepper
    4 tablespoons grated Parmesan cheese, divided

Cook the cheese tortellini according to the package directions. Meanwhile, in a large skillet, saute the pepper strips in the butter until crisp-tender. Add the ham and garlic; saute 1 minute longer. Combine the cornstarch, chicken broth, basil, parsley and pepper; stir into pepper mixture. Bring to a boil; cook and stir for 2 minutes or until thickened.

Add 2 tablespoons Parmesan cheese. Drain tortellini; toss with ham mixture. Sprinkle with remaining cheese. **Yield:** 4 servings.

Shrimp Burritos

Week 4

Black Bean Spinach Salad

Shopping List

Check for these staples:

- all-purpose flour
- beef broth
- butter
- chicken broth
- chili powder
- cornstarch
- garlic powder
- ground ginger
- Italian seasoning
- ketchup
- lemon juice
- maple syrup
- minced garlic
- olive oil
- oregano
- pepper
- rice
- salad dressing
- salt
- sesame seeds
- soy sauce

Shop for these items:

- 2 cans (15 ounces each) black beans
- 1 package (12 ounces) bow tie pasta
- 2 packages (2.25 ounces each) chopped walnuts
- 1 can (6 ounces) tomato paste
- 3 packages (6 ounces each) fresh baby spinach
- 2 medium green peppers
- 5 medium onions
- 6 medium tomatoes
- 2 medium yellow peppers
- 2 medium zucchini
- 1 package (16 ounces) shredded cheddar cheese
- 2 tubes (8 ounces each) refrigerated crescent rolls
- 1-1/2 pounds boneless skinless chicken breasts
- 2 pounds ground beef
- 4 boneless pork loin chops (1 inch thick and 6 ounces each)

Time-Saving Tips

- While preparing Black Bean Spinach Salad on Monday, save yourself some time later in the week by chopping an extra yellow pepper and storing it in the fridge. It'll be ready to add to Vegetable Beef Bow Tie Skillet on Wednesday.
- Want to use fresh ginger in Tuesday's Ginger Sesame Chicken? Use 1 teaspoon of peeled and minced fresh ginger and add it to the skillet with the peppers and onions.
- If you're not a fan of tomato paste, simply substitute 1 cup of tomato sauce for the tomato paste and 1/2 cup of water when putting together Sloppy Joe Calzones on Friday.

Monday

Black Bean Spinach Salad

(Pictured above)

Prep/Total Time: 15 min.

Enjoy a meatless Monday night with this satisfying salad chock-full of black beans, baby spinach, tomatoes and toasted walnuts. With these nutritious ingredients, you'll be starting your week off on the right foot.

- 4 cups fresh baby spinach
- 1 can (15 ounces) black beans, rinsed and drained
- 1 cup chopped sweet yellow pepper
- 2 medium tomatoes, cut into wedges
- 1 cup shredded zucchini
- 1 cup (4 ounces) shredded cheddar cheese
- 1/2 cup chopped walnuts, toasted

Salad dressing of your choice

In a large salad bowl, combine the spinach, black beans and yellow pepper. Top with tomatoes and zucchini; sprinkle with cheddar cheese and walnuts. Serve with salad dressing. **Yield:** 4 servings.

Try Toasting

TOASTING NUTS before using them in a recipe (such as Black Bean Spinach Salad above) intensifies their flavor. To toast nuts, simply spread them on a baking sheet and bake them at 350° for 5 to 10 minutes or until they're lightly toasted. Be sure to watch them carefully so they don't burn.

Ginger Sesame Chicken

(Pictured below)

Prep/Total Time: 30 min.

Want an Asian-style dinner made easy? Here, tender chunks of chicken and vegetables are coated in a sweet and salty sauce flavored with ginger and a hint of maple syrup. It all comes together in a mere 30 minutes.

      1 tablespoon cornstarch
  3/4 cup chicken broth
      2 tablespoons sesame seeds
      2 tablespoons maple syrup
      4 teaspoons soy sauce
  1/2 teaspoon ground ginger
  1/4 teaspoon pepper
1-1/2 pounds boneless skinless chicken breasts, cut into 1-inch cubes
      2 tablespoons olive oil, *divided*
      1 cup chopped green pepper
  1/2 cup chopped onion
Hot cooked rice

In a small bowl, combine the first seven ingredients until blended; set aside.

In a large skillet or wok, stir-fry chicken in 1 tablespoon oil for 4-6 minutes or until no longer pink. Remove and keep warm.

Stir-fry green pepper and onion in remaining oil for 2 minutes. Stir cornstarch mixture and add to the pan. Bring to a boil; cook and stir for 1 minute or until thickened. Add chicken; heat through. Serve with rice. **Yield:** 4 servings.

Vegetable Beef Bow Tie Skillet

Ginger Sesame Chicken

Vegetable Beef Bow Tie Skillet

(Pictured above and on page 114)

Prep: 15 min. **Cook:** 25 min.

This one-dish wonder has everything you need to please a family—filling ground beef, fun bow tie pasta and plenty of vegetables. No one will leave the table hungry!

      1 pound ground beef
      1 cup chopped onion
      1 can (14-1/2 ounces) beef broth
1-1/2 cups uncooked bow tie pasta
  1/2 cup water
      1 teaspoon Italian seasoning
      1 teaspoon chili powder
  1/2 teaspoon salt
  1/2 teaspoon garlic powder
  1/4 teaspoon pepper
      1 cup chopped sweet yellow pepper
      1 cup chopped zucchini
      2 cups chopped tomatoes
      1 cup (4 ounces) shredded cheddar cheese

In a large skillet, cook beef and onion over medium heat until meat is no longer pink; drain. Stir in the broth, pasta, water and seasonings. Bring to a boil. Reduce heat; cover and simmer for 15 minutes.

Add yellow pepper and zucchini; cover and cook 2-4 minutes longer or until pasta and vegetables are tender, stirring occasionally. Stir in tomatoes; sprinkle with cheese. **Yield:** 4 servings.

Thursday

Spinach Pork Chops With Lemon Gravy
(Pictured below)
Prep: 20 min. **Cook:** 20 min.

Spinach-stuffed pork chops with walnuts and lemon gravy make for a surprising twist on a down-home meal. It might feel elegant, but it really couldn't be any easier.

- 1/2 cup chopped onion
- 1 tablespoon butter
- 1 package (6 ounces) fresh baby spinach
- 3 teaspoons minced garlic
- 1/4 cup chopped walnuts, *divided*
- 4 boneless pork loin chops (1 inch thick and 6 ounces *each*)
- 1/4 teaspoon pepper
- 1 tablespoon olive oil
- 2 tablespoons all-purpose flour
- 1/4 teaspoon salt
- 3/4 cup chicken broth
- 1 tablespoon lemon juice

In a large skillet, saute onion in butter until tender. Add the spinach, garlic and 2 tablespoons walnuts; cook and stir just until spinach is wilted. Remove from the heat; set aside.

Cut a deep slit in each pork chop, forming a pocket. Stuff 1/4 cup spinach mixture into each chop; secure with toothpicks. Sprinkle with pepper. In the same skillet, cook chops in oil for 8-10 minutes on each side until pork is no longer pink and a meat thermometer reads 160°. Remove and keep warm.

Stir flour and salt into the skillet until blended. Gradually stir in broth and lemon juice, scraping up any browned bits from bottom of pan. Bring to a boil; cook and stir for 2 minutes or until thickened. Serve over chops; sprinkle with remaining nuts. **Yield:** 4 servings.

Spinach Pork Chops with Lemon Gravy

Sloppy Joe Calzones

Friday

Sloppy Joe Calzones
(Pictured above)
Prep: 20 min. **Bake:** 15 min.

Create a kid-friendly supper—and put a delightfully different twist on ordinary sloppy joes—with these simple calzones. The hot sandwiches take advantage of convenient refrigerated crescent roll dough.

- 1 pound ground beef
- 1 cup chopped onion
- 1 cup chopped green pepper
- 1 can (15 ounces) black beans, rinsed and drained
- 1 can (6 ounces) tomato paste
- 1/2 cup water
- 1/2 cup ketchup
- 1 teaspoon dried oregano
- 1/4 teaspoon salt
- 2 tubes (8 ounces *each*) refrigerated crescent rolls
- 1 cup (4 ounces) shredded cheddar cheese

In a large skillet, cook the beef, onion and pepper over medium heat until meat is no longer pink; drain. Stir in the black beans, tomato paste, water, ketchup, oregano and salt.

Separate crescent dough into four rectangles; seal perforations. Spoon a fourth of the meat mixture onto half of each rectangle; sprinkle with cheese. Fold dough over filling; pinch edges to seal. Cut slits in tops.

Place the calzones on an ungreased baking sheet. Bake at 375° for 13-15 minutes or until golden brown. **Yield:** 4 servings.

Week 5

Ham & Sun-Dried Tomato Alfredo

Shopping List

Check for these staples:

- all-purpose flour
- brown sugar
- butter
- cider vinegar
- eggs
- grated Parmesan cheese
- olive oil
- pepper
- salt

Shop for these items:

- 1 jar (8 ounces) oil-packed sun-dried tomatoes
- 1 jar (12 ounces) honey Dijon mustard
- 1 package (16 ounces) linguine
- 1 package (12-1/2 ounces) nacho tortilla chips
- 1 package (2 ounces) onion soup mix
- 1 envelope taco seasoning
- 1 can (8 ounces) tomato sauce
- 1 bottle (12 ounces) beer
- 1 bunch broccoli
- 1 large red onion
- 1 carton (8 ounces) heavy whipping cream
- 1 package (8 ounces) shredded Monterey Jack cheese
- 1 package (5 ounces) shredded Swiss cheese
- 1 broiler/fryer chicken (3 to 4 pounds)
- 1 package (16 ounces) cubed fully cooked ham
- 1-1/2 pounds ground beef
- 4 boneless pork loin chops (5 ounces each)

Time-Saving Tips

- It pays to plan ahead on Monday—you're sure to appreciate it later in the week! If you have a few spare moments while preparing Ham & Sun-Dried Tomato Alfredo, chop your broccoli for Wednesday's Ham & Broccoli Frittata. If you have any extra carrots or onion, dice them as well to saute with the broccoli for the frittata.
- The frittata—which is an omelet that hasn't been flipped—would be perfect for brunch, too. Keep it in mind when entertaining on the weekend.
- Prepare your favorite mashed potatoes to soak up the gravy in Savory Onion Chicken on Tuesday for a simply delicious meal.
- The honey Dijon flavor in Thursday's main course, Onion-Dijon Pork Chops, also complements chicken or cubed steak.
- Get the kids involved in making Friday's Southwest Beef Pie. They'll love crushing the chips—just place the chips into large resealable plastic bags.

Monday

Ham & Sun-Dried Tomato Alfredo
(Pictured above)
Prep/Total Time: 20 min.

This quick Alfredo dish seems decadent and special—something you might enjoy in a fancy Italian restaurant, not at home on a busy weeknight. No one will guess that the recipe comes together with just five ingredients! Sun-dried tomatoes add an elegant touch.

- 8 ounces uncooked linguine
- 1/4 cup chopped oil-packed sun-dried tomatoes
- 1 cup heavy whipping cream
- 1/2 cup grated Parmesan cheese
- 1 cup cubed fully cooked ham

Cook the linguine according to the package directions. Meanwhile, in a large skillet coated with cooking spray, saute the tomatoes for 1 minute.

Reduce the heat; stir in the heavy whipping cream and Parmesan cheese. Bring to a gentle boil over medium heat. Simmer, uncovered, for 5-7 minutes or until thickened.

Drain linguine; stir into sauce mixture. Add ham; heat through. **Yield:** 4 servings.

Tuesday

Savory Onion Chicken

(Pictured below)

Prep/Total Time: 30 min.

Dinner doesn't get any easier than this tasty, 30-minute chicken entree. Buy chicken that's already cut up to save even more time. —Julia Anderson, Ringgold, Georgia

☑ This recipe includes Nutrition Facts and Diabetic Exchanges.

- 1/4 cup all-purpose flour, *divided*
- 1 broiler/fryer chicken (3 to 4 pounds), skin removed and cut up
- 2 tablespoons olive oil
- 1 envelope onion soup mix
- 1 bottle (12 ounces) beer *or* nonalcoholic beer

Place 2 tablespoons flour in a large resealable plastic bag. Add chicken, a few pieces at a time, and shake to coat. In a large skillet, brown chicken in oil on all sides. Remove and keep warm.

Add soup mix and remaining flour, stirring to loosen browned bits from pan. Gradually whisk in beer. Bring to a boil; cook and stir for 2 minutes or until thickened. Return chicken to the pan. Bring to a boil. Reduce heat; cover and simmer for 12-15 minutes or until chicken juices run clear. **Yield:** 6 servings.

Nutrition Facts: 1 serving equals 231 calories, 11 g fat (2 g saturated fat), 73 mg cholesterol, 469 mg sodium, 7 g carbohydrate, trace fiber, 25 g protein. **Diabetic Exchanges:** 3 lean meat, 1 fat, 1/2 starch.

Savory Onion Chicken

Wednesday

Ham & Broccoli Frittata

(Pictured above)

Prep/Total Time: 25 min.

This cheesy entree is bound to become a regular in your monthly dinner plans. Keep the recipe in mind when you need something fast but simple for breakfast as well.

- 6 eggs
- 1-1/4 cups (5 ounces) shredded Swiss cheese, *divided*
- 1 cup cubed fully cooked ham
- 1/4 teaspoon pepper
- 1 cup chopped fresh broccoli
- 1 tablespoon butter

In a small bowl, whisk eggs, 1 cup cheese, ham and pepper; set aside. In a 10-in. ovenproof skillet, saute broccoli in butter until tender. Reduce heat; add egg mixture. Cover and cook for 4-6 minutes or until nearly set.

Uncover skillet; sprinkle with the remaining cheese. Broil 3-4 in. from the heat for 2-3 minutes or until the eggs are completely set. Let stand for 5 minutes. Cut into wedges. **Yield:** 4 servings.

Broccoli Basics

WHEN purchasing fresh broccoli for Ham & Broccoli Frittata (recipe above) or other recipes, look for bunches that have a deep green color, tightly closed buds and crisp leaves. Store fresh broccoli in a resealable plastic bag in the refrigerator for up to 4 days. Wash broccoli just before using.

Onion-Dijon Pork Chops

Southwest Beef Pie

(Pictured below)

Prep/Total Time: 30 min.

This south-of-the-border sensation is sure to have your family coming back for second helpings! Hearty and filling, it really hits the spot after a busy day...and is on the dinner table in only half an hour.

2 cups coarsely crushed nacho tortilla chips
1-1/2 pounds ground beef
1 can (8 ounces) tomato sauce
1/2 cup water
1 envelope taco seasoning
1/4 teaspoon pepper
1 cup (4 ounces) shredded Monterey Jack cheese

Place the nacho tortilla chips in an ungreased 9-in. pie plate; set aside. In a large skillet, cook the ground beef over medium heat until meat is no longer pink; drain. Add the tomato sauce, water, taco seasoning and pepper. Bring to a boil; cook and stir for 2 minutes or until thickened.

Spoon half of the meat mixture over the tortilla chips; sprinkle with half of the cheese. Repeat layers. Bake, uncovered, at 375° for 10-15 minutes or until heated through and cheese is melted. Serve immediately. **Yield:** 6 servings.

Onion-Dijon Pork Chops

(Pictured above)

Prep/Total Time: 25 min.

Coated in a lip-smacking mustard sauce, these pork chops are cooked to tender perfection. To round out your meal, serve them alongside rice and carrots.

✓ This recipe includes Nutrition Facts and Diabetic Exchanges.

4 boneless pork loin chops (5 ounces *each*)
1/4 teaspoon salt
1/4 teaspoon pepper
3/4 cup thinly sliced red onion
1/4 cup water
1/4 cup cider vinegar
3 tablespoons brown sugar
2 tablespoons honey Dijon mustard

Sprinkle pork chops with salt and pepper. In a large non-stick skillet coated with cooking spray, cook pork over medium heat for 4-6 minutes on each side or until lightly browned. Remove and keep warm.

Add the remaining ingredients to the skillet; stir to loosen browned bits. Bring to a boil; cook and stir for 2 minutes or until thickened. Return chops to the pan. Reduce heat; cover and simmer for 4-5 minutes or until a meat thermometer reads 160°. **Yield:** 4 servings.

Nutrition Facts: 1 pork chop with 2 tablespoons onion mixture equals 261 calories, 9 g fat (3 g saturated fat), 69 mg cholesterol, 257 mg sodium, 17 g carbohydrate, 1 g fiber, 28 g protein. **Diabetic Exchanges:** 4 lean meat, 1 starch.

Southwest Beef Pie

Week 6

Shopping List

Check for these staples:

- beef broth
- butter
- chicken broth
- cornstarch
- dried parsley flakes
- dried thyme
- eggs
- garlic salt
- ground ginger
- honey
- Italian seasoning
- mayonnaise
- milk
- minced garlic
- olive oil
- onions
- pepper
- poultry seasoning
- prepared horseradish
- rubbed sage
- salt
- seasoned bread crumbs
- soy sauce
- Worcestershire sauce

Shop for these items:

- 1 can (10-3/4 ounces) condensed cream of broccoli soup
- 1 jar (15 ounces) marinara or spaghetti sauce
- 1 package (8 ounces) raisins
- 1 package (6 ounces) stuffing mix
- 1 package (8 ounces) shredded Colby cheese
- 1-1/2 pounds boneless skinless chicken breasts
- 4 boneless skinless chicken breast halves (6 ounces each)
- 1 package (10 ounces) julienned carrots
- 4 large baking potatoes
- 1 container (15 ounces) ricotta cheese
- 1 pound ground pork
- 1 pound sliced deli roast beef
- 1/2 pound cooked medium shrimp
- 1 package (16 ounces) frozen broccoli florets
- 1 package (12 ounces) frozen home-style egg noodles
- 1 package (14 ounces) frozen pepper strips

Time-Saving Tips

- You'll have an extra 2-1/2 cups of julienned carrots, 1-1/4 cups of raisins and 1-1/2 cups of stuffing mix left over from this week's menu. The carrots and raisins are perfect for snacking or a lunchbox. For a quick side, prepare the stuffing with 1 cup of water and 2-1/2 tablespoons of honey butter.
- Chop an extra 1/2 cup of onion on Tuesday and save it for Friday night's Italian Pork Skillet.
- Can't find frozen noodles for Wednesday's Shrimp Egg Drop Soup? Use linguine. Cook it in the broth and water for 6 minutes before adding the veggies.

Monday

Broccoli Chicken Skillet

(Pictured below)

Prep/Total Time: 25 min.

Thanks to this recipe, you're only 25 minutes away from a comforting, cheesy, veggie-and-chicken dish that the whole family is sure to love. And because it all comes together in one skillet, cleanup is a breeze.

- 1-1/2 pounds boneless skinless chicken breasts, cubed
- 2 cups frozen broccoli florets, thawed
- 1 cup julienned carrots
- 1/2 cup chopped onion
- 1 tablespoon olive oil
- 1 can (10-3/4 ounces) condensed cream of broccoli soup, undiluted
- 1 cup stuffing mix
- 1 cup milk
- 1/4 cup raisins
- 1/8 teaspoon pepper
- 1 cup (4 ounces) shredded Colby cheese

In a large skillet, saute the chicken, broccoli, carrots and onion in oil for 5-6 minutes or until chicken is no longer pink.

Stir in the soup, stuffing mix, milk, raisins and pepper. Cook, uncovered, over medium heat for 8-10 minutes or until heated through. Sprinkle with cheese. Remove from the heat; cover and let stand until cheese is melted. **Yield:** 4 servings.

Broccoli Chicken Skillet

Philly Steak Potatoes

Shrimp Egg Drop Soup

(Pictured below)

Prep/Total Time: 30 min.

Who knew that egg drop soup could be so easy? The recipe for this better-than-restaurant-quality soup requires just three simple steps and 30 minutes.

    4 teaspoons cornstarch
  1/2 teaspoon soy sauce
  1/8 teaspoon ground ginger
1-1/2 cups water, *divided*
    2 cans (14-1/2 ounces *each*) chicken broth
1-1/2 cups frozen home-style egg noodles
    1 cup frozen broccoli florets, thawed and coarsely chopped
  1/2 cup julienned carrot
    1 egg, beaten
  1/2 pound cooked medium shrimp, peeled and deveined

In a small bowl, combine the cornstarch, soy sauce, ginger and 1/2 cup water; set aside.

In a large saucepan, combine broth and remaining water. Bring to a simmer; add noodles. Cook, uncovered, for 15 minutes. Add broccoli and carrot; simmer 3-4 minutes longer or until noodles are tender.

Drizzle beaten egg into hot soup, stirring constantly. Stir cornstarch mixture and add to the pan. Bring to a boil; cook and stir for 2 minutes or until slightly thickened. Add shrimp; heat through. **Yield:** 4 servings.

Tuesday

Philly Steak Potatoes

(Pictured above)

Prep/Total Time: 25 min.

This is one packed potato! With pepper strips, onion, deli roast beef and cheese on top of a baked spud, you've got everything you need for a one-dish meal. Dollop it with a blend of horseradish and mayonnaise.

    4 large baking potatoes
1-1/2 cups frozen pepper strips
    1 cup chopped onion
  1/4 cup butter, cubed
    1 pound sliced deli roast beef, cut into thin strips
    1 cup (4 ounces) shredded Colby cheese
  1/4 cup mayonnaise
  3/4 teaspoon prepared horseradish

Scrub and pierce potatoes; place on a microwave-safe plate. Microwave, uncovered, on high for 15-17 minutes or until tender, turning once.

Meanwhile, in a large skillet, cook peppers and onion in butter over medium heat until tender. Stir in roast beef; heat through.

Cut an "X" in the top of each potato; fluff pulp with a fork. Spoon meat mixture into potatoes; sprinkle with cheese. Combine mayonnaise and horseradish; spoon over tops. **Yield:** 4 servings.

Editor's Note: This recipe was tested in a 1,100-watt microwave.

Shrimp Egg Drop Soup

Herb Chicken with Honey Butter

Italian Pork Skillet

(Pictured below)

Prep/Total Time: 30 min.

This meaty, cheesy pasta dinner is guaranteed to please after a busy day. If you can't find ground pork, simply replace it with ground beef or ground turkey.

1-1/2 cups frozen home-style egg noodles
   1 pound ground pork
  1/2 cup chopped onion
   1 teaspoon minced garlic
   1 jar (15 ounces) marinara *or* spaghetti sauce
   1 cup frozen pepper strips, thawed and chopped
  3/4 cup beef broth, *divided*
1-1/2 teaspoons dried parsley flakes
  1/2 teaspoon Worcestershire sauce
  1/4 teaspoon salt
  1/4 teaspoon rubbed sage
  1/4 teaspoon dried thyme
  1/4 teaspoon pepper
   2 teaspoons cornstarch
  1/2 cup ricotta cheese

Cook the noodles according to the package directions. Meanwhile, in a large skillet, cook the pork, onion and garlic over medium heat until meat is no longer pink; drain. Add the marinara sauce, peppers, 1/2 cup broth, parsley, Worcestershire sauce, salt, sage, thyme and pepper. Bring to a boil. Reduce heat; simmer, uncovered, for 5 minutes.

Combine cornstarch and remaining broth until smooth. Gradually stir into the skillet. Bring to a boil; cook and stir for 2 minutes or until thickened. Drain noodles; stir into pork mixture. Remove from the heat; dollop with ricotta cheese. **Yield:** 4 servings.

Herb Chicken with Honey Butter

(Pictured above)

Prep/Total Time: 25 min.

When you want a comforting, home-style supper, this one really fills the bill. You'll love how the honey's sweetness mixes perfectly with the salty herb flavor.

   1 egg, beaten
  3/4 cup seasoned bread crumbs
   2 tablespoons dried parsley flakes
   1 teaspoon Italian seasoning
  3/4 teaspoon garlic salt
  1/2 teaspoon poultry seasoning
   4 boneless skinless chicken breast halves (6 ounces *each*)
   3 tablespoons butter
HONEY BUTTER:
  1/4 cup butter, softened
  1/4 cup honey

Place egg in a shallow bowl. In another shallow bowl, combine the bread crumbs and seasonings. Dip chicken in egg, then coat with bread crumb mixture.

In a large skillet over medium heat, cook chicken in butter for 4-5 minutes on each side or until chicken juices run clear. Meanwhile, combine butter and honey. Serve with chicken. **Yield:** 4 servings.

Butter Bonus

IF YOU have honey butter left over from Herb Chicken with Honey Butter (recipe above), add some garlic salt to the extra butter for a great spread on grilled French Bread or shrimp kabobs. Or, whip up an extra batch and refrigerate it for sandwiches.

Italian Pork Skillet

Chapter 8

⊛ Speedy Sides and Salads

YOU'VE found the perfect main course...now, what are you going to serve with it? The answer is right here in this chapter!

Your meal will get even better when you add accompaniments such as Flavorful Red Potatoes, Broccoli with Asiago, Couscous with Mushrooms, Fancy Green Beans and Herb-Crusted Sweet Onion Rings.

And don't forget the salads! Choose from a variety of sensational creations, from Romaine Pecan Salad with Shrimp Skewers to Fruit Flower Garden and Tuna Salad in Tomato Cups.

Whichever favorites you decide to prepare, one thing's for sure—your sides and salads will be among the main attractions!

TASTY TOSS-UP. Chicken-Melon Spinach Salad (p. 144).

Cranberry Pear Salad

Summer Squash Casserole

(Pictured below)

Prep: 20 min. **Bake:** 25 min.

Need something for a summer potluck or picnic? This rich, creamy comfort food is a wonderful choice. Everyone loves the buttery taste and crunchy cracker topping. Plus, the casserole pairs beautifully with a variety of entrees.
—*Jennifer Wallace, Grove City, Ohio*

      2 medium yellow summer squash, diced
      1 large zucchini, diced
  1/2 pound sliced fresh mushrooms
      1 cup chopped onion
      2 tablespoons olive oil
      2 cups (8 ounces) shredded cheddar cheese
      1 can (10-3/4 ounces) condensed cream of mushroom soup, undiluted
  1/2 cup sour cream
  1/2 teaspoon salt
      1 cup crushed butter-flavored crackers (about 25 crackers)
      1 tablespoon butter, melted

In a large skillet, saute the summer squash, zucchini, mushrooms and onion in oil until tender; drain.

In a large bowl, combine the vegetable mixture, cheese, soup, sour cream and salt. Transfer to a greased 11-in. x 7-in. baking dish. In a small bowl, combine cracker crumbs and butter. Sprinkle over vegetable mixture. Bake, uncovered, at 350° for 25-30 minutes or until bubbly. **Yield:** 10 servings.

Cranberry Pear Salad

(Pictured above)

Prep/Total Time: 15 min.

With a blend of fresh ingredients and crunchy walnuts, this salad is a favorite. It's quick to toss together, yet looks very elegant—special enough to go on your holiday menu. I think the chopped pear and dried cranberries make it especially nice for Thanksgiving and Christmas.
—*Irene Fenlason, East Helena, Montana*

      9 cups torn red leaf lettuce
      1 medium pear, chopped
      1 small red onion, halved and sliced
  1/2 cup crumbled blue cheese
  1/3 cup dried cranberries
  1/3 cup chopped walnuts, toasted
DRESSING:
  1/2 cup canola oil
  1/4 cup sugar
  1/4 cup red wine vinegar
  1/2 teaspoon poppy seeds
  1/8 teaspoon Worcestershire sauce

In a large serving bowl, combine the first six ingredients. In a jar with a tight-fitting lid, combine the dressing ingredients; shake well.

Just before serving, shake the dressing and pour over the salad; toss to coat. **Yield:** 13 servings.

Summer Squash Casserole

Asian Chicken Salad

Asian Chicken Salad

(Pictured above)

Prep/Total Time: 20 min.

I serve this salad in lettuce leaves or pita pockets to friends who enjoy something a bit out of the ordinary. If you like peanut butter, this is the chicken salad for you! It's also great as a cool main dish on a hot summer day.
—Mary Bergfeld, Eugene, Oregon

- 3/4 cup reduced-fat sesame ginger salad dressing
- 1/2 cup creamy peanut butter
- 1 tablespoon sesame oil
- 2 to 3 teaspoons cider vinegar
- 1 teaspoon salt
- 1/2 teaspoon crushed red pepper flakes
- 1/4 teaspoon pepper
- 3 packages (6 ounces *each*) ready-to-use grilled chicken breast strips
- 4 cups chopped cucumbers
- 1 cup chopped sweet red pepper
- 3/4 cup chopped green onions
- 1/4 cup grated carrot
- 8 Bibb *or* Boston lettuce leaves
Chopped fresh cilantro, optional

In a small bowl, whisk the first seven ingredients. In a large bowl, combine the chicken, cucumbers, pepper, green onions and carrot. Drizzle with dressing; toss to coat. Chill until serving.

Serve on lettuce leaves. Garnish with cilantro if desired. **Yield:** 8 servings.

Broccoli with Asiago

Prep/Total Time: 20 min.

This is one of the best and most simple ways I've found to serve broccoli. It gets dressed up with only five ingredients! If you don't have Asiago cheese, just use Parmesan.
—cjintexas, tasteofhome.com Community

- 1 bunch broccoli, cut into spears
- 4 teaspoons minced garlic
- 2 tablespoons olive oil
- 1/4 teaspoon salt
Dash pepper
- 1 cup (4 ounces) shaved Asiago cheese

Place broccoli in a large skillet; cover with water. Bring to a boil. Reduce heat; cover and simmer for 5-7 minutes or until broccoli is tender. Drain well. Remove and keep warm.

In the same skillet, saute garlic in oil for 1 minute. Stir in the broccoli, salt and pepper. Top with cheese. **Yield:** 4 servings.

Broccoli Dish Hints

WHEN MAKING Broccoli with Asiago (recipe above), keep these handy tips in mind:

Using a vegetable peeler on a block of Asiago will give you nice, thin slices of cheese. Also, four teaspoons minced garlic is equal to four garlic cloves.

Romaine Pecan Salad With Shrimp Skewers

(Pictured above)

Prep/Total Time: 25 min.

From our Test Kitchen staff, this delightfully different medley tops off convenient packaged salad greens with shrimp skewers and flavors it all with a from-scratch dressing. You'll love the refreshing tang of oranges and the crunch of toasted pecans, too.

1/4 cup white vinegar
1 cup canola oil
1/2 cup sugar
1 teaspoon salt
1/2 small red onion, chopped
1 teaspoon ground mustard
2 tablespoons water
1 pound uncooked medium shrimp, peeled and deveined
Coarsely ground pepper, optional
2 packages (10 ounces *each*) ready-to-serve romaine lettuce
2 oranges, peeled and segmented
3/4 cup pecan halves, toasted

In a blender or food processor, combine first seven ingredients. Cover and blend until smooth and creamy. Reserve 1/4 cup dressing; set aside. Cover and refrigerate remaining dressing.

On metal or soaked bamboo skewers, thread shrimp. Brush shrimp with one-half of reserved dressing. Sprinkle with pepper if desired. Arrange skewers on rack in broiler pan. Broil 3-4 in. from heat for 3-4 minutes on each side or until shrimp turn pink, basting with remaining reserved dressing halfway through cooking time. Serve warm or refrigerate shrimp until serving.

In a salad bowl, combine lettuce, orange segments and pecans. Drizzle dressing over salad; toss gently to coat. Divide salad among plates. Arrange shrimp skewers over salad. Serve immediately. **Yield:** 6-8 servings.

Taco Salad with a Twist

(Pictured below)

Prep/Total Time: 30 min.

My husband and son say this is the best taco salad they've ever had. They can't get enough of the combination of ground beef, cheese, beans, chips and more. I fix it on crazy days when I don't have much time to cook.
—*Vivian Schuler, Cheboygan, Michigan*

> 1 pound ground beef
> 1 package (11 ounces) torn iceberg and romaine
> 2 medium tomatoes, chopped
> 1 cup sliced green onions
> 1 can (16 ounces) kidney beans, rinsed and drained
> 2 cups (8 ounces) shredded Mexican cheese blend
> 8 cups corn chips, coarsely crushed
> 1 cup green goddess salad dressing
> 1/2 cup sour cream

In a large skillet, cook beef over medium heat until no longer pink; drain and cool slightly.

In a large bowl, combine the lettuce, tomatoes and onions. Add the beef, beans, cheese and corn chips. Drizzle with salad dressing; toss to coat. Dollop with sour cream. Serve immediately. **Yield:** 12 servings.

Taco Salad with a Twist

Tuna Salad in Tomato Cups

Tuna Salad in Tomato Cups

(Pictured above)

Prep/Total Time: 25 min.

Have an abundance of garden tomatoes? Put them to use in this fun recipe. An Asian twist makes the tuna salad stand out. —*Edie Farm, Farmington, New Mexico*

> 1 can (6 ounces) light water-packed tuna, drained and flaked
> 5 tablespoons mayonnaise
> 1/4 cup chopped celery
> 2 tablespoons chopped green pepper
> 1 tablespoon finely chopped onion
> 1/2 teaspoon lemon juice
> 1/2 teaspoon soy sauce

Dash white pepper
Lettuce leaves
> 2 medium tomatoes
> 1/3 cup chow mein noodles

In a small bowl, combine the first eight ingredients; chill.

Line two serving plates with lettuce. Cut tomatoes, but not all the way through, into six wedges; place on lettuce and separate wedges slightly.

Gently stir chow mein noodles into tuna salad; spoon into the center of each tomato. **Yield:** 2 servings.

Salad Add-Ins

I like to jazz up tuna salad by adding shredded cheddar cheese. It tastes great and thickens the mixture, which is especially nice if I'm making sandwiches—the filling doesn't squeeze out as easily! Sometimes I also add shredded carrots for extra crunch.
—*Deanne Bagley, Bath, New York*

Flavorful Red Potatoes

(Pictured below)

Prep/Total Time: 30 min.

This 30-minute side is so hearty and satisfying, it could even make a late-night meatless supper. It's delicious with baby red, white or Yukon gold potatoes. If you can't find those, just use larger potatoes cut in quarters.
—Wolfgang Hanau, West Palm Beach, Florida

  12 small red potatoes
1/2 cup grated Parmesan cheese
1/2 cup olive oil
   2 tablespoons minced fresh parsley
   2 tablespoons capers, drained
   2 tablespoons sliced Greek olives
   1 tablespoon thinly sliced green onion
   1 teaspoon white wine vinegar
1/4 teaspoon pepper

Place potatoes in a large saucepan and cover with water. Bring to a boil. Reduce the heat; cover and cook for 15-20 minutes or until tender.

Meanwhile, in a small bowl, combine the remaining ingredients. Drain potatoes; cool slightly. Cut each in half; place in a serving bowl. Add cheese mixture; toss gently to coat. **Yield:** 6 servings.

Super Spinach Salad

Flavorful Red Potatoes

Super Spinach Salad

(Pictured above)

Prep/Total Time: 15 min.

The name says it all! Thanks to this super recipe, an elegant salad is a snap to toss together. Fresh baby spinach forms the backdrop for salty bacon bits, hard-cooked egg, fresh mushrooms and tangy balsamic vinaigrette. It's a terrific way to get your good-for-you greens.
—Mary Harris, Shively, Kentucky

✓ This recipe includes Nutrition Facts and Diabetic Exchanges.

   1 package (9 ounces) fresh baby spinach
1/2 pound sliced fresh mushrooms
   2 hard-cooked eggs, chopped
   2 tablespoons real bacon bits
1/2 cup balsamic vinaigrette

In a large salad bowl, combine the spinach, mushrooms, eggs and bacon. Drizzle with vinaigrette; toss to coat. **Yield:** 8 servings.

Nutrition Facts: 1 cup equals 68 calories, 4 g fat (1 g saturated fat), 54 mg cholesterol, 225 mg sodium, 4 g carbohydrate, 1 g fiber, 4 g protein. **Diabetic Exchanges:** 1 vegetable, 1 fat.

Fresh Mozzarella & Tomato Salad

(Pictured at right)

Prep: 25 min. + chilling

A splash of lemon juice and hint of refreshing mint really brighten up this medley of tomatoes, mozzarella and avocados. —Lynn Scully, Rancho Santa Fe, California

   6 plum tomatoes, chopped
   2 cartons (8 ounces *each*) fresh mozzarella
      cheese pearls, drained
1/3 cup minced fresh basil
   1 tablespoon minced fresh parsley
   2 teaspoons minced fresh mint
1/4 cup lemon juice
1/4 cup olive oil
3/4 teaspoon salt
1/4 teaspoon pepper
   2 medium ripe avocados, peeled and chopped

In a large bowl, combine the tomatoes, cheese, basil, parsley and mint; set aside.

In a small bowl, whisk the lemon juice, oil, salt and pepper. Pour over tomato mixture; toss to coat. Cover and refrigerate for at least 1 hour before serving.

Just before serving, stir in avocados. Serve with a slotted spoon. **Yield:** 8 servings.

Couscous with Mushrooms

(Pictured below)

Prep/Total Time: 15 min.

Fluffy and flavorful, this stovetop side dish takes only moments to prepare. I like to use couscous a lot because it cooks quickly. —Claudia Ruiss, Massapequa, New York

Couscous with Mushrooms

Fresh Mozzarella & Tomato Salad

1-1/4 cups water
    2 tablespoons butter
    2 teaspoons chicken bouillon granules
 1/4 teaspoon salt
 1/4 teaspoon pepper
    1 cup uncooked couscous
    1 can (7 ounces) mushroom stems and pieces, drained

In a large saucepan, bring the water, butter, chicken bouillon, salt and pepper to a boil.

Stir in the couscous and mushrooms. Cover and remove from the heat; let stand for 5 minutes. Fluff with a fork. **Yield:** 4 servings.

Couscous Clues

WONDERFULLY versatile, couscous is a great choice as a side dish to round out menus. Try it in place of the usual rice for a refreshing change of pace.

Couscous with Mushrooms (recipe above left) calls for chicken bouillon granules. If you'd like to serve this dish with an entree of beef, replace the chicken bouillon with beef bouillon to better complement your main course.

Plan on serving stew? You could also use couscous as a bed for the stew in place of the usual noodles.

Salads with Pistachio-Crusted Goat Cheese

In a small nonstick skillet coated with cooking spray, cook cheese slices over medium heat for 1-2 minutes on each side or until golden brown. Place on salads. **Yield:** 4 servings.

Fancy Green Beans

(Pictured below)

Prep/Total Time: 30 min.

You'll love the sweet-salty sauce, nutty cashews and sprinkle of bacon in this side dish. It's a great way to jazz up green beans. —Kelly Waller, Madison, Florida

```
1-1/2  pounds fresh green beans, trimmed
    2  bacon strips, diced
    2  tablespoons teriyaki sauce
    1  tablespoon honey
    1  tablespoon butter, melted
  1/2  cup sliced sweet red pepper
    1  small onion, cut into thin wedges
  1/2  cup salted whole cashews
    2  teaspoons lemon juice
```

Place beans in a large saucepan and cover with water. Bring to a boil. Cover and cook for 4-6 minutes or until crisp-tender. Drain and immediately place beans in ice water. Drain and pat dry.

In a large skillet, cook the bacon over medium heat until crisp. Using a slotted spoon, remove to paper towels to drain.

Meanwhile, in a small bowl, combine the teriyaki sauce, honey and butter. Saute the red pepper and onion in bacon drippings until tender. Add the beans, teriyaki mixture, bacon, cashews and lemon juice; heat through. **Yield:** 8 servings.

Salads with Pistachio-Crusted Goat Cheese

(Pictured above)

Prep/Total Time: 30 min.

Want something impressive and elegant? This vegetarian salad blends walnuts, oranges and tomatoes with warm, pistachio-crusted goat cheese medallions and a splash of vinaigrette. —Gloria Bradley, Naperville, Illinois

```
    6  cups torn mixed salad greens
    2  medium oranges, peeled and segmented
    1  cup cherry tomatoes
  1/2  cup chopped walnuts, toasted
  1/4  medium red onion, thinly sliced
    2  tablespoons orange juice
    1  tablespoon white wine vinegar
    1  teaspoon grated orange peel
    1  teaspoon honey
  1/2  teaspoon salt
  1/4  teaspoon ground cumin
    6  tablespoons walnut or olive oil, divided
  1/3  cup pistachios
4-1/2  teaspoons seasoned bread crumbs
    1  log (4 ounces) fresh goat cheese
```

In a large bowl, combine the first five ingredients. In a small bowl, whisk the orange juice, vinegar, orange peel, honey, salt, cumin and 5 tablespoons oil. Pour over salad; toss to coat. Divide among four serving plates.

Place the pistachios in a food processor; cover and process until ground. Transfer to a small bowl; stir in bread crumbs. Cut goat cheese into four slices; brush slices with remaining oil. Coat in crumb mixture.

Fancy Green Beans

Balsamic Chicken Pasta Salad

Radish Asparagus Salad
(Pictured below)
Prep/Total Time: 25 min.

A dressing with lemon zest and mustard adds the perfect punch to crisp asparagus and crunchy radishes in this fresh spring salad. —Nancy Latulippe, Simcoe, Ontario

☑ This recipe includes Nutrition Facts and Diabetic Exchanges.

    1 **pound fresh asparagus, trimmed and cut into 2-inch pieces**
    7 **radishes, thinly sliced**
    2 **tablespoons sesame seeds**
DRESSING:
    2 **tablespoons olive oil**
    2 **tablespoons thinly sliced green onion**
    1 **tablespoon white wine vinegar**
    1 **tablespoon lemon juice**
    2 **teaspoons honey**
    1 **teaspoon Dijon mustard**
1/4 **teaspoon garlic powder**
1/4 **teaspoon grated lemon peel**
1/4 **teaspoon pepper**

In a large saucepan, bring 6 cups water to a boil. Add the asparagus; cover and boil for 3 minutes. Drain and immediately place the asparagus in ice water. Drain and pat dry.

Transfer to a large bowl; add the radishes and sesame seeds. Place dressing ingredients in a jar with a tight-fitting lid; shake well. Pour over the salad; toss to coat. **Yield:** 6 servings.

Nutrition Facts: 2/3 cup equals 73 calories, 6 g fat (1 g saturated fat), 0 cholesterol, 28 mg sodium, 5 g carbohydrate, 1 g fiber, 2 g protein. **Diabetic Exchanges:** 1 vegetable, 1 fat.

Balsamic Chicken Pasta Salad
(Pictured above)
Prep/Total Time: 25 min.

Pick up a rotisserie chicken on your way home, and you'll be halfway done with dinner—thanks to this winning pasta salad! Serve it with a crusty loaf of bread and glasses of iced tea for a fantastic meal-in-minutes on busy weeknights.
—Terri McCarty, Oro Grande, California

    3 **cups uncooked bow tie pasta**
    4 **cups cubed cooked chicken breast**
    2 **cups chopped tomatoes**
1/2 **cup chopped red onion**
    4 **bacon strips, cooked and crumbled**
1/4 **cup crumbled Gorgonzola cheese**
1/2 **cup olive oil**
1/4 **cup minced fresh basil**
1/4 **cup balsamic vinegar**
    2 **tablespoons brown sugar**
    1 **teaspoon minced garlic**
1/4 **teaspoon salt**
1/4 **teaspoon pepper**
1/2 **cup grated Parmesan cheese**

Cook the pasta according to the package directions. Drain and rinse in cold water; transfer to a large bowl. Add the chicken, tomatoes, onion, bacon and Gorgonzola cheese.

For dressing, in a small bowl, whisk the oil, basil, vinegar, brown sugar, garlic, salt and pepper. Drizzle over salad and toss to coat; sprinkle with Parmesan cheese. **Yield:** 8 servings.

Radish Asparagus Salad

Chicken-Melon Spinach Salad

(Pictured above and on page 134)

Prep/Total Time: 30 min.

Different colors and flavors mix beautifully in this distinctive salad. It's a favorite choice for hot summer days.
—Lorie Fritsch, Dublin, California

    4 cups fresh baby spinach
2-1/2 cups cubed cantaloupe
    2 cups cubed cooked chicken
    1 medium sweet red pepper, chopped
    1 medium ripe avocado, peeled and cubed
1/4 cup chopped onion
SALAD DRESSING:
    2 tablespoons plus 1-1/2 teaspoons canola oil
4-1/2 teaspoons sugar
4-1/2 teaspoons cider vinegar
4-1/2 teaspoons ketchup
1/2 teaspoon Worcestershire sauce
1/4 teaspoon salt
    2 tablespoons salted soy nuts

In a large salad bowl, combine the first six ingredients. In a small bowl, whisk the oil, sugar, cider vinegar, ketchup, Worcestershire and salt. Pour over the salad; toss to coat. Sprinkle with soy nuts. Serve immediately. **Yield:** 5 servings.

Festive Corn 'n' Broccoli

Prep/Total Time: 15 min.

This is always a popular side. If you like, use 1 tablespoon minced fresh basil instead of dried and two to three ears of sweet corn—cut fresh from the cob, about 1 cup—for the Mexicorn. —Lucile Throgmorton, Clovis, New Mexico

    1 package (16 ounces) frozen chopped broccoli, thawed
    1 can (7 ounces) Mexicorn, drained
1/4 cup butter, cubed
    1 teaspoon dried basil
1/2 teaspoon salt
1/8 teaspoon garlic powder
1/8 teaspoon pepper

In a large skillet, combine the broccoli, corn and butter; cook over medium heat until butter is melted. Stir in the basil, salt, garlic powder and pepper. Cover and cook for 8-10 minutes or until vegetables are tender, stirring occasionally. **Yield:** 5 servings.

Crab Pasta Salad

(Pictured below)

Prep/Total Time: 15 min.

A woman at work made this for a party, and boy, did word spread fast! Everyone was talking about the delicious medley of pasta shells, crabmeat, onion, dill and convenient deli coleslaw. Keep the recipe in mind for your summertime picnics and backyard barbecues.
—Cheryl Seweryn, Lemont, Illinois

  8 ounces uncooked medium pasta shells
  1 pound creamy coleslaw
1/2 cup mayonnaise
  1 tablespoon chopped onion
  1 teaspoon dill weed
Dash salt
  2 cups chopped imitation crabmeat

Cook the pasta according to package directions. Meanwhile, in a large serving bowl, combine the coleslaw, mayonnaise, onion, dill and salt. Stir in crab.

    Drain the pasta and rinse in cold water. Add to the coleslaw mixture; toss to coat. Chill until serving. **Yield:** 4 servings.

Crab Pasta Salad

Fruit Flower Garden

Fruit Flower Garden

(Pictured above)

Prep/Total Time: 30 min.

Brighten any get-together with this surprisingly simple fruit platter from our Test Kitchen cooks. It makes a festive centerpiece because it's as fun to look at as it is to eat. Guests will ask for your secrets—but only you will know that the "garden" took just 30 minutes to "grow!"

Fresh parsley sprigs
Fresh strawberries
Sliced fresh honeydew melon, pineapple and kiwi
Seedless red grapes, halved
ANTS:
Seedless red grapes
Pretzel sticks
Dried currants
GARNISHES:
Orange slices
Orange peel strips

Line a large serving platter with parsley. With a small sharp knife, cut a strawberry vertically toward the cap. Repeat, cutting to form petals resembling a rose. Repeat with remaining berries.

    Using cookie cutters, cut the honeydew, pineapple and kiwi into desired shapes. Decorate with grape halves as desired.

    For ants, skewer three grapes with a pretzel stick. With a small sharp knife, cut two small holes in a grape for the eyes; insert dried currants. Arrange three pretzel sticks on the platter for the legs; top with an ant body. Repeat as desired.

    Decorate platter with berry roses, fruit cutouts, ants, orange slices and peel. **Yield:** 1 fruit flower garden.

Spinach Tortellini Salad

(Pictured below)

Prep/Total Time: 25 min.

Pretty and packed with nutrition, this fresh-tasting salad is special enough for company and can even make a light meal paired with your favorite bread. Sometimes I add diced purple onion and red bell pepper...or substitute diced cooked chicken and bow-tie pasta for the tortellini.
—Emily Hanson, Logan, Utah

- 1 package (9 ounces) refrigerated cheese tortellini
- 1/2 cup sugar
- 1/4 cup red wine vinegar
- 1/4 cup olive oil
- 1 tablespoon sesame seeds, toasted
- 1 tablespoon grated onion
- 1/2 teaspoon salt
- 1/4 teaspoon paprika
- 1 package (6 ounces) fresh baby spinach
- 2 cups sliced cucumbers
- 1 can (11 ounces) mandarin oranges, drained
- 1/4 cup honey-roasted sliced almonds
- 1/4 cup real bacon bits

Cook tortellini according to package directions. Meanwhile, for dressing, in a small heavy saucepan, combine the sugar, vinegar and oil. Cook and stir over low heat just until sugar is dissolved. Remove from the heat. Stir in the sesame seeds, onion, salt and paprika; set aside.

Drain tortellini and rinse with cold water. In a large bowl, combine the tortellini, spinach, cucumbers, oranges, almonds and bacon. Pour dressing over salad; toss to coat. Serve immediately. **Yield:** 6 servings.

Green Salad with Pepperoni and Cheese

Prep/Total Time: 20 min.

Here, just a few simple additions turn plain-Jane salad greens into a taste-tempting side dish. Pepperoni and bacon add zip. —Joeanne Steras, Garrett, Pennsylvania

✓ This recipe includes Nutrition Facts and Diabetic Exchanges.

- 1 package (3 ounces) sliced pepperoni
- 1 package (10 ounces) ready-to-serve salad greens
- 2 medium tomatoes, chopped
- 1 cup cubed cheddar cheese
- 1/2 cup real bacon bits

Salad dressing of your choice

Cut pepperoni slices in half. In a large salad bowl, combine the salad greens, tomatoes, cheese, bacon and pepperoni. Serve with salad dressing. **Yield:** 12 servings.

Nutrition Facts: 3/4 cup salad (calculated without dressing) equals 105 calories, 8 g fat (4 g saturated fat), 21 mg cholesterol, 359 mg sodium, 2 g carbohydrate, 1 g fiber, 7 g protein. **Diabetic Exchanges:** 1 lean meat, 1 fat.

Herb-Crusted Sweet Onion Rings

Prep/Total Time: 30 min.

These are truly the ultimate onion rings! Lightly battered and seasoned, they fry up crisp, golden and irresistible.
—Denise Patterson, Bainbridge, Ohio

- 1 cup all-purpose flour
- 1 cup beer *or* nonalcoholic beer
- 2 tablespoons Dijon mustard
- 2 teaspoons salt-free Italian herb seasoning
- 1 teaspoon salt
- 1/4 teaspoon cayenne pepper
- 2 large sweet onions

Oil for deep-fat frying

In a shallow bowl, whisk the first six ingredients. Cut onions into 1/4-in. slices and separate into rings. Dip in flour mixture.

In an electric skillet, heat 1 in. of oil to 375°. Fry onion rings, a few at a time, for 1-2 minutes on each side or until golden brown. Drain on paper towels. Serve immediately. **Yield:** 8 servings.

Spinach Tortellini Salad

Mediterranean Green Salad

Szechuan Shrimp Salad

(Pictured below)

Prep/Total Time: 25 min.

This Asian-style dish is a definite crowd pleaser—it's as good as many similar specialties served at restaurants. Packed with shrimp, veggies, pasta and nuts, the salad also keeps well for several days in the refrigerator.
—Tish Stevenson, Grand Rapids, Michigan

- 10 ounces uncooked thin spaghetti
- 1/3 cup canola oil
- 1/3 cup honey
- 2 tablespoons rice vinegar
- 2 tablespoons sesame oil
- 2 tablespoons soy sauce
- 1 tablespoon minced ginger
- 1/2 teaspoon crushed red pepper flakes
- 1 pound deveined peeled cooked medium shrimp
- 1 package (10 ounces) julienned carrots
- 2 cups fresh sugar snap peas
- 1 large sweet red pepper, sliced
- 1/2 cup sliced green onions
- 3 tablespoons minced fresh cilantro
- 3/4 cup coarsely chopped dry roasted peanuts

Cook spaghetti according to package directions. Meanwhile, in a jar with a tight-fitting lid, combine the canola oil, honey, vinegar, sesame oil, soy sauce, ginger and pepper flakes; shake well.

Drain spaghetti; rinse in cold water. Place in a large bowl. Add the shrimp, carrots, peas, red pepper, onions and cilantro. Drizzle with dressing; toss to coat. Sprinkle with peanuts. Chill until serving. **Yield:** 8 servings.

Mediterranean Green Salad

(Pictured above)

Prep/Total Time: 30 min.

Looking for a great way to use up those fresh vegetables from your summer garden? Here's a beautiful and colorful option. It's always a hit with my friends and family. On especially hot days, I buy a rotisserie chicken, shred it and add it to the salad for a complete meal.
—Angela Larson, Tomahawk, Wisconsin

- 1 package (16 ounces) ready-to-serve salad greens
- 2 cups grape tomatoes
- 6 green onions, thinly sliced
- 1 jar (7-1/2 ounces) marinated quartered artichoke hearts, drained and coarsely chopped
- 1 cup (4 ounces) crumbled feta cheese
- 1 medium sweet yellow pepper, cut into thin strips
- 3/4 cup pitted Greek olives, halved
- 1/2 cup sunflower kernels
- 1/2 cup Italian salad dressing

In a large salad bowl, combine the first eight ingredients. Just before serving, drizzle with salad dressing; toss to coat. **Yield:** 10 servings.

Szechuan Shrimp Salad

Chapter 9

☉ *Plan an Instant Party*

IF HOSTING family members and friends for some food and fun seems too time-consuming for your hectic schedule, check out the surprisingly easy ideas in this chapter.

Each themed party gives you a festive but fast menu you can quickly throw together for an event. Choose from an outdoor pizza feast, eye-opening slumber party, fan-favorite spread for tailgates and swashbuckling pirate birthday.

Whether you'd like to have an event for children or adults, you'll find delightful, fuss-free recipes that'll make your preparations a snap...and make the party just as much fun for the host as it is for the guests!

FUN-FILLED FINALE. Coconut Berry Pizza (p. 155).

Pirate Birthday Bash, Ahoy!

SHIVER ME TIMBERS! Summer's the perfect time to host a pirate-theme party, whether at the beach or in your backyard. Start with invitations written on brown paper bags with torn edges, like a treasure map to your house, then rolled up and tied with ribbon.

At the party, thrill all of your "mateys" with swashbuckling foods such as a shipshape sandwich and treasure-chest cupcakes...all featured here. Arrr!

Out-to-Sea Pasta Shell Salad

(Pictured below)

Prep/Total Time: 20 min.

Here's a healthier version of a popular boxed salad mix. You can also add a little cooked chicken breast to make it heartier. —Ann Timmerman, Northfield, Minnesota

- 3 cups uncooked medium pasta shells
- 2/3 cup shredded carrots
- 2/3 cup frozen peas, thawed
- 4 turkey bacon strips, diced and cooked
- 4 ounces reduced-fat cream cheese
- 1/2 cup reduced-fat sour cream
- 3/4 cup fat-free milk
- 1 envelope ranch salad dressing mix

Cook shells according to package directions. Meanwhile, in a large bowl, combine the carrots, peas and bacon. In a small bowl, beat cream cheese and sour cream. Add milk and dressing mix; beat until combined.

Drain pasta and rinse in cold water; add to vegetable mixture. Add dressing mixture; toss to coat. Chill until serving. **Yield:** 8 servings.

Hidden Treasure Cupcakes

Hidden Treasure Cupcakes

(Pictured above)

Prep: 1 hour **Bake:** 20 min. + cooling

Let kids discover the "hidden treasure" inside these fun-as-can-be cupcakes from our Test Kitchen. They offer make-ahead convenience, ensure even-steven portions of cake for all party guests and are almost too cute to eat!

- 1 package (18-1/4 ounces) chocolate cake mix
- 1/4 cup strawberry pie filling
- 24 Swiss cake rolls
- 1 can (16 ounces) vanilla frosting
- Blue food coloring, optional
- Assorted candies: Jolly Ranchers, Nerds, skull and fish hard candies
- Yellow food coloring, optional

Prepare cake mix according to package directions. Fill paper-lined muffin cups half full. Drop 1/2 teaspoon pie filling in the center of each; top with remaining batter. Bake at 350° for 19-23 minutes or until a toothpick inserted in the cake portion comes out clean. Cool for 10 minutes before removing from pans to wire racks to cool completely.

Meanwhile, cut cake rolls lengthwise (do not cut through); set aside. Place two tablespoons frosting in a

Out-to-Sea Pasta Shell Salad

small bowl; set aside. Tint remaining frosting with blue food coloring if desired; frost cupcakes.

Place a cake roll on each cupcake. Decorate with assorted candies. Tint reserved frosting with yellow food coloring if desired; place in a resealable plastic bag. Cut a small hole in a corner of bag; pipe latches onto chests. **Yield:** 24 servings.

Pirate Ship Sandwich

(Pictured below)

Prep/Total Time: 25 min.

This clever seafaring sandwich from our home economists is easy to assemble and, more importantly, a cinch for young party guests to pull apart and eat.

   1 small bunch romaine
1/4 cup Italian salad dressing
   1 loaf (1 pound) Italian bread, unsliced
 10 slices Colby cheese
1/3 pound sliced deli turkey
1/3 pound sliced deli ham
1/3 pound thinly sliced hard salami
   3 pretzel rods

Remove three outer leaves of romaine for sails; set aside. Chop remaining romaine; toss with dressing. Cut bread into 20 slices, leaving slices attached at the bottom. Between every other slice of bread, layer the cheese, turkey, ham, salami and romaine mixture.

Poke two holes in each reserved lettuce leaf, one about 2 in. from the top and one about 2 in. from the

Snack Loot

bottom. Place a pretzel rod through both holes on each lettuce leaf to form a sail. Place sails in the sandwich.

To serve, cut completely through the bread between the plain slices. **Yield:** 10 servings.

Snack Loot

(Pictured above)

Prep/Total Time: 15 min.

Looking for "loot" to fill take-home sacks? This crisp mix is sure to satisfy little buccaneers with apple-cinnamon cereal, gummy candy shapes and goldfish crackers.
          —John Slivon, Navarre Beach, Florida

    6 cups Apple Cinnamon Cheerios
1-1/2 cups animal crackers
1-1/2 cups miniature cheddar cheese fish-shaped
      crackers
1-1/2 cups miniature pretzels
  1/2 cup sugar
  1/3 cup honey
    1 teaspoon ground cinnamon
Dash salt
  1/2 cup gummy candy shapes

In a large bowl, combine Cheerios, animal crackers, fish-shaped crackers and pretzels. In a small saucepan, combine the sugar, honey, cinnamon and salt. Cook and stir over low heat until sugar is dissolved. Pour over cereal mixture and toss to coat.

Transfer to two greased 15-in. x 10-in. x 1-in. baking pans. Bake at 275° for 20 minutes, stirring once. Cool completely. Stir in candy shapes. **Yield:** 2 quarts.

Pirate Ship Sandwich

Slumber Party Spread

HOSTING a sleepover for kids? No matter what their age, these late-night snacks and breakfast treats will help you throw the ultimate bedtime bash!

Party Nachos, Olive Pepperoni Spread and Popcorn Bars will guarantee that everyone goes to bed with a full stomach. And sweet dreams will lead to a breakfast of Chocolate Pecan Waffles, sure to start the day in a delectable way.

So get the sleepover party started—and look forward to getting plenty of sleep yourself, stress-free!

Olive Pepperoni Spread
(Pictured below)
Prep/Total Time: 20 min.

Pizza lovers will go crazy for this quick-and-easy dip. If you're serving picky eaters, keep the black olives on the side. —Cheri Authement, Appleton, Wisconsin

   1 package (8 ounces) cream cheese, softened
1/2 cup pizza sauce
   1 cup (4 ounces) shredded Italian cheese blend
1/4 cup sliced and quartered pepperoni
   2 tablespoons sliced ripe olives, drained
Bagel chips

Spread cream cheese into a 9-inch pie plate. Layer with pizza sauce, Italian cheese and pepperoni. Bake at 350° for 10-15 minutes or until cheese is melted. Sprinkle with olives. Serve with bagel chips. **Yield:** 11 servings.

Party Nachos

Olive Pepperoni Spread

Party Nachos
(Pictured above)
Prep/Total Time: 20 min.

Put a new, delicious spin on nachos with this recipe that uses barbecued shredded pork. Consider setting up a build-your-own nacho bar so guests can choose their toppings. —Mike Tchou, Pepper Pike, Ohio

   1 carton (18 ounces) refrigerated fully cooked barbecued shredded pork
   1 package (12-1/2 ounces) nacho tortilla chips
   2 cups (8 ounces) shredded Mexican cheese blend
1/2 cup sour cream
1/2 cup salsa
1/2 cup shredded lettuce
1/4 cup thinly sliced green onions
1/4 cup sliced ripe olives, optional
1/4 cup pickled pepper rings, optional

Heat pork according to package directions. Place tortilla chips on a large microwave-safe serving plate. Layer with pork and cheese.

Microwave, uncovered, on high for 1-2 minutes or until cheese is melted. Top with sour cream, salsa, lettuce and onions. Sprinkle with olives and pepper rings if desired. **Yield:** 12 servings.

Editor's Note: This recipe was tested in a 1,100-watt microwave.

Chocolate Pecan Waffles

(Pictured below)

Prep/Total Time: 30 min.

Made-from-scratch waffles are such a treat, and this crisp, chocolaty version will have everyone drooling! The recipe calls for raspberries but is just as luscious with strawberries or bananas. —Lucille Mead, Ilion, New York

   3 eggs
   1 cup sugar
   1 cup milk
  1/2 cup butter, melted
  1/4 teaspoon vanilla extract
   2 squares (1 ounce *each*) unsweetened
     chocolate, melted and cooled
1-1/2 cups all-purpose flour
   1 teaspoon baking powder
  1/2 teaspoon salt
  1/4 teaspoon baking soda
  1/4 cup chopped pecans
Fresh raspberries and whipped topping

In a large bowl, beat eggs and sugar until foamy; beat in the milk, butter and vanilla. Stir in the chocolate.

In a large bowl, combine the flour, baking powder, salt and baking soda. Stir in chocolate mixture just until combined; fold in pecans. Bake in a preheated waffle iron according to manufacturer's directions until golden brown. Serve with raspberries and whipped topping. **Yield:** 16 waffles.

Popcorn Bars

Popcorn Bars

(Pictured above)

Prep: 20 min. + cooling

Forget the fuss of creating homemade popcorn balls—these sweet-salty bars dotted with mini M&M's give you terrific taste without the hassle. An added bonus: They're not too sticky, so they're great for little hands. —Cathy Tang, Redmond, Washington

  1/4 cup butter
  1/4 cup light corn syrup
   1 package (10 ounces) large marshmallows
   2 quarts popped popcorn
  3/4 cup dry roasted peanuts, chopped
1-1/4 cups M&M's miniature baking bits

In a Dutch oven, melt the butter; add the corn syrup and marshmallows. Cook and stir over low heat for 3-4 minutes or until smooth. Add the popcorn; stir until coated. Stir in the peanuts and miniature baking bits until combined.

Spread into a greased 13-in. x 9-in. pan. Cool to room temperature. Cut into bars. **Yield:** 2 dozen.

Editor's Note: This recipe was prepared with popcorn popped in oil.

Chocolate Pecan Waffles

Wonderful Waffles

For a refreshing change of pace when making from-scratch waffles, stir a bit of grated orange peel into your waffle batter. That touch of citrus will add a yummy tang the whole family is sure to enjoy. —Ruth Harrow, Alexandria, New Hampshire

Outdoor Pizza Party

WHAT would summertime parties be without grilled food? This year, put something different on the backyard barbie! Grilled pizzas are surprisingly simple to make and easy to vary for any taste. With the crowd-pleasing recipes here, you'll have popular new main dishes to fire up—plus a refreshing pizza dessert.

Pepperoni Provolone Pizzas

(Pictured below)

Prep/Total Time: 25 min.

These grilled pies use two kinds of sauce for a great blend of flavors. And with just five other ingredients, the recipe is a breeze to make. —Randy Armbruster, Waverly, Ohio

        1 can (13.8 ounces) refrigerated pizza crust
        2 teaspoons olive oil
    2/3 cup pizza sauce
    1/2 cup prepared pesto
        3 ounces sliced turkey pepperoni
        1 large tomato, thinly sliced
        3 cups (12 ounces) shredded provolone cheese

Coat grill rack with cooking spray before starting the grill. Divide dough in half. On a lightly floured surface, roll each portion into a 12-in. x 10-in. rectangle.

Lightly brush both sides of dough with oil; place on grill. Cover and grill over medium heat for 1-2 minutes or until the bottom is lightly browned.

Remove from grill. Top the grilled side of each pizza with pizza sauce, pesto, pepperoni, tomato and cheese. Return to grill. Cover and cook each pizza for 4-5 minutes or until the bottom is lightly browned and cheese is melted. **Yield:** 2 pizzas (4 pieces each).

Pepperoni Provolone Pizzas

Grilled Artichoke-Mushroom Pizza

Grilled Artichoke-Mushroom Pizza

(Pictured above)

Prep: 20 min. **Grill:** 15 min.

We entertain a lot and are always looking for something new to grill. When we found this deliciously different pizza, it quickly became a favorite summer meal.
—Brenda Waters, Clarkesville, Georgia

☑ This recipe includes Nutrition Facts and Diabetic Exchanges.

        1 prebaked Italian bread shell crust
            (14 ounces)
    1/2 teaspoon olive oil
    2/3 cup tomato and basil spaghetti sauce
        2 plum tomatoes, sliced
    1/4 cup sliced fresh mushrooms
    1/4 cup water-packed artichoke hearts, rinsed,
            drained and chopped
        2 tablespoons sliced ripe olives, optional
        1 cup (4 ounces) shredded part-skim
            mozzarella cheese
    1/2 cup crumbled tomato and basil feta cheese
1-1/2 teaspoons minced fresh basil *or*
            1/2 teaspoon dried basil
1-1/2 teaspoons minced fresh rosemary *or*
            1/2 teaspoon dried rosemary, crushed
1-1/2 teaspoons minced chives

Brush crust with oil. Spread spaghetti sauce over crust to within 1 in. of edges. Top with tomatoes, mushrooms, artichokes and olives if desired. Sprinkle with cheeses.

Prepare grill for indirect heat. Grill, covered, over medium indirect heat for 12-15 minutes or until cheese is melted and crust is lightly browned. Sprinkle with herbs during the last 5 minutes of cooking. Let stand for 5 minutes before slicing. **Yield:** 6 servings.

Nutrition Facts: 1 slice (calculated without olives) equals 283 calories, 10 g fat (3 g saturated fat), 17 mg cholesterol, 712 mg sodium, 34 g carbohydrate, 1 g fiber, 14 g protein. **Diabetic Exchanges:** 2 starch, 1-1/2 fat, 1 lean meat.

Grilled BBQ Meatball Pizzas

Coconut Berry Pizza

(Pictured below and on page 148)

Prep: 10 min. + chilling **Bake:** 15 min.

With a bounty of fresh berries, coconut and more, this makes a scrumptious dessert for picnics. Keep it in mind when you need a breakfast dish or appetizer, too!
—*Joan Warner Carr, Kingwood, West Virginia*

    2 tubes (8 ounces *each*) refrigerated crescent
        rolls
    1 package (8 ounces) cream cheese, softened
    1 cup confectioners' sugar
    2 tablespoons seedless raspberry jam
    1 carton (8 ounces) frozen whipped topping,
        thawed
    4 medium kiwifruit, peeled and sliced
1-1/3 cups sliced fresh strawberries
1-1/3 cups *each* fresh raspberries, blueberries and
        blackberries
    1/2 cup flaked coconut, toasted

Unroll crescent dough and place in a greased 15-in. x 10-in. x 1-in. baking pan. Press onto the bottom and up the sides of pan; seal seams. Bake at 375° for 15-20 minutes or until golden brown. Cool on a wire rack.

Meanwhile, in a small bowl, beat the cream cheese, confectioners' sugar and jam until smooth. Fold in whipped topping. Spread over crust. Arrange fruit over top. Sprinkle with coconut. Chill until serving. **Yield:** 16 servings.

Grilled BBQ Meatball Pizzas

(Pictured above)

Prep: 25 min. + rising **Grill:** 5 min.

You'll be the hit of the party with these slices featuring ever-popular frozen meatballs. Barbecue sauce adds to the terrific taste. —*Willie DeWaard, Coralville, Iowa*

    2 cups all-purpose flour
    1 package (1/4 ounce) quick-rise yeast
    1/2 teaspoon sugar
    1/2 teaspoon salt
    3/4 cup warm water (120° to 130°)
    1 tablespoon olive oil
    20 frozen cooked Italian meatballs (1/2 ounce
        each)
    1/2 cup barbecue sauce
    1/4 cup apricot preserves
    2 cups (8 ounces) shredded Colby-Monterey
        Jack cheese
    1/4 cup thinly sliced green onions

In a large bowl, combine the flour, yeast, sugar and salt. Add the water and oil; mix until a soft dough forms. Turn dough onto a floured surface; knead until smooth and elastic, about 6-8 minutes. Cover and let stand for 15 minutes.

Meanwhile, cook meatballs according to package directions. Cut each meatball in half. In a large bowl, combine barbecue sauce and preserves. Add meatball halves; stir to coat.

Divide dough into fourths. Roll each portion into a 6-in. circle. Coat grill rack with cooking spray before starting the grill.

Grill dough, covered, over medium heat for 1-2 minutes or until the crust is lightly browned. Remove from grill. Layer the grilled side of each pizza with meatball mixture, cheese and onions. Return pizzas to grill. Cover and cook for 4-5 minutes or until crust is lightly browned and cheese is melted. **Yield:** 4 pizzas.

Coconut Berry Pizza

Game for Tailgating

PULL OUT the grill, gather some friends and get ready to cheer! Fall is a great time to tailgate, and when the food's good, you're guaranteed to have fun.

Instead of the usual burgers and hot dogs, jazz up your next parking-lot picnic with some delicious new recipes. Whether you're grilling on-site or taking the food to-go, you'll find versatile dishes that are perfect for the occasion. Even if your favorite sports team doesn't come out on top, your tailgate party will!

Game Day Brats

(Pictured below)

Prep/Total Time: 25 min.

Looking for a twist on the usual game-day fare? With French salad dressing and Monterey Jack cheese, these brats kick things up a notch. If you like, try replacing the brats in this recipe with cooked Italian sausage links.
—Laura McDowell, Lake Villa, Illinois

- **6 fully cooked bratwurst links (1 to 1-1/4 pounds)**
- **3/4 cup sauerkraut, rinsed and well drained**
- **6 tablespoons French salad dressing**
- **6 tablespoons shredded Monterey Jack cheese**
- **6 brat buns, split**

Make a lengthwise slit three-fourths of the way through each bratwurst to within 1/2 in. of each end. Fill with sauerkraut; top with dressing and cheese.

Place bratwurst in buns; wrap individually in a double thickness of heavy-duty foil (about 12 in. x 10 in.). Grill, covered, over medium-hot heat for 10-15 minutes or until heated through and cheese is melted. **Yield:** 6 servings.

Pecan Butterscotch Cookies

Pecan Butterscotch Cookies

(Pictured above)

Prep/Total Time: 25 min.

These are both the fastest and yummiest cookies I've ever made! They can be varied endlessly, but I always come back to this version. —Trisha Kruse, Eagle, Idaho

✓ This recipe includes Nutrition Facts and Diabetic Exchanges.

- **1 cup complete buttermilk pancake mix**
- **1 package (3.4 ounces) instant butterscotch pudding mix**
- **1/3 cup butter, melted**
- **1 egg**
- **1/2 cup chopped pecans, toasted**

In a large bowl, beat the pancake mix, pudding mix, butter and egg until blended. Stir in pecans. Roll into 1-1/2-in. balls. Place 2 in. apart on greased baking sheets. Flatten with the bottom of a glass.

Bake at 350° for 8-10 minutes or until edges begin to brown. Remove to wire racks to cool. **Yield:** about 1-1/2 dozen.

Editor's Note: You may substitute regular biscuit/baking mix for the buttermilk pancake mix.

Nutrition Facts: 1 cookie equals 88 calories, 6 g fat (2 g saturated fat), 18 mg cholesterol, 188 mg sodium, 8 g carbohydrate, trace fiber, 1 g protein. **Diabetic Exchanges:** 1 fat, 1/2 starch.

Game Day Brats

Chicken Pesto Sandwiches
Mediterranean Broccoli Slaw

Chicken Pesto Sandwiches

(Pictured above)

Prep/Total Time: 30 min.

These are terrific for a sports party. Even the heartiest of appetites will be satisfied with the grilled chicken, mozzarella and peppers. As the cook, I like the fact that the sandwiches are easy to prep ahead and assemble later at the event.
—Colleen Sturma, Milwaukee, Wisconsin

  6 boneless skinless chicken breast halves
     (4 ounces *each*)
3/4 cup prepared pesto, *divided*
1/2 teaspoon salt
1/4 teaspoon pepper
 12 slices Italian bread (1/2 inch thick), toasted
  1 jar (12 ounces) roasted sweet red peppers,
     drained
1/4 pound fresh mozzarella cheese, cut into six
     slices

Flatten chicken to 1/4-in. thickness. Spread 1 tablespoon pesto over each chicken breast; sprinkle with salt and pepper. Grill chicken, covered, over medium heat for 3-5 minutes on each side or until juices run clear.

Spread 3 tablespoons pesto over six slices of toast; layer with red peppers, chicken and cheese. Spread remaining pesto over remaining toast; place over top. **Yield:** 6 servings.

Mediterranean Broccoli Slaw

(Pictured above)

Prep/Total Time: 10 min.

Pair your favorite burger or sandwich with this simple slaw, and you'll have the perfect side. Kalamata olives give it extra zip, but a 4-ounce can of sliced ripe olives works well, too. —Nancy Hammond, Beverly Hills, Michigan

  1 package (12 ounces) broccoli coleslaw mix
  1 cup (4 ounces) crumbled feta cheese
 15 Greek olives, sliced
3/4 cup Greek vinaigrette

In a salad bowl, combine the coleslaw mix, cheese and olives. Add vinaigrette; toss to coat. Chill until serving. **Yield:** 5 servings.

Chapter 10

⏱ *Slow-Cooked Sensations*

IMAGINE walking in the door after a long, busy day and having a delicious, home-cooked dinner ready and waiting for you and your family to enjoy. Think it's too good to be true? It's not—when you take advantage of a slow cooker!

Just fill up this convenient appliance in the morning, then let it cook while you're off at work or running errands. By the time you return home, you'll be able to sit down to a hot supper in a matter of moments.

With mouth-watering recipes such as Smoked Sausage Gumbo, Fiesta Chicken Burritos and Tender Beef Brisket, your slow cooker just might become your favorite part of the kitchen!

SLOWLY BUT SURELY. Tex-Mex Beef Barbecues (p. 168).

Spicy Sausage Hash Browns

(Pictured above)

Prep: 15 min. **Cook:** 5 hours

I love to develop my own recipes and am thrilled when people call me to request them. My family members and friends from church tend to be my favorite and most honest critics! They always give this sausage dish a big thumbs-up.
—Angela Sheridan, Opdyke, Illinois

- 1 tube (16 ounces) bulk spicy pork sausage
- 1 package (30 ounces) frozen shredded hash brown potatoes, thawed
- 2 cups (16 ounces) sour cream
- 1 jar (16 ounces) double-cheddar cheese sauce
- 2 cans (4 ounces *each*) chopped green chilies
- 1/2 teaspoon crushed red pepper flakes

In a large skillet, cook sausage over medium heat until no longer pink; drain. In a 4-qt. slow cooker, combine all ingredients. Cover and cook on low for 5-6 hours or until heated through. **Yield:** 9 servings.

Editor's Note: This recipe was tested with Ragu double-cheddar cheese sauce.

Tangy Pot Roast

Prep: 15 min. **Cook:** 7 hours

This super-tender roast gets its lip-smacking flavor from zippy Catalina dressing and wine. Cooked with potatoes, carrots and onion, this is a dinner-in-one. And best of all, it's ready to eat when I get home after a long day.
—Paula Beach, Milton, New York

- 3 medium potatoes, thinly sliced
- 1-1/3 cups thinly sliced fresh carrots
- 2/3 cup sliced onion
- 1 boneless beef chuck roast (3 pounds)
- 1 teaspoon salt
- 1/2 teaspoon pepper
- 1/2 cup Catalina salad dressing
- 1/4 cup dry red wine *or* beef broth

Place the potatoes, carrots and onion in a 5-qt. slow cooker. Cut the roast in half; rub with salt and pepper. Place over vegetables. In a small bowl, combine salad dressing and red wine; pour over roast.

Cover and cook on low for 7-8 hours or until meat is tender. Skim fat from cooking juices; thicken juices if desired. **Yield:** 6 servings.

Teriyaki Chicken

(Pictured below)

Prep: 15 min. **Cook:** 4 hours

Here, chicken and a sweet-salty sauce come together for an entree that's packed with Asian flair. And you don't have to run to a restaurant to get it—you simply fill your slow cooker and let it do the work for you. Just whip up a quick batch of rice to complete a family-pleasing meal.
—Gigi Miller, Stoughton, Wisconsin

   12 **boneless skinless chicken thighs (4 ounces**
      ***each*)**
  3/4 **cup sugar**
  3/4 **cup soy sauce**
    6 **tablespoons cider vinegar**
  3/4 **teaspoon ground ginger**
  3/4 **teaspoon minced garlic**
  1/4 **teaspoon pepper**
4-1/2 **teaspoons cornstarch**
4-1/2 **teaspoons cold water**
Hot cooked rice, optional

Place chicken in a 4-qt. slow cooker. In a large bowl, combine the sugar, soy sauce, vinegar, ginger, garlic and pepper. Pour over chicken. Cover and cook on low for 4-5 hours or until chicken juices run clear.

Remove chicken to a serving platter; keep warm. Transfer cooking juices to a small saucepan. Bring to a boil. Combine cornstarch and water until smooth. Gradually stir into pan. Bring to a boil; cook and stir for 2 minutes or until thickened. Serve with chicken and rice. **Yield:** 6 servings.

Party Meatballs

Party Meatballs

(Pictured above)

Prep: 10 min. **Cook:** 3 hours

Meatballs are always a popular choice at parties. This is an easy twist on the usual recipe, and it's very fast to fix.
—Debbie Paulsen, Apollo Beach, Florida

☑ **This recipe includes Nutrition Facts.**

    1 **package (38 ounces) frozen cooked**
      meatballs, thawed
    1 **bottle (14 ounces) ketchup**
  1/4 **cup A.1. steak sauce**
    1 **tablespoon minced garlic**
    1 **teaspoon Dijon mustard**

Place the meatballs in a 3-qt. slow cooker. In a small bowl, combine the ketchup, steak sauce, garlic and mustard. Pour over meatballs. Cover and cook on low for 3-4 hours or until meatballs are heated through. **Yield:** about 6 dozen.

Nutrition Facts: 1 meatball equals 52 calories, 4 g fat (2 g saturated fat), 11 mg cholesterol, 193 mg sodium, 3 g carbohydrate, trace fiber, 2 g protein.

On the Go

NEED to take your food-filled slow cooker with you to a party or other event? Completely cook the food at home, then use a slow cooker traveling case...or tightly pack the slow cooker in a sturdy box with clean towels or crumpled newspapers.

Teriyaki Chicken

Hearty Minestrone Soup

(Pictured below)

Prep: 25 min. **Cook:** 6-1/4 hours

I got this minestrone recipe in California many years ago and have been making it ever since. I love it for both its taste and its effortless slow-cooked preparation.
—Bonnie Hosman, Young, Arizona

> 2 cans (one 28 ounces, one 14-1/2 ounces)
>   diced tomatoes, undrained
> 2 cups water
> 2 medium carrots, sliced
> 1 medium onion, chopped
> 1 medium zucchini, chopped
> 1 package (3-1/2 ounces) sliced pepperoni
> 2 teaspoons minced garlic
> 2 teaspoons chicken bouillon granules
> 1/2 teaspoon dried basil
> 1/2 teaspoon dried oregano
> 2 cans (16 ounces *each*) kidney beans, rinsed
>   and drained
> 1 package (10 ounces) frozen chopped
>   spinach, thawed and squeezed dry
> 1-1/4 cups cooked elbow macaroni
> Shredded Parmesan cheese

In a 5-qt. slow cooker, combine the first 10 ingredients. Cover and cook on low for 6-7 hours or until vegetables are tender.

Stir in the kidney beans, spinach and macaroni. Cover and cook 15 minutes longer or until heated through. Sprinkle with the Parmesan cheese. **Yield:** 7 servings (2-3/4 quarts).

Hearty Minestrone Soup

Soy-Garlic Chicken

Soy-Garlic Chicken

(Pictured above)

Prep: 10 min. **Cook:** 4 hours

Being a full-time mother as well as helping my husband on our ranch, I rely on simple, fuss-free meals. My family is always happy to see this chicken on the table.
—Colleen Faber, Buffalo, Montana

☑ This recipe includes Nutrition Facts and Diabetic Exchange.

> 6 chicken leg quarters, skin removed
> 1 can (8 ounces) tomato sauce
> 1/2 cup soy sauce
> 1/4 cup packed brown sugar
> 2 teaspoons minced garlic

With a sharp knife, cut leg quarters at the joints if desired. Place in a 4-qt. slow cooker. In a small bowl, combine the tomato sauce, soy sauce, brown sugar and garlic; pour over chicken.

Cover and cook on low for 4-5 hours or until a meat thermometer inserted into the chicken reads 180°. **Yield:** 6 servings.

Nutrition Facts: 1 leg quarter equals 201 calories, 8 g fat (2 g saturated fat), 90 mg cholesterol, 389 mg sodium, 3 g carbohydrate, trace fiber, 27 g protein. **Diabetic Exchange:** 4 lean meat.

Under Cover

UNLESS your slow cooker recipe instructs you to stir in or add ingredients, resist the temptation to lift the lid while the slow cooker is cooking. The loss of steam can result in an additional 15 to 30 minutes of cooking every time you lift the lid.

Apricot Pork Roast

(Pictured below)

Prep: 15 min. **Cook:** 6 hours

While this delightful roast is cooking, I have plenty of time to fix a side dish to go with it. The pork is great with everything from rice to potatoes and veggies. We like the leftovers served on buns with gravy the next day. —Patricia Defosse Wilmington, Delaware

✓ This recipe includes Nutrition Facts and Diabetic Exchanges.

1 boneless whole pork loin roast
  (2 to 3 pounds)
1 jar (12 ounces) apricot preserves
1 cup vegetable broth
2 tablespoons cornstarch
1/4 cup cold water

Place roast in a 3-qt. slow cooker. In a small bowl, combine preserves and broth; pour over roast. Cover and cook on low for 6-7 hours or until a meat thermometer reads 160°.

Remove meat to a serving platter; keep warm. Skim fat from cooking juices; transfer to a small saucepan. Bring liquid to a boil. Combine cornstarch and water until smooth. Gradually stir into pan. Bring to a boil; cook and stir for 2 minutes or until thickened. Serve with pork. **Yield:** 6 servings.

Nutrition Facts: 4 ounces cooked pork with 1/3 cup gravy equals 337 calories, 7 g fat (3 g saturated fat), 75 mg cholesterol, 223 mg sodium, 39 g carbohydrate, trace fiber, 30 g protein. **Diabetic Exchanges:** 4 lean meat, 2 starch.

Apricot Pork Roast

Maple Mustard Chicken

Maple Mustard Chicken

(Pictured above)

Prep: 5 min. **Cook:** 3 hours

This main-dish recipe is one of my husband's all-time favorites. Plus, it calls for only five ingredients—chicken, maple syrup, mustard, tapioca and rice. Because we like this recipe so much, we try to keep everything on hand so we can whip up this delicious dinner any time we want. —Jennifer Seidel, Midland, Michigan

✓ This recipe includes Nutrition Facts and Diabetic Exchanges.

6 boneless skinless chicken breast halves
  (6 ounces *each*)
1/2 cup maple syrup
1/3 cup whole grain mustard
2 tablespoons quick-cooking tapioca
Hot cooked brown rice

Place chicken in a 3-qt. slow cooker. In a small bowl, combine the maple syrup, mustard and tapioca; pour over the chicken.

Cover and cook on low for 3-4 hours or until the chicken juices run clear. Serve the chicken with rice. **Yield:** 6 servings.

Nutrition Facts: 1 chicken breast half with 3 tablespoons sauce (calculated without rice) equals 289 calories, 4 g fat (1 g saturated fat), 94 mg cholesterol, 296 mg sodium, 24 g carbohydrate, 2 g fiber, 35 g protein. **Diabetic Exchanges:** 5 very lean meat, 1-1/2 starch.

Chicken and Red Potatoes

cook on low for 3-1/2 to 4 hours or until chicken juices run clear and vegetables are tender. **Yield:** 4 servings.

Editor's Note: This recipe was tested with McCormick's Montreal Chicken Seasoning. Look for it in the spice aisle.

Smoked Sausage Gumbo

(Pictured below)

Prep: 20 min. **Cook:** 4 hours

You can serve up the flavors of the bayou with this zesty recipe. Chock-full of vegetables, seasonings and sausage, it'll satisfy the heartiest appetites at your table. Add even more Cajun flavor with Andouille sausage if you like.
—Sharon Delaney-Chronis, South Milwaukee, Wisconsin

>   2 celery ribs, chopped
>   1 medium onion, chopped
>   1 medium green pepper, chopped
>   1 medium carrot, chopped
>   2 tablespoons olive oil
>   1/4 cup all-purpose flour
>   1 cup chicken broth
>   1 pound smoked kielbasa *or* Polish sausage,
>   cut into 1/2-inch pieces
>   1 can (14-1/2 ounces) diced tomatoes,
>   undrained
>   2 teaspoons dried oregano
>   2 teaspoons dried thyme
>   1/8 teaspoon cayenne pepper
> Hot cooked rice

In a large skillet, saute the celery, onion, green pepper and carrot in oil until tender. Stir in flour until blended; gradually add broth. Bring to a boil. Cook and stir for 2 minutes or until thickened.

Transfer to a 3-qt. slow cooker. Stir in the sausage, tomatoes, oregano, thyme and cayenne. Cover and cook on low for 4-5 hours or until heated through. Serve with rice. **Yield:** 5 servings.

Chicken and Red Potatoes

(Pictured above)

Prep: 20 min. **Cook:** 3-1/2 hours

Wondering what to serve for dinner tonight? Try this moist, tender chicken-and-potato dish featuring a creamy gravy. It's a comforting meal any day of the week.
—Michele Trantham, Waynesville, North Carolina

>   3 tablespoons all-purpose flour
>   4 boneless skinless chicken breast halves
>   (6 ounces *each*)
>   2 tablespoons olive oil
>   4 medium red potatoes, cut into wedges
>   2 cups fresh baby carrots, halved lengthwise
>   1 can (4 ounces) mushroom stems and pieces,
>   drained
>   4 canned whole green chilies, cut into 1/2-inch
>   slices
>   1 can (10-3/4 ounces) condensed cream of
>   onion soup, undiluted
>   1/4 cup milk
>   1/2 teaspoon chicken seasoning
>   1/4 teaspoon salt
>   1/4 teaspoon dried rosemary, crushed
>   1/4 teaspoon pepper

Place flour in a large resealable plastic bag. Add chicken, one piece at a time, and shake to coat. In a large skillet, brown chicken in oil on both sides.

Meanwhile, place the potatoes, carrots, mushrooms and chilies in a greased 5-qt. slow cooker. In a small bowl, combine the remaining ingredients. Pour half of soup mixture over vegetables. Transfer chicken to slow cooker; top with remaining soup mixture. Cover and

Smoked Sausage Gumbo

Home-Style Stew

(Pictured above)

Prep: 20 min. **Cook:** 6 hours

My husband and I work full-time and have three daughters, so good, quick meals are a must. This stew is a regular menu item. —Marie Shanks, Terre Haute, Indiana

    2 packages (16 ounces *each*) frozen vegetables
      for stew
1-1/2 pounds beef stew meat, cut into 1-inch
      cubes
    1 can (10-3/4 ounces) condensed cream of
      mushroom soup, undiluted
    1 can (10-3/4 ounces) condensed tomato
      soup, undiluted
    1 envelope reduced-sodium onion soup mix

Place the vegetables in a 5-qt. slow cooker. In a large nonstick skillet coated with cooking spray, brown beef on all sides. Transfer to slow cooker.

Combine the remaining ingredients; pour over top. Cover and cook on low for 6-7 hours or until beef is tender. **Yield:** 5 servings.

Slow Cooker Sloppy Joes

Prep: 15 min. **Cook:** 4 hours

Slow cook your way to a crowd-pleasing main dish with this convenient recipe. Just a few kitchen staples transform ordinary ground beef into a classic sandwich filling.
—Joeanne Steras, Garrett, Pennsylvania

    2 pounds ground beef
    1 cup chopped green pepper
  2/3 cup chopped onion
    2 cups ketchup
    2 envelopes sloppy joe mix
    2 tablespoons brown sugar
    1 teaspoon prepared mustard
   12 hamburger buns, split

In a large skillet, cook the ground beef, green pepper and onion over medium heat until the meat is no longer pink; drain. Stir in the ketchup, sloppy joe mix, brown sugar and mustard.

Transfer to a 3-qt. slow cooker. Cover and cook on low for 4 hours or until the flavors are blended. Spoon 1/2 cup onto each bun. **Yield:** 12 servings.

Beef & Vegetable Soup

(Pictured below)

Prep: 20 min. **Cook:** 8 hours

I've been making this hearty soup packed with ground beef and vegetables for over 20 years. The beer always makes people pause and wonder what the unique flavor is.
—Tammy Landry, Saucier, Massachusetts

- 1 pound lean ground beef
- 1/2 cup chopped sweet onion
- 1 bottle (12 ounces) beer *or* nonalcoholic beer
- 1 can (10-1/2 ounces) condensed beef broth, undiluted
- 1-1/2 cups sliced fresh carrots
- 1-1/4 cups water
- 1 cup chopped peeled turnip
- 1/2 cup sliced celery
- 1 can (4 ounces) mushroom stems and pieces, drained
- 1 teaspoon salt
- 1 teaspoon pepper
- 1 bay leaf
- 1/8 teaspoon ground allspice

In a large skillet, cook beef and onion over medium heat until the meat is no longer pink; drain. Transfer to a 5-qt. slow cooker. Stir in the remaining ingredients. Cover and cook on low for 8-10 hours or until heated through. Discard bay leaf. **Yield:** 6 servings.

Fiesta Chicken Burritos

Beef & Vegetable Soup

Fiesta Chicken Burritos

(Pictured above)

Prep: 30 min. **Cook:** 4-1/4 hours

Looking for some heat in your meal—but want to keep your kitchen cool? Try these spicy, slow-cooked burritos. When I'm hosting guests who prefer a spicier dish, I add a teaspoon of cayenne pepper instead of just a dash.
—Margaret Latta, Paducah, Kentucky

- 1-1/2 pounds boneless skinless chicken breasts
- 1 can (15-1/4 ounces) whole kernel corn, drained
- 1 can (15 ounces) black beans, rinsed and drained
- 1 can (10 ounces) diced tomatoes and green chilies, undrained
- 1 jalapeno pepper, seeded and finely chopped
- 3 tablespoons ground cumin
- 1 teaspoon salt
- 1 teaspoon paprika
- 1/2 teaspoon pepper
- Dash cayenne pepper
- Dash crushed red pepper flakes
- 1 package (8 ounces) reduced-fat cream cheese
- 8 flour tortillas (8 inches), warmed
- Optional toppings: sour cream, shredded cheddar cheese, shredded lettuce and chopped tomatoes

Place chicken in a greased 4-qt. slow cooker. In a large bowl, combine the corn, beans, tomatoes, jalapeno and seasonings; pour over chicken. Cover and cook on low for 4-5 hours or until chicken is tender.

Remove the chicken; cool slightly. Shred and return

to the slow cooker. Stir in the cream cheese. Cover and cook 15 minutes longer or until heated through. Spoon 3/4 cup chicken mixture down the center of each tortilla; add toppings of your choice. Fold sides and ends over filling and roll up. **Yield:** 8 servings.

Editor's Note: When cutting hot peppers, disposable gloves are recommended. Avoid touching your face.

Fruity Pork Roast

Picante Beef Roast

(Pictured below)

Prep: 15 min. **Cook:** 8 hours

Everyone loves the south-of-the-border taste of this beef roast. Before putting the meat in your slow cooker, trim the fat so the gravy isn't greasy. Also, if your roast weighs 3 or more pounds, cut it in half to ensure even cooking.
—*Margaret Thiel, Levittown, Pennsylvania*

1 beef bottom round roast (3 pounds), trimmed and halved
1 jar (16 ounces) picante sauce
1 can (15 ounces) tomato sauce
1 envelope taco seasoning
3 tablespoons cornstarch
1/4 cup water

Cut roast in half; place in a 4-qt. slow cooker. In a large bowl, combine the picante sauce, tomato sauce and taco seasoning; pour over roast. Cover and cook on low for 8-9 hours or until meat is tender.

Remove the meat to a serving platter; keep warm. Skim fat from cooking juices; transfer 3 cups to a small saucepan. Bring liquid to a boil. Combine cornstarch and water until smooth. Gradually stir into pan. Bring to a boil; cook and stir for 2 minutes or until thickened. Slice roast; serve with gravy. **Yield:** 8 servings.

Fruity Pork Roast

(Pictured above)

Prep: 25 min. **Cook:** 8 hours + standing

This dressed-up pork roast is so attractive and delicious, it's special enough for a holiday feast. The meat gets gorgeous color from ruby-red cranberries and golden raisins.
—*Mary Davis, St. Cloud, Minnesota*

✓ This recipe includes Nutrition Facts and Diabetic Exchanges.

1/2 medium lemon, sliced
1/2 cup dried cranberries
1/3 cup golden raisins
1/3 cup unsweetened apple juice
3 tablespoons sherry *or* additional unsweetened apple juice
1 teaspoon minced garlic
1/2 teaspoon ground mustard
1 boneless whole pork loin roast (about 3 pounds)
1/2 teaspoon salt
1/4 teaspoon pepper
1/8 to 1/4 teaspoon ground ginger
1 medium apple, peeled and sliced
1/2 cup packed fresh parsley sprigs

In a small bowl, combine the first seven ingredients; set aside. Sprinkle the roast with salt, pepper and ginger. Transfer to a 3-qt. slow cooker. Pour fruit mixture over roast. Place apple and parsley around roast. Cover and cook on low for 8-9 hours or until a meat thermometer reads 160°.

Transfer the meat to a serving platter. Let stand for 10 minutes before slicing. **Yield:** 8 servings.

Nutrition Facts: 5 ounces cooked meat with 1/4 cup fruit mixture equals 272 calories, 8 g fat (3 g saturated fat), 85 mg cholesterol, 200 mg sodium, 15 g carbohydrate, 1 g fiber, 33 g protein. **Diabetic Exchanges:** 4 lean meat, 1 fruit, 1 fat.

Picante Beef Roast

Tex-Mex Beef Barbecues

(Pictured above and on page 158)

Prep: 20 min. **Cook:** 5 hours

I took this to a potluck and received many compliments. The recipe came from my mom, and it's equally good with ground beef. —Lynda Zuniga, Crystal City, Texas

  1 fresh beef brisket (3-1/2 pounds)
  1 jar (18 ounces) hickory smoke-flavored barbecue sauce
1/2 cup finely chopped onion
  1 envelope chili seasoning
  1 tablespoon Worcestershire sauce
  1 teaspoon minced garlic
  1 teaspoon lemon juice
14 hamburger buns, split

Cut brisket in half; place in a 5-qt. slow cooker. In a small bowl, combine the barbecue sauce, onion, chili seasoning, Worcestershire sauce, garlic and lemon juice. Pour over beef. Cover and cook on high for 5-6 hours or until meat is tender.

Remove beef; cool slightly. Shred and return to the slow cooker. Heat through. Serve on hamburger buns. **Yield:** 14 servings.

   Editor's Note: This is a fresh beef brisket, not corned beef.

Slow-Cooked Pork & Beans

Prep: 25 min. **Cook:** 6 hours

Bacon adds subtle smokiness to this hearty side dish. Serve it over rice, and presto—you have a filling main course. —Sue Livermore, Detroit Lakes, Minnesota

  1 package (1 pound) sliced bacon, chopped
  1 cup chopped onion
  2 cans (15 ounces *each*) pork and beans, undrained
  1 can (16 ounces) kidney beans, rinsed and drained
  1 can (15-1/4 ounces) lima beans, rinsed and drained
  1 can (15 ounces) butter beans, rinsed and drained
  1 can (15 ounces) black beans, rinsed and drained
  1 cup packed brown sugar
1/2 cup cider vinegar
  1 tablespoon molasses
  2 teaspoons garlic powder
1/2 teaspoon ground mustard

In a large skillet, cook the bacon and onion over medium heat until the bacon is crisp. Remove to paper towels to drain.

In a 4-qt. slow cooker, combine the remaining ingredients; stir in bacon mixture. Cover and cook on low for 6-7 hours or until heated through. **Yield:** 12 servings.

Italian Pot Roast

(Pictured below)

Prep: 20 min. **Cook:** 5 hours

This zesty pot roast, a favorite of my husband's, is an entree I make regularly. The tender meat seems to melt in your mouth. —Debbie Daly, Buckingham, Illinois

      1 boneless beef chuck roast (3 to 4 pounds)
      1 can (28 ounces) diced tomatoes, drained
   3/4 cup chopped onion
   3/4 cup burgundy wine *or* beef broth
 1-1/2 teaspoons salt
      1 teaspoon dried basil
   1/2 teaspoon dried oregano
   1/2 teaspoon minced garlic
   1/4 teaspoon pepper
   1/4 cup cornstarch
   1/2 cup cold water

Cut roast in half. Place in a 5-qt. slow cooker. Add the tomatoes, onion, wine, salt, basil, oregano, garlic and pepper. Cover and cook on low for 5 to 5-1/2 hours.

Remove the meat to a serving platter; keep warm. Skim the fat from the cooking juices; transfer to a small saucepan. Combine the cornstarch and water until smooth. Gradually stir into the pan. Bring to a boil; cook and stir for 2 minutes or until thickened. Serve with meat. **Yield:** 8 servings.

Herbed Chicken with Wild Rice

Italian Pot Roast

Herbed Chicken with Wild Rice

(Pictured above)

Prep: 20 min. **Cook:** 4 hours

My family is busy with after-school and evening activities, so it's nice to come home to a meal that's already prepared and ready to eat. This comforting chicken-and-rice dinner is a mainstay. —Becky Gifford, Conway, Arkansas

      1 package (6 ounces) long grain and wild rice
        mix
      6 boneless skinless chicken breast halves
        (5 ounces *each*)
      1 tablespoon canola oil
      1 teaspoon butter
   1/2 pound sliced fresh mushrooms
      1 can (10-3/4 ounces) condensed cream of
        chicken soup, undiluted
      1 cup water
      3 bacon strips, cooked and crumbled
      1 teaspoon dried parsley flakes
   1/2 teaspoon dried thyme
   1/4 teaspoon dried tarragon

Place rice in a 5-qt. slow cooker; set aside seasoning packet. In a large skillet, brown chicken in oil and butter. Add to slow cooker. In the same skillet, saute mushrooms until tender; place over chicken.

In a small bowl, combine the soup, water, bacon, herbs and contents of seasoning packet. Pour over top. Cover and cook on low for 4 hours or until chicken juices run clear. **Yield:** 6 servings.

Beef Barley Soup

(Pictured below)

Prep: 15 min. **Cook:** 9 hours

My husband doesn't usually consider a bowl of soup to be "dinner." But this beefy, chunky recipe changed his mind. I served it with a side of corn bread, and it got his enthusiastic approval! —Ginny Perkins, Columbiana, Ohio

1-1/2 pounds beef stew meat
   1 tablespoon canola oil
   1 can (14-1/2 ounces) diced tomatoes
   1 cup chopped onion
   1 cup diced celery
   1 cup sliced fresh carrots
 1/2 cup chopped green pepper
   4 cups beef broth
   2 cups water
   1 cup spaghetti sauce
 2/3 cup medium pearl barley
   1 tablespoon dried parsley flakes
   2 teaspoons salt
1-1/2 teaspoons dried basil
 3/4 teaspoon pepper

In a large skillet, brown meat in oil over medium heat; drain. Meanwhile, in a 5-qt. slow cooker, combine the vegetables, broth, water, spaghetti sauce, barley and seasonings. Stir in beef. Cover and cook on low for 9-10 hours or until meat is tender. Skim fat from cooking juices. **Yield:** 8 servings (2-1/2 quarts).

Citrus Chicken

Beef Barley Soup

Citrus Chicken

(Pictured above)

Prep: 15 min. **Cook:** 4 hours

Here, moist and flavorful chicken is jazzed up with oranges, green pepper, chili sauce and soy sauce. It's an easy main dish that'll impress everyone at the table.
—Barbara Easton, North Vancouver, British Columbia

   2 medium oranges, cut into wedges
   1 medium green pepper, chopped
   1 broiler/fryer chicken (3 to 4 pounds), cut up and skin removed
   1 cup orange juice
 1/2 cup chili sauce
   2 tablespoons soy sauce
   1 tablespoon molasses
   1 teaspoon ground mustard
   1 teaspoon minced garlic
 1/4 teaspoon pepper
Hot cooked rice

Place oranges and green pepper in a 5-qt. slow cooker coated with cooking spray. Top with chicken. Combine the remaining ingredients; pour over chicken.

Cover and cook on low for 4-5 hours or until chicken juices run clear. Serve with rice. **Yield:** 4 servings.

Easy Accompaniments

WONDERING what to serve with Citrus Chicken (recipe above)? This entree would work well with any of a number of different sides. For example, pair it with buttered noodles, fettuccine alfredo, mashed potatoes, steamed broccoli or green beans.

Tender Beef Brisket

(Pictured below)

Prep: 15 min. **Cook:** 8 hours

Beef brisket can sometimes be a challenge to make, but I never have to worry with this recipe—it always turns out great. Fixed in the slow cooker, it's so easy! And combined with tomato sauce, Worcestershire sauce, mustard and other ingredients, the meat has an incredible taste.
—Jenni Arnold, Woodbury, Tennessee

- 1 fresh beef brisket (4 pounds)
- 1 can (15 ounces) tomato sauce
- 1 can (12 ounces) beer *or* nonalcoholic beer
- 1 cup chopped green pepper
- 2/3 cup chopped onion
- 2 tablespoons brown sugar
- 2 tablespoons balsamic vinegar
- 2 tablespoons Worcestershire sauce
- 2 teaspoons prepared mustard
- 1 teaspoon salt
- 1 teaspoon garlic powder
- 1/2 teaspoon pepper

Cut brisket into thirds; place in a 5-qt. slow cooker. In a large bowl, combine the remaining ingredients; pour over beef. Cover and cook on low for 8-9 hours or until meat is tender.

Thinly slice meat across the grain. If desired, thicken pan juices. **Yield:** 10 servings.

Editor's Note: This is a fresh beef brisket, not corned beef.

Saucy Chicken with Veggies and Rice

Tender Beef Brisket

Saucy Chicken with Veggies and Rice

(Pictured above)

Prep: 15 min. **Cook:** 4-1/2 hours

I came up with this recipe many years ago and entered it in a slow cooker contest. I was thrilled when the recipe won first place, and now I'm proud to share it.
—Teri Lindquist, Gurnee, Illinois

- 3 cups sliced celery
- 3 cups sliced fresh carrots
- 2 cups sliced onion
- 6 boneless skinless chicken breast halves (5 ounces *each*)
- 1 can (10-3/4 ounces) condensed cream of mushroom soup, undiluted
- 1 envelope onion soup mix
- 1 teaspoon dried thyme
- 1 teaspoon pepper
- 1/2 teaspoon dried tarragon
- 2 tablespoons cornstarch
- 1/3 cup white wine *or* chicken broth

Hot cooked rice

Place the celery, carrots, onion and chicken in a 5-qt. slow cooker. In a small bowl, combine the cream of mushroom soup, onion soup mix, thyme, pepper and tarragon; pour over chicken. Cover and cook on low for 4-5 hours or until a meat thermometer inserted into the chicken reads 170°.

Mix cornstarch and wine until smooth; stir into slow cooker. Cover and cook on high for 30 minutes or until gravy is thickened. Serve with rice. **Yield:** 6 servings.

Chapter 11

Breakfast & Brunch Favorites

WHAT snooze button? You and your family will want to jump out of bed instantly when these taste-tempting dishes are on the morning menu!

Baked Blueberry Pancake... Sausage & Egg Breakfast Pizza... Iced Coffee Latte...Orange Cinnamon Rolls...these treats are so good, it's hard to believe you won't have to rise at the crack of dawn to make them.

In fact, most of the recipes featured in this chapter can be prepared from start to finish in just 30 minutes or less.

Whether you need a quick weekday breakfast to get your family going or a special brunch for weekend guests, look here for the perfect wake-up fare.

A.M. SENSATIONS. Chocolate-Orange Scones (p. 182).

Glazed Apple and Sausage with Pancakes

(Pictured above)

Prep/Total Time: 20 min.

With sausage links and fruit built right in, this comforting pancake breakfast is a treat the whole family can enjoy. You could also use frozen waffles in place of the pancakes. If your children don't care for onion, simply leave it out.

—Cheryl Reisen, Ashland, Nebraska

2 packages (7 ounces *each*) brown-and-serve sausage links
1 teaspoon all-purpose flour
3 tablespoons water
1 large apple, peeled and sliced
1/2 cup chopped onion
3 tablespoons brown sugar
8 pancakes *or* frozen waffles, warmed

Heat sausage links according to package directions. Meanwhile, in a 1-1/2-qt. microwave-safe dish, combine flour and water. Add apple and onion. Cover and microwave on high for 3 minutes.

Stir in the brown sugar. Cover and cook on high for 1-2 minutes or until sugar is dissolved.

Cut sausage links into bite-size pieces. Add sausage pieces to the apple mixture. Serve with the pancakes. **Yield:** 4 servings.

Editor's Note: This recipe was tested in a 1,100-watt microwave.

Summer Fruit Salad

(Pictured below)

Prep/Total Time: 25 min.

My friends are always requesting this tangy medley. The colorful fruit slices are dressed up with a sauce of citrus juices and honey. For a special touch, I sometimes add strawberries.   —Anneliese Deising, Plymouth, Michigan

☑ This recipe includes Nutrition Facts and Diabetic Exchange.

   2 medium navel oranges, peeled and sectioned
   2 medium kiwifruit, peeled and sliced
1-1/2 cups halved seedless red grapes
   1 cup sliced peeled apple
   1 cup diced honeydew
   1 cup fresh blueberries
  1/4 cup orange juice
   2 tablespoons honey
   1 tablespoon lime juice
1-1/2 cups sliced ripe bananas

In a large salad bowl, combine the first six ingredients. In a small bowl, combine the orange juice, honey and lime juice. Drizzle over fruit mixture; toss to coat. Chill until serving.

Add bananas just before serving. Serve with a slotted spoon. **Yield:** 8 servings.

Nutrition Facts: 3/4 cup equals 120 calories, 1 g fat (trace saturated fat), 0 cholesterol, 4 mg sodium, 31 g carbohydrate, 3 g fiber, 1 g protein. **Diabetic Exchange:** 2 fruit.

Crustless Chicken Quiche

Crustless Chicken Quiche

(Pictured above)

Prep: 15 min. **Bake:** 35 min. + standing

This savory, hard-to-resist brunch dish may sound complicated, but it's actually super-easy. Plus, any leftovers keep well.   —Susie Baumberger, Lancaster, California

   1 large sweet onion, chopped
   2 teaspoons minced garlic
   2 tablespoons olive oil
   6 eggs
  3/4 cup heavy whipping cream
   2 cups cubed cooked rotisserie chicken (skin removed)
   2 cups (8 ounces) shredded cheddar cheese
   5 bacon strips, cooked and crumbled

In a small skillet, saute onion and garlic in oil until tender. In a large bowl, combine eggs and cream. Stir in the chicken, cheese, bacon and onion mixture. Pour into a greased 9-in. deep-dish pie plate.

Bake at 375° for 35-45 minutes or until a knife inserted near the center comes out clean. Let stand for 10 minutes before cutting. **Yield:** 6 servings.

Summer Fruit Salad

Quiche Clue

TO AVOID water on the bottom of the pie when making a quiche, use an oven thermometer to check the accuracy of your oven temperature. Then, to avoid overbaking the quiche, do the "knife test" as instructed in the recipe to check for doneness.

Orange Zucchini Muffins

(Pictured below)

Prep: 15 min. **Bake:** 20 min.

Put some of that garden zucchini to yummy use in these tender muffins. They're nicely spiced and feature a burst of orange flavor. —Chris Snyder, Boulder, Colorado

    1 cup shredded zucchini
1-1/4 cups all-purpose flour
  3/4 teaspoon ground nutmeg, *divided*
  1/2 teaspoon baking powder
  1/2 teaspoon baking soda
  1/2 teaspoon ground cinnamon
  1/4 teaspoon salt
    2 eggs
  3/4 cup packed brown sugar
  1/3 cup canola oil
    2 tablespoons orange juice
    1 teaspoon grated orange peel
    1 teaspoon vanilla extract
  1/2 cup raisins
    1 tablespoon sugar

Squeeze zucchini until dry; set aside. In a large bowl, combine the flour, 1/2 teaspoon nutmeg, baking powder, baking soda, cinnamon and salt.

In another bowl, beat the eggs, brown sugar, oil, orange juice, orange peel and vanilla. Stir into the dry ingredients just until moistened. Fold in raisins and reserved zucchini.

Fill paper-lined muffin cups two-thirds full. Combine sugar and remaining nutmeg; sprinkle over batter. Bake at 350° for 18-22 minutes or until a toothpick comes out clean. Cool for 5 minutes before removing from pan to a wire rack. **Yield:** 10 muffins.

Apple Yogurt Parfaits

Apple Yogurt Parfaits

(Pictured above)

Prep/Total Time: 10 min.

Even on your most rushed mornings, you can get the day started off right with this super-simple, four-ingredient parfait that takes mere moments to fix. For variety, try chunky or flavored applesauce, such as strawberry.
—Rebekah Radewahn, Wauwatosa, Wisconsin

☑ This recipe includes Nutrition Facts and Diabetic Exchanges.

    1 cup sweetened applesauce
Dash ground nutmeg
  1/2 cup granola with raisins
1-1/3 cups vanilla yogurt

In a small bowl, combine applesauce and nutmeg. Spoon 1 tablespoon granola into each of four parfait glasses. Layer each with 1/3 cup yogurt and 1/4 cup applesauce; sprinkle with remaining granola. Serve immediately. **Yield:** 4 servings.

Nutrition Facts: 1 parfait equals 170 calories, 4 g fat (2 g saturated fat), 8 mg cholesterol, 69 mg sodium, 30 g carbohydrate, 1 g fiber, 5 g protein. **Diabetic Exchanges:** 1 starch, 1/2 milk.

Orange Zucchini Muffins

My Favorite Granola

Prep: 10 min. **Bake:** 30 min. + cooling

I first made this when I was a teenager, and I've never found a granola recipe I like as much. Sometimes I toss fresh fruit in with the oats, coconut, wheat germ, sunflower seeds and nuts, but this mix is good just as it is.
—Sarah Wilson, Republic, Washington

2-1/2 cups old-fashioned oats
1/2 cup flaked coconut
1/3 cup chopped walnuts
1/3 cup sunflower kernels
2 tablespoons toasted wheat germ
1/4 teaspoon salt
1/3 cup water
1/3 cup canola oil
3 tablespoons brown sugar
2 tablespoons honey

In a large bowl, combine the first six ingredients; set aside. In a small saucepan, combine the water, oil, brown sugar and honey. Cook and stir over medium heat for 2-3 minutes or until heated through. Pour over oat mixture and toss to coat.

Transfer to a greased 15-in. x 10-in. x 1-in. baking pan. Bake at 300° for 30-40 minutes or until golden brown, stirring once. Cool on a wire rack. Store in an airtight container. **Yield:** 4 cups.

Iced Coffee Latte

Prep/Total Time: 10 min.

This 10-minute latte is a refreshing alternative to regular hot coffee...and much easier on your budget than store-bought or restaurant beverages. Sweetened condensed milk and a hint of chocolate lend a special touch.
—Heather Nandell, Johnston, Iowa

1/2 cup instant coffee granules
1/2 cup boiling water
4 cups chocolate milk
2 cups cold water
1 can (14 ounces) sweetened condensed milk
Ice cubes

In a large bowl, dissolve instant coffee granules in the boiling water. Stir in the chocolate milk, cold water and sweetened condensed milk. Serve coffee over ice. **Yield:** 8 servings.

Bacon Vegetable Quiche

(Pictured at right)

Prep: 25 min. **Bake:** 35 min.

I love the versatility of this flavorful quiche. You can prepare it with Vidalia onions, green onions or leeks. Asparagus can take the place of broccoli, and you can use whatever fresh herbs or cheese you have on hand. I especially like this dish in spring, when I have an abundance of fresh greens. —Shannon Koene, Blacksburg, Virginia

1 unbaked pastry shell (9 inch)
2 cups fresh baby spinach
1 cup sliced fresh mushrooms
1 cup chopped fresh broccoli
3/4 cup chopped sweet onion
2-1/2 teaspoons olive oil
3 eggs, lightly beaten
1 can (5 ounces) evaporated milk
1 tablespoon minced fresh rosemary *or*
1 teaspoon dried rosemary, crushed
1/4 teaspoon salt
1/4 teaspoon pepper
1 cup (4 ounces) shredded cheddar cheese
6 bacon strips, cooked and crumbled
1/2 cup crumbled tomato and basil feta cheese

Line unpricked pastry shell with a double thickness of heavy-duty foil. Bake at 450° for 8 minutes. Remove foil; bake 5 minutes longer.

Meanwhile, in a large skillet, saute the spinach, mushrooms, broccoli and onion in oil until tender. In a large bowl, whisk the eggs, milk, rosemary, salt and pepper. Using a slotted spoon, transfer vegetables to egg mixture. Stir in cheddar cheese and bacon. Pour into crust. Sprinkle with feta cheese.

Cover edges loosely with foil. Bake at 375° for 30-35 minutes or until a knife inserted near the center comes out clean. Let stand for 5 minutes before cutting. **Yield:** 6 servings.

Bacon Vegetable Quiche

Mustard Ham Strata

(Pictured below)

Prep: 15 min. + chilling **Bake:** 45 min.

I first had this hearty bake at a bed-and-breakfast years ago. They were kind enough to give me the recipe, and I've prepared it many times since. Keep it in mind when you need to use up deli ham or ham leftovers from Easter.
—Dolores Zornow, Poynette, Wisconsin

   12 slices day-old bread, crusts removed and
      cubed
1-1/2 cups cubed fully cooked ham
    1 cup chopped green pepper
  3/4 cup shredded cheddar cheese
  3/4 cup shredded Monterey Jack cheese
  1/3 cup chopped onion
    7 eggs
    3 cups milk
    3 teaspoons ground mustard
    1 teaspoon salt

In a greased 13-in. x 9-in. baking dish, layer the bread cubes, ham, green pepper, cheeses and onion. In a large bowl, combine the eggs, milk, mustard and salt. Pour over top. Cover and refrigerate overnight.

Remove from the refrigerator 30 minutes before baking. Bake, uncovered, at 325° for 45-50 minutes or until a knife inserted near the center comes out clean. Let stand for 5 minutes before cutting. **Yield:** 12 servings.

Eggs Benedict with Jalapeno Hollandaise

Eggs Benedict with Jalapeno Hollandaise

(Pictured above)

Prep/Total Time: 20 min.

Make a memorable morning or evening meal with this special dish. Cool, creamy avocado balances the jalapeno perfectly.   —Laura Denney, Redondo Beach, California

    1 tablespoon white vinegar
    4 eggs
  1/4 cup butter, cubed
    1 cup milk
    1 package hollandaise sauce mix
    2 tablespoons chopped seeded jalapeno
      pepper
    2 English muffins, split and toasted
    4 slices Canadian bacon, warmed
    4 slices tomato
    1 medium ripe avocado, peeled and sliced

Place 2-3 in. of water in a large skillet with high sides; add the vinegar. Bring to a boil; reduce the heat and simmer gently. Break the cold eggs, one at a time, into a custard cup or saucer. Holding the cup close to the surface of the water, slip each egg into the water. Cook, uncovered, until whites are completely set and yolks

Mustard Ham Strata

Avocado Advice

PLAN on preparing delicious Eggs Benedict with Jalapeno Sauce (recipe above)? When choosing an avocado, keep in mind that the easiest avocados to peel and slice are those that are ripe yet firm. Very ripe, soft avocados are best used for mashing.

begin to thicken (but are not hard), about 4-5 minutes.

Meanwhile, in a small saucepan, melt the butter over medium heat; whisk in the milk and sauce mix. Bring to a boil. Reduce heat; simmer, uncovered, for 1 minute or until thickened. Stir in jalapeno. Set aside and keep warm.

With a slotted spoon, lift each egg out of the water. On each muffin half, layer the Canadian bacon, tomato, avocado and an egg; spoon sauce over tops. Serve immediately. **Yield:** 4 servings.

Editor's Note: When cutting hot peppers, disposable gloves are recommended. Avoid touching your face.

Crescent Zucchini Pie

(Pictured below)

Prep: 20 min. **Bake:** 20 min.

With a tender, flaky crust, this egg-and-zucchini-based pie is a wonderful treat. Cheese, herbs and seasonings add delectable flavor.   —Zelda Dehoedt, Cedar Rapids, Iowa

- 1 tube (8 ounces) refrigerated crescent rolls
- 2 teaspoons Dijon mustard
- 4 cups sliced zucchini
- 1 cup chopped onion
- 6 tablespoons butter, cubed
- 2 eggs, lightly beaten
- 1 cup (4 ounces) shredded part-skim mozzarella cheese
- 1 cup (4 ounces) shredded Colby-Monterey Jack cheese
- 2 tablespoons dried parsley flakes
- 1/2 teaspoon salt
- 1/2 teaspoon pepper
- 1/4 teaspoon dried basil
- 1/4 teaspoon dried oregano

Blueberry Banana Smoothies

Separate the crescent roll dough into eight triangles and place in a greased 9-in. deep-dish pie plate with the points toward the center. Press dough onto the bottom and up the sides of plate to form a crust; seal seams. Spread with mustard.

In a large skillet, saute zucchini and onion in butter until tender. In a large bowl, combine the eggs, cheeses, seasonings and zucchini mixture. Pour into crust.

Bake at 375° for 20-25 minutes or until a knife inserted near the center comes out clean. Cover the edges loosely with foil if the crust browns too quickly. **Yield:** 6 servings.

Blueberry Banana Smoothies

(Pictured above)

Prep/Total Time: 5 min.

We often make smoothies to use up overripe bananas. This yummy combination with blueberries and cherry juice is a favorite. —Lisa DeMarsh, Mt. Solon, Virginia

☑ **This recipe includes Nutrition Facts.**

- 1 medium ripe banana, cut into chunks
- 1 cup frozen unsweetened blueberries
- 1 cup cherry juice blend
- 3/4 cup vanilla yogurt
- 1/2 cup crushed ice
- Dash ground cinnamon

In a blender, combine all ingredients; cover and process for 30 seconds or until smooth. Pour into chilled glasses; serve immediately. **Yield:** 3 servings.

Nutrition Facts: 1 cup equals 164 calories, 2 g fat (1 g saturated fat), 6 mg cholesterol, 44 mg sodium, 33 g carbohydrate, 2 g fiber, 4 g protein.

Crescent Zucchini Pie

Sausage & Egg Breakfast Pizza

Baked Blueberry Pancake

(Pictured below)

Prep/Total Time: 20 min.

For a no-fuss breakfast that still has the comforting, homey taste we crave, I rely on this recipe. Sometimes I make one large pancake the night before, then cut it into squares. In the morning, all I have to do is pop them in the microwave and serve.
—*Norna Detig, Lindenwood, Illinois*

✓ This recipe includes Nutrition Facts and Diabetic Exchanges.

　　2 cups pancake mix
1-1/2 cups fat-free milk
　　1 egg
　　1 tablespoon canola oil
　　1 teaspoon ground cinnamon
　　1 cup fresh *or* frozen blueberries
Butter and maple syrup

In a large bowl, combine the pancake mix, milk, egg, oil and cinnamon just until blended (batter will be lumpy). Fold in blueberries.

Spread into a greased 15-in. x 10-in. x 1-in. baking pan. Bake at 400° for 10-12 minutes or until golden brown. Serve with butter and syrup. **Yield:** 6 servings.

Editor's Note: If using frozen blueberries, do not thaw before adding to batter.

Nutrition Facts: 1 serving (calculated without butter and syrup) equals 200 calories, 4 g fat (1 g saturated fat), 36 mg cholesterol, 527 mg sodium, 34 g carbohydrate, 3 g fiber, 7 g protein. **Diabetic Exchanges:** 2 starch, 1 fat.

Sausage & Egg Breakfast Pizza

(Pictured above)

Prep: 30 min. **Bake:** 5 min.

I came up with this recipe after trying something similar at a restaurant. My husband likes my version better and often requests it, whether in the morning or for supper.
—*Julie Tucker, Columbus, Nebraska*

　　2 packages (8 ounces *each*) refrigerated
　　　crescent rolls
　　1 pound bulk pork sausage
1/3 cup chopped onion
　　1 small green pepper, chopped
　　1 envelope country gravy mix
　　6 eggs
　　2 tablespoons milk
1/2 teaspoon salt
1/4 teaspoon pepper
　　1 tablespoon butter
1-1/4 cups sliced fresh mushrooms
　　2 cups (8 ounces) shredded cheddar cheese
　　1 cup (4 ounces) pepper Jack cheese

Separate crescent dough into 16 triangles and place on a greased 14-in. round pizza pan with points toward the center. Press onto the bottom and up the sides of pan to form a crust; seal seams. Bake at 375° for 11-13 minutes or until golden brown.

Meanwhile, in a skillet, cook the sausage, onion and green pepper over medium heat until sausage is no longer pink; drain. Prepare gravy according to package directions. Stir into sausage mixture; set aside.

In a small bowl, whisk the eggs, milk, salt and pepper. In a large skillet, heat butter over medium heat. Add egg mixture; cook and stir until almost set. Spread gravy mixture over crust. Top with egg mixture, mushrooms and cheeses. Bake 5-10 minutes longer or until cheese is melted. Cut into wedges. **Yield:** 8 servings.

Baked Blueberry Pancake

Breakfast Biscuits 'n' Eggs

Breakfast Biscuits 'n' Eggs

(Pictured above)

Prep/Total Time: 15 min.

With just the two of us, my husband and I never eat a whole batch of biscuits. I can fix these easy sandwiches using either leftover biscuits or ones baked fresh.
— *Teresa Huff, Nevada, Missouri*

    4 individually frozen biscuits
    2 teaspoons butter
    4 eggs
    4 slices process American cheese
    4 thin slices deli ham

Prepare biscuits according to package directions. Meanwhile, in a large skillet, heat butter until hot. Add eggs; reduce heat to low. Fry until whites are completely set and yolks begin to thicken but are not hard.

Split the biscuits. Layer the bottom of each biscuit with cheese, ham and an egg; replace top. Microwave, uncovered, for 30-45 seconds or until cheese is melted. **Yield:** 4 biscuits.

Editor's Note: This recipe was tested in a 1,100-watt microwave.

Stacking Up

FEEL FREE to vary the recipe for Breakfast Biscuits 'n' Eggs (recipe above) to suit your family's tastes. For example, use cooked bacon, Canadian bacon or sausage patties in place of the deli ham. Try a different type of cheese...or English muffins instead of biscuits.

Pull-Apart Sticky Bun Ring

(Pictured below)

Prep: 25 min. **Bake:** 25 min.

Moist and loaded with rich maple flavor, this treat tastes as scrumptious as it looks. The gooey cream cheese inside each piece will have everyone's mouth watering.
— *Doreen Wright-Laukaitis, Oxford, Massachusetts*

    3/4 cup chopped pecans
    1/2 cup butter, melted, *divided*
    1/3 cup maple syrup
      2 tubes (6 ounces *each*) refrigerated flaky
        buttermilk biscuits
    1/2 cup sugar
      1 teaspoon ground cinnamon
      1 package (8 ounces) cream cheese

Sprinkle pecans into a greased 10-in. fluted tube pan. In a small bowl, combine 2 tablespoons butter and maple syrup; pour over pecans. Set aside.

Separate biscuits; split each in half horizontally. Place remaining butter in a shallow bowl. In another shallow bowl, combine sugar and cinnamon.

Cut the cream cheese into 20 cubes; roll in the sugar mixture. Place one cube in the center of each piece of dough. Fold dough over cheese cube; pinch edges to seal tightly. Dip one side of each biscuit in butter, then sugar mixture.

Arrange biscuits in prepared pan, sugar side up. Pour remaining butter over top; sprinkle with remaining sugar mixture. Bake at 375° for 25-30 minutes or until golden brown. Immediately invert onto a serving platter. Serve warm. Refrigerate leftovers. **Yield:** 20 servings.

Pull-Apart Sticky Bun Ring

Three-Fruit Smoothies

(Pictured below)
Prep/Total Time: 10 min.

There's nothing more refreshing than a cold, fruit-filled smoothie in the morning, as a pick-me-up snack in the afternoon or just as a special treat on a hot summer's day. This version features a tongue-tingling blend of peaches, strawberries, banana, vanilla yogurt and honey.
—Jenny Flake, Gilbert, Arizona

1 can (11-1/2 ounces) frozen strawberry breeze juice concentrate, thawed
1 cup (8 ounces) vanilla yogurt
1/2 cup milk
1 tablespoon honey
1 teaspoon vanilla extract
1 pint fresh strawberries, hulled
1 large banana, cut into chunks
1 cup chopped peeled fresh peaches *or* frozen unsweetened sliced peaches
1 cup crushed ice

Place half of all ingredients in a blender; cover and process for 15 seconds or until smooth. Pour into chilled glasses. Repeat. Serve immediately. **Yield:** 6 servings.

Three-Fruit Smoothies

Chocolate-Orange Scones

Chocolate-Orange Scones

(Pictured above and on page 172)
Prep/Total Time: 25 min.

Yes, you can make scones! They're not as difficult to prepare as some may think—especially when you have a recipe as simple as this one. Pancake mix is the key ingredient in these light and fluffy wedges, which are great with everything from coffee and milk to herbal tea.
—Margaret Wilson, Sun City, California

1-1/2 cups complete buttermilk pancake mix
3/4 cup heavy whipping cream
2 to 3 teaspoons grated orange peel
2 milk chocolate candy bars (1.55 ounces *each*), chopped

In a small bowl, combine the pancake mix, cream and orange peel. Turn onto a lightly floured surface, knead 6 times. Knead in chocolate.

Pat into a 9-in. circle. Cut into eight wedges. Separate wedges and place on a greased baking sheet. Bake at 400° for 9-11 minutes or until lightly browned. Serve warm. **Yield:** 8 scones.

Orange Cinnamon Rolls

(Pictured below)

Prep: 25 min. + rising **Bake:** 15 min.

I've been making this comforting recipe from my grand-mother for years. It's a must on Sunday mornings! The orange zest, juice and nuts give the iced rolls great flavor.
—Donna Taylor, Southbridge, Massachusetts

☑ This recipe includes Nutrition Facts and Diabetic Exchanges.

   1 loaf (1 pound) frozen bread dough, thawed
1/4 cup butter, softened
1/2 cup chopped pecans
1/4 cup sugar
1/4 cup packed brown sugar
   1 tablespoon grated orange peel
   1 teaspoon ground cinnamon
ICING:
   1 cup confectioners' sugar
   1 tablespoon butter, melted
1/2 teaspoon vanilla extract
   2 to 3 tablespoons orange juice

On a lightly floured surface, roll dough into a 14-in. square. Spread with butter. In a small bowl, combine the pecans, sugar, brown sugar, orange peel and cinnamon. Sprinkle over dough to within 1/2 inch of edges.

Roll up jelly-roll style; pinch seams to seal. Cut into 28 slices. Place cut side down in two greased 9-in. round baking pans. Cover and let rise in a warm place until doubled, about 40 minutes.

Bake at 350° for 14-16 minutes or until the rolls are golden brown. Combine the confectioners' sugar, butter, vanilla and enough orange juice to achieve the desired consistency; drizzle the icing over the warm rolls. **Yield:** about 2 dozen.

Nutrition Facts: 1 roll equals 110 calories, 4 g fat (1 g saturated fat), 5 mg cholesterol, 106 mg sodium, 16 g carbohydrate, 1 g fiber, 2 g protein. **Diabetic Exchanges:** 1 starch, 1/2 fat.

Eggs in Muffin Cups

Orange Cinnamon Rolls

Eggs in Muffin Cups

(Pictured above)

Prep/Total Time: 30 min.

My mother used to fix these all the time for my family, and now I'm carrying on the tradition. The cups are formed with deli roast beef and then filled with cheese and eggs. While they're in the oven, I can go get ready for the day.
—Lisa Walder, Urbana, Illinois

12 thin slices deli roast beef
  6 slices process American cheese, quartered
12 eggs

Press one slice of beef onto the bottom and up the sides of each greased muffin cup, forming a shell. Arrange two cheese pieces in each shell. Break one egg into each cup. Bake, uncovered, at 350° for 20-25 minutes or until eggs are completely set. **Yield:** 6 servings.

Chapter 12

◷ *Snappy Soups & Sandwiches*

WHEN IT COMES to that classic combination of soup and a sandwich, why settle for the same-old, same-old? Thanks to the easy ideas in this chapter, you can enjoy an exciting new taste sensation—and still keep kitchen time to a minimum.

Fire up Grilled Pizza Burgers at your next barbecue...warm your family with Macaroni Vegetable Soup on a winter's day... or prepare Chicken Salad Croissants for a luncheon. No matter what the occasion, you'll find memorable recipes here.

With speedy options such as Pesto-Turkey Layered Loaf and Summer Strawberry Soup, you get perfect choices for parties and brown bags, too!

GRAB AND GO. Mango Shrimp Pitas (p. 193).

Macaroni Vegetable Soup

(Pictured below)

Prep/Total Time: 25 min.

Soup doesn't have to simmer for hours on end to be delicious—this recipe proves it! Ready to eat in just 25 minutes, this satisfying veggie-pasta combination couldn't be much easier to get on the table. Simply open the ingredients, pour 'em in, and dinner's practically done.
—Metzel Turley, South Charleston, West Virginia

- 1 package (1.4 ounces) vegetable soup mix
- 1 envelope (.6 ounce) cream of chicken soup mix
- 2 cans (5-1/2 ounces *each*) spicy tomato juice
- 4 cups water
- 2 cans (15 ounces *each*) mixed vegetables, drained
- Dash crushed red pepper flakes
- Dash dried minced garlic
- 1/2 cup uncooked elbow macaroni

In a Dutch oven, combine the soup mixes and spicy tomato juice. Stir in the water, mixed vegetables, red pepper flakes and garlic; bring to a boil. Add the macaroni. Reduce the heat; cook, uncovered, for 10-15 minutes or until the macaroni is tender, stirring occasionally. **Yield:** 7 servings.

Chicken Salad Croissants

Macaroni Vegetable Soup

Chicken Salad Croissants

(Pictured above)

Prep/Total Time: 20 min.

I wanted a sandwich that's on the healthier side but still tasty, so I experimented in the kitchen and came up with this chicken salad recipe loaded with wholesome carrot bits, pineapple, celery, dried cranberries and more. When I took these croissants to a party, they disappeared fast.
—Cheryl Lafferty, Incline Village, Nevada

- 2 cups cooked rotisserie chicken
- 1/2 cup chopped celery
- 1/2 cup crushed pineapple
- 1/4 cup chopped carrot
- 1/4 cup golden raisins
- 1/4 cup dried cranberries
- 1/4 cup sunflower kernels
- 1 tablespoon chopped green onion
- 1/4 cup mayonnaise
- 1/4 cup sour cream
- 3/4 teaspoon lemon juice
- 1/8 teaspoon curry powder
- 1/8 teaspoon cayenne pepper
- 6 croissants, split

In a large bowl, combine the first eight ingredients. In another bowl, combine the mayonnaise, sour cream, lemon juice, curry powder and cayenne. Pour over the chicken mixture; toss to coat. Place 3/4 cup chicken salad on each croissant bottom. Replace the tops. **Yield:** 6 servings.

Creamy Cauliflower And Bacon Soup

(Pictured below)

Prep: 15 min. **Cook:** 30 min.

Asiago cheese, cream and bacon make this such a rich soup that you don't need to serve a lot with it. In fact, it can make a satisfying meal all by itself. For a garnish that has a bit of a kick, add a drop of hot sauce to the top of each bowlful and drag a butter knife through it.
—Mildred Caruso, Brighton, Tennessee

- 1 medium head cauliflower (2 pounds), cut into florets
- 2 cups half-and-half cream, *divided*
- 1/2 cup shredded Asiago cheese
- 1/2 teaspoon salt
- 1/2 teaspoon ground nutmeg
- 1/8 teaspoon pepper
- 1/2 to 1 cup water
- 4 bacon strips, cooked and crumbled

Place cauliflower in a steamer basket; place in a large saucepan over 1 in. of water. Bring to a boil; cover and steam for 8-10 minutes or until tender. Cool slightly.

Place cauliflower and 1/2 cup cream in a food processor; cover and process until pureed. Transfer to a large saucepan.

Stir in the cheese, salt, nutmeg, pepper and remaining cream. Add enough water to reach desired consistency; heat through. Sprinkle each serving with bacon. **Yield:** 4 servings.

Creamy Cauliflower and Bacon Soup

Grilled Pizza Burgers

Grilled Pizza Burgers

(Pictured above)

Prep: 20 min. **Grill:** 15 min.

Pizza burgers are usually a hit with kids, but these please adults, too. The patties are well spiced and served on English muffins. *—Mitzi Sentiff, Annapolis, Maryland*

- 1 egg, lightly beaten
- 3/4 cup grated Parmesan cheese
- 1/2 cup chopped onion
- 1/4 cup minced fresh parsley
- 3/4 teaspoon dried basil
- 3/4 teaspoon dried oregano
- 3/4 teaspoon dried rosemary, crushed
- 3/4 teaspoon pepper
- 1 pound ground beef
- 4 slices provolone cheese
- 4 English muffins, split and toasted
- 1/2 cup pizza sauce

In a large bowl, combine the first eight ingredients. Crumble beef over mixture and mix well. Shape into four patties.

Grill burgers, covered, over medium heat for 5-7 minutes on each side or until a meat thermometer reads 160° and juices run clear. Top burgers with cheese; cover and grill 2-3 minutes longer or until cheese is melted. Serve on muffins with pizza sauce. **Yield:** 4 servings.

Mess-Free Mixing

IF YOU don't like getting your hands messy when mixing the meat mixture for hamburger patties, put the ingredients in a large resealable plastic bag and then mix. Or, if you do use your hands, first dampen them with water so nothing will stick.

Grilled Vegetable Sandwich

(Pictured above)

Prep: 20 min. + marinating **Grill:** 10 min.

This recipe's a keeper! Even meat lovers you know will rave about the simply fabulous flavor in this hearty veggie sandwich cooked on the grill. I like to stack the ingredients on ciabatta bread because of its crispy crust and light, airy texture.
—Diana Tseperkas, Hamden, Connecticut

  1 **medium zucchini, thinly sliced lengthwise**
  1 **medium sweet red pepper, quartered**
  1 **small red onion, cut into 1/2-inch slices**
1/4 **cup prepared Italian salad dressing**
  1 **loaf ciabatta bread (14 ounces), halved lengthwise**
  2 **tablespoons olive oil**

1/4 **cup reduced-fat mayonnaise**
  1 **tablespoon lemon juice**
  2 **teaspoons grated lemon peel**
  1 **teaspoon minced garlic**
1/2 **cup crumbled feta cheese**

In a large resealable plastic bag, combine the zucchini, pepper, onion and salad dressing. Seal bag and turn to coat; refrigerate for at least 1 hour. Drain and discard marinade.

  Brush cut sides of bread with oil; set aside. Place the vegetables on grill rack. Grill, covered, over medium heat for 4-5 minutes on each side or until crisp-tender. Remove and keep warm. Grill bread, oil side down, over medium heat for 30-60 seconds or until toasted.

  In a small bowl, combine the mayonnaise, lemon juice, lemon peel and garlic. Spread over the bottom of the bread; sprinkle with the feta cheese. Top with the vegetables and remaining bread. Cut into four slices.
Yield: 4 servings.

Chicken Cheese Soup

(Pictured at right)

Prep/Total Time: 30 min.

Children won't think twice about eating their vegetables when you serve this creamy, cheesy soup. It's yummy!
—Lavonne Lundgren, Sioux City, Iowa

4 cups cubed cooked chicken breast
3-1/2 cups water
2 cans (10-3/4 ounces *each*) condensed cream of chicken soup, undiluted
1 package (16 ounces) frozen mixed vegetables, thawed
1 can (14-1/2 ounces) diced potatoes, drained
1 package (16 ounces) process cheese (Velveeta), cubed

In a Dutch oven, combine the first five ingredients. Bring to a boil. Reduce heat; cover and simmer for 8-10 minutes or until vegetables are tender. Stir in cheese just until melted (do not boil). **Yield:** 7 servings.

Chicken Cheese Soup

Open-Faced Pizza Sandwiches

(Pictured below)

Prep/Total Time: 15 min.

This warm-from-the-oven pizza bread is always a winner with my grandkids...and nothing could be easier for Saturday lunch. —Dorothy Eriksen, Salem, Oregon

1/4 cup butter, softened
6 slices white bread
1 can (15 ounces) chili, warmed
1/2 teaspoon garlic salt
3/4 cup pizza sauce
1 cup (4 ounces) shredded part-skim mozzarella cheese
1 teaspoon Italian seasoning

Butter bread on both sides. On a greased griddle, toast bread on one side until lightly browned. Turn; spoon about 1/4 cup chili on each slice. Sprinkle with garlic salt. Top each with 2 tablespoons pizza sauce and about 2 tablespoons cheese. Sprinkle with Italian seasoning. Cook until bottom is golden brown and cheese is melted. **Yield:** 6 servings.

Greek-Stuffed Hamburgers

Prep: 15 min. **Cook:** 20 min.

Stuffed with traditional Greek ingredients, these open-face hamburgers look impressive but are actually simple to fix.
—Jessica Ring, Chicago, Illinois

2 pounds ground beef
1/2 cup crumbled feta cheese
1/2 cup chopped tomato
2 tablespoons chopped red onion
2 tablespoons chopped ripe olives
1 tablespoon olive oil
1/4 teaspoon dried oregano
1/2 teaspoon salt
1/4 teaspoon pepper
6 whole gyro-style pitas (6 inch)
6 lettuce leaves
6 slices tomato
1 small cucumber, sliced
1/3 cup cucumber ranch salad dressing

Shape beef into 12 patties. In a small bowl, combine the cheese, chopped tomato, onion, olives, oil and oregano. Top half of the patties with cheese mixture. Cover with remaining patties and firmly press edges to seal. Sprinkle with salt and pepper.

Grill patties, covered, over medium-hot heat or broil 4 in. from heat for 6-8 minutes on each side or until a meat thermometer reads 160° and juices run clear. Serve each burger on a pita with lettuce, sliced tomato, cucumber and salad dressing. **Yield:** 6 servings.

Open-Faced Pizza Sandwiches

Sausage Tortellini Soup

(Pictured below)

Prep: 10 min. **Cook:** 30 min.

Always on the lookout for new and different soup recipes, I came across one in an old church cookbook and made a few changes to suit my family. Now, it's a favorite.
—Heather Persch, Hudsonville, Michigan

  1 pound bulk Italian sausage
  2 cups water
  2 cups chopped cabbage
  1 can (14-1/2 ounces) Italian stewed tomatoes, undrained and cut up
  1 can (14-1/2 ounces) beef broth
  1 can (10-1/2 ounces) condensed French onion soup
  1 package (9 ounces) refrigerated cheese tortellini
1/2 cup grated Parmesan cheese

In a large saucepan, cook the Italian sausage over medium heat until no longer pink; drain. Stir in the water, cabbage, tomatoes, beef broth and French onion soup. Bring to a boil. Reduce the heat; simmer, uncovered, for 8 minutes.

Stir in tortellini; cook 7-9 minutes longer or until pasta is tender. Sprinkle with cheese. **Yield:** 10 servings (2-1/2 quarts).

Sausage Tortellini Soup

Ham and Brie Melts

Ham and Brie Melts

(Pictured above)

Prep/Total Time: 20 min.

Tired of the same old BLTs or grilled cheese? You'll want to try these very special sandwiches. It's hard to believe that five ingredients can add up to such great taste!
—Bonnie Bahler, Ellington, Connecticut

  8 slices multigrain bread
1/4 cup apricot preserves
  8 ounces sliced deli ham
  1 round (8 ounces) Brie cheese, rind removed and cut into four slices
  3 tablespoons butter, softened

Spread four bread slices with half of preserves. Layer with ham and cheese. Spread remaining bread with remaining preserves; place on top. Butter outsides of sandwiches.

In a large skillet over medium heat, toast sandwiches for 2-3 minutes on each side or until bread is lightly browned and cheese is melted. **Yield:** 4 servings.

Facts on Freezing

MOST SOUPS freeze nicely for future meals. The exceptions are soups made with cream and potatoes, which are better when eaten fresh. Also, pasta in soup can get mushy in the freezer. It's best to add the pasta when ready to eat, not before freezing.

To help retain their fantastic flavor, don't freeze soups for longer than 3 months. Thaw soup completely in the refrigerator and reheat in a saucepan.

Taco Turkey Burgers

(Pictured below)

Prep/Total Time: 30 min.

We love the flavor of Tex-Mex foods, and I decided to combine them with ground turkey. Try these unique sandwiches when you want to shake up your grilling routine.
—Jennifer Feindt, Milford, Delaware

  1 egg
  1 tablespoon Worcestershire sauce
1/4 cup dry bread crumbs
1/4 cup finely chopped onion
1/4 cup finely chopped green pepper
1/2 teaspoon ground cumin
1/2 teaspoon chili powder
1/4 teaspoon salt
1/4 teaspoon garlic powder
1/4 teaspoon pepper
  1 pound ground turkey
  1 tablespoon canola oil
1/2 cup shredded cheddar-Monterey Jack cheese
  4 hamburger buns, split and toasted
1/2 cup salsa
1/4 cup sour cream

In a large bowl, combine the first 10 ingredients. Crumble the turkey over the mixture and mix well. Shape into four patties.

In a large skillet, cook burgers in oil over medium heat for 6-8 minutes on each side or until a meat thermometer reads 165° and juices run clear.

Sprinkle with cheese. Serve on buns with salsa and sour cream. **Yield:** 4 servings.

Italian Sausage Sandwiches

Taco Turkey Burgers

Italian Sausage Sandwiches

(Pictured above)

Prep/Total Time: 30 min.

Perfect for summer cookouts, these hearty sandwiches are popular picnic fare. Just add a simple side of chips or potato salad. —Mariela Petrosk, Helena, Montana

  6 Italian sausage links (4 ounces *each*)
  1 bottle (14.9 ounces) dark beer *or*
    nonalcoholic beer
  2 cups julienned green peppers
  1 cup sliced onion
  2 teaspoons minced garlic
  2 tablespoons olive oil
1/2 cup chopped fresh tomato
3/4 teaspoon salt
1/2 teaspoon pepper
  6 brat buns, split
  6 slices provolone cheese, halved

Place sausages in a large saucepan; add beer. Bring to a boil. Reduce heat; cover and simmer for 8-10 minutes or until meat is no longer pink.

Meanwhile, in a large skillet, saute the green peppers, onion and garlic in oil until tender. Add the tomato, salt and pepper; heat through.

Drain and discard beer. Grill sausages, covered, over direct medium heat for 4-5 minutes or until browned, turning occasionally. Serve on buns with green pepper mixture and cheese. **Yield:** 6 servings.

Egg Salad Sandwiches

Zesty Hamburger Soup

(Pictured below)

Prep/Total Time: 30 min.

This quick recipe is especially nice for chilly winter days. I usually pair it with garlic bread or crusty French bread.
—*Kelly Milan, Lake Jackson, Texas*

☑ This recipe includes Nutrition Facts and Diabetic Exchanges.

    1 **pound ground beef**
    2 **cups sliced celery**
    1 **cup chopped onion**
    2 **teaspoons minced garlic**
    4 **cups hot water**
    2 **medium red potatoes, peeled and cubed**
    2 **cups frozen corn**
1-1/2 **cups uncooked small shell pasta**
    4 **jarred jalapeno slices**
    1 **bottle (32 ounces) V8 juice**
    2 **cans (10 ounces *each*) diced tomatoes with green chilies**
    1 **to 2 tablespoons sugar**

In a Dutch oven, cook the beef, celery, onion and garlic over medium heat until meat is no longer pink; drain. Stir in the water, potatoes, corn, pasta and jalapeno.

Bring to a boil. Reduce the heat; cover and simmer for 10-15 minutes or until the pasta is tender. Stir in the remaining ingredients. Cook and stir until heated through. **Yield:** 10 servings (3-3/4 quarts).

Nutrition Facts: 1-1/2 cups equals 221 calories, 5 g fat (2 g saturated fat), 22 mg cholesterol, 548 mg sodium, 33 g carbohydrate, 4 g fiber, 13 g protein. **Diabetic Exchanges:** 2 vegetable, 1-1/2 starch, 1 lean meat.

Egg Salad Sandwiches

(Pictured above)

Prep/Total Time: 15 min.

The ingredients in this sandwich may be basic, but each one accentuates the flavor—making it hard to stop with just one bite! You'll love the sweet pickles, cheddar cheese and horseradish. Keep this recipe in mind as brown-bag fare or when hosting friends for a casual summer lunch.
—*Anna Jean Allen, West Liberty, Kentucky*

    6 **hard-cooked eggs**
    1 **cup (4 ounces) shredded cheddar cheese**
1/2 **cup chopped green pepper**
1/2 **cup sweet pickles, chopped**
1/4 **cup mayonnaise**
    2 **tablespoons horseradish sauce**
    1 **tablespoon sweet pickle juice**
1/4 **teaspoon salt**
  12 **slices white bread**
Lettuce leaves and tomato slices, optional

In a small bowl, combine the first eight ingredients. On six slices of bread, layer 1/2 cup egg salad, lettuce and tomato slices if desired. Top with remaining bread slices. **Yield:** 6 servings.

Zesty Hamburger Soup

Mango Shrimp Pitas

spoon the reserved chutney mixture over filling. **Yield:** 4 servings.

Nutrition Facts: 1 filled pita half equals 313 calories, 2 g fat (trace saturated fat), 138 mg cholesterol, 638 mg sodium, 49 g carbohydrate, 2 g fiber, 22 g protein.

Summer Strawberry Soup

(Pictured below)

Prep: 15 min. + chilling

Yogurt, orange juice, berries and sugar are all you'll need to create this spectacular summer soup. It's a fun treat on a warm day. —*Verna Bollin, Powell, Tennessee*

☑ This recipe includes Nutrition Facts.

    2 cups vanilla yogurt
1/2 cup orange juice
    2 pounds fresh strawberries, halved (8 cups)
1/2 cup sugar
Additional vanilla yogurt and fresh mint leaves, optional

In a blender, combine the yogurt, orange juice, strawberries and sugar in batches; cover and process until blended. Refrigerate for at least 2 hours. Garnish soup with additional yogurt and mint leaves if desired. **Yield:** 6 servings.

Nutrition Facts: 1 cup (calculated without additional yogurt) equals 204 calories, 3 g fat (2 g saturated fat), 8 mg cholesterol, 54 mg sodium, 41 g carbohydrate, 3 g fiber, 5 g protein.

Mango Shrimp Pitas

(Pictured above and on page 184)

Prep: 15 min. + marinating **Grill:** 10 min.

Here, refreshing mango, ginger and curry combine with a splash of lime juice to coat juicy grilled shrimp. Stuffed in pitas, it all makes for an easy-to-hold, fabulous lunch or dinner. If you like, serve the filling on a bed of rice instead.
—*Beverly O'Ferrall, Linkwood, Maryland*

☑ This recipe includes Nutrition Facts.

1/2 cup mango chutney
  3 tablespoons lime juice
  1 teaspoon grated fresh gingerroot
1/2 teaspoon curry powder
  1 pound uncooked large shrimp, peeled and deveined
  2 pita breads (6 inches), halved
  8 Bibb *or* Boston lettuce leaves
  1 large tomato, thinly sliced

In a small bowl, combine the chutney, lime juice, ginger and curry. Pour 1/2 cup marinade into a large resealable plastic bag; add the shrimp. Seal bag and turn to coat; refrigerate for at least 15 minutes. Cover and refrigerate remaining marinade.

Coat grill rack with cooking spray before starting the grill. Drain and discard marinade. Thread shrimp onto four metal or soaked wooden skewers. Grill shrimp, covered, over medium heat for 6-8 minutes or until shrimp turn pink, turning once.

Fill the pita halves with lettuce, tomato and shrimp;

Summer Strawberry Soup

Veggie Tortellini Soup

Chili Chicken Sandwiches

(Pictured below)

Prep/Total Time: 20 min.

We often serve these when we have friends over to watch a game on TV. I also use this recipe when I need a quick dinner on a weeknight but don't want to spend a lot of time in the kitchen. The creamy, cheesy chicken sandwiches always come out of the oven hot and delicious.
—Dena Peterson, LaPorte, Texas

    1 package (8 ounces) cream cheese, softened
    2 cups cubed cooked chicken
1-1/2 cups shredded cheddar cheese
    1 can (4 ounces) chopped green chilies
    3 tablespoons chopped green onions
    1 teaspoon ground cumin
  1/4 teaspoon crushed red pepper flakes
  1/4 teaspoon chili powder
    4 hard rolls
    2 tablespoons minced fresh cilantro

In a small bowl, beat the cream cheese until fluffy. Stir in the chicken, cheddar cheese, chilies, green onions and seasonings.

Cut the top fourths off of the hard rolls; carefully hollow out the bottoms, leaving 1/4-in. shells (discard the removed bread or save for another use). Fill the bottom portions of rolls with the chicken mixture; replace the tops.

Place on a baking sheet. Bake at 375° for 5-7 minutes or until golden brown. Sprinkle with cilantro. **Yield:** 4 servings.

Veggie Tortellini Soup

(Pictured above)

Prep/Total Time: 30 min.

Make the best of frozen vegetables and dried cheese tortellini with this fuss-free recipe. For a special touch, add a sprinkling of Parmesan to the top...or a small drizzle of balsamic vinegar. You could also try different veggie blends.
—Helen Rehberger, Pewaukee, Wisconsin

5 cups chicken broth
1 package (16 ounces) frozen California-blend vegetables
1 package (8 ounces) dried cheese tortellini
1 can (14-1/2 ounces) Italian diced tomatoes, undrained

In a Dutch oven, bring the chicken broth to a boil. Stir in the vegetables and dried cheese tortellini. Return to a boil. Reduce the heat; simmer, uncovered, for 10-12 minutes or until the vegetables are tender, stirring occasionally.

Stir in the Italian diced tomatoes. Cover and cook for 5-6 minutes or until soup is heated through. **Yield:** 6 servings.

Chili Chicken Sandwiches

Pesto-Turkey Layered Loaf

bread or save for another use.) Spread pesto on the inside of top and bottom of bread. Set top aside.

In bottom of bread, layer the turkey, cheese, zucchini, tomatoes and onion. Gently press the layers together. Replace bread top and wrap tightly in foil. Place on a baking sheet. Bake at 350° for 25-30 minutes or until heated through. Let stand for 10 minutes before cutting. **Yield:** 6 servings.

Egg Salad & Cucumber Sandwiches

(Pictured below)

Prep/Total Time: 15 min.

Cool, crisp cucumber adds a summery crunch to these out-of-the-ordinary egg salad sandwiches. Sometimes I add celery and substitute rye bread for the sourdough bread.
—Kelly McCune, Westerville, Ohio

  1/2 cup chopped red onion
  1/2 cup mayonnaise
  1/4 cup sour cream
    2 tablespoons Dijon mustard
  1/2 teaspoon pepper
  1/4 teaspoon salt
    8 hard-cooked eggs, chopped
    1 large cucumber, sliced
    1 tablespoon dill weed
  12 slices sourdough bread, toasted

In a small bowl, combine the first six ingredients. Add eggs; stir gently to combine. In another bowl, toss cucumber and dill. Spread egg salad over six slices of toast; top with cucumbers and remaining toast. Serve immediately. **Yield:** 6 servings.

Pesto-Turkey Layered Loaf

(Pictured above)

Prep: 20 min. **Cook:** 25 min. + standing

This big sandwich may look complicated, but it's actually easy to assemble. Plus, it travels well to tailgate parties, picnics or other events. Make several when you're feeding a crowd and use any meat, veggies and cheese you like.
—Marion Sundberg, Yorba Linda, California

    1 loaf (1 pound) French bread
    1 cup prepared pesto
    1 pound thinly sliced deli turkey
  1/2 pound provolone cheese, thinly sliced
    2 small zucchini, thinly sliced
    2 medium tomatoes, thinly sliced
    1 medium red onion, thinly sliced

Cut the top fourth off loaf of bread. Carefully hollow out the bottom, leaving a 1/2-in. shell. (Discard removed

Egg Salad & Cucumber Sandwiches

Egg Salad Ideas

I spruce up my egg salad with lemon juice—about a tablespoon for every six eggs. It allows me to use a little less mayonnaise while enhancing the flavor. Occasionally, I also toss in some chopped green olives.
—Lee Levy, Tamarac, Florida

Chapter 13

⏱ *Easy Half-Hour Entrees*

BURGUNDY STEAK...Balsamic Almond Chicken...Fruit-Glazed Pork Chops...Thai Shrimp Linguine...can these memorable main courses really be table-ready in just 30 minutes? The answer is, yes!

Busy cooks from all around rely on the speedy dishes in this chapter to feed their own families, and now they've shared the recipes here for you. Each one goes together from start to finish in only half an hour—or less.

After a long day at work or running errands, come home to Smoked Sausage Pasta, Enchilada Beef, Crumb-Topped Baked Fish and other simple-to-fix entrees that'll have your family sitting down to eat in a flash.

MAIN EVENT. Fruit-Glazed Pork Chops (p. 215).

Raspberry Chicken

(Pictured above)

Prep/Total Time: 30 min.

Here, a tongue-tingling raspberry sauce gives basic skillet-cooked chicken a slightly sweet kick. You'll need just four ingredients to whip up the ruby-red topping, which looks beautiful on the table for a dinner party or holiday feast. On weeknights, serve this entree over rice for a full meal.
—Anita Hennesy, Hagerstown, Maryland

☑ This recipe includes Nutrition Facts and Diabetic Exchanges.

> **4 boneless skinless chicken breast halves**
>   **(5 ounces** *each***)**
> **1/4 teaspoon salt**
> **1/4 teaspoon pepper**
> **1/2 cup seedless raspberry jam**
>   **2 tablespoons balsamic vinegar**
>   **1 tablespoon reduced-sodium soy sauce**
> **1/8 teaspoon crushed red pepper flakes**

Sprinkle chicken with salt and pepper. In a large nonstick skillet coated with cooking spray, cook chicken over medium heat for 5-7 minutes on each side or until juices run clear.

Meanwhile, in a small saucepan, combine the remaining ingredients. Bring to a boil; cook until the liquid is reduced to 1/2 cup. Serve sauce with chicken. **Yield:** 4 servings.

Nutrition Facts: 1 chicken breast half with 2 tablespoons sauce equals 260 calories, 3 g fat (1 g saturated fat), 78 mg cholesterol, 369 mg sodium, 28 g carbohydrate, trace fiber, 29 g protein. **Diabetic Exchanges:** 4 very lean meat, 1-1/2 starch.

Enchilada Beef

(Pictured below)

Prep/Total Time: 20 min.

When it comes to family-pleasing food, you just can't go wrong going Southwestern. This favorite has lots of chips and melted cheese. —Loraine Meyer, Bend, Oregon

- 1/2 cup chopped onion
- 1 pound lean ground beef
- 1 cup tomato juice
- 1 can (6 ounces) tomato paste
- 1 can (4 ounces) chopped green chilies, drained
- 2 tablespoons plus 2 teaspoons enchilada sauce mix
- 2 cups (8 ounces) shredded Monterey Jack cheese, *divided*
- 1/2 cup coarsely crushed corn chips

Additional corn chips, optional

Place the onion in a microwave-safe bowl; cover and microwave on high for 2-3 minutes or until tender. Crumble beef over onion and mix well. Cover and cook on high for 4-6 minutes or until beef is no longer pink, stirring once; drain.

Stir in the tomato juice, tomato paste, green chilies and sauce mix. Spread half of beef mixture in a 2-qt. microwave-safe dish; sprinkle with 1 cup cheese. Top with the remaining beef mixture. Cover; microwave for 2-3 minutes or until heated through.

Sprinkle with the crushed corn chips and remaining cheese. Microwave 1 minute longer or until cheese is melted. Serve with additional corn chips if desired. **Yield:** 4 servings.

Editor's Note: This recipe was tested in a 1,100-watt microwave.

Enchilada Beef

Muffuletta Pasta

Muffuletta Pasta

(Pictured above)

Prep/Total Time: 25 min.

After discovering that I love muffulettas, a friend of mine gave me this recipe. Rich and filling, the no-fuss stovetop supper has all the taste of the classic Italian sandwiches I crave. Plus, it goes together quickly on a busy weekday. Round out your menu with fresh-baked garlic bread. —Jan Hollingsworth, Houston, Mississippi

- 1 package (16 ounces) bow tie pasta
- 1 bunch green onions, chopped
- 1 tablespoon minced garlic
- 2 teaspoons plus 1/4 cup butter, *divided*
- 1 package (16 ounces) cubed fully cooked ham
- 1 jar (12.36 ounces) tapenade *or* ripe olive bruschetta topping, drained
- 1 package (3-1/2 ounces) sliced pepperoni
- 1 cup heavy whipping cream
- 2 cups (8 ounces) shredded Italian cheese blend

Cook the pasta according to the package directions. Meanwhile, in a large skillet, saute the onions and garlic in 2 teaspoons butter until tender. Add the ham, tapenade and pepperoni; saute 2 minutes longer.

Cube the remaining butter; stir the butter and heavy whipping cream into the skillet. Bring to a boil over medium heat. Reduce the heat; simmer, uncovered, for 3 minutes.

Drain pasta; toss with ham mixture. Sprinkle with cheese. **Yield:** 8 servings.

Pasta Carbonara

Crumb-Coated Cubed Steaks

(Pictured below)

Prep/Total Time: 30 min.

I always buy steaks like this—ones that are already cubed and tenderized at the meat counter. Mashed potatoes and peas are great plate fillers alongside this home-style main course. —Agnes Ward, Stratford, Ontario

    1 egg
  1/2 cup milk
   23 saltines, crushed
  2/3 cup all-purpose flour
  3/4 teaspoon salt
  1/4 teaspoon baking powder
  1/4 teaspoon cayenne pepper
  1/4 teaspoon pepper
    4 beef cubed steaks (4 ounces *each*)
    3 tablespoons canola oil
GRAVY:
    2 tablespoons all-purpose flour
1-1/3 cups milk
  1/4 teaspoon salt
  1/4 teaspoon pepper

In a shallow bowl, whisk the egg and milk. In another shallow bowl, combine the cracker crumbs, flour, salt, baking powder, cayenne and pepper. Dip steaks in egg mixture, then cracker crumb mixture.

In a large skillet, cook steaks in oil over medium heat for 3-4 minutes on each side or until no longer pink. Remove and keep warm.

Add flour to the skillet, stirring to blend and loosen browned bits from pan. Gradually add milk. Bring to a boil; cook and stir for 2 minutes or until thickened. Season with salt and pepper. Serve with steaks. **Yield:** 4 servings.

Pasta Carbonara

(Pictured above)

Prep/Total Time: 30 min.

This creamy and delicious recipe gives you a restaurant-quality pasta entree in just half an hour. I serve it with a side salad and warm-from-the-oven rolls for a full meal. —Cindi Bauer, Marshfield, Wisconsin

2-1/2 cups uncooked mostaccioli
    8 bacon strips, diced
    1 jar (4-1/2 ounces) whole mushrooms, drained
  3/4 cup half-and-half cream
  1/3 cup butter, cubed
    1 teaspoon dried parsley flakes
    1 teaspoon minced garlic
    6 to 8 drops hot pepper sauce
  1/2 teaspoon salt, optional
  1/3 cup grated Parmesan cheese
  1/4 cup sliced green onions

Cook the mostaccioli according to the package directions. Meanwhile, in a large skillet, cook bacon over medium heat until crisp. Using a slotted spoon, remove to paper towels to drain. Brown mushrooms in drippings; remove to paper towels. Drain drippings from pan.

Add the cream, butter, parsley, garlic, pepper sauce and salt if desired to skillet; cook and stir over medium heat until butter is melted.

Drain the mostaccioli; add to the cream mixture. Stir in the bacon, mushrooms and Parmesan cheese; heat through. Remove from the heat. Sprinkle with green onions. **Yield:** 4 servings.

Crumb-Coated Cubed Steaks

Macadamia-Crusted Mahi Mahi

(Pictured above)

Prep/Total Time: 30 min.

Transform mahi mahi fillets into fancy company fare—or a special weekday dinner for your family—with this easy recipe. I give the fish a crunchy coating of macadamia nuts and panko bread crumbs, then drizzle on a gingery sauce. Carrot coins make a colorful, nutritious side.
—Idana Mooney, Moreno Valley, California

 1 cup panko (Japanese) bread crumbs
3/4 cup macadamia nuts
1/4 teaspoon salt
1/4 teaspoon white pepper
 1 egg
 2 teaspoons water
1/3 cup all-purpose flour
 4 mahi mahi fillets (4 ounces *each*)
1/4 cup canola oil
 2 tablespoons brown sugar
 2 tablespoons reduced-sodium soy sauce
 2 teaspoons minced fresh gingerroot

Place bread crumbs, macadamia nuts, salt and pepper in a food processor; cover and pulse until the nuts are finely chopped.

In a shallow bowl, whisk the egg and water. Place the flour and nut mixture in separate shallow bowls. Coat fillets with flour, then dip in egg mixture and coat with nut mixture.

In a large skillet, heat oil over medium heat; cook fillets for 3-4 minutes on each side or until golden brown.

Meanwhile, in a small microwave-safe bowl, combine the brown sugar, soy sauce and ginger. Microwave, uncovered, on high for 30-60 seconds or until sugar is dissolved. Drizzle over fish. **Yield:** 4 servings.

Veggie Chicken Pitas

(Pictured below)

Prep/Total Time: 30 min.

These satisfying pita pockets are stuffed to the brim with wholesome vegetables, protein-packed chicken and two kinds of cheese. Plus, I add a kick of cayenne pepper. They're super for on-the-go meals... but don't forget a napkin! —Bill Parkis Wilmington, North Carolina

☑ This recipe includes Nutrition Facts and Diabetic Exchanges.

1 medium red onion, sliced
1 cup julienned carrots
1 cup chopped fresh broccoli
1 cup fresh snow peas
1/2 teaspoon minced garlic
2 tablespoons olive oil
1 cup cubed cooked chicken
1 jar (7 ounces) roasted sweet red peppers, drained and chopped
1/4 cup white wine *or* chicken broth
1/2 teaspoon dried oregano
1/2 teaspoon cayenne pepper
5 pita breads (6 inches), halved
1/3 cup shredded part-skim mozzarella cheese
1/3 cup shredded cheddar cheese

In a large skillet, saute the onion, carrots, broccoli, peas and garlic in oil for 4-5 minutes or until tender.

Stir in the chicken, red peppers, wine, oregano and cayenne. Bring to a boil. Reduce the heat; simmer, uncovered, for 5-6 minutes or until heated through. Spoon mixture into pita breads; sprinkle with cheeses. **Yield:** 5 servings.

Nutrition Facts: 2 stuffed pita halves equals 373 calories, 12 g fat (4 g saturated fat), 37 mg cholesterol, 595 mg sodium, 43 g carbohydrate, 4 g fiber, 19 g protein. **Diabetic Exchanges:** 2 starch, 2 vegetable, 2 fat, 1 lean meat.

Linguine Pesto with Italian Chicken Strips

Linguine Pesto with Italian Chicken Strips

(Pictured above)

Prep/Total Time: 20 min.

This linguine dinner came together by chance one night when I was scrambling to get a meal together in a short time. It's now one of the tastiest pasta recipes in my file. It's also incredibly fuss-free to make using packaged grilled chicken strips and other convenience items.
—Beckie Perez, Port Washington, Wisconsin

8 ounces uncooked linguine
1 package (6 ounces) ready-to-use grilled Italian chicken strips
1 cup (4 ounces) shredded sharp cheddar cheese
3/4 cup frozen corn, thawed
1 jar (3-1/2 ounces) prepared pesto
1/4 cup seasoned bread crumbs
1/4 teaspoon crushed red pepper flakes
1/4 teaspoon pepper

Cook the linguine according to the package directions; drain. Add the chicken, cheddar cheese, corn, pesto, bread crumbs, red pepper flakes and pepper. Toss to coat. **Yield:** 4 servings.

Veggie Chicken Pitas

Asparagus Scallop Stir-Fry

(Pictured below)

Prep/Total Time: 25 min.

With plenty of fresh asparagus, this all-in-one meal truly captures the essence of spring...but is delicious any time of year. The recipe mixes in scallops, mushrooms, crunchy water chestnuts and slivered almonds for a stir-fry your family is sure to love. Serve it over your favorite rice.
—*Mary Ann Griffin, Saginaw, Michigan*

> 1 pound bay scallops
> 3 tablespoons cornstarch
> 2 cups chicken broth
> 2 tablespoons soy sauce
> 2 cups cut fresh asparagus (2-inch pieces)
> 1/2 cup chopped onion
> 1/2 cup chopped celery
> 2 tablespoons canola oil, *divided*
> 1 cup sliced fresh mushrooms
> 1 can (8 ounces) sliced water chestnuts, drained
> 1/4 cup slivered almonds

Hot cooked rice, optional

If scallops are large, cut in half and set aside. In a small bowl, combine the cornstarch, chicken broth and soy sauce until smooth; set aside.

In a large skillet, saute the asparagus, onion and celery in 1 tablespoon oil for 3 minutes. Add mushrooms and water chestnuts; stir-fry for 2-3 minutes or until crisp-tender. Remove vegetable mixture and set aside.

In the same skillet, stir-fry scallops in remaining oil for 2-3 minutes or until scallops are firm and opaque. Stir chicken broth mixture; add to pan. Bring to a boil; cook and stir for 2 minutes or until thickened. Add the vegetables; heat through. Sprinkle with almonds. Serve with rice if desired. **Yield:** 4 servings.

Asparagus Scallop Stir-Fry

Broiled Halibut Steaks with Raspberry Sauce

Broiled Halibut Steaks With Raspberry Sauce

(Pictured above)

Prep/Total Time: 15 min.

This elegant fish entree is also versatile. You can replace the halibut with salmon...and the raspberry jam with blackberry. —*Allene Bary-Cooper, Wichita Falls, Texas*

> 1/4 cup butter, cubed
> 1/4 teaspoon garlic powder
> 1/4 teaspoon salt
> 1/4 teaspoon pepper
> 4 halibut steaks (6 ounces *each*)
> 3/4 cup seedless raspberry jam
> 2 green onions, sliced
> 2 teaspoons Dijon mustard

Fresh raspberries and lemon wedges, optional

In a microwave-safe bowl, melt butter; stir in the garlic powder, salt and pepper.

Broil halibut 4-6 in. from the heat for 5-6 minutes on each side or until fish flakes easily with a fork, basting occasionally with butter mixture.

Meanwhile, in a microwave-safe bowl, heat the jam, onions and mustard until jam is melted, stirring once. Serve with fish. Garnish with raspberries and lemon wedges if desired. **Yield:** 4 servings.

Stirring Success

STIR-FRY RECIPES such as Asparagus Scallop Stir-Fry (above left) make great family dinners. When fixing a stir-fry, select a skillet or wok that is large enough to accommodate the volume of food you'll be stir-frying. If the food is crowded in the pan, it will steam. If necessary, stir-fry the food in batches.

Sausage & Spinach Calzones

(Pictured above)

Prep/Total Time: 30 min.

Hot and hearty, these pockets are perfect as either a meal or a satisfying afternoon snack. My co-workers always ask me to fix them when it's my turn to bring in lunch.
—*Kourtney Williams, Mechanicsville, Virginia*

1/2 pound bulk Italian sausage
1 tube (13.8 ounces) refrigerated pizza crust
3/4 cup shredded part-skim mozzarella cheese
2-2/3 cups fresh baby spinach
1/2 cup part-skim ricotta cheese
1/4 teaspoon salt
1/4 teaspoon pepper

In a large skillet, cook sausage over medium heat until no longer pink. Meanwhile, unroll pizza crust; pat into a 15-in. x 11-in. rectangle. Cut into four rectangles. Sprinkle mozzarella cheese over half of each rectangle to within 1 in. of edges.

Drain sausage. Add the spinach; cook and stir over medium heat until spinach is wilted. Remove from the heat. Stir in the ricotta cheese, salt and pepper; spread over mozzarella cheese. Fold dough over filling; press edges with a fork to seal.

Transfer to a greased baking sheet. Bake at 400° for 10-15 minutes or until lightly browned. **Yield:** 4 servings.

Crumb-Topped Baked Fish

Prep/Total Time: 25 min.

A coating of bread crumbs, seasonings and cheese makes these fillets something special. It's fish your family will be hooked on! —*Jean Barcroft, Clarksville, Michigan*

4 haddock *or* cod fillets (6 ounces *each*)
Salt and pepper to taste
1-1/4 cups seasoned bread crumbs
1/4 cup shredded cheddar cheese
1/4 cup butter, melted
1 tablespoon minced fresh parsley
1/2 teaspoon dried marjoram
1/4 teaspoon garlic powder
1/4 teaspoon dried rosemary, crushed

Place the fish fillets on a greased baking sheet; season with salt and pepper. In a small bowl, combine the remaining ingredients; pat onto the fillets. Bake at 400° for 15-20 minutes or until the fish flakes easily with a fork. **Yield:** 4 servings.

Lemon Chicken and Veggies

(Pictured below)

Prep/Total Time: 30 min.

Drizzled with a lemony hollandaise sauce, this chicken-and-vegetable dinner from our Test Kitchen brings both great taste and nutrition to the table.

   1/4 cup all-purpose flour
   1 teaspoon lemon-pepper seasoning
   4 boneless skinless chicken breast halves
     (6 ounces *each*)
   1 package (0.9 ounce) hollandaise sauce mix
   1 tablespoon lemon juice
   4 tablespoons butter, *divided*
   1/4 cup chicken broth
   2 cups shredded carrots
   1 package (9 ounces) fresh baby spinach

In a large resealable bag, combine flour and lemon-pepper. Flatten chicken to 1/2-in. thickness. Add the chicken, one piece at a time, and shake to coat.

Prepare the hollandaise sauce mix according to the package directions. Stir in lemon juice. Meanwhile, in a Dutch oven, saute the chicken in 2 tablespoons butter for 4-6 minutes on each side or until no longer pink. Remove and keep warm.

In the same pan, add the chicken broth, stirring to loosen brown bits. Add the carrots and remaining butter; cook for 2 minutes or until crisp-tender. Add the spinach; cook 3-5 minutes longer or until the spinach is wilted. Serve the chicken with sauce and vegetables. **Yield:** 4 servings.

Lemon Chicken and Veggies

Mac and Cheese Chicken Skillet

Mac and Cheese Chicken Skillet

(Pictured above)

Prep/Total Time: 30 min.

Does your family love macaroni and cheese? For a change of pace from the plain boxed mix, jazz things up with this recipe. It stirs in chunks of chicken, zucchini, onion and tomatoes for an Italian-style entree everyone will like. And it takes a mere 30 minutes to prepare from start to finish.
   —Margaret Wilson, Hemet, California

   1 pound boneless skinless chicken breasts, cut
     into 1-inch cubes
   1 teaspoon olive oil
   1 package (7-1/4 ounces) macaroni and cheese
     dinner mix
2-1/2 cups chicken broth
   1 cup chopped zucchini
   1/2 cup chopped onion
   1 teaspoon dried oregano
   1 can (14-1/2 ounces) Italian stewed tomatoes

In a large skillet, cook chicken in oil over medium-high heat until no longer pink.

Set aside the cheese packet from the macaroni dinner mix. Stir in the pasta, chicken broth, zucchini, onion and oregano. Bring to a boil. Reduce the heat; cover and simmer for 7-8 minutes or until the pasta is tender, stirring occasionally.

Stir in tomatoes and the contents of the reserved cheese packet. Cook and stir for 3-4 minutes or until heated through. **Yield:** 6 servings.

Chicken and Artichoke Pasta

(Pictured below)

Prep/Total Time: 30 min.

Without a doubt, this is the meal my husband requests most often. I like to serve it with a loaf of crusty French bread. —Laurel Johnson, Sterling Heights, Michigan

> 4 cups uncooked bow tie pasta
> 1 pound chicken tenderloins, cut into 1-inch pieces
> 2 tablespoons olive oil, *divided*
> 1/2 pound sliced fresh mushrooms
> 1/2 cup chopped green onions
> 2 tablespoons white wine *or* chicken broth
> 1 can (14-1/2 ounces) diced tomatoes with roasted garlic, undrained
> 1 can (14 ounces) water-packed quartered artichoke hearts, rinsed and drained
> 1/4 teaspoon salt
> 2 teaspoons cornstarch
> 2 teaspoons cold water
> 1 tablespoon thinly sliced fresh basil *or* 1 teaspoon dried basil
> 1/2 cup shaved Parmesan cheese

Cook pasta according to package directions. Meanwhile, in a large skillet, saute chicken in 1 tablespoon oil until no longer pink. Remove and keep warm.

In the same skillet, saute mushrooms and onions in remaining oil until tender; add wine, stirring to loosen browned bits from pan. Reduce heat to medium. Stir in the tomatoes, artichokes, salt and chicken. Cook and stir for 4-5 minutes or until heated through.

Combine the cornstarch and cold water until smooth. Gradually stir into the pan. Bring to a boil; cook and stir for 1 minute or until thickened. Stir in the basil. Drain the pasta; serve with the chicken mixture and cheese. **Yield:** 5 servings.

Chicken and Artichoke Pasta

Orange Roughy with Tartar Sauce

Orange Roughy with Tartar Sauce

(Pictured above)

Prep/Total Time: 30 min.

These foil-wrapped fillets come out perfect every time. And you may never buy tartar sauce again once you've tried this version! —Michelle Stromko, Forest Hill, Maryland

> 6 orange roughy fillets (6 ounces *each*)
> 1 tablespoon seafood seasoning
> 2 tablespoons butter, cubed
> **TARTAR SAUCE:**
> 2/3 cup chopped dill pickles
> 1/2 cup mayonnaise
> 3 tablespoons finely chopped onion
> **Dash pepper**

Place three fillets on each of two double thicknesses of heavy-duty foil (about 18 in. square). Sprinkle each with seasoning; dot with butter. Fold the foil around the fish and seal tightly. Grill, covered, over medium heat for 10-15 minutes or until fish flakes easily with a fork. Open foil carefully to allow steam to escape.

In a small bowl, combine the sauce ingredients; serve with fish. **Yield:** 6 servings (1 cup sauce).

Herb Ease

TO QUICKLY cut basil for recipes such as Chicken and Artichoke Pasta (above left), create basil chiffonade (thin shredded strips).

Before cutting basil chiffonade, sprinkle a few drops of canola oil on the leaves and gently rub to evenly coat the leaves. This will prevent them from darkening. Then, stack several basil leaves and roll them into a tight tube. Slice the leaves widthwise into narrow pieces to create long thin strips. If you'd prefer smaller pieces, simply chop the strips.

Smoked Kielbasa with Rice

(Pictured above)
Prep/Total Time: 25 min.

With a little zip and just the right amount of smokiness, this sausage-and-rice combo is guaranteed to please. You could also serve the sausage pieces alone as an appetizer with toothpicks. —Nicole Jackson, El Paso, Texas

   2 pounds smoked kielbasa *or* Polish sausage, halved lengthwise and cut into 1/4-inch slices
1/4 cup finely chopped onion
   3 bacon strips, finely chopped
3/4 cup honey barbecue sauce
1/4 cup packed brown sugar
   1 tablespoon prepared horseradish
   2 teaspoons water
   2 teaspoons minced garlic
1/2 teaspoon crushed red pepper flakes
Hot cooked rice

In a Dutch oven, saute the smoked kielbasa, onion and bacon until the onion is tender; drain. Add the honey barbecue sauce, brown sugar, horseradish, water, garlic and red pepper flakes. Bring to a boil; cook and stir for 2-3 minutes or until the sauce is thickened. Serve with rice. **Yield:** 6 servings.

Balsamic Almond Chicken

Prep/Total Time: 25 min.

Brown sugar and balsamic vinegar lend sweet and subtly tangy flavor to this tender, almond-crusted chicken.
—Lisa Ruehlow, Blaine, Minnesota

1/2 cup ground almonds
1/4 cup all-purpose flour
   2 eggs
   4 boneless skinless chicken breast halves (4 ounces *each*)
   2 tablespoons canola oil
   1 teaspoon cornstarch
1/2 cup chicken broth
   2 tablespoons balsamic vinegar
   1 tablespoon brown sugar

In a shallow bowl, combine the almonds and flour. In another shallow bowl, whisk eggs. Flatten chicken to 1/4-in. thickness. Dip chicken in eggs; then coat with almond mixture. In a large skillet, cook chicken in oil over medium heat for 4-6 minutes on each side or until juices run clear.

Meanwhile, in a small saucepan, combine cornstarch, broth, vinegar and brown sugar until smooth. Bring to a boil; cook and stir for 2 minutes or until slightly thickened. Serve with chicken. **Yield:** 4 servings.

Thai Shrimp Linguine

Thai Shrimp Linguine

(Pictured above)

Prep/Total Time: 15 min.

My family loves this restaurant-style pasta. For even more flavor, add a squeeze of lime juice and a bit of cilantro on top. —Paula Marchesi, Lenhartsville, Pennsylvania

- 1 package (9 ounces) refrigerated linguine
- 1 cup fresh snow peas
- 2 cups shredded carrots
- 1/2 pound sliced fresh mushrooms
- 1 tablespoon olive oil
- 1/2 pound uncooked medium shrimp, peeled and deveined
- 1 cup Thai peanut sauce

Cook linguine according to package directions, adding snow peas and linguine at the same time.

Meanwhile, in a large skillet, cook the carrots and mushrooms in oil over medium heat for 3 minutes. Add shrimp; cook and stir 3 minutes longer or until shrimp turn pink. Stir in peanut sauce; heat through. Drain linguine and snow peas; transfer to a serving bowl. Top with shrimp mixture; toss to coat. **Yield:** 3 servings.

Sausage Skillet Dinner

Prep/Total Time: 30 min.

Quick to assemble, this is our favorite go-to recipe when all we need is something simple, satisfying and good! —Tinda Davis, Franklin, Tennessee

- 3/4 pound smoked sausage, cut into 1-inch pieces
- 2 tablespoons butter
- 2 cups refrigerated red potato wedges

- 1 medium onion, cut into wedges
- 1 medium apple, cut into wedges
- 1/4 cup cider vinegar
- 3 tablespoons sugar
- 1/2 teaspoon caraway seeds
- 2 tablespoons minced fresh parsley

In a large skillet, saute sausage in butter for 3 minutes. Add the potatoes, onion and apple; saute 4-5 minutes longer or until apple is tender and potatoes are golden brown. Stir in the vinegar, sugar and caraway seeds.

Bring to a boil. Reduce the heat; simmer, uncovered, for 2-3 minutes or until heated through. Sprinkle with parsley. **Yield:** 4 servings.

Buttery Grilled Shrimp

(Pictured below)

Prep/Total Time: 25 min.

These shrimp are fantastic alongside steak. For an extra-special occasion, brush the sauce on lobster tails and then grill. —Sheryl Shenberger, Albuquerque, New Mexico

- 1/2 cup butter, melted
- 3 tablespoons lemon juice
- 2 teaspoons chili powder
- 1 teaspoon ground ginger
- 1/4 teaspoon salt
- 2 pounds uncooked jumbo shrimp, peeled and deveined

In a small bowl, combine the first five ingredients; set aside 1/4 cup. Thread shrimp onto eight metal or soaked wooden skewers.

Grill the shrimp, covered, over medium heat for 3-5 minutes on each side or until the shrimp turn pink, basting occasionally with the butter mixture. Remove from the grill; brush with the reserved butter mixture. **Yield:** 8 servings.

Buttery Grilled Shrimp

Barbecue Pork and Penne Skillet

(Pictured above)

Prep/Total Time: 25 min.

I'm the mother of four active children, so speedy but delicious meals are a must. This stovetop supper is perfect for us to enjoy together following after-school activities and errands. —Judy Armstrong, Prairieville, Louisiana

  1 package (16 ounces) penne pasta
  1 cup chopped sweet red pepper
3/4 cup chopped onion
  1 tablespoon butter
  1 tablespoon olive oil
  3 teaspoons minced garlic
  1 carton (18 ounces) refrigerated fully cooked
    barbecued shredded pork
  1 can (14-1/2 ounces) diced tomatoes with
    mild green chilies, undrained
1/2 cup beef broth
  1 teaspoon ground cumin
  1 teaspoon pepper
1/4 teaspoon salt
1-1/4 cups (5 ounces) shredded cheddar cheese
1/4 cup chopped green onions

Cook the pasta according to the package directions. Meanwhile, in a large skillet, saute the red pepper and onion in the butter and oil until tender. Add the garlic; saute 1 minute longer. Stir in the pork, tomatoes, beef broth, cumin, pepper and salt; heat through.

Drain pasta. Add pasta and cheese to pork mixture. Sprinkle with green onions. **Yield:** 8 servings.

Mexican Hat Dance Spuds

Prep/Total Time: 20 min.

These out-of-the-ordinary potatoes stuffed with sloppy joe meat, cheese and onions come together with only five basic ingredients. Best of all, the recipe takes just 20 minutes to make. In no time, your family will be saying, "Olé!"
—Nancee Melin, Tucson, Arizona

  4 large baking potatoes
  1 pound ground beef
  1 can (16 ounces) bold sloppy joe sauce
1/2 cup shredded cheddar cheese
  3 green onions, thinly sliced

Scrub and pierce potatoes; place on a microwave-safe plate. Microwave, uncovered, on high for 15-17 minutes or until tender, turning once.

Meanwhile, in a large skillet, cook the beef over medium heat until no longer pink; drain. Stir in the sloppy joe sauce; heat through. Cut an "X" in the top of each potato; fluff the pulp with a fork. Spoon the meat mixture into potatoes; sprinkle with cheese and green onions. **Yield:** 4 servings.

Editor's Note: This recipe was tested in a 1,100-watt microwave.

Grilled Halibut Steaks

(Pictured below)

Prep/Total Time: 25 min.

After sampling this grilled fish, guests never guess that I use only basic ingredients such as brown sugar, soy sauce and lemon juice to prepare it. The simple butter sauce goes together quickly on the stovetop to give the halibut terrific flavor. It's an entree that always gets compliments.
—Mary Ann Dell, Phoenixville, Pennsylvania

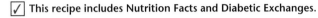

✓ This recipe includes Nutrition Facts and Diabetic Exchanges.

2 tablespoons brown sugar
2 tablespoons butter
1 tablespoon lemon juice
2 teaspoons soy sauce
1 teaspoon minced garlic
1/2 teaspoon pepper
4 halibut steaks (5 ounces *each*)

In a small saucepan, combine the first six ingredients. Cook and stir until butter is melted. Remove from the heat; set aside.

Coat grill rack with cooking spray before starting the grill. Grill halibut, covered, over medium-hot heat for 4-5 minutes on each side or until fish flakes easily with a fork, basting frequently with the butter mixture. **Yield:** 4 servings.

Nutrition Facts: 1 halibut steak equals 236 calories, 9 g fat (4 g saturated fat), 60 mg cholesterol, 273 mg sodium, 7 g carbohydrate, trace fiber, 30 g protein. **Diabetic Exchanges:** 4 very lean meat, 1 fat, 1/2 starch.

Zippy BLT Wraps

Zippy BLT Wraps

(Pictured above)

Prep/Total Time: 15 min.

I love BLT sandwiches and whole-wheat wraps, so I did some experimenting in the kitchen and created this version that combines both. Use mild, medium or hot salsa to give the filling as much of a kick as you'd like.
—Trisha Thielen, Aberdeen, South Dakota

3 tablespoons mayonnaise
4 teaspoons salsa
4 whole wheat tortillas (8 inches), room temperature
1/4 teaspoon garlic powder
Dash *each* salt and pepper
12 slices ready-to-serve fully cooked bacon
4 lettuce leaves
1 large tomato, sliced
1/2 medium ripe avocado, peeled and sliced

Spread mayonnaise and salsa down the center of each tortilla. Sprinkle with garlic powder, salt and pepper. Top with bacon strips, lettuce, tomato and avocado; roll up tightly. **Yield:** 4 servings.

Grilled Halibut Steaks

Covered Up

WHEN a recipe (such as Grilled Halibut Steaks, above left) in this book says to grill an item "covered," it means to put the cover on the grill during cooking—not to cover the item with foil. Cover it with foil if the recipe specifically instructs you to do so.

Bacon Cheeseburger Spaghetti

(Pictured below)

Prep/Total Time: 30 min.

I run a daycare center, and it's always a challenge to find different foods the children will eat. I spruced up a variation of this quick-and-easy recipe to suit my taste, and now the kids—and my husband—request it all the time!
—Nichelle Nell, Isle, Minnesota

    10 ounces uncooked spaghetti
     1 pound lean ground beef
    2/3 cup chopped onion
     6 slices ready-to-serve fully cooked bacon,
         chopped
    1-1/2 cups ketchup
     1 cup chopped dill pickles
     1 cup barbecue sauce
    1/2 cup prepared mustard
     2 cups (8 ounces) shredded cheddar cheese

Cook the spaghetti according to the package directions. Meanwhile, in a large skillet, cook the beef and onion over medium heat until the meat is no longer pink; drain. Stir in the bacon, ketchup, pickles, barbecue sauce and mustard. Bring to a boil. Reduce the heat; simmer, uncovered, for 5 minutes. Drain the spaghetti; stir into the meat mixture.

Sprinkle with cheese. Remove from the heat; cover and let stand until cheese is melted. **Yield:** 6 servings.

Bacon Cheeseburger Spaghetti

Kielbasa Chili

Kielbasa Chili

(Pictured above)

Prep/Total Time: 20 min.

This recipe is like eating a chili dog in a bowl! Try it on hectic weeknights or when the gang is over for the big game on TV. —Audra Duvall, Canoga Park, California

     1 pound smoked kielbasa *or* Polish sausage,
         halved and sliced
     2 cans (14-1/2 ounces *each*) diced tomatoes,
         undrained
     1 can (15 ounces) chili with beans
     1 can (8-3/4 ounces) whole kernel corn,
         drained
     1 can (2-1/4 ounces) sliced ripe olives, drained

In a Dutch oven coated with cooking spray, saute kielbasa until browned. Stir in the remaining ingredients. Bring to a boil. Reduce heat; simmer, uncovered, for 4-5 minutes or until heated through. **Yield:** 7 servings.

Skillet Catfish

Prep/Total Time: 25 min.

It takes only three ingredients to prepare this tasty fish, thanks to a simple-as-can-be coating of corn bread/muffin mix and seafood seasoning. For a fast tartar sauce to serve on the side, simply combine mayo with pickle relish.
—Kim Hardison, Maitland, Florida

    3/4 cup corn bread/muffin mix
     2 teaspoons seafood seasoning
     4 catfish fillets (6 ounces *each*)

In a large resealable plastic bag, combine corn bread mix and seafood seasoning. Add catfish, one fillet at a time, and shake to coat.

In a large nonstick skillet coated with cooking spray, cook fillets in batches over medium heat for 5-6 minutes on each side or until fish flakes easily with a fork. **Yield:** 4 servings.

Turkey Club Pizza

(Pictured above)

Prep/Total Time: 20 min.

Bored with the usual sausage or pepperoni pie? Here's a terrific option, especially when you have leftovers from your Thanksgiving bird. The pizza features popular club sandwich ingredients—turkey, bacon, mayo and tomatoes. Using a prebaked crust ensures quick prep, too.
—Pippa Milburn, Dover, Ohio

> 1 prebaked Italian bread shell crust
> (14 ounces)
> 1/2 cup mayonnaise
> 1-1/2 cups (6 ounces) shredded Monterey Jack
> cheese
> 1 cup diced cooked turkey
> 1/2 cup real bacon bits
> 2 plum tomatoes, sliced

Place the Italian bread shell crust on a baking sheet; spread with the mayonnaise. Top with 1 cup Monterey Jack cheese, turkey, bacon and plum tomatoes. Sprinkle with remaining cheese.

Bake pizza at 450° for 10-12 minutes or until the cheese is melted. **Yield:** 8 servings.

Ramen-Vegetable Beef Skillet

Prep/Total Time: 30 min.

This stovetop supper has a deliciously different combination of beef, cabbage, ramen noodles and more. It's an all-in-one meal. —Marlene McAllister, Portland, Michigan

> 1 pound ground beef
> 1-1/2 cups sliced fresh carrots
> 3/4 cup sliced onion
> 1 cup water
> 1 cup shredded cabbage
> 1 cup sliced fresh mushrooms
> 1 cup chopped green pepper
> 3 tablespoons soy sauce
> 1 package (3 ounces) beef ramen noodles

In a large skillet, cook the beef, carrots and onion over medium heat until meat is no longer pink and carrots are crisp-tender; drain.

Add the water, cabbage, mushrooms, green pepper, soy sauce and the contents of the seasoning packet from the beef ramen noodles. Break the ramen noodles into small pieces; add to the pan. Cover and cook for 10 minutes or until the liquid is absorbed and the ramen noodles are tender. **Yield:** 4 servings.

Ham Caesar Salad

(Pictured below)

Prep/Total Time: 25 min.

One bite, and you're sure to fall in love with this refreshing medley. Boasting a homemade dressing, it's a great dinner for hot summer days when you want to cool off—not heat up the kitchen by turning on the stove or oven. Serve the salad with iced tea and banana splits for dessert.
—Mary Ann Schlabach, Sarasota, Florida

    3 cups hearts of romaine salad mix
    2 medium nectarines, chopped
    2 cups fully cooked turkey ham, julienned
    1 tablespoon minced fresh cilantro
    1/2 cup Caesar salad croutons
    1/4 cup shredded Parmesan cheese
CREAMY CAESAR DRESSING:
    1/3 cup mayonnaise
    2 tablespoons sour cream
    4 teaspoons chopped onion
    4 teaspoons half-and-half cream
    1 teaspoon lemon juice
    1/4 teaspoon minced garlic
    1/8 teaspoon dried basil
    1/8 teaspoon dried oregano
Dash pepper

In a serving bowl, combine the romaine salad mix, nectarines, turkey ham, cilantro, Caesar salad croutons and Parmesan cheese.

In a small bowl, whisk the dressing ingredients; drizzle over salad. **Yield:** 4 servings.

Ham Caesar Salad

Zesty Tacos

Zesty Tacos

(Pictured above)

Prep/Total Time: 30 min.

I jazz up ordinary tacos in a snap to bring a little excitement to dinner. Black-eyed peas and a drizzle of bottled Italian salad dressing are the surprise ingredients in this recipe. Add shredded cheese, lettuce, tomatoes or whatever toppings you like.
—Susie Bonham, Fairview, Oklahoma

    1 pound ground beef
    1 cup water
    1 envelope taco seasoning
    8 taco shells
    1 can (15-1/2 ounces) black-eyed peas, rinsed
      and drained
    1 cup chopped tomatoes
    1 cup shredded lettuce
    1 cup (4 ounces) shredded cheddar cheese
  1/2 cup zesty Italian salad dressing

In a large skillet, cook the beef over medium heat for 5-6 minutes or until the meat is no longer pink; drain. Stir in the water and taco seasoning. Bring to a boil. Reduce the heat; simmer, uncovered, for 4-5 minutes or until thickened.

Meanwhile, prepare the taco shells according to the package directions. Stir peas into skillet; heat through. Spoon 1/4 cup beef mixture into each taco shell. Top with tomatoes, lettuce and cheese. Drizzle with salad dressing. **Yield:** 8 servings.

Salmon with Vegetable Salsa

Salmon with Vegetable Salsa

(Pictured above)
Prep/Total Time: 30 min.

The veggie salsa in this recipe is fantastic not only with salmon, but also with grilled chicken breasts and barbe-cued shrimp kabobs. The only fresh ingredient not available for it in my son's garden was the avocado! Make a double batch of the condiment to serve with tortilla chips.
—Priscilla Gilbert, Indian Harbour Beach, Florida

1-1/2 cups grape tomatoes, halved
1-1/2 cups chopped peeled cucumber
   1 medium ripe avocado, peeled and cubed
   1 small red onion, chopped
   2 tablespoons minced fresh cilantro
   1 jalapeno pepper, seeded and minced
   3 tablespoons lime juice, *divided*
   1 teaspoon salt, *divided*
   4 salmon fillets (6 ounces *each*)
1/4 teaspoon cayenne pepper
   1 tablespoon butter

In a large bowl, combine tomatoes, cucumber, avocado, onion, cilantro, jalapeno, 2 tablespoons lime juice and 1/2 teaspoon salt; set aside.

Sprinkle the salmon fillets with cayenne and the re-maining lime juice and salt. In a large skillet, cook the fil-lets in butter for 3-4 minutes on each side or until the fish flakes easily with a fork. Serve fish with prepared sal-sa. **Yield:** 4 servings.

Editor's Note: When cutting hot peppers, disposable gloves are recommended. Avoid touching your face.

Burgundy Steak

(Pictured below)
Prep/Total Time: 30 min.

A sped-up version of a crowd-pleasing classic, this home-style main course gets to the table quickly but doesn't skimp on taste. Serve the beef-and-pasta dish with your favorite tossed green salad or vegetable medley.
—Jennifer Hess, Cupertino, California

☑ This recipe includes Nutrition Facts and Diabetic Exchanges.

1/4 cup all-purpose flour
1/4 teaspoon paprika
   1 pound boneless beef sirloin steak, cut into 1-inch strips
   1 tablespoon canola oil
   1 can (10-1/2 ounces) condensed French onion soup, undiluted
1/2 cup burgundy wine *or* beef broth
   3 cups hot cooked egg noodles

In a large resealable plastic bag, combine the flour and paprika. Add the beef strips, a few pieces at a time, and shake to coat.

In a large skillet, brown beef in oil. Add soup and wine; bring to a boil. Reduce heat; simmer, uncovered, for 10-12 minutes or until sauce is thickened. Serve with noodles. **Yield:** 4 servings.

Nutrition Facts: 3/4 cup burgundy steak with 3/4 cup noodles equals 360 calories, 11 g fat (3 g satu-rated fat), 90 mg cholesterol, 617 mg sodium, 31 g car-bohydrate, 2 g fiber, 28 g protein. **Diabetic Exchanges:** 3 lean meat, 2 starch, 1/2 fat.

Burgundy Steak

Fruit-Glazed Pork Chops

(Pictured above and on page 196)

Prep/Total Time: 30 min.

Here, apricot preserves lend fruity flavor to the homemade sauce that dresses up pork chops. It goes together in mere minutes with just five basic ingredients. Feel free to substitute a different variety of preserves for a change of pace...or to broil in the oven instead of grilling.
—Edie DeSpain, Logan, Utah

    1/3 cup hickory smoke-flavored barbecue sauce
    1/2 cup apricot *or* peach preserves
      1 tablespoon corn syrup
      1 teaspoon prepared mustard
    1/4 teaspoon ground cloves
      6 bone-in pork loin chops (3/4 inch thick
        and 8 ounces *each*)
    1/2 teaspoon salt
    1/2 teaspoon pepper

In a small bowl, combine the barbecue sauce, preserves, corn syrup, mustard and cloves; set aside.

Coat the grill rack with cooking spray before starting the grill. Sprinkle the pork chops with salt and pepper. Grill the pork chops, covered, over medium heat for 6-8 minutes on each side or until a meat thermometer reads 160°, basting frequently with the sauce mixture. **Yield:** 6 servings.

Smoked Sausage Pasta

Prep/Total Time: 20 min.

One of the things I like most about this recipe is that you can chill any leftovers you have, then enjoy an equally delicious sausage pasta salad later in the week. In fact, after trying this meaty and tangy dish, you may want to prepare a double batch just to ensure you have extras!
—Jasen Guillermo, Tucson, Arizona

    2-2/3 cups uncooked tricolor spiral pasta
        1 pound smoked sausage, cut into 1/4-inch
          slices
    1-1/2 cups sliced fresh carrots
        1 cup coarsely chopped green pepper
        1 small onion, halved and sliced
        1 tablespoon canola oil
        1 can (2-1/4 ounces) sliced ripe olives,
          drained
      1/2 cup Italian salad dressing

Cook the spiral pasta according to the package directions. Meanwhile, in a large skillet, saute the sausage, carrots, green pepper and onion in oil until the vegetables are tender.

Drain the spiral pasta; place in a large bowl. Add the sausage mixture and ripe olives. Drizzle with the Italian salad dressing and toss to coat. Serve warm or chilled. **Yield:** 4 servings.

Chapter 14

✴ *Delectable Desserts*

ALMOND BROWNIES...Gooey Butterscotch Bars...Chocolate Zucchini Cupcakes...Raspberry-Glazed Pie...these sweet treats sound too good to be speedy recipes. But, they are!

You'll see for yourself when you page through this dessert-filled chapter. From crisps and parfaits to cookies and candies, each decadent delight goes together in a snap to thrill everyone at the table.

With these time-saving temptations, even the busiest cooks will be able to whip up something special to top off meals. So whether you want to surprise your family on a weeknight or serve a real showstopper on a holiday, look here!

FAST FINALE. Coconut Rhubarb Dessert (p. 227).

Almond Brownies

at 350° for 25-30 minutes or until a toothpick inserted near the center comes out clean (brownies may appear moist). Cool on a wire rack.

For the frosting, in a microwave-safe bowl, melt the chocolate chips and 1 cup whipped topping; stir until smooth. Cool. Fold in extract and remaining whipped topping. Spread over cooled brownies. Sprinkle with almonds. Store in the refrigerator. **Yield:** 3 dozen.

Nutrition Facts: 1 brownie equals 149 calories, 6 g fat (4 g saturated fat), 30 mg cholesterol, 67 mg sodium, 21 g carbohydrate, 1 g fiber, 2 g protein. **Diabetic Exchanges:** 1-1/2 starch, 1 fat.

Easy Grasshopper Ice Cream Pie

(Pictured below)

Prep: 15 min. + freezing

This easy ice cream dessert goes together in 15 minutes and is such an ego booster for the cook. My family compliments me the entire time they're eating the chocolaty, minty slices. And the pie virtually "hops" off the plate!
—*Kim Murphy, Albia, Iowa*

    4 **cups mint chocolate chip ice cream, softened**
    1 **chocolate crumb crust (8 inches)**
    5 **cream-filled chocolate sandwich cookies, chopped**
1/3 **cup chocolate-covered peppermint candies**
Chocolate hard-shell ice cream topping

Spread ice cream into crust. Sprinkle with cookies and candies; drizzle with ice cream topping. Freeze until firm. Remove from the freezer 15 minutes before serving. **Yield:** 8 servings.

Editor's Note: This recipe was tested with Junior Mints chocolate-covered peppermint candies.

Almond Brownies

(Pictured above)

Prep: 20 min. **Bake:** 25 min. + cooling

A boxed mixed just can't compare to these home-baked treats, sure to thrill brownie lovers. With a creamy made-from-scratch frosting and touch of almond flavor, these goodies may not seem fuss-free—but they actually are!
—*Didi Desjardins, Dartmouth, Massachusetts*

☑ This recipe includes Nutrition Facts and Diabetic Exchanges.

1/2 **cup butter, softened**
    1 **cup sugar**
    4 **eggs**
    1 **can (16 ounces) chocolate syrup**
1/2 **teaspoon almond extract**
    1 **cup plus 1 tablespoon all-purpose flour**
1/2 **teaspoon salt**
FROSTING:
    1 **cup (6 ounces) semisweet chocolate chips**
    1 **carton (8 ounces) frozen whipped topping, thawed, *divided***
1/4 **teaspoon almond extract**
1/2 **cup chopped almonds**

In a large bowl, cream the butter and sugar until light and fluffy. Add the eggs, one at a time, beating well after each addition. Stir in the chocolate syrup and extract. Combine the flour and salt; gradually add to the chocolate mixture.

Pour into a greased 13-in. x 9-in. baking pan. Bake

Easy Grasshopper Ice Cream Pie

Peanut Butter Cake Bars

Nutty Orange Snowballs
(Pictured below)

Prep: 30 min. **Bake:** 10 min./batch + cooling

These nutty, buttery cookies will melt in your mouth and give you a refreshing hint of orange flavor. An old recipe from my mom, they used to be reserved only for weddings and other special events. But they're perfect for Christmas because they look just like snowballs!
—*Judith Weidner, Spearfish, South Dakota*

☑ This recipe includes Nutrition Facts and Diabetic Exchanges.

    1 cup butter, softened
1-1/4 cups confectioners' sugar, *divided*
    1 teaspoon grated orange peel
  1/2 teaspoon orange extract
  1/2 teaspoon vanilla extract
    2 cups all-purpose flour
  1/4 teaspoon salt
  1/2 cup finely chopped walnuts
  1/2 cup finely chopped hazelnuts

In a large bowl, cream butter and 3/4 cup confectioners' sugar until light and fluffy. Beat in the orange peel and extracts. Combine the flour and salt; gradually add to creamed mixture and mix well. Stir in nuts.

Shape into 3/4-in. balls. Place 1 in. apart on ungreased baking sheets. Bake at 350° for 10-12 minutes or until bottoms are lightly browned. Remove to wire racks to cool completely.

Place the remaining confectioners' sugar in a large resealable plastic bag. Add the cookies, a few at a time, and shake to coat. Store cookies in an airtight container. **Yield:** 3 dozen.

Nutrition Facts: 1 cookie equals 107 calories, 7 g fat (3 g saturated fat), 13 mg cholesterol, 52 mg sodium, 10 g carbohydrate, trace fiber, 1 g protein. **Diabetic Exchanges:** 1 fat, 1/2 starch.

Peanut Butter Cake Bars
(Pictured above)

Prep: 15 min. **Bake:** 45 min. + cooling

Packed with the ever-popular combination of peanut butter and chocolate chips, these cake-like bars are perfect for practically any occasion—from school events and picnics to potlucks and bake sales. Children and adults alike are in for a treat when you put out a platter of these gems.
—*Charlotte Ennis, Lake Arthur, New Mexico*

2/3 cup butter, softened
2/3 cup peanut butter
  1 cup sugar
  1 cup packed brown sugar
  4 eggs
  2 teaspoons vanilla extract
  2 cups all-purpose flour
  2 teaspoons baking powder
1/2 teaspoon salt
  1 package (11-1/2 ounces) milk chocolate chips

In a large bowl, cream the butter, peanut butter, sugar and brown sugar. Add eggs, one at a time, beating well after each addition. Beat in vanilla. Combine the flour, baking powder and salt; gradually add to creamed mixture. Stir in chocolate chips.

Spread into a greased 13-in. x 9-in. baking pan. Bake at 350° for 45-50 minutes or until a toothpick inserted near the center comes out clean. Cool on a wire rack. Cut into bars. **Yield:** 2 dozen.

Nutty Orange Snowballs

Lemon Fluff Dessert

(Pictured below)

Prep: 25 min. + chilling

Wondering what to do with the evaporated milk and graham crackers in your pantry? Try this lovely light dessert.
— Leola McKinney, Morgantown, West Virginia

☑ This recipe includes Nutrition Facts and Diabetic Exchanges.

    1 can (12 ounces) evaporated milk
    1 package (3 ounces) lemon gelatin
    1 cup sugar
1-1/3 cups boiling water
    1/4 cup lemon juice
1-3/4 cups graham cracker crumbs (about
        28 squares)
    5 tablespoons butter, melted

Pour milk into a small metal bowl; place mixer beaters in the bowl. Cover and refrigerate for at least 2 hours.

Meanwhile, in a large bowl, dissolve gelatin and sugar in boiling water. Stir in lemon juice. Cover and refrigerate until syrupy, about 1-1/2 hours.

In a small bowl, combine crumbs and butter; set aside 2 tablespoons for garnish. Press remaining crumbs onto the bottom of a 13-in. x 9-in. dish. Beat chilled milk until soft peaks form. Beat gelatin until tiny bubbles form. Fold milk into gelatin. Pour over prepared crust. Sprinkle with reserved crumbs. Cover and refrigerate until set. Cut into squares. **Yield:** 12 servings.

Nutrition Facts: 1 piece equals 221 calories, 8 g fat (5 g saturated fat), 22 mg cholesterol, 151 mg sodium, 35 g carbohydrate, trace fiber, 3 g protein. **Diabetic Exchanges:** 2 starch, 1 fat.

Lemon Fluff Dessert

Gooey Butterscotch Bars

Gooey Butterscotch Bars

(Pictured above)

Prep: 20 min. **Bake:** 20 min. + cooling

The name says it all for these gotta-have-'em bars. With caramels, butterscotch chips and pudding, they're ooey, gooey and finger-lickin' good! Packaged sugar cookie mix speeds up preparation, and the recipe makes a big batch—ideal for potlucks, bakes sales or other events.
— Carol Brewer, Fairborn, Ohio

    1 package (17-1/2 ounces) sugar cookie mix
    1 package (3.4 ounces) instant butterscotch
        pudding mix
    1/2 cup butter, softened
    1 egg
    1 package (14 ounces) caramels
    1/2 cup evaporated milk
    2 cups mixed nuts
    1 teaspoon vanilla extract
    1 cup butterscotch chips

In a large bowl, combine the sugar cookie mix, pudding mix, butter and egg. Press into an ungreased 13-in. x 9-in. baking pan. Bake at 350° for 20-25 minutes or until set.

In a large saucepan, combine the caramels and milk. Cook and stir over medium-low heat until melted. Remove from heat. Stir in the nuts and vanilla.

Pour over crust. Sprinkle with butterscotch chips. Cool completely. Cut into bars. Store in an airtight container. **Yield:** about 3 dozen.

Chocolate Zucchini Cupcakes

(Pictured below)

Prep: 25 min. **Bake:** 20 min. + cooling

Our grandchildren love these cupcakes and don't believe us when we tell them there are vegetables in each one! I'm always asked for the recipe, which makes a fun treat after school, packed in lunches or after dinner. It's also a great way to use up your garden-grown zucchini.
—Carole Fraser, North York, Ontario

    1-1/4 cups butter, softened
    1-1/2 cups sugar
        2 eggs
        1 teaspoon vanilla extract
    2-1/2 cups all-purpose flour
        3/4 cup baking cocoa
        1 teaspoon baking powder
        1 teaspoon baking soda
        1/2 teaspoon salt
        1/2 cup plain yogurt
        1 cup grated zucchini
        1 cup grated carrots
        1 can (16 ounces) chocolate frosting

In a large bowl, cream the butter and sugar until light and fluffy. Add the eggs, one at a time, beating well after each addition. Stir in the vanilla. Combine the flour, baking cocoa, baking powder, baking soda and salt; add to the creamed mixture alternately with the plain yogurt, beating well after each addition. Fold in the zucchini and carrots.

Fill paper-lined muffin cups two-thirds full. Bake at 350° for 18-22 minutes or until a toothpick comes out clean. Cool for 10 minutes before removing from pans to wire racks to cool completely. Frost cupcakes. **Yield:** 21 cupcakes.

Strawberry Cheesecake Ice Cream

Strawberry Cheesecake Ice Cream

(Pictured above)

Prep: 10 min. + freezing

Light and refreshing, this dreamy, creamy dessert is perfect for steamy afternoons...and nice for scooping into cones because it won't melt too quickly. Try changing up the recipe with a variety of frozen berries or fruits.
—Debra Goforth, Newport, Tennessee

    1 package (8 ounces) cream cheese, softened
    1/3 cup refrigerated French vanilla nondairy
        creamer
    1/4 cup sugar
    1 teaspoon grated lemon peel
    1 carton (16 ounces) frozen whipped topping,
        thawed
    1 package (16 ounces) frozen sweetened
        sliced strawberries, thawed

In a large bowl, beat the cream cheese, creamer, sugar and lemon peel until blended. Fold in the whipped topping and strawberries. Transfer to a freezer container; freeze for 4 hours or until firm. Remove from the freezer 10 minutes before serving. **Yield:** 2 quarts.

Cone Clue

You can keep ice cream from dripping out the bottom of a sugar cone by stuffing a miniature marshmallow into the bottom before adding scoops of ice cream. It'll help ensure you enjoy every last drop!
—Cheryl Maczko, Arthurdale, West Virginia

Chocolate Zucchini Cupcakes

Berry Delicious Rhubarb Crisp

Stir in water. Bring to a boil; cook and stir for 1-2 minutes or until thickened. Stir in remaining vanilla. Pour over fruit; sprinkle with remaining crumb mixture. Bake at 350° for 25-30 minutes or until bubbly. Serve with ice cream. **Yield:** 9 servings.

Editor's Note: If using frozen rhubarb, measure rhubarb while still frozen, then thaw completely. Drain in a colander, but do not press liquid out.

Caramel Pear Dessert

(Pictured below)

Prep/Total Time: 15 min.

I hit on this treat when my sister and a friend came over for lunch. They liked it so much, they threatened to lick their plates. After that, I knew I had a winner!
—*Shirley Stubblefield, Chino, California*

    1/2 cup chopped pecans
1-1/2 teaspoons butter
    1 cup packed brown sugar
    1 cup heavy whipping cream
    1 prepared angel food cake (8 inches),
       cut into 12 slices
    6 cups vanilla ice cream
    3 cans (15-1/4 ounces *each*) pear halves,
       drained

In a small skillet, saute the pecans in the butter until toasted; set aside. In a small saucepan, combine the brown sugar and heavy whipping cream. Bring to a boil; cook and stir for 3 minutes.

Place the angel food cake slices on individual dessert plates. Top with vanilla ice cream and pears. Drizzle with the cream mixture; sprinkle with the reserved pecans. **Yield:** 12 servings.

Berry Delicious Rhubarb Crisp

(Pictured above)

Prep: 15 min. **Bake** 25 min.

What a perfect spring dessert! With rhubarb, strawberries and blackberries, this crisp is so pretty and has tangy flavor the whole family will enjoy. I sometimes grate about a tablespoonful of orange or lemon zest and add it to the crumb mixture. —*Shannon Hadinger, Dublin, Ohio*

    1 cup all-purpose flour
    1 cup packed brown sugar
    3/4 cup old-fashioned oats
    1/2 cup butter, melted
1-1/2 teaspoons vanilla extract, *divided*
    1 teaspoon ground cinnamon
1-1/2 cups diced fresh *or* frozen rhubarb
1-1/2 cups sliced fresh strawberries
1-1/2 cups fresh blackberries
    1/2 cup sugar
    1 tablespoon cornstarch
    1/2 cup water
Vanilla ice cream

In a small bowl, combine the flour, brown sugar, oats, butter, 1 teaspoon vanilla and cinnamon. Set aside 1 cup for the topping; press remaining crumb mixture into a greased 8-in. square baking dish. Top with rhubarb, strawberries and blackberries.

In a small saucepan, combine sugar and cornstarch.

Caramel Pear Dessert

Raspberry-Glazed Pie

least 4 hours or until set. Serve with whipped topping if desired. **Yield:** 8 servings.

Nutrition Facts: 1 piece (calculated without whipped topping) equals 291 calories, 8 g fat (4 g saturated fat), 15 mg cholesterol, 255 mg sodium, 54 g carbohydrate, 4 g fiber, 3 g protein.

Cranberry Pecan Cookies

(Pictured below)

Prep: 10 min. **Bake:** 10 min./batch

These goodies are so yummy and simple to prepare using refrigerated sugar cookie dough. The dried cranberries, pecans and vanilla chips really dress them up.
—*Louise Hawkins, Lubbock, Texas*

☑ This recipe includes Nutrition Facts and Diabetic Exchanges.

> 1 tube (16-1/2 ounces) refrigerated sugar cookie dough, softened
> 1 cup chopped pecans
> 2/3 cup vanilla *or* white chips
> 2/3 cup dried cranberries
> 1 teaspoon vanilla extract

In a large bowl, combine the cookie dough, pecans, chips, cranberries and vanilla. Drop by tablespoonfuls 2 in. apart onto ungreased baking sheets.

Bake at 350° for 10-12 minutes or until lightly browned. Cool for 2 minutes before removing from pans to wire racks. Store in an airtight container. **Yield:** about 3-1/2 dozen.

Nutrition Facts: 1 cookie equals 87 calories, 5 g fat (1 g saturated fat), 4 mg cholesterol, 50 mg sodium, 10 g carbohydrate, trace fiber, 1 g protein. **Diabetic Exchanges:** 1 fat, 1/2 starch.

Raspberry-Glazed Pie

(Pictured above)

Prep: 15 min. **Bake:** 15 min. + chilling

Everyone raves about this quick pie that gives you a delightful burst of summer in every bite. Biscuit mix speeds up the crust, and the filling comes together in a jiffy. Just add a dollop of whipped topping for the perfect finish.
—*Kathy Voss, Jackson, Michigan*

☑ This recipe includes Nutrition Facts.

> 1 cup biscuit/baking mix
> 1/4 cup cold butter
> 3 tablespoons cold water
> FILLING:
> 1 cup sugar
> 3 tablespoons plus 1-1/2 teaspoons cornstarch
> 1 cup water
> 2 teaspoons corn syrup
> 1 package (3 ounces) raspberry gelatin
> 3-1/2 cups fresh raspberries
> Whipped topping, optional

Place baking mix in a small bowl; cut in butter until crumbly. Gradually add water, tossing with a fork until dough forms a ball. Press onto the bottom and up the sides of a 9-in. pie plate coated with cooking spray.

Line unpricked pastry shell with a double thickness of heavy-duty foil. Bake at 450° for 8 minutes. Remove foil; bake 5 minutes longer. Cool on a wire rack.

In a small saucepan, combine sugar and cornstarch. Stir in the water and corn syrup until smooth. Bring to a boil, stirring constantly. Cook and stir for 2-3 minutes or until thickened. Remove from the heat; stir in gelatin until dissolved.

Place the raspberries in the pie crust; pour the gelatin mixture over the top. Cover and refrigerate for at

Cranberry Pecan Cookies

Blondie Nut Bars

(Pictured below)

Prep: 15 min. **Bake:** 25 min. + cooling

Looking for a treat that will not only please sweet tooths but also travel well? These moist, chewy bars are chock-full of chocolate chips and two kinds of nuts. Plus, the recipe makes a nice big batch. What's not to love?
—Lori Phillips, Corona, California

  4 eggs
  2 tablespoons heavy whipping cream
  2 tablespoons butter, melted
  2 teaspoons instant coffee granules
  1 teaspoon vanilla extract
  2 cups all-purpose flour
  2 cups sugar
  2 tablespoons baking powder
  1/4 teaspoon salt
  1 cup chopped almonds
  1 cup chopped walnuts
  1 cup (6 ounces) semisweet chocolate chips
Confectioners' sugar

In a large bowl, beat the eggs, cream, butter, coffee granules and vanilla until blended. Combine the flour, sugar, baking powder and salt; gradually add to butter mixture. Stir in the almonds, walnuts and chocolate chips (batter will be stiff).

Spread into a greased 13-in. x 9-in. baking pan. Bake at 350° for 25-30 minutes or until lightly browned. Cool on a wire rack. Cut into bars. Dust with confectioners' sugar. **Yield:** 2 dozen.

Blondie Nut Bars

Banana Cheesecake Pie

Banana Cheesecake Pie

(Pictured above)

Prep: 25 min. + chilling

I came up with this quick combo of two classic desserts when I needed to make something for a gathering. It was a hit! —Kelly Whitaker, West Carrollton, Ohio

  1 package (11.1 ounces) no-bake home-style
     cheesecake mix
  1/2 cup crushed vanilla wafers (about 15 wafers)
  2 tablespoons sugar
  1/2 cup cold butter
  1 cup plus 1-1/2 cups milk, *divided*
  1 package (3.4 ounces) instant banana cream
     pudding mix
  2 medium bananas, cut into 1/4-inch slices
  1 cup whipped topping
  1/4 cup chopped pecans, toasted

In a large bowl, combine the contents of the crust mix, vanilla wafers and sugar; cut in the butter until the mixture resembles coarse crumbs. Press onto the bottom and up the sides of an ungreased 9-in. deep-dish pie plate.

In a large bowl, beat 1 cup milk and contents of filling mix on low speed until blended. Beat on medium for 3 minutes or until smooth (filling will be thick). Spoon into the crust. Chill for 30 minutes.

Meanwhile, in a small bowl, whisk remaining milk and pudding mix for 2 minutes. Let stand for 2 minutes or until soft-set (pudding will be stiff). Arrange banana slices over filling. Spread with pudding, then whipped topping. Sprinkle with pecans. Chill for at least 1 hour before serving. **Yield:** 8 servings.

Berry Chocolate Dessert

(Pictured below)

Prep: 20 min. + chilling

Here's a deceptively simple treat that's sure to get attention on a dessert table. Our Test Kitchen home economists topped their creamy and chocolaty concoction with fresh raspberries, blueberries and blackberries. Time-crunched cooks will love the easy, no-bake preparation.

  2/3 cup sliced almonds, toasted
1-1/3 cups semisweet chocolate chips
    2 packages (8 ounces *each*) cream cheese, softened
  2/3 cup sugar
    1 carton (12 ounces) frozen whipped topping, thawed
    1 cup *each* fresh raspberries, blueberries and blackberries
    2 tablespoons seedless strawberry jam

Place almonds in a small food processor; cover and pulse until chopped. Sprinkle into a greased 9-in. springform pan; set aside.

In a microwave, melt the chocolate chips; stir until smooth. Cool completely. In a large bowl, beat cream cheese and sugar until smooth. Beat in the melted chocolate; fold in whipped topping.

Spread the cream cheese mixture evenly into the prepared pan. Mound the fruit on top. Microwave strawberry jam on high for 15 seconds or until melted; drizzle over the fruit.

Cover and refrigerate for at least 3 hours. Remove sides of pan before serving. **Yield:** 12 servings.

Pistachio Pudding Parfaits

Berry Chocolate Dessert

Pistachio Pudding Parfaits

(Pictured above)

Prep/Total Time: 20 min.

I tried this recipe when my kids needed a treat for school on St. Patrick's Day, and the parfaits went over big. You can fix them right before serving or a few hours earlier.
—Rosanna Fowler, Bedford, Indiana

    1 package (8 ounces) cream cheese, softened
    1 cup confectioners' sugar
1-1/2 cups whipped topping
    1 package (3.4 ounces) instant pistachio pudding mix
  10 pecan shortbread cookies, coarsely crushed

In a small bowl, beat the cream cheese and confectioners' sugar. Fold in the whipped topping; set aside. Prepare the pistachio pudding according to the package directions; set aside.

Spoon 1 tablespoon shortbread cookie crumbs into each of eight parfait glasses. Top with half the pistachio pudding and whipped topping mixture. Repeat layers. Top with remaining cookie crumbs. Chill until serving. **Yield:** 8 servings.

Maple Walnut Crisps

Maple Walnut Crisps

(Pictured above)

Prep: 15 min. **Bake:** 10 min. + cooling

If you like maple, you'll love these dainty, sweet-and-salty crisps. Give them as a homemade gift at Christmastime.
—*Mary Shivers, Ada, Oklahoma*

✓ This recipe includes Nutrition Facts and Diabetic Exchanges.

    44 Club crackers (2-1/2-inch x 1-inch)
     1 cup unsalted butter, cubed
     1 cup packed brown sugar
     2 tablespoons maple syrup
    1/2 cup chopped pecans
    1/2 cup chopped walnuts
    1/3 cup finely chopped almonds
    1/4 teaspoon maple flavoring

Place the crackers in a single layer in a parchment paper-lined 15-in. x 10-in. x 1-in. baking pan. Set aside.

In a small heavy saucepan, melt butter over medium heat. Stir in brown sugar and syrup. Bring to a boil; cook and stir for 3-4 minutes or until sugar is dissolved. Stir in remaining ingredients. Spread evenly over crackers.

Bake at 350° for 10-12 minutes or until tops appear dry. Cool completely on a wire rack. Break into pieces. Store in an airtight container. **Yield:** 44 crisps.

Nutrition Facts: 1 crisp equals 104 calories, 8 g fat (3 g saturated fat), 11 mg cholesterol, 47 mg sodium, 9 g carbohydrate, trace fiber, 1 g protein. **Diabetic Exchanges:** 1 fat, 1/2 starch.

Toffee Bars

(Pictured below)

Prep: 15 min. **Bake:** 20 min. + cooling

With a yummy coconut-pecan topping, this simple-to-make treat is the perfect end to a casual meal with family or friends. If you have leftovers, send a few bars home with each of your guests. They'll be thrilled!
—*Joeanne Steras, Garrett, Pennsylvania*

✓ This recipe includes Nutrition Facts and Diabetic Exchanges.

     1 cup all-purpose flour
    3/4 cup packed brown sugar
    1/2 cup cold butter
TOPPING:
     1 egg
     1 cup packed brown sugar
     1 teaspoon vanilla extract
     1 teaspoon baking powder
     1 cup flaked coconut
    1/2 cup chopped pecans *or* walnuts

In a large bowl, combine flour and brown sugar. Cut in butter until crumbly. Press into an ungreased 13-in. x 9-in. baking pan. Bake at 350° for 8-10 minutes or until golden brown; cool slightly.

In a small bowl, beat the egg, brown sugar, vanilla and baking powder until blended. Stir in coconut and pecans. Spread over the crust. Bake for 12-15 minutes or until golden brown. Cool on a wire rack. Cut into bars. **Yield:** 2 dozen.

Nutrition Facts: 1 bar equals 153 calories, 7 g fat (4 g saturated fat), 19 mg cholesterol, 63 mg sodium, 22 g carbohydrate, 1 g fiber, 1 g protein. **Diabetic Exchanges:** 1-1/2 starch, 1 fat.

Toffee Bars

Coconut Rhubarb Dessert

In a large saucepan, combine the rhubarb, sugar, water and food coloring if desired. Cook over medium heat for 8-10 minutes or until rhubarb is tender; cool slightly. Transfer to a greased 13-in. x 9-in. baking dish; sprinkle with cake mix. Top with coconut and pecans. Drizzle with butter.

Bake at 350° for 25-30 minutes or until a toothpick inserted near the center comes out clean. Serve with ice cream if desired. **Yield:** 12 servings.

Cherry Fluff

(Pictured below)

Prep/Total Time: 15 min.

This fruit-filled fluff is my own concoction from a revised recipe. It's so easy to whip up in just 15 minutes. Pop it in the fridge, and you'll have dessert for a crowd ready to go.
—Naomi Cross, Millwood, Kentucky

  1 package (8 ounces) cream cheese, softened
  1 can (20 ounces) crushed pineapple, undrained
  1 can (21 ounces) cherry pie filling
1/2 cup chopped pecans
  1 carton (8 ounces) frozen whipped topping, thawed
Additional whipped topping and cherries, optional

In a large bowl, beat cream cheese and pineapple. Stir in the pie filling and pecans. Fold in whipped topping. Spoon into individual dessert dishes. Garnish each with additional whipped topping and a cherry if desired. Cover and chill until serving. **Yield:** 10 servings.

Coconut Rhubarb Dessert

(Pictured above and on page 216)

Prep: 25 min. **Bake:** 25 min.

Want a special treat? Here, tart rhubarb is sweetened and combined with crunchy pecans and flaked coconut for a comforting, homey dessert. Serve it warm and top off each bowlful with a scoop of vanilla ice cream. Yum! —Connie Korger Green Bay, Wisconsin

  4 cups sliced fresh *or* frozen rhubarb
1-1/2 cups sugar
1-1/2 cups water
1/8 teaspoon red food coloring, optional
  1 package (18-1/4 ounces) butter pecan cake mix
  1 cup flaked coconut
1/2 cup chopped pecans
1/2 cup butter, melted
Vanilla ice cream, optional

Ready for Rhubarb

WANT to make luscious Coconut Rhubarb Dessert (recipe above) using fresh rhubarb? Choose rhubarb stalks that are crisp and brightly colored. Tightly wrap them in a plastic bag and store them in the refrigerator for up to 3 days. Wash the stalks and remove the poisonous leaves before using them.

Cherry Fluff

Chocolate Peanut Crunch Ice Cream Cake

(Pictured below)

Prep: 30 min. + freezing

I bring this simple but impressive dessert to family get-togethers, and it seems no one is ever too full to have a piece! With chocolate chips, cookies and ice cream, it's a can't-miss treat.   —Karen Scaglione, Sanford, Maine

- 1 cup milk chocolate chips
- 2 cups crushed peanut butter cream-filled sandwich cookies (about 18 cookies)
- 1 quart vanilla ice cream, softened
- 1 quart chocolate ice cream, softened
- 1 cup heavy whipping cream
- 1 tablespoon confectioners' sugar
- 1 teaspoon vanilla extract

In a small saucepan, melt chocolate chips over low heat. Stir in cookie crumbs until coated. Spread on waxed paper to cool. Coarsely chop.

Spread the vanilla ice cream into a 9-in. springform pan; sprinkle with 2 cups cookie mixture. Freeze for 30 minutes. Spread with chocolate ice cream. Cover and freeze for 4 hours or until firm.

In a small bowl, beat cream until it begins to thicken. Add confectioners' sugar and vanilla; beat until stiff peaks form. Carefully run a knife around edge of pan to loosen. Remove sides of pan.

Spread the whipped cream over the top and sides of dessert; press the remaining cookie mixture into the sides. Freeze for 1 hour or until the whipped cream is set. Remove from the freezer 15 minutes before serving.
Yield: 14 servings.

Chocolate Peanut Crunch Ice Cream Cake

Strawberries with Chocolate Cream Filling

Strawberries with Chocolate Cream Filling

(Pictured above)

Prep/Total Time: 30 min.

When you want just a sweet little something to top off a meal and make it special, this is the recipe for you! These party-pretty bites are as easy to make as they are scrumptious. Plus, they can be served after breakfast, lunch or dinner. Try them as a refreshing appetizer, too.
—Lisa Huff, Clive, Iowa

- 1-1/2 squares (1-1/2 ounces) semisweet chocolate, grated, *divided*
- 1 package (8 ounces) cream cheese, softened
- 1 teaspoon vanilla extract
- 1 cup whipped topping
- 18 large fresh strawberries, halved

Set aside 2 tablespoons chocolate. In a microwave, melt remaining chocolate; stir until smooth. Cool to room temperature.

In a small bowl, beat the cream cheese and vanilla until smooth. Beat in the melted chocolate. Fold in the whipped topping and 1 tablespoon reserved chocolate. Cut a small hole in the corner of pastry or plastic bag; insert #21 star pastry tip. Fill the bag with cream cheese mixture.

Place the strawberries cut side up on a serving platter. Pipe cream cheese mixture onto strawberries. Sprinkle with remaining chocolate. Refrigerate leftovers.
Yield: 3 dozen.

Peanut Butter Turtle Candies

(Pictured below)

Prep: 30 min. + chilling

During the holiday season, I share these candies with family, friends and coworkers. I get lots of requests for more and have even been told not to bother visiting if I don't bring my turtles—talk about a compliment! They're also good made with dark chocolate and salted pecans.
—Misty Schwotzer, Groveport, Ohio

☑ This recipe includes Nutrition Facts and Diabetic Exchanges.

72 pecan halves (about 1-3/4 cups)
1/4 cup peanut butter
2 tablespoons butter, softened
1/2 cup confectioners' sugar
5 ounces milk chocolate candy coating, chopped
2 teaspoons shortening

On waxed paper-lined pans, arrange pecan halves in clusters of three.

In a small bowl, beat peanut butter and butter until blended; gradually beat in confectioners' sugar. In a microwave, melt candy coating and shortening; stir until smooth.

Spoon 1/4 teaspoon melted chocolate into the center of each pecan cluster. Place teaspoonfuls of the peanut butter mixture into the center of each cluster; press down slightly. Spoon remaining melted chocolate over tops. Chill for 10 minutes or until set. Store in an airtight container in the refrigerator. **Yield:** 2 dozen.

Nutrition Facts: 1 candy equals 97 calories, 7 g fat (3 g saturated fat), 3 mg cholesterol, 19 mg sodium, 8 g carbohydrate, 1 g fiber, 1 g protein. **Diabetic Exchanges:** 1 fat, 1/2 starch.

Peanut Butter Turtle Candies

Raspberry Oatmeal Bars

Raspberry Oatmeal Bars

(Pictured above)

Prep: 10 min. **Bake:** 35 min. + cooling

Cake mix hurries along the prep work for these yummy bars. Raspberry jam adds a pop of color and sweetness.
—Trish Bosman-Golata, Rock Hill, South Carolina

☑ This recipe includes Nutrition Facts and Diabetic Exchanges.

1 package (18-1/4 ounces) yellow cake mix
2-1/2 cups quick-cooking oats
3/4 cup butter, melted
1 jar (12 ounces) seedless raspberry preserves
1 tablespoon water

In a large bowl, combine the dry cake mix, oats and butter until crumbly. Press 3 cups of the crumb mixture into a greased 13-in. x 9-in. baking pan. Bake at 350° for 10 minutes. Cool on a wire rack for 5 minutes.

In a small bowl, stir the preserves and water until blended. Spread over the crust. Sprinkle with the remaining crumb mixture. Bake for 25-28 minutes or until lightly browned. Cool on a wire rack. Cut into bars. **Yield:** 2 dozen.

Nutrition Facts: 1 bar equals 202 calories, 8 g fat (4 g saturated fat), 15 mg cholesterol, 181 mg sodium, 32 g carbohydrate, 1 g fiber, 2 g protein. **Diabetic Exchanges:** 2 starch, 1 fat.

Treat Technique

Use a measuring cup to press the crust for Raspberry Oatmeal Bars (recipe above) into the pan. This spreads the crust more uniformly for even baking—and keeps hands clean!

Chapter 15

☾ *Make-Ahead Marvels*

A LITTLE PLANNING can go a long way...especially when it comes to feeding your family on hectic weeknights.

On days that aren't as busy, take a bit of time to assemble delicious recipes such as Ranch Bean Chili, Pork Chops Creole, Chicken Cordon Bleu Bake and Southwestern Shepherd's Pie, then pop them in the freezer. You'll be glad you did!

That's because, on a later day when you barely have a minute to spare, you'll have a delicious dinner that's already prepared and ready to cook.

In this chapter, you'll also find make-in-advance desserts, breakfasts and more. Mealtime just doesn't get much easier!

FROM THE FREEZER. Turkey Tetrazzini (p. 234).

Potato-Topped Chicken Casserole

Divide mixture between two greased 13-in. x 9-in. baking dishes. Drain potatoes; place in a large bowl. Add milk and butter; mash until smooth. Stir in cheese. Spread over chicken mixture.

Cover and freeze one casserole for up to 3 months. Bake the remaining casserole, uncovered, at 400° for 15-20 minutes or until bubbly.

To use frozen casserole: Thaw in the refrigerator overnight. Remove from the refrigerator 30 minutes before baking. Bake, uncovered, at 400° for 50-55 minutes or until bubbly. **Yield:** 2 casseroles (6 servings each).

Berry Compote Topping

(Pictured below)

Prep/Total Time: 20 min.

This tongue-tingling dessert sauce is fantastic served over scoops of vanilla ice cream, as well as toasted slices of pound cake and warm-from-the-oven biscuits.
—Wanda Wedekind, West Frankfort, Illinois

  1 cup sugar
1/3 cup cornstarch
  1 cup cold water
1/2 cup lemon juice
1/2 cup maple syrup
  4 cups fresh strawberries, halved
  2 cups fresh raspberries
  2 cups fresh blackberries

In a large saucepan, combine sugar and cornstarch. Stir in the water, lemon juice and syrup. Stir in the berries. Bring to a boil over medium heat; cook and stir for 2 minutes or until thickened.

Serve immediately or transfer to freezer containers. May be frozen for up to 3 months.

To use frozen sauce: Thaw sauce in the refrigerator overnight. Place in a saucepan and heat through. **Yield:** 6 cups.

Berry Compote Topping

Potato-Topped Chicken Casserole

(Pictured above)

Prep: 45 min. **Bake:** 15 min.

A friend gave me this delicious dinner recipe, which is perfect for nights when you want something hearty and homemade. Any cheese you have on hand will work fine.
—Mary Ann Dell, Phoenixville, Pennsylvania

    4 pounds medium red potatoes, quartered
    3 pounds ground chicken
    4 medium carrots, finely chopped
    2 medium onions, finely chopped
1/4 cup all-purpose flour
    2 tablespoons tomato paste
1-1/2 teaspoons salt
  3/4 teaspoon pepper
1/4 teaspoon minced fresh thyme
1-1/4 cups chicken broth
    1 cup milk
    6 tablespoons butter, cubed
1-3/4 cups (7 ounces) shredded cheddar cheese

Place potatoes in a Dutch oven and cover with water. Bring to a boil. Reduce the heat; cover and simmer for 15-20 minutes or until tender.

Meanwhile, in a Dutch oven, cook the chicken, carrots and onions over medium heat until meat is no longer pink; drain. Stir in the flour, tomato paste, salt, pepper and thyme. Add chicken broth; bring to a boil. Reduce heat; simmer, uncovered, for 6-8 minutes or until thickened.

Ranch Bean Chili

Peaches & Cream French Toast

(Pictured below)

Prep: 20 min. + chilling **Bake:** 50 min.

Wake up the sleepyheads in your house with the warm, comforting aroma of peaches and brown sugar in this delectable breakfast bake. It's a wonderful overnight dish.
—Susan Westerfield, Albuquerque, New Mexico

    1 **cup packed brown sugar**
1/2 **cup butter, cubed**
    2 **tablespoons corn syrup**
    1 **can (29 ounces) sliced peaches, drained**
    1 **loaf (1 pound) day-old French bread, cubed**
    1 **package (8 ounces) cream cheese, cubed**
  12 **eggs**
1-1/2 **cups half-and-half cream**
    1 **teaspoon vanilla extract**

In a small saucepan, combine the brown sugar, butter and corn syrup. Cook and stir over medium heat until sugar is dissolved; pour into a greased 13-in. x 9-in. baking dish.

Arrange peaches in dish. Place half of the bread cubes over peaches. Layer with cream cheese and remaining bread. Place the eggs, cream and vanilla in a blender; cover and process until smooth. Pour over top. Cover and refrigerate overnight.

Remove from the refrigerator 30 minutes before baking. Bake, uncovered, at 350° for 50-60 minutes or until a knife inserted near the center comes out clean. **Yield:** 12 servings.

Ranch Bean Chili

(Pictured above)

Prep: 25 min. **Cook:** 20 min.

Loaded with beans, peppers, tomatoes and corn, this colorful chili is a surefire hit. I often take it to potluck suppers and always come home with an empty pot.
—Nancy Foreman, East Wenatchee, Washington

    1 **pound lean ground beef**
3/4 **cup chopped onion**
    1 **teaspoon minced garlic**
    1 **medium green pepper, chopped**
    1 *each* **small sweet orange, red and yellow pepper, chopped**
    2 **cans (16 ounces *each*) kidney beans, rinsed and drained**
    1 **can (15-1/2 ounces) chili beans, undrained**
    1 **can (14-1/2 ounces) diced tomatoes, undrained**
    1 **can (11-1/2 ounces) tomato juice**
1-1/3 **cups fresh *or* frozen corn**
    1 **cup water**
    1 **envelope ranch salad dressing mix**

In a Dutch oven, cook the beef, onion and garlic over medium heat until meat is no longer pink; drain. Add peppers; cook and stir for 3 minutes. Stir in the remaining ingredients. Bring to a boil. Reduce heat; cover and simmer for 15 minutes.

Serve desired amount of chili. Cool remaining chili; transfer to freezer containers. Cover and freeze for up to 3 months.

To use frozen chili: Thaw in the refrigerator. Place in a saucepan; heat through. **Yield:** 8 servings (3 quarts).

Peaches & Cream French Toast

Chicken Cordon Bleu Bake

(Pictured below)

Prep: 20 min. **Bake:** 40 min.

A friend gave me this recipe years ago. I freeze it in disposable pans to share with neighbors or to enjoy at home when I'm short on time. —Rea Newell, Decatur, Illinois

- 2 packages (6 ounces *each*) reduced-sodium stuffing mix
- 1 can (10-3/4 ounces) condensed cream of chicken soup, undiluted
- 1 cup milk
- 8 cups cubed cooked chicken
- 1/2 teaspoon pepper
- 3/4 pound sliced deli ham, cut into 1-inch strips
- 1 cup (4 ounces) shredded Swiss cheese
- 3 cups (12 ounces) shredded cheddar cheese

Prepare the stuffing mixes according to the package directions. Meanwhile, in a large bowl, combine soup and milk; set aside. Divide the chicken between two greased 13-in. x 9-in. baking dishes. Sprinkle with pepper. Layer with ham, Swiss cheese, 1 cup cheddar cheese, soup mixture and stuffing. Sprinkle with remaining cheddar cheese.

Cover and freeze one casserole for up to 3 months. Cover and bake the remaining casserole at 350° for 30 minutes. Uncover; bake 10-15 minutes longer or until cheese is melted.

To use frozen casserole: Thaw in the refrigerator overnight. Remove from the refrigerator 30 minutes before baking. Cover and bake at 350° for 45 minutes. Uncover; bake 10-15 minutes longer or until heated through and the cheese is melted. **Yield:** 2 casseroles (6 servings each).

Chicken Cordon Bleu Bake

Turkey Tetrazzini

Turkey Tetrazzini

(Pictured above and on page 230)

Prep: 50 min. **Cook:** 30 min.

My mom came up with this tasty casserole. It's great for weeknights, but the pasta, Parmesan cheese and splash of sherry make it nice enough for dinner parties, too.
  —Peggy Kroupa, Leawood, Kansas

- 1 pound uncooked spaghetti
- 1/2 pound sliced fresh mushrooms
- 1 cup chopped onion
- 1/2 teaspoon minced garlic
- 2 tablespoons olive oil
- 3 cans (10-3/4 ounces *each*) condensed cream of mushroom soup, undiluted
- 3 cups cubed cooked turkey
- 1 cup chicken broth
- 1/3 cup sherry *or* additional chicken broth
- 1 teaspoon Italian seasoning
- 3/4 teaspoon pepper
- 2 cups grated Parmesan cheese, *divided*

Cook spaghetti according to package directions. Meanwhile, in a Dutch oven, saute the mushrooms, onion and garlic in oil until tender. Stir in the soup, turkey, broth, sherry, Italian seasoning, pepper and 1 cup cheese. Drain spaghetti; stir into turkey mixture.

Transfer to two greased 8-in. square baking dishes. Sprinkle with remaining cheese. Cover and freeze one casserole for up to 3 months. Cover and bake the remaining casserole at 350° for 30-40 minutes or until heated through.

To use frozen casserole: Thaw in the refrigerator overnight. Remove from the refrigerator 30 minutes before baking. Cover and bake at 350° for 45 minutes. Uncover; bake 5-10 minutes longer or until bubbly. **Yield:** 2 casseroles (4 servings each).

Carrot Cookie Bites

(Pictured below)

Prep: 15 min. **Bake:** 10 min./batch

This recipe is a longtime family favorite. The cookies are soft and delicious…and the aroma while baking is simply irresistible! —Jeanie Petrik, Greensburg, Kentucky

☑ **This recipe includes Nutrition Facts and Diabetic Exchanges.**

  2/3 cup shortening
    1 cup packed brown sugar
    2 eggs
  1/2 cup buttermilk
    1 teaspoon vanilla extract
    2 cups all-purpose flour
    1 teaspoon ground cinnamon
  1/2 teaspoon salt
  1/4 teaspoon baking powder
  1/4 teaspoon baking soda
  1/4 teaspoon ground nutmeg
  1/4 teaspoon ground cloves
    2 cups quick-cooking oats
    1 cup shredded carrots
  1/2 cup chopped pecans

In a large bowl, cream shortening and brown sugar until light and fluffy. Beat in the eggs, buttermilk and vanilla. Combine the flour, cinnamon, salt, baking powder, baking soda, nutmeg and cloves; gradually add to creamed mixture. Stir in the oats, carrots and pecans.

To freeze cookie dough, drop desired amount of dough by rounded teaspoonfuls onto baking sheets; cover and freeze until firm. Transfer frozen cookie dough balls into a resealable plastic freezer bag. May be frozen for up to 3 months.

Drop remaining cookie dough by rounded teaspoonfuls 2 in. apart onto ungreased baking sheets. Bake at 375° for 6-8 minutes or until lightly browned. Remove to wire racks to cool.

To use frozen cookie dough: Place dough balls 2 in. apart onto ungreased baking sheets. Bake at 375°

Carrot Cookie Bites

Italian Sausage Spaghetti Sauce

for 10-15 minutes or until lightly browned. Remove to wire racks to cool. **Yield:** 7 dozen.

Nutrition Facts: 1 cookie equals 50 calories, 2 g fat (trace saturated fat), 5 mg cholesterol, 24 mg sodium, 6 g carbohydrate, trace fiber, 1 g protein. **Diabetic Exchanges:** 1/2 starch, 1/2 fat.

Italian Sausage Spaghetti Sauce

(Pictured above)

Prep: 20 min. **Cook:** 25 min.

A jarred sauce from the store offers convenience, but the taste of this meaty homemade version just can't be beat. —Angus Barsch, Milwaukee, Wisconsin

    2 pounds bulk Italian sausage
  2/3 cup chopped onion
    2 teaspoons minced garlic
    2 pounds plum tomatoes, diced
    2 cans (14-1/2 ounces *each*) beef broth
    2 cans (6 ounces *each*) tomato paste
    2 tablespoons brown sugar
    2 teaspoons Italian seasoning
  1/4 teaspoon ground cinnamon
    2 cups (8 ounces) shredded part-skim
      mozzarella cheese
Hot cooked spaghetti

In a Dutch oven, cook the sausage, onion and garlic over medium heat until sausage is no longer pink; drain. Add the tomatoes, broth, tomato paste, brown sugar, Italian seasoning and cinnamon. Bring to a boil. Reduce heat; simmer, uncovered, for 15-20 minutes or until heated through. Stir in cheese.

Serve desired amount over spaghetti. Cool remaining sauce; transfer to freezer containers. Freeze for up to 3 months.

To use frozen sauce: Thaw sauce in the refrigerator overnight. Place in a saucepan and heat through. **Yield:** 12 servings (about 2 quarts).

Italian Quiches

Italian Quiches

(Pictured above)

Prep: 25 min. **Bake:** 35 min. + standing

Love pizza? This meaty dish gives you that delicious taste for breakfast. Chances are, you'll want to fix it for dinner, too! —Bernice Hancock, Greenville, Pennsylvania

　2　unbaked pastry shells (9 inches)
　1　pound bulk Italian sausage
　4　cups (16 ounces) finely shredded part-skim
　　　mozzarella cheese
　1　medium onion, thinly sliced
　1　medium green pepper, thinly sliced
　1　medium sweet red pepper, thinly sliced
　6　eggs
　2　cups milk
　1　teaspoon minced garlic
1/4　cup grated Parmesan cheese

Line unpricked pastry shells with a double thickness of heavy-duty foil. Bake at 400° for 4 minutes. Remove foil; bake 4 minutes longer.

In a large skillet, cook sausage over medium heat until no longer pink; drain. Spoon sausage into pastry shells; sprinkle with mozzarella cheese. Top with onion and peppers. In a large bowl, whisk the eggs, milk and garlic. Pour over peppers; sprinkle with Parmesan cheese.

Cover and freeze one quiche for up to 3 months. Cover edges of remaining quiche loosely with foil; place on a baking sheet. Bake at 400° for 35-40 minutes or until a knife inserted near the center comes out clean. Let stand for 10 minutes before cutting.

To use frozen quiche: Remove from the freezer 30 minutes before baking (do not thaw). Cover edges of crust loosely with foil; place on a baking sheet. Bake at 400° for 50-60 minutes or until a knife inserted near the center comes out clean. Let stand for 10 minutes before cutting. **Yield:** 2 quiches (6 servings each).

Ham & Cheese Potato Casserole

Prep: 15 min. **Bake:** 50 min. + standing

Having this cheesy dish on hand is like money in the bank on hectic nights. Just let the frozen casserole thaw in the fridge, then bake. —Kari Adams, Fort Collins, Colorado

　　2　cans (10-3/4 ounces *each*) condensed cream
　　　　of celery soup, undiluted
　　2　cups (16 ounces) sour cream
　1/2　cup water
　1/2　teaspoon pepper
　　2　packages (28 ounces *each*) frozen O'Brien
　　　　potatoes
　　1　package (16 ounces) process cheese
　　　　(Velveeta), cubed
2-1/2　cups cubed fully cooked ham

In a large bowl, combine the soup, sour cream, water and pepper. Stir in the potatoes, cheese and ham.

Transfer to two greased 11-in. x 7-in. baking dishes. Cover and freeze one casserole for up to 3 months. Cover and bake remaining casserole at 375° for 40 minutes. Uncover and bake 10-15 minutes longer or until bubbly. Let stand for 10 minutes before serving.

To use frozen casserole: Thaw in the refrigerator overnight. Remove from the refrigerator 30 minutes before baking. Bake as directed. **Yield:** 2 casseroles (5 servings each).

Spinach Pesto

Banana Sundae Dessert

(Pictured below)

Prep: 25 min. + freezing

You get chocolate, banana and cherries in every spoonful of this frosty layered treat. It's simple to make but looks special. —Caroline Wamelink, Cleveland Heights, Ohio

    1 package (12 ounces) vanilla wafers, crushed
    1/2 cup butter, melted
    2 tablespoons sugar
    6 cups chocolate chip ice cream, softened
    4 large firm bananas, sliced
    2 jars (11-3/4 ounces *each*) hot fudge ice
        cream topping, *divided*
    6 cups cherry vanilla ice cream, softened
Maraschino cherries

In a small bowl, combine the wafer crumbs, butter and sugar; press onto the bottom of a 13-in. x 9-in. dish. Freeze for 15 minutes.

Spread chocolate chip ice cream over crust. Layer with bananas and 1-1/2 cups fudge topping. Cover and freeze for at least 30 minutes. Spread cherry vanilla ice cream evenly over topping. Cover and freeze for 6 hours or overnight.

Remove from the freezer 10 minutes before cutting. Warm remaining fudge topping. Drizzle over each serving; top each with a cherry. **Yield:** 16 servings.

Banana Sundae Dessert

Spinach Pesto

(Pictured above)

Prep/Total Time: 15 min.

Serve this vibrant pesto on pasta, pizza, sandwiches and more. If you don't have fresh oregano handy, feel free to omit it. —Susan Westerfield, Albuquerque, New Mexico

    2 cups fresh baby spinach
    2 cups loosely packed basil leaves
    1 cup grated Romano cheese
    2 tablespoons fresh oregano
    2 teaspoons minced garlic
    1/2 teaspoon salt
    1/2 cup chopped walnuts, toasted
    1 tablespoon lemon juice
    2 teaspoons grated lemon peel
    1 cup olive oil
Hot cooked pasta

Place the first six ingredients in a food processor; cover and pulse until chopped. Add the walnuts, lemon juice and peel; cover and process until blended. While processing, gradually add oil in a steady stream.

Serve desired amount of pesto with pasta. Transfer remaining sauce to ice cube trays. Cover and freeze for up to 1 month.

To use frozen pesto: Thaw pesto in the refrigerator for 3 hours. Serve with pasta. **Yield:** 2 cups.

Soft Touch

TO SOFTEN ice cream, transfer it from the freezer to the refrigerator about 20-30 minutes before using. Or let it stand at room temperature for 10-15 minutes. Hard ice cream can also be softened in the microwave at 30 percent power for about 30 seconds.

Creamed Turkey with Puff Pastry

(Pictured below)

Prep/Total Time: 25 min.

Warm and hearty, with lots of veggies in every creamy bite, this is classic comfort food. It tastes a lot like pot pie but is much quicker! —Nila Grahl, Gurnee, Illinois

- 1 package (17.3 ounces) frozen puff pastry
- 4 cans (18.8 ounces *each*) chunky chicken corn chowder soup
- 4 cups cubed cooked turkey
- 2 packages (16 ounces *each*) frozen peas and carrots, thawed
- 1 package (8 ounces) cream cheese, softened
- 1/4 teaspoon pepper

Thaw one sheet of puff pastry. Cut into six squares. Cut each square in half diagonally; transfer to two greased baking sheets. Bake at 400° for 10-15 minutes or until golden brown.

Meanwhile, in a Dutch oven, combine soup, turkey, peas and carrots, cream cheese and pepper. Bring to a boil, stirring frequently. Reduce heat; simmer, uncovered, for 5 minutes or until cream cheese is melted. Serve half of the soup mixture with puff pastry triangles. Cool the remaining soup mixture; transfer to freezer containers. May be frozen for up to 3 months.

To use frozen soup mixture: Thaw soup mixture in the refrigerator overnight. Thaw remaining puff pastry. Cut into six squares. Cut each square in half diagonally; transfer to two greased baking sheets. Bake at 400° for 10-15 minutes or until golden brown.

Meanwhile, place soup mixture in a Dutch oven. Bring to a boil over medium heat. Reduce heat; simmer, uncovered, for 3-5 minutes. Serve with puff pastry triangles. **Yield:** 12 servings.

Creamed Turkey with Puff Pastry

Southwestern Shepherd's Pie

Southwestern Shepherd's Pie

(Pictured above)

Give classic shepherd's pie a southwestern kick with this recipe. The ground beef, corn and potatoes create a complete dinner in one. —Suzette Jury, Keene, California

- 3 pounds ground beef
- 1 cup chopped onion
- 2 cans (10 ounces *each*) enchilada sauce
- 2 tablespoons all-purpose flour
- 2 teaspoons chopped chipotle peppers in adobo sauce
- 1 teaspoon ground cumin
- 1 teaspoon dried oregano
- 2-1/2 cups water
- 2 cups milk
- 1/3 cup butter, cubed
- 1 teaspoon salt
- 4 cups mashed potato flakes
- 2 cans (4 ounces *each*) chopped green chilies, undrained
- 2 cups (8 ounces) shredded Mexican cheese blend, *divided*
- 2 cans (11 ounces *each*) Mexicorn, drained
- 2/3 cup chopped green onions

Paprika

In a Dutch oven, cook ground beef and onion over medium heat until the meat is no longer pink; drain. Add the enchilada sauce, flour, chipotle peppers, cumin and oregano; bring to a boil. Reduce heat; simmer, uncovered, for 5 minutes.

Meanwhile, in a large saucepan, combine the water, milk, butter and salt; bring to a boil. Remove from the heat. Stir in the mashed potato flakes until combined. Add green chilies and 1/2 cup cheese.

Transfer ground beef mixture to two greased 11-in. x 7-in. baking dishes. Layer with the corn, mashed potato mixture and remaining cheese. Sprinkle with the green onions. Cover and freeze one casserole for up to 3 months.

Cover and bake the remaining casserole at 375° for 20 minutes. Uncover and bake 5-10 minutes longer or until bubbly. Sprinkle with paprika.

To use frozen casserole: Thaw the frozen casserole in the refrigerator overnight. Remove from refrigerator 30 minutes before baking. Cover and bake at 375° for 20 minutes. Uncover and bake 15-20 minutes longer or until bubbly. Sprinkle with paprika. **Yield:** 2 casseroles (7 servings each).

Creamy Chicken Casserole

Prep: 20 min. **Bake:** 40 min.

My husband was craving a dish his aunt used to make, so I did some experimenting in the kitchen and came up with this noodle casserole. It tastes great and is now a mealtime staple. For variety, try substituting different frozen vegetable blends.
—*Mari Warnke, Fremont, Wisconsin*

4 cups uncooked egg noodles
4 cups cubed cooked chicken
1 package (16 ounces) frozen peas and carrots
2 cups milk
2 cans (10-3/4 ounces *each*) condensed cream of celery soup, undiluted
2 cans (10-3/4 ounces *each*) condensed cream of chicken soup, undiluted
1 cup chopped onion
2 tablespoons butter, melted
1/2 teaspoon salt
1/2 teaspoon pepper

Cook the egg noodles according to the package directions. Meanwhile, in a large bowl, combine the remaining ingredients. Drain the egg noodles; add to the chicken mixture.

Transfer to two greased 8-in. square baking dishes. Cover and freeze one casserole for up to 3 months. Cover and bake remaining casserole at 350° for 30 minutes. Uncover and bake 10-15 minutes longer or until heated through.

To use frozen casserole: Thaw casserole in the refrigerator overnight. Remove from refrigerator 30 minutes before cooking. Cover and microwave on high for 10-12 minutes or until heated through, stirring twice. **Yield:** 2 casseroles (5 servings each).

Grilled Flank Steak

(Pictured below)

Prep: 5 min. + marinating **Grill:** 15 min. + standing

Friends shared this three-ingredient marinade with me years ago, and it's been a favorite ever since. Serve this steak with salad and grilled potatoes for a quick meal.
—*Beverly Dietz, Surprise, Arizona*

☑ This recipe includes Nutrition Facts and Diabetic Exchanges.

1 cup barbecue sauce
1/2 cup burgundy wine *or* beef broth
1/4 cup lemon juice
1 beef flank steak (2 pounds)

In a bowl, combine the barbecue sauce, wine and lemon juice. Pour 1 cup marinade into a large resealable plastic bag; add the steak. Seal bag and turn to coat; refrigerate for 4 hours or overnight. Cover and refrigerate remaining marinade.

Drain and discard marinade. Grill steak, covered, over medium heat 6-8 minutes on each side or until meat reaches desired doneness (for medium-rare, a meat thermometer should read 145°; medium, 160°; well-done, 170°). Let stand for 10 minutes before slicing. To serve, thinly slice across the grain. Serve with reserved marinade. **Yield:** 8 servings.

Nutrition Facts: 3 oz. cooked steak with 1-1/2 tablespoons marinade equals 195 calories, 9 g fat (4 g saturated fat), 54 mg cholesterol, 271 mg sodium, 4 g carbohydrate, trace fiber, 22 g protein. **Diabetic Exchanges:** 3 lean meat, 1 fat.

Grilled Flank Steak

Pork Chops Creole

tuted for 1 teaspoon Creole seasoning: 1/4 teaspoon each salt, garlic powder and paprika; and a pinch each of dried thyme, ground cumin and cayenne pepper.

Nutrition Facts: 1 pork chop with 1/2 cup sauce mixture (calculated without rice) equals 221 calories, 9 g fat (3 g saturated fat), 54 mg cholesterol, 412 mg sodium, 11 g carbohydrate, 1 g fiber, 23 g protein. **Diabetic Exchanges:** 3 lean meat, 1 vegetable, 1 fat, 1/2 starch.

Italian Sausage Strata

(Pictured below)

Prep: 25 min. + chilling **Bake:** 1 hour + standing

Everyone at the table will love this pretty, puffy casserole… and you'll love the fact that it can be made ahead of time for convenience.   —Suzette Jury, Keene, California

  1 pound bulk Italian sausage
  1 loaf (1 pound) sourdough bread, cubed
  1 jar (4-1/2 ounces) sliced mushrooms, drained
  1/4 cup thinly sliced green onions
  10 eggs
  3 cups half-and-half cream
  1 teaspoon ground mustard
  1/2 teaspoon salt
  1 cup (4 ounces) shredded Italian cheese blend

In a large skillet, cook sausage over medium heat until no longer pink; drain. Place bread cubes in a greased 13-in. x 9-in. baking dish. Layer with mushrooms, onions and sausage. In a large bowl, whisk the eggs, cream, mustard and salt. Pour over top; sprinkle with cheese. Cover and refrigerate overnight.

Remove from the refrigerator 30 minutes before baking. Bake, uncovered, at 350° for 60-65 minutes or until a knife inserted near the center comes out clean. (Cover loosely with foil if top browns too quickly.) Let stand for 10 minutes before serving. **Yield:** 12 servings.

Pork Chops Creole

(Pictured above)

Prep: 25 min. **Cook:** 15 min.

This recipe is a family favorite, and it usually becomes a favorite of guests, too. Plus, it's so easy to make—you can't beat a one-skillet dish!   —Amy Gross, Swanton, Ohio

☑ This recipe includes Nutrition Facts and Diabetic Exchanges.

  8 boneless pork loin chops (3/4 inch thick and 6 ounces *each*)
  4 teaspoons canola oil
  2 large onions, sliced
  1 medium green pepper, cut into strips
  1 medium sweet yellow pepper, cut into strips
  1 can (10-3/4 ounces) condensed tomato soup, undiluted
  2/3 cup water
  1 teaspoon Creole seasoning
  1/2 teaspoon pepper
  1/4 teaspoon salt
Hot cooked rice, optional

In a large skillet, brown pork chops in oil on both sides in batches. Set aside and keep warm. In the same skillet, saute the onions, green pepper and yellow pepper until tender.

Return pork chops to the skillet. Combine the soup, water, Creole seasoning, pepper and salt; pour over chops. Bring to a boil. Reduce heat; cover and simmer for 12-14 minutes or until meat is tender.

Serve immediately with rice if desired, or cool before placing in a freezer container. Cover and freeze for up to 3 months.

To use frozen pork chops: Thaw in the refrigerator overnight. Place in a skillet; bring to a boil. Reduce heat; cover and simmer for 8-12 minutes or until a meat thermometer reads 165°. **Yield:** 8 servings.

Editor's Note: The following spices may be substi-

Italian Sausage Strata

Cherry Chocolate Pie

Cherry Chocolate Pie

(Pictured above)

Prep: 20 min. + chilling

We have a large family, and they like trying all of my pies and cakes. This recipe is one of the most-requested. It's a no-bake treat I can keep in the fridge overnight.
—Bonnie Phillips, Cedar Hill, Missouri

- 11 large marshmallows
- 1/3 cup milk
- 1 piece (3 ounces) milk chocolate candy bar, chopped
- 1 container (8 ounces) frozen whipped topping, thawed and *divided*
- 1 graham cracker crust (10 inches)
- 1 can (21 ounces) cherry pie filling

In a large saucepan, combine the marshmallows, milk and chocolate. Cook and stir over medium-low heat until smooth. Cool completely.

Fold 3/4 cup whipped topping into chocolate mixture. Pour into prepared crust. Cover and refrigerate for at least 30 minutes. Top with pie filling and remaining whipped topping. Cover and refrigerate for 8 hours or overnight. **Yield:** 8 servings.

Editor's Note: This recipe uses half of a 6-ounce milk chocolate candy bar.

Mostaccioli Casserole

(Pictured at right)

Prep: 25 min. **Bake:** 25 min.

This rich and cheesy casserole freezes so well that no one would ever guess it had been on ice! The pasta, ground beef, spaghetti sauce and mozzarella appeal to all ages.
—Margaret McNeil, Germantown, Tennessee

✓ **This recipe includes Nutrition Facts and Diabetic Exchanges.**

- 1 package (16 ounces) mostaccioli
- 1-1/2 pounds ground beef
- 1-1/4 cups chopped green pepper
- 1 cup chopped onion
- 1 jar (26 ounces) spaghetti sauce
- 1 can (10-3/4 ounces) condensed cheddar cheese soup, undiluted
- 1-1/2 teaspoons Italian seasoning
- 3/4 teaspoon pepper
- 2 cups (8 ounces) shredded part-skim mozzarella cheese, *divided*

Cook mostaccioli according to the package directions. Meanwhile, in a large skillet, cook the beef, green pepper and onion over medium heat until meat is no longer pink; drain. Stir in the spaghetti sauce, soup, Italian seasoning and pepper.

Drain mostaccioli. Add mostaccioli and 1-1/2 cups cheese to beef mixture. Transfer to two greased 11-in. x 7-in. baking dishes. Sprinkle with remaining cheese. Cover and freeze one casserole for up to 3 months. Cover and bake remaining casserole at 350° for 20 minutes. Uncover; bake 5-10 minutes longer or until bubbly and cheese is melted.

To use frozen casserole: Thaw in the refrigerator overnight. Remove from the refrigerator 30 minutes before baking. Cover and bake at 350° for 50-60 minutes or until heated through and cheese is melted. **Yield:** 2 casseroles (6 servings each).

Nutrition Facts: 1 cup equals 351 calories, 12 g fat (5 g saturated fat), 42 mg cholesterol, 633 mg sodium, 39 g carbohydrate, 3 g fiber, 22 g protein. **Diabetic Exchanges:** 2-1/2 starch, 2 lean meat, 1 fat.

Mostaccioli Casserole

Chapter 16

Casseroles and Oven Suppers

IT'S A SURE WAY to please your family—pulling a piping-hot casserole or other baked entree out of the oven for the dinner table. And you won't need as much time in the kitchen as you may think!

Most of the delicious dishes featured in this chapter can be assembled in a mere 20 minutes or less. After that, you can let them bake while you're free to take care of other things.

Before long, you'll be serving up a hearty supper such as Pizza Lover's Pie, Scalloped Potatoes with Ham & Cheese and Pesto Chicken Mostaccioli.

So go ahead—open the door to a speedy, fuss-free meal by relying on your oven!

HEAT IT UP. Saucy Parmesan Chicken (p. 245).

Honey Mustard Chicken

(Pictured above)

Prep: 15 min. **Bake:** 45 min.

Moist and flavorful, this chicken entree is a real treat. And with just 15 minutes of prep time, you'll be out of the kitchen quickly! —Richard Gallop, Pueblo, Colorado

☑ This recipe includes Nutrition Facts and Diabetic Exchanges.

  1/2 cup honey
  1/4 cup prepared mustard
    1 envelope ranch salad dressing mix
    1 tablespoon dried parsley flakes
1-1/2 teaspoons Italian seasoning
  1/2 teaspoon dried basil
  1/2 teaspoon chili powder
  1/4 teaspoon garlic powder
  1/4 teaspoon pepper
    6 chicken drumsticks
    6 bone-in chicken thighs

For sauce, in a small bowl, combine first nine ingredients. Set aside 1/2 cup for serving. Place the chicken in a greased 15-in. x 10-in. x 1-in. baking pan; brush with the remaining sauce.

Bake, uncovered, at 350° for 45-50 minutes or until a meat thermometer reads 180° and chicken juices run clear, basting occasionally with pan juices. Warm the reserved sauce; serve with chicken. **Yield:** 6 servings.

Nutrition Facts: 1 chicken thigh and drumstick with 4 teaspoons sauce equals 322 calories, 12 g fat (3 g saturated fat), 93 mg cholesterol, 576 mg sodium, 27 g carbohydrate, 1 g fiber, 28 g protein. **Diabetic Exchanges:** 4 lean meat, 2 starch.

Swiss Broccoli Bake

(Pictured above)

Prep: 15 min. **Bake:** 35 min. + standing

Even people who usually don't care for broccoli end up enjoying this rich and creamy side dish. It's good with just about any main course and also travels well to potlucks. —Elaine Grimme, Sioux Falls, South Dakota

    3 packages (16 ounces *each*) frozen chopped broccoli, thawed
    1 can (10-3/4 ounces) condensed cream of mushroom soup, undiluted
    1 can (10-3/4 ounces) condensed cream of broccoli soup, undiluted
2-1/2 cups (10 ounces) shredded Swiss cheese, *divided*
    1 can (5 ounces) evaporated milk

In a large bowl, combine broccoli, soups, 2 cups Swiss cheese and evaporated milk. Pour into a greased 13-in. x 9-in. baking dish. Bake, uncovered, at 350° for 30 minutes or until heated through.

Sprinkle with the remaining cheese. Bake 5-10 minutes longer or until the cheese is melted. Let stand for 10 minutes before serving. Refrigerate the leftovers. **Yield:** 10 servings.

Ravioli Casserole

(Pictured below)

Prep: 25 min. **Bake:** 35 min. + standing

You'll need less than 30 minutes to assemble this hearty, crowd-pleasing meal. Then just pop it in the oven, and in less than an hour it'll be on the table. The recipe takes advantage of convenient frozen cheese ravioli, but the nutmeg, white wine and basil give it a special flair.
— Margie Williams, Mt. Juliet, Tennessee

    1 package (25 ounces) frozen cheese ravioli
1/4 cup butter, cubed
1/4 cup all-purpose flour
1/4 teaspoon salt
1/4 teaspoon ground nutmeg
    2 cups milk
1/4 cup white wine *or* vegetable broth
1/2 cup minced fresh basil
    3 cups (12 ounces) shredded part-skim
       mozzarella cheese, *divided*
3/4 cup grated Parmesan cheese, *divided*
2-1/2 cups marinara *or* spaghetti sauce

Cook the cheese ravioli according to the package directions. Meanwhile, in a large saucepan, melt the butter. Stir in the flour, salt and nutmeg until smooth; gradually add the milk and wine. Bring to a boil; cook and stir for 1 minute or until thickened. Remove from heat. Stir in the basil, 1 cup mozzarella cheese and 1/4 cup Parmesan cheese.

Drain the ravioli; toss with the sauce mixture. Transfer to a greased 13-in. x 9-in. baking dish. Top with 1 cup mozzarella cheese and marinara sauce; sprinkle with the remaining cheeses. Cover and bake at 375° for 30 minutes. Uncover; bake 5-10 minutes longer or until bubbly. Let stand for 15 minutes before serving. **Yield:** 8 servings.

Ravioli Casserole

Saucy Parmesan Chicken

Saucy Parmesan Chicken

(Pictured above and on page 242)

Prep: 20 min. **Bake:** 25 min.

This chicken dinner recipe has been in my file for years. Curry powder adds a unique taste but can easily be omitted if you prefer. — Bobby Taylor, Michigan City, Indiana

1/2 cup chopped onion
    2 tablespoons butter
    1 can (10-3/4 ounces) condensed tomato
       soup, undiluted
1/3 cup beer *or* nonalcoholic beer
1/2 teaspoon curry powder
1/2 teaspoon dried oregano
1/4 teaspoon salt
1/8 teaspoon pepper
    6 boneless skinless chicken breast halves
       (7 ounces *each*)
1/4 cup grated Parmesan cheese

In a large skillet, saute the onion in butter until tender. Add the soup, beer, curry, oregano, salt and pepper; bring to a boil. Reduce heat; simmer, uncovered, for 8-10 minutes or until thickened, stirring occasionally.

Place chicken in a greased 13-in. x 9-in. baking dish. Pour soup mixture over chicken. Bake, uncovered, at 375° for 24-28 minutes or until chicken juices run clear. Sprinkle with cheese. **Yield:** 6 servings.

Choosing Chicken

BUYING skinned, boned chicken breasts for recipes such as Saucy Parmesan Chicken (above) can cut up to 15 minutes from your cooking time. Save money by buying larger packages, then rewrap the breasts individually or in family-size portions and freeze.

Scalloped Potatoes With Ham & Cheese

(Pictured below)

Prep: 20 min. **Bake:** 65 min. + standing

This recipe gives you comfort food at its absolute best! The creamy main dish is loaded with red potatoes, mozzarella cheese, onion and chunks of ham. Bring the pan to your next family gathering, community event or church potluck and watch 'em come back for second helpings.
—Alisa Hanson, Duluth, Minnesota

    1 can (10-3/4 ounces) condensed cream of
      mushroom soup, undiluted
    1 cup milk
  2/3 cup condensed cream of potato soup,
      undiluted
  1/2 cup chopped onion
  1/4 cup butter, melted
  1/2 teaspoon minced garlic
  1/2 teaspoon pepper
  1/4 teaspoon seasoned salt
    8 medium red potatoes, peeled and thinly
      sliced
    3 cups cubed fully cooked ham
1-1/2 cups (6 ounces) shredded part-skim
      mozzarella cheese

In a large bowl, combine the first eight ingredients. Add the potatoes, ham and cheese; toss to coat. Transfer to a greased 13-in. x 9-in. baking dish.

Bake, uncovered, at 350° for 65-70 minutes or until bubbly and potatoes are tender. Let stand for 10 minutes before serving. **Yield:** 10 servings.

Chinese Beef Casserole

Scalloped Potatoes with Ham & Cheese

Chinese Beef Casserole

(Pictured above)

Prep: 15 min. **Bake:** 45 min.

Crispy chow mein noodles top this twist on traditional chop suey. With plenty of ground beef, rice and crunchy water chestnuts, it's sure to become a family favorite. Plus, it takes a mere 15 minutes to get in the oven.
—Willie DeWaard, Coralville, Iowa

    2 pounds ground beef
    1 cup chopped onion
    1 cup chopped celery
    2 cans (10-3/4 ounces *each*) condensed cream
      of mushroom soup, undiluted
    1 can (14 ounces) bean sprouts, undrained
  1/4 cup soy sauce
  1/2 teaspoon pepper
    1 cup uncooked long grain rice
    1 can (8 ounces) sliced water chestnuts,
      drained
    2 cups frozen peas, thawed
    1 can (5 ounces) chow mein noodles

In a large skillet, cook the beef, onion and celery over medium heat until the meat is no longer pink; drain. Return to skillet. Stir in the soup, bean sprouts, soy sauce and pepper. Bring to a boil. Pour into a greased 3-qt. baking dish. Stir in rice and water chestnuts.

Cover and bake at 350° for 30 minutes. Uncover; stir in peas and sprinkle with noodles. Bake 15-20 minutes longer or until heated through. **Yield:** 8 servings.

Pesto Chicken Mostaccioli

(Pictured below)

Prep: 25 min. **Bake:** 25 min.

I was looking for something new to fix and decided to try inventing my own recipe. This one, which yields two 11-inch x 7-inch casseroles, was the result. We love pesto and mac and cheese, but we never guessed what a yummy combination they would make with chicken tenders!
—Rebecca Stablein, Lake Forest, California

  1 package (16 ounces) mostaccioli
  1 package (16 ounces) frozen breaded chicken tenders
  4 cups (16 ounces) shredded cheddar cheese
  1 container (16 ounces) sour cream
  1 container (15 ounces) ricotta cheese
3/4 cup prepared pesto
2/3 cup heavy whipping cream
1/2 cup grated Parmesan cheese
1/2 cup dry bread crumbs
1/4 cup butter, melted

Cook mostaccioli and chicken according to package directions. Meanwhile, in a large bowl, combine the cheddar cheese, sour cream, ricotta, pesto, cream and Parmesan cheese.

Chop the chicken tenders and drain the mostaccioli; add to the cheese mixture. Toss to coat. Transfer to two greased 11-in. x 7-in. baking dishes (dishes will be full). Combine the bread crumbs and butter; sprinkle over the top. Bake, uncovered, at 350° for 25-30 minutes or until heated through and golden brown. **Yield:** 2 casseroles (5 servings each).

Tater Brat Bake

Pesto Chicken Mostaccioli

Tater Brat Bake

(Pictured above)

Prep: 25 min. **Bake:** 25 min.

My husband suggested a brats-and-sauerkraut lunch for friends who were back for their high school reunion, and I served this. It was so simple but went over big.
—Pauline Lentz, Mesa, Arizona

  1 package (1-1/4 pounds) uncooked bratwurst links
  2 bottles (12 ounces *each*) beer *or* non-alcoholic beer
  2 tablespoons butter
  1 can (16 ounces) sauerkraut, rinsed, drained and chopped
  1 can (10-3/4 ounces) condensed cheddar cheese soup, undiluted
1/2 cup milk
  1 package (32 ounces) frozen Tater Tots
  1 cup (4 ounces) shredded cheddar cheese

In a large saucepan, combine the bratwurst and beer. Bring to a boil. Reduce the heat. Cover and simmer for 10-15 minutes or until meat is no longer pink. Drain and cut into 1/4-in. slices. In a large skillet, brown brats in butter over medium-high heat; drain on paper towels.

Spoon the sauerkraut into a greased 13-in. x 9-in. baking dish. Top with brats. Combine soup and milk; drizzle over brats. Top with Tater Tots. Bake at 450° for 20-25 minutes or until potatoes are lightly browned.

Sprinkle with cheese; bake 5 minutes longer or until cheese is melted. **Yield:** 6 servings.

Lasagna Roll-Ups

Orzo-Stuffed Peppers

(Pictured below)

Prep: 30 min. **Bake:** 15 min.

Filled with orzo pasta, Italian sausage and garden-fresh flavor, these cheese-topped veggie cups make a fun, fast-to-fix dinner for your family. If you like, adjust the heat level by changing the amount of pepper flakes.
—Kelly Evans, Smithville, Texas

 4 large green peppers
 1 cup uncooked orzo pasta
 1 pound bulk Italian sausage
 1/2 cup chopped red onion
 2 teaspoons minced garlic
 2 cups marinara *or* spaghetti sauce
 1 medium tomato, chopped
 1/4 cup minced fresh basil *or* 1 tablespoon
    dried basil
 2 teaspoons dried rosemary, crushed
 1 teaspoon crushed red pepper flakes
 1/4 cup shredded part-skim mozzarella cheese
 2 tablespoons grated Parmesan cheese

Cut tops off peppers and remove the seeds. In a large kettle, cook peppers in boiling water for 3-5 minutes. Drain and rinse in cold water; set aside.

Cook the orzo according to package directions. Meanwhile, in a large skillet, cook the sausage, onion and garlic over medium heat until meat is no longer pink; drain. Drain orzo; stir into meat mixture. Add the marinara sauce, tomato, basil, rosemary and pepper flakes. Spoon into peppers.

Place in a greased 11-in. x 7-in. baking dish. Cover and bake at 350° for 10 minutes. Uncover; sprinkle with cheeses. Bake 5 minutes longer or until cheese is melted. **Yield:** 4 servings.

Lasagna Roll-Ups

(Pictured above)

Prep: 20 min. **Bake:** 30 min.

This crowd-pleasing take on lasagna offers a new way to enjoy a classic. Round out the meal with a simple salad.
—Susan Sabia, Windsor, California

 10 uncooked lasagna noodles
 1 package (19-1/2 ounces) Italian turkey
    sausage links, casings removed
 1 package (8 ounces) cream cheese, softened
 1 jar (26 ounces) spaghetti sauce, *divided*
 1-3/4 cups (7 ounces) shredded cheddar cheese,
    divided

Cook the noodles according to the package directions. Meanwhile, in a large skillet, cook the sausage over medium heat until no longer pink; drain. Stir in cream cheese and 1/3 cup spaghetti sauce. Drain noodles; spread 1/4 cup meat mixture on each noodle. Sprinkle each with 2 tablespoons cheese; carefully roll up.

Spread 2/3 cup spaghetti sauce into an ungreased 13-in. x 9-in. baking dish. Place roll-ups seam side down over sauce. Top with the remaining sauce and cheese. Cover and bake at 350° for 20 minutes. Uncover; bake 10-15 minutes longer or until bubbly. **Yield:** 10 servings.

Sausage Specifics

NOT SURE what kind of Italian sausage to use in a recipe? When a recipe in this book (such as Orzo-Stuffed Peppers, above right) calls for Italian sausage, it is referring to sweet Italian sausage. Recipes using hot Italian sausage specifically call for that type.

Orzo-Stuffed Peppers

Ham Mac and Cheese

(Pictured above)

Prep: 30 min. **Bake:** 35 min.

I've been serving this recipe for years—you just can't go wrong with mac and cheese! Chunks of ham make this version hearty. —*Susan Taul, Birmingham, Alabama*

- 1 package (7-1/4 ounces) macaroni and cheese dinner mix
- 3/4 cup soft bread crumbs
- 2 tablespoons grated Parmesan cheese
- 1 tablespoon minced fresh parsley
- 1 tablespoon butter, melted
- 1 cup cubed fully cooked ham
- 1 cup (8 ounces) cream-style cottage cheese
- 1/2 cup sour cream
- 2 tablespoons sliced green onion
- 1 tablespoon diced pimientos, optional
- 1/4 teaspoon salt
- 1/4 teaspoon ground mustard

Prepare the macaroni dinner mix according to the package directions. Meanwhile, in a small bowl, combine the bread crumbs, Parmesan cheese, parsley and butter; set aside.

In a large bowl, combine the macaroni and cheese, ham, cottage cheese, sour cream, green onion, pimientos if desired, salt and mustard. Pour into a greased 1-1/2-qt. baking dish. Sprinkle with crumb mixture.

Bake, uncovered, at 350° for 35-40 minutes or until heated through. **Yield:** 4 servings.

Meaty Noodle Casserole

Prep: 20 min. **Bake:** 30 min.

With both sausage and ground beef, this pasta bake is perfect for big, hearty appetites. If your family doesn't like green olives, use black instead or skip them altogether. —*Lana Backus, Vonore, Tennessee*

- 1 package (12 ounces) wide egg noodles
- 1 pound ground beef
- 1/2 pound bulk pork sausage
- 3 tablespoons chopped onion
- 1/4 teaspoon garlic powder
- 1 can (14-3/4 ounces) cream-style corn
- 1 can (14-1/2 ounces) stewed tomatoes, cut up
- 1 can (10-3/4 ounces) condensed cream of chicken soup, undiluted
- 1 cup chopped pimiento-stuffed olives
- 2 tablespoons minced fresh parsley
- 1-1/2 cups (6 ounces) shredded cheddar cheese

Cook pasta according to package directions. Meanwhile, in a Dutch oven, cook the beef, pork sausage, onion and garlic powder over medium heat until meat is no longer pink; drain. Add the corn, tomatoes, soup, olives and parsley; heat through.

Drain the pasta; stir into the meat mixture. Transfer to a greased 13-in. x 9-in. baking dish. Sprinkle with the cheese. Cover and bake at 350° for 25 minutes. Uncover; bake 5-10 minutes longer or until cheese is melted. **Yield:** 8 servings.

Loaded Spaghetti Bake

cream of chicken soup, Alfredo sauce and Parmesan cheese; spread over cheddar cheese. In another bowl, combine cornflake crumbs and the remaining cheddar cheese; sprinkle over the top.

Bake, uncovered, at 350° for 30 minutes or until bubbly and cheese is melted. Let stand for 5 minutes before serving. **Yield:** 8 servings.

Southwest Tuna Noodle Bake

(Pictured below)

Prep: 15 min. **Bake:** 30 min.

None of my coworkers had ever tried tuna noodle casserole, and—since we live near the Mexican border—they challenged me to make my version "culturally sensitive" to the area. After sampling this creation, everyone wanted the recipe.   —Sandra Crane, Las Cruces, New Mexico

  1 package (16 ounces) egg noodles
2-1/2 cups milk
  2 cans (6 ounces *each*) light
    water-packed tuna, drained
  1 can (10-3/4 ounces) condensed cream of
    chicken soup, undiluted
  1 can (10-3/4 ounces) condensed cream of
    mushroom soup, undiluted
  1 cup (4 ounces) shredded cheddar cheese
  1 can (4 ounces) chopped green chilies
  2 cups crushed tortilla chips

Cook the noodles according to the package directions. Meanwhile, in a large bowl, combine the milk, tuna, soups, cheese and chilies. Drain noodles; gently stir into tuna mixture.

Transfer to an ungreased 13-in. x 9-in. baking dish. Sprinkle with tortilla chips. Bake, uncovered, at 350° for 30-35 minutes or until bubbly. **Yield:** 6 servings.

Loaded Spaghetti Bake

(Pictured above)

Prep: 25 min. **Bake:** 30 min.

You'll want to add this versatile recipe to your own kitchen files. Everyone loves it! Instead of making the casserole with ground beef, you could use leftover chicken from last night's dinner. Feel free to substitute another hard cheese for the Parmesan, too...or just go with the cheddar.
    —Marian Pappas, Lake Stevens, Washington

  12 ounces uncooked spaghetti
  1 pound lean ground beef
  1 cup chopped onion
  1 cup chopped green pepper
  1 jar (26 ounces) spaghetti sauce
  1 can (4 ounces) mushroom stems and pieces,
    drained
  1 can (2-1/4 ounces) sliced ripe olives, drained
  2 cups (8 ounces) shredded cheddar cheese,
    divided
  1 can (10-3/4 ounces) condensed cream of
    chicken soup, undiluted
  1 carton (10 ounces) refrigerated Alfredo sauce
1/4 cup grated Parmesan cheese
1/2 cup cornflake crumbs

Cook the spaghetti according to package directions. In a large skillet, cook the beef, onion and pepper over medium heat until meat is no longer pink; drain. Add the spaghetti sauce, mushrooms and olives. Drain spaghetti; add to skillet.

Transfer to a greased 13-in. x 9-in. baking dish. Sprinkle with 1 cup cheddar cheese. In a small bowl, combine the

Southwest Tuna Noodle Bake

Pecan Chicken with Blue Cheese Sauce

Pecan Chicken with Blue Cheese Sauce

(Pictured above)

Prep: 15 min. **Bake:** 20 min.

Special enough for a holiday feast, this moist chicken is coated with crunchy pecans and drizzled with a rich blue cheese sauce. No one guesses how easy it is to prepare! You could also use turkey breast and adjust the cook time.
—Maggie Ruddy, Altoona, Iowa

  4 boneless skinless chicken breast halves
    (5 ounces *each*)
1/4 teaspoon salt
1/8 teaspoon pepper
1/4 cup all-purpose flour
  1 tablespoon minced fresh rosemary *or*
    1 teaspoon dried rosemary, crushed
1/4 cup butter, melted
  1 tablespoon brown sugar
3/4 cup finely chopped pecans
SAUCE:
  1 cup heavy whipping cream
1/3 cup crumbled blue cheese
  1 tablespoon finely chopped green onion
1/4 teaspoon salt
1/4 teaspoon pepper

Sprinkle the chicken with salt and pepper. In a shallow bowl, combine the flour and rosemary; in a separate shallow bowl, combine the butter and brown sugar. Place the pecans in another shallow bowl. Coat chicken with the flour mixture, then dip in the butter mixture and coat with pecans.

Transfer to a greased baking sheet. Bake at 375° for

20-25 minutes or until juices run clear.

Meanwhile, place the cream in a small saucepan. Bring to a boil; cook and stir for 8-10 minutes or until thickened. Stir in the cheese, onion, salt and pepper. Serve with chicken. **Yield:** 4 servings.

Sun-Dried Tomato Chicken Roll-Ups

(Pictured below)

Prep: 20 min. **Bake:** 20 min.

The filling ingredients complement each other so well and give these roll-ups great flavor. Add a side of veggies for a full meal. —Christine Maddox, Prattville, Alabama

  4 boneless skinless chicken breast halves
    (6 ounces *each*)
  1 egg, lightly beaten
1/2 cup seasoned bread crumbs
3/4 cup shredded part-skim mozzarella cheese
1/2 cup chopped oil-packed sun-dried tomatoes
  2 turkey bacon strips, halved
  2 tablespoons olive oil

Flatten chicken to 1/4-in. thickness. Place egg and bread crumbs in separate shallow bowls. Dip chicken in egg, then coat with bread crumbs.

Combine the mozzarella cheese and tomatoes. Place 1/4 cup cheese mixture down the center of each chicken breast; top each with bacon. Roll up from a short side; secure with toothpicks. Place on a greased baking sheet; drizzle with oil. Bake at 400° for 20-25 minutes or until chicken juices run clear. Discard the toothpicks before serving. **Yield:** 4 servings.

Sun-Dried Tomato Chicken Roll-Ups

Potato Beef Lasagna

Potato Beef Lasagna

(Pictured above)

Prep: 20 min. **Bake:** 70 min. + standing

This recipe comes from our family cookbook. We're big fans of casseroles, and this distinctive lasagna is a cherished favorite. —Suzette Jury, Keene, California

    1 pound lean ground beef
  1/2 pound bulk Italian sausage
    1 can (19 ounces) ready-to-serve tomato-basil soup
    1 can (14-1/2 ounces) Italian diced tomatoes, undrained
    1 package (20 ounces) refrigerated sliced potatoes
    1 medium onion, thinly sliced
    1 cup (4 ounces) shredded part-skim mozzarella cheese
1-1/2 cups (6 ounces) shredded Gruyere *or* Swiss cheese
    3 tablespoons minced fresh parsley

In a large skillet, cook beef and sausage over medium heat until no longer pink; drain. Stir in the soup and tomatoes; set aside. In a greased 13-in. x 9-in. baking dish, layer half of the potatoes and onion. Repeat with the remaining potatoes and onion. Top with mozzarella cheese and meat mixture.

Cover and bake at 350° for 1 hour. Uncover; sprinkle with Gruyere cheese. Bake 10-15 minutes longer or until potatoes are tender and cheese is melted. Let stand 10 minutes before serving. Sprinkle with parsley. **Yield:** 8 servings.

Corned Beef Cabbage Bake

Prep: 20 min. **Bake:** 20 min.

When I was growing up, my parents made every holiday and special occasion fun by preparing festive foods and playing games. I carried on that tradition with our own children and my students. It just wouldn't be St. Patrick's Day without this corned-beef-and-cabbage casserole. —Stephanie Norton, Bettendorf, Iowa

  1/4 cup butter, cubed
    4 cups chopped cabbage
  3/4 cup chopped onion
    1 teaspoon caraway seeds
    1 can (12 ounces) corned beef *or* 12 ounces deli corned beef, chopped
    2 cups (8 ounces) shredded Swiss cheese
  1/4 cup Thousand Island salad dressing
    2 tubes (12 ounces *each*) refrigerated buttermilk biscuits

In a large skillet, melt butter; stir in the cabbage, onion and caraway seeds. Cover and cook over medium heat for 8-10 minutes or until cabbage is crisp-tender, stirring occasionally; set aside.

Meanwhile, in a large bowl, combine the corned beef, Swiss cheese and salad dressing. Separate the biscuits; place 10 biscuits in each of two ungreased 9-in. round baking pans. Press biscuits onto the bottom and halfway up the sides of pans. Add cabbage mixture; top with corned beef mixture.

Bake, uncovered, at 350° for 20-25 minutes or until heated through and the biscuits are golden brown. Cut into wedges. **Yield:** 2 casseroles (4 servings each).

Parmesan Cornflake Chicken

Prep: 10 min. **Bake:** 45 min.

This oven recipe gives you that irresistible fried-chicken taste without the mess or lengthy frying time. I love it!
—Claudia Ruiss, Massapequa, New York

1/2 cup crushed cornflakes
1/3 cup grated Parmesan cheese
1/4 cup seasoned bread crumbs
1-1/2 teaspoons dried parsley flakes
1/2 teaspoon salt
1/8 teaspoon pepper
6 tablespoons butter, melted
1 broiler/fryer chicken (2 to 3 pounds), cut up and skin removed

In a shallow bowl, combine the first six ingredients. Place butter in another shallow bowl. Dip chicken in butter, then roll in cornflake mixture.

Arrange chicken on a rack in a foil-lined 15-in. x 10-in. x 1-in. baking pan. Bake, uncovered, at 350° for 45-50 minutes or until chicken juices run clear. **Yield:** 4 servings.

Apricot-Glazed Ham

Round Steak with Potatoes

(Pictured below)

Prep: 20 min. **Bake:** 2-1/2 hours

When you're craving a meat-and-potatoes meal, try this terrific dinner. Braising the steak will ensure tenderness.
—Taryn Kuebelbeck, Plymouth, Minnesota

2 pounds boneless beef top round steak
1 teaspoon salt
1/2 teaspoon pepper
2 tablespoons canola oil
1 can (10-3/4 ounces) condensed golden mushroom soup, undiluted
1-1/4 cups water
1 cup chopped celery
1 cup chopped sweet red pepper
1/2 cup chopped onion
1/4 teaspoon dried thyme
12 small red potatoes

Cut steak into six pieces; sprinkle with salt and pepper. In a Dutch oven, brown meat in oil on both sides. Stir in the soup, water, celery, red pepper, onion and thyme. Cover and bake at 350° for 1 hour.

Add potatoes; cover and bake 1-1/2 hours longer or until steak and vegetables are tender. **Yield:** 6 servings.

Apricot-Glazed Ham

(Pictured above)

Prep: 20 min. **Bake:** 2 hours + standing

Chutney adds a delightful sweetness to the glaze on this tender ham. Serve it to guests and prepare to hear raves!
—Chinarose, tasteofhome.com Community

1 boneless fully cooked ham (6 pounds)
2 teaspoons whole cloves
2 cups apple cider *or* juice
1/4 cup apricot preserves
3 tablespoons mango chutney
3 tablespoons Dijon mustard
1 cup packed brown sugar

Place ham on a rack in a shallow roasting pan. Score the surface of the ham, making diamond shapes 1/2 in. deep; insert a clove in each diamond. Pour cider into pan.

In a small saucepan, combine the preserves, chutney and mustard. Cook and stir over medium heat until preserves are melted; brush over ham. Press brown sugar onto ham. Bake, uncovered, at 325° for 2 to 2-1/2 hours or until a meat thermometer reads 140°, basting occasionally with pan drippings. Cover loosely with foil if ham browns too quickly.

Let the ham stand for 10 minutes before slicing. **Yield:** 18 servings.

Round Steak with Potatoes

Cajun Chicken Fettuccine

(Pictured below)

Prep: 25 min. **Bake:** 25 min.

For this fast-to-fix casserole, I combined two pasta sauces and mixed in Cajun seasoning for a kick. Using frozen onions and peppers speeds up the preparation even more. You could also try adding mushrooms or frozen peas.
—Rebecca Reece, Henderson, Nevada

  8 ounces uncooked fettuccine
  1 large sweet onion, halved and sliced
  1 medium green pepper, cut into 1/4-inch
    strips
  1 medium sweet red pepper, cut into 1/4-inch
    strips
  2 tablespoons olive oil
  2 cups cubed cooked chicken
  4 teaspoons Cajun seasoning
  1 teaspoon minced garlic
  1 jar (17 ounces) Alfredo sauce
1/2 cup spaghetti sauce
  2 cups (8 ounces) shredded part-skim
    mozzarella cheese
1/2 cup grated Parmesan cheese

Cook the fettuccine according to package directions. Meanwhile, in a large skillet, saute onion and peppers in oil until tender. Add the chicken, Cajun seasoning and garlic; heat through. Transfer to a large bowl. Drain the fettuccine; add to chicken mixture. Stir in Alfredo and spaghetti sauces.

Transfer to a greased 13-in. x 9-in. baking dish. Sprinkle with cheeses. Cover and bake at 375° for 15 minutes. Uncover; bake 10-15 minutes longer or until golden brown. **Yield:** 8 servings.

Cajun Chicken Fettuccine

Tuna Mac and Cheese Bake

Tuna Mac and Cheese Bake

(Pictured above)

Prep: 15 min. **Bake:** 30 min.

You'll want to toss out your other tuna casserole recipes because this one's the ultimate! It's easy, tasty and economical, too. —Bonnie Hord, Lee's Summit, Missouri

  1 package (7-1/4 ounces) macaroni and cheese
    dinner mix
  1 can (12 ounces) light water-packed tuna,
    drained and flaked
  1 can (10-3/4 ounces) condensed cream of
    mushroom soup, undiluted
1-1/3 cups milk
  2 packages (9 ounces *each*) frozen peas and
    pearl onions
  1 can (4 ounces) mushroom stems and pieces,
    drained
  1 can (2.8 ounces) french-fried onions, *divided*

Prepare macaroni dinner mix according to package directions. Add tuna, soup, milk, peas, mushrooms and half of the fried onions. Place in a greased 11-in. x 7-in. baking dish. Bake, uncovered, at 325° for 25 minutes.

Sprinkle with remaining onions; bake 5 minutes longer or until heated through. **Yield:** 8 servings.

Mac and Cheese Mix-Ins

TAKE plain mac and cheese from ordinary to exciting by mixing in any of these additional ingredients:

Diced cooked bacon	Sauteed mushrooms
Cooked peas	Sliced cooked hot dogs
Roasted peppers	Fresh or dried herbs
Sloppy joe meat	Steamed broccoli

Pizza Lover's Pie

(Pictured below)

Prep: 20 min. **Bake:** 20 min.

Can't get enough pizza? Dig into this fun pie filled with sausage, mushrooms, onion, mozzarella cheese and more.
—Carol Gillespie, Chambersburg, Pennsylvania

☑ This recipe includes Nutrition Facts and Diabetic Exchanges.

- 1/4 pound bulk pork sausage
- 1/2 cup chopped green pepper
- 1/4 cup chopped onion
- 1 loaf (1 pound) frozen bread dough, thawed and halved
- 2 cups (8 ounces) shredded part-skim mozzarella cheese
- 1/2 cup grated Parmesan cheese
- 1 can (8 ounces) pizza sauce
- 8 slices pepperoni
- 1 can (4 ounces) mushroom stems and pieces, drained
- 1/4 teaspoon dried oregano, *divided*

In a large skillet, cook the sausage, pepper and onion over medium heat until meat is no longer pink; drain. Set aside.

Roll half of dough into a 12-in. circle. Transfer to a greased 9-in. deep-dish pie plate. Layer with half of the mozzarella cheese, Parmesan cheese and pizza sauce. Top with sausage mixture, pepperoni, mushrooms and 1/8 teaspoon oregano. Roll out remaining dough to fit top of pie. Place over filling; seal edges. Layer with the remaining pizza sauce, cheeses and oregano.

Bake at 400° for 18-22 minutes or until golden brown. **Yield:** 8 servings.

Nutrition Facts: 1 piece equals 305 calories, 12 g fat (5 g saturated fat), 27 mg cholesterol, 743 mg sodium, 32 g carbohydrate, 3 g fiber, 17 g protein. **Diabetic Exchanges:** 2 starch, 1 lean meat, 1 fat.

Pizza Lover's Pie

Creamy Spinach Sausage Pasta

Creamy Spinach Sausage Pasta

(Pictured above)

Prep: 15 min. **Bake:** 45 min.

So rich and cheesy, this pasta dinner featuring creamed spinach and Italian sausage practically guarantees full stomachs and satisfied smiles. For time-saving convenience, I like to assemble this dish the night before, store it in the refrigerator and pop it in the oven the next day.
—Susie Sizemore, Collinsville, Virginia

- 3 cups uncooked rigatoni *or* large tube pasta
- 1 pound bulk Italian sausage
- 1 cup finely chopped onion
- 1 can (14-1/2 ounces) Italian diced tomatoes, undrained
- 1 package (10 ounces) frozen creamed spinach, thawed
- 1 package (8 ounces) cream cheese, softened
- 2 cups (8 ounces) shredded part-skim mozzarella cheese, *divided*

Cook the pasta according to the package directions. Meanwhile, in a Dutch oven, cook sausage and onion over medium heat until sausage is no longer pink; drain. Stir in the tomatoes, spinach, cream cheese and 1 cup mozzarella cheese. Transfer to a greased 11-in. x 7-in. baking dish.

Cover and bake at 350° for 35 minutes. Uncover; sprinkle with remaining cheese. Bake 10 minutes longer or until cheese is melted. **Yield:** 5 servings.

Six-Cheese Lasagna

Six-Cheese Lasagna
(Pictured above)
Prep: 25 min. **Bake:** 1 hour + standing

This amazing lasagna looks and tastes so good, it's hard to believe that it takes less than 30 minutes to assemble! No-boil noodles and jarred sauce save time and cut down on pots and pans, too. —Jodi Anderson, Vassar, Kansas

- 1 pound ground beef
- 1 pound bulk Italian sausage
- 1 jar (26 ounces) meatless spaghetti sauce
- 2 eggs, beaten
- 1 carton (15 ounces) ricotta cheese
- 1-1/2 cups (12 ounces) 4% cottage cheese
- 1/4 cup grated Parmesan cheese
- 1/4 cup grated Romano *or* Asiago cheese
- 8 no-cook lasagna noodles
- 4 cups (16 ounces) shredded part-skim mozzarella cheese
- 6 slices provolone cheese, quartered

In a large skillet, cook beef and sausage over medium heat until no longer pink; drain. Stir in spaghetti sauce. In a large bowl, combine the eggs, ricotta, cottage, Parmesan and Romano cheeses.

Spread 1-1/2 cups sauce mixture in a greased 13-in. x 9-in. baking dish. Top with four noodles. Spread 1-1/2 cups sauce to edges of noodles. Sprinkle with 2 cups mozzarella cheese. Top with the ricotta mixture, provolone cheese and the remaining noodles, sauce and mozzarella cheese.

Cover and bake at 350° for 50 minutes. Uncover; bake 10 minutes longer or until cheese is melted. Let stand for 15 minutes before cutting. **Yield:** 12 servings.

Cornish Game Hens
(Pictured below)
Prep: 15 min. **Bake:** 35 min.

Sprinkled with crunchy almonds and parsley, these special hens are delectable and so impressive on the table. Keep them in mind for your next holiday feast or dinner party. —Kara de la Vega, Santa Rosa, California

- 1/2 teaspoon salt
- 1/2 teaspoon dill weed
- 1/2 teaspoon dried oregano
- 1/2 teaspoon pepper
- 1/4 teaspoon paprika
- 2 Cornish game hens (20 ounces *each*), split lengthwise
- 1 tablespoon olive oil
- 1/4 cup chopped green onions
- 1/2 teaspoon minced garlic
- 1/2 cup chicken broth
- 1/4 cup orange juice concentrate
- 2 tablespoons slivered almonds, toasted
- 1 tablespoon minced fresh parsley

In a small bowl, combine first five ingredients; sprinkle over hens. In a large skillet, cook hens over medium-high heat in oil until browned on both sides. Transfer to an ungreased 13-in. x 9-in. baking dish; set aside and keep warm.

In the same skillet, saute the green onions and garlic until tender. Stir in broth and orange juice concentrate; pour over hens. Bake, uncovered, at 350° for 35-40 minutes or until meat is tender and juices run clear. To serve, drizzle with pan juices and sprinkle with almonds and parsley. **Yield:** 4 servings.

Cornish Game Hens

Ham & Spinach Casserole

Ham & Spinach Casserole

(Pictured above)

Prep: 25 min. **Bake:** 20 min.

This is down-home cooking at its best! Ham and veggies combine with a creamy sauce and pretty topping to create the hearty meal-in-one from our Test Kitchen staff. To easily form a lattice crust, see the tip box at right.

   3 cups cubed fully cooked ham
   1 package (16 ounces) frozen sliced carrots, thawed
   1 can (10-3/4 ounces) condensed cream of potato soup, undiluted
   1 package (10 ounces) frozen creamed spinach, thawed
1/4 cup water
1/4 teaspoon pepper
1/8 teaspoon salt
   1 tube (4 ounces) refrigerated crescent rolls

In a large nonstick skillet coated with cooking spray, cook ham over medium heat for 3-5 minutes or until lightly browned. Stir in carrots, soup, spinach, water, pepper and salt. Bring to a boil. Reduce heat, simmer for 5-10 minutes or until heated through. Pour into a greased 8-in. square baking dish.

Unroll the crescent roll dough; separate into two rectangles. Seal the seams and perforations. Cut each rectangle lengthwise into four strips; make a lattice crust. Bake at 375° for 18-22 minutes or until bubbly and crust is golden brown. **Yield:** 4 servings.

How To Make a Lattice Crust

Lay out strips of dough vertically. Fold every other strip back roughly halfway. Lay another strip horizontally at the fold. Unfold the strips.

Fold the alternate strips about halfway up; lay another strip horizontally at the fold. Unfold the strips.

Add the remaining strips, lifting and weaving strips to complete the lattice design.

Chapter 17

Fast, Delicious...and Nutritious

SPEEDY RECIPES are a must for most family cooks. But what if you also want foods that are on the lighter side?

Page through this doubly delightful chapter, and you'll find delicious dishes that are both quick to fix and better for you. See for yourself by checking the complete Nutrition Facts at the end of each recipe.

Whether someone in your household is on a special diet or you just want to cook healthier for your family, you'll love favorites such as Salsa Chicken Skillet, Marinated Flank Steak, Herb Bubble Bread and Basil Parmesan Puffs.

And you won't want to skip dessert—luscious Tropical Pie!

GUILT-FREE FARE. Eggplant Zucchini Bolognese (p. 267).

 All recipes in this chapter include Nutrition Facts. Most include Diabetic Exchanges.

Fruited Turkey Salad

(Pictured above)

Prep/Total Time: 25 min.

 *This tangy, refreshing salad is ideal for lunch or even dinner on a warm day. The creamy dressing coating the turkey and fruit never lets on that it's light...but it is, thanks to fat-free cream cheese as well as reduced-fat mayo and sour cream.*
—Angela Miller, Nampa, Idaho

1 medium apple, diced
1-1/4 cups cubed cooked turkey
1 can (8 ounces) unsweetened pineapple chunks, drained
1 cup halved seedless grapes
1/4 cup fat-free cream cheese
2 tablespoons reduced-fat sour cream
1 tablespoon lemon juice
1 tablespoon reduced-fat mayonnaise

In a serving bowl, combine the apple, turkey, pineapple and grapes. In another bowl, beat cream cheese until smooth. Add sour cream, lemon juice and mayonnaise. Fold into turkey mixture. **Yield:** 4 servings.

Nutrition Facts: 1 cup equals 182 calories, 5 g fat (1 g saturated fat), 38 mg cholesterol, 146 mg sodium, 20 g carbohydrate, 2 g fiber, 16 g protein. **Diabetic Exchanges:** 2 lean meat, 1 fruit.

Orange Corn Bread

(Pictured at left)

Prep/Total Time: 30 min.

You'll need only 30 minutes to whip up this made-from-scratch corn bread. Because the recipe takes advantage of lighter ingredients, you can enjoy a piece guilt-free. Serve it warm or cold...either way, you'll love the citrus flavor.
—Sharon Runyan, Fort Wayne, Indiana

- 1 cup all-purpose flour
- 1 cup cornmeal
- 1/3 cup sugar
- 2 teaspoons baking powder
- 1/2 teaspoon baking soda
- 1/2 teaspoon salt
- 1 cup fat-free milk
- 1/2 cup egg substitute
- 1/4 cup orange juice
- 2 tablespoons canola oil

In a large bowl, combine the first six ingredients. In a small bowl, combine the milk, egg substitute, orange juice and oil; stir into dry ingredients just until combined (batter will be thin).

Pour the batter into a greased 9-in. square baking pan. Bake at 400° for 18-22 minutes or until a toothpick inserted near the center of bread comes out clean. **Yield:** 9 servings.

Nutrition Facts: 1 piece equals 182 calories, 4 g fat (trace saturated fat), 1 mg cholesterol, 330 mg sodium, 32 g carbohydrate, 2 g fiber, 5 g protein. **Diabetic Exchanges:** 2 starch, 1/2 fat.

Tomato Zucchini Saute

Prep/Total Time: 15 min.

Add a burst of color and garden-fresh flavor to your plate with this tasty side. I usually serve it in a bowl with a spoon because the vegetables produce their own delicious broth—no one will want to leave it behind!
—Claudia Ruiss, Massapequa, New York

- 2 medium zucchini, cut into 3/4-inch cubes
- 1 medium yellow summer squash, cut into 3/4-inch cubes
- 1/3 cup chopped onion
- 1 tablespoon olive oil
- 6 medium plum tomatoes, chopped
- 3/4 teaspoon salt
- 1/4 teaspoon pepper

Grated Parmesan cheese

In a large skillet, saute the zucchini, squash and onion in oil for 5 minutes.

Add the tomatoes, salt and pepper. Cook and stir until the vegetables are tender. Sprinkle with Parmesan cheese. **Yield:** 6 servings.

Nutrition Facts: 3/4 cup equals 52 calories, 3 g fat (trace saturated fat), 0 cholesterol, 306 mg sodium, 7 g carbohydrate, 2 g fiber, 2 g protein. **Diabetic Exchanges:** 1 vegetable, 1/2 fat.

Herb Bubble Bread

(Pictured below)

Prep: 20 min. + rising **Bake:** 25 min. + cooling

This well-seasoned, cheesy bread is an absolute must-try! I never have leftovers when I present a loaf to family and friends. Fun to eat, it's a hit with everyone.
—Joan Anderson, West Covina, California

- 1/2 cup grated Parmesan cheese
- 3/4 teaspoon dried parsley flakes
- 1/4 teaspoon dill weed
- 1/8 teaspoon *each* dried thyme, basil and rosemary, crushed
- 1/4 cup butter, melted
- 2 teaspoons minced garlic
- 1 loaf (1 pound) frozen bread dough, thawed

In a small bowl, combine the cheese and seasonings. In another bowl, combine butter and garlic; set aside.

Divide dough into 16 pieces. Roll into balls. Coat balls in butter mixture, then dip in cheese mixture. Place in a greased 9-in. x 5-in. loaf pan.

Cover and let rise in a warm place until doubled, about 1 hour. Bake at 350° for 22-26 minutes or until golden brown. (Cover loosely with foil if top browns too quickly.) Cool for 10 minutes before removing from pan to a wire rack. Serve warm. **Yield:** 16 servings.

Nutrition Facts: 1 piece equals 110 calories, 4 g fat (2 g saturated fat), 8 mg cholesterol, 212 mg sodium, 14 g carbohydrate, 1 g fiber, 4 g protein. **Diabetic Exchanges:** 1 starch, 1/2 fat.

Herb Bubble Bread

Asian Chicken with Pasta

(Pictured below)

Prep/Total Time: 25 min.

Even picky eaters like this fast main course. A convenient coleslaw mix brings a pleasing crunch to the mild-flavored pasta. —Rebecca Sams, Oak Harbor, Ohio

- 1/2 pound uncooked angel hair pasta
- 1 pound chicken tenderloins, cut into 1-inch cubes
- 1/3 cup prepared balsamic vinaigrette
- 1/3 cup prepared Italian salad dressing
- 1 package (12 ounces) broccoli coleslaw mix
- 1/2 pound sliced fresh mushrooms
- 3/4 cup julienned sweet red pepper
- 1/2 cup sliced onion
- 1/2 teaspoon garlic powder
- 1/2 teaspoon ground ginger
- 1/4 teaspoon salt
- 1/8 teaspoon pepper

Cook pasta according to package directions. Meanwhile, in a large skillet, saute chicken in vinaigrette and salad dressing until no longer pink. Remove and keep warm.

In the same skillet, saute coleslaw mix, mushrooms, red pepper and onion until tender. Add the seasonings. Stir in the chicken; heat through. Drain pasta. Add to chicken mixture; toss to coat. **Yield:** 6 servings.

Nutrition Facts: 1-1/2 cups equals 320 calories, 8 g fat (1 g saturated fat), 44 mg cholesterol, 474 mg sodium, 38 g carbohydrate, 4 g fiber, 25 g protein. **Diabetic Exchanges:** 3 very lean meat, 2 starch, 1 vegetable, 1 fat.

Asian Chicken with Pasta

Watermelon Gazpacho

Watermelon Gazpacho

(Pictured above)

Prep/Total Time: 25 min.

This cool soup is delightfully simple and elegant. Serve it as a side...or with pita and hummus for a light summer meal. It's so refreshing, my guests always love it. —Nicole Deelah, Nashville, Tennessee

- 4 cups cubed watermelon, seeded, *divided*
- 2 tablespoons lime juice
- 1 tablespoon grated lime peel
- 1 teaspoon minced fresh gingerroot
- 1 teaspoon salt
- 1 cup chopped tomato
- 1/2 cup chopped cucumber
- 1/2 cup chopped green pepper
- 1/4 cup minced fresh cilantro
- 2 tablespoons chopped green onions
- 1 tablespoon finely chopped seeded jalapeno pepper

Puree 3 cups watermelon in a blender. Cut remaining watermelon into 1/2-in. pieces; set aside.

In a large bowl, combine watermelon puree, lime juice, lime peel, ginger and salt. Stir in tomato, cucumber, green pepper, cilantro, onions, jalapeno and cubed watermelon. Chill until serving. **Yield:** 4 servings.

Editor's Note: When cutting hot peppers, disposable gloves are recommended. Avoid touching your face.

Nutrition Facts: 1 cup equals 58 calories, trace fat (trace saturated fat), 0 cholesterol, 599 mg sodium, 18 g carbohydrate, 2 g fiber, 1 g protein. **Diabetic Exchange:** 1 fruit.

Turkey Stir-Fry with Cabbage

(Pictured below)

Prep/Total Time: 30 min.

Cabbage makes a crunchy alternative to rice in this delicious stir-fry coated with a sweet-savory sauce. Packed with flavor, it's a terrific dinner solution on busy nights.
—Didi Desjardins, Dartmouth, Massachusetts

    1 tablespoon cornstarch
1-1/4 cups reduced-sodium chicken broth
  1/3 cup plus 2 tablespoons mango chutney
4-1/4 teaspoons reduced-sodium soy sauce
    1 teaspoon Chinese five-spice powder
    1 teaspoon minced garlic
    1 package (20 ounces) turkey breast
       tenderloins, cut into thin strips
    7 teaspoons sesame oil, *divided*
    1 large sweet red pepper, julienned
1-1/2 cups fresh snow peas
    6 cups shredded cabbage

In a small bowl, combine cornstarch and broth until smooth; stir in the chutney, soy sauce, five-spice powder and garlic.

In a large skillet, saute turkey in 3 teaspoons oil for 6-8 minutes or until no longer pink; set aside. In same skillet, saute red pepper and snow peas in 2 teaspoons oil for 2-3 minutes or until crisp-tender. Stir soy sauce mixture and add to skillet. Bring to a boil; cook and stir for 2 minutes or until thickened. Add the turkey; heat through.

Meanwhile, in a large nonstick skillet coated with cooking spray, saute the cabbage in the remaining oil for 5 minutes or until crisp-tender. Serve with the turkey mixture. **Yield:** 4 servings.

Nutrition Facts: 1-1/4 cups stir-fry with 1 cup cabbage equals 410 calories, 10 g fat (2 g saturated fat), 69 mg cholesterol, 803 mg sodium, 42 g carbohydrate, 5 g fiber, 38 g protein.

Turkey Stir-Fry with Cabbage

Marinated Flank Steak

Marinated Flank Steak

(Pictured above)

Prep: 10 min. + marinating **Grill:** 20 min.

Here, seven simple ingredients come together in a flavorful marinade to perk up grilled or broiled flank steak. Try putting the strips on a salad with your favorite dressing, then round out the menu with fresh bread or rolls.
—Lisa Ruehlow, Blaine, Minnesota

    3 tablespoons canola oil
    2 tablespoons lemon juice
    2 tablespoons Worcestershire sauce
    1 tablespoon dried minced garlic
    1 tablespoon Greek seasoning
    1 tablespoon brown sugar
    1 teaspoon onion powder
    1 beef flank steak (1-1/2 pounds)

In a large resealable plastic bag, combine the first seven ingredients; add the steak. Seal bag and turn to coat; refrigerate for 6 hours or overnight.

If grilling the steak, coat the grill rack with cooking spray before starting the grill. Drain and discard the marinade. Grill the steak, covered, over medium heat or broil 4-6 in. from heat for 9-11 minutes on each side or until steak reaches desired doneness (for medium-rare, a meat thermometer should read 145°; medium, 160°; well-done, 170°).

To serve the steak, thinly slice across the grain. **Yield:** 6 servings.

Nutrition Facts: 3 ounces cooked beef equals 196 calories, 11 g fat (4 g saturated fat), 54 mg cholesterol, 269 mg sodium, 2 g carbohydrate, trace fiber, 22 g protein. **Diabetic Exchanges:** 3 lean meat, 1 fat.

Vegetable Pasta Salad

(Pictured below)

Prep: 20 min. + chilling

Filled with the goodness of garden-fresh veggies, this pasta bowl is colorful, refreshing and perfect for potlucks. It makes a wonderful partner for a variety of meats.
—*Joy Beck, Cincinnati, Ohio*

　4 cups uncooked tricolor spiral pasta
　1 jar (16 ounces) salsa
　2 cups frozen corn, thawed
1-1/2 cups sliced halved cucumber
　1 cup halved cherry tomatoes
　1 medium red onion, chopped
　1 can (8 ounces) no-salt-added tomato sauce
　2 tablespoons minced fresh parsley
　1 tablespoon red wine vinegar

Cook the pasta according to package directions; rinse in cold water and drain. In a large serving bowl, combine pasta and the remaining ingredients. Refrigerate for at least 30 minutes before serving. **Yield:** 13 servings.

Nutrition Facts: 3/4 cup equals 144 calories, 1 g fat (trace saturated fat), 0 cholesterol, 173 mg sodium, 29 g carbohydrate, 3 g fiber, 4 g protein. **Diabetic Exchanges:** 1-1/2 starch, 1 vegetable.

Tropical Pie

Vegetable Pasta Salad

Tropical Pie

(Pictured above)

Prep: 20 min. + chilling

I came up with this recipe when we needed a light dessert on a hot day—and I didn't want to heat up the kitchen by turning on the oven. I just grabbed ingredients from the fridge and pantry, and it took no time at all to create a cool, creamy pie bursting with pineapple and bananas.
—*Audrey Arno, Enid, Oklahoma*

　1 can (20 ounces) unsweetened crushed
　　pineapple
　2 medium firm bananas, cut into 1/4-inch slices
　4 ounces fat-free cream cheese, softened
　4 teaspoons sugar substitute equivalent to
　　4 teaspoons sugar
　2 cups reduced-fat whipped topping, *divided*
　1 reduced-fat graham cracker crust (9 inches)
　4 maraschino cherries, halved
　2 tablespoons chopped walnuts, toasted

Drain the pineapple, reserving the juice. Place the sliced bananas in the juice; set aside. In a small bowl, beat the cream cheese, sugar substitute and 1 tablespoon reserved pineapple juice until smooth. Fold in 1/4 cup whipped topping.

Drain bananas. Arrange half of bananas in bottom of crust. Carefully spread with cream cheese mixture. Top with pineapple, remaining bananas and whipped topping. Garnish with cherries and walnuts. Refrigerate for 4 hours. **Yield:** 8 servings.

Nutrition Facts: 1 piece equals 240 calories, 6 g fat (3 g saturated fat), 1 mg cholesterol, 173 mg sodium, 41 g carbohydrate, 1 g fiber, 4 g protein.

Sauteed Corn with Tomatoes & Basil

(Pictured above)

Prep/Total Time: 15 min.

We harvest the vegetables and basil from our backyard garden right before preparing this recipe. It's so fresh-tasting, easy and delicious with grilled fish or meat.
—Patricia Nieh, Portola Valley, California

- 1 cup fresh *or* frozen corn
- 1 tablespoon olive oil
- 2 cups cherry tomatoes, halved
- 1/4 teaspoon salt
- 1/4 teaspoon pepper
- 3 fresh basil leaves, thinly sliced

In a large skillet, saute the corn in oil until crisp-tender. Stir in the tomatoes, salt and pepper; cook 1 minute longer. Remove from the heat; sprinkle with basil. **Yield:** 4 servings.

Nutrition Facts: 3/4 cup equals 85 calories, 4 g fat (1 g saturated fat), 0 cholesterol, 161 mg sodium, 12 g carbohydrate, 2 g fiber, 2 g protein. **Diabetic Exchanges:** 1 starch, 1/2 fat.

Baked Tilapia

(Pictured above)

Prep/Total Time: 20 min.

A quick and easy crumb coating makes this flavorful fish entree ideal for dinner on busy weeknights. Try the breading on cod instead of tilapia for a change of pace.
—Patricia Nieh, Portola Valley, California

- 3/4 cup soft bread crumbs
- 1/3 cup grated Parmesan cheese
- 1 teaspoon garlic salt
- 1 teaspoon dried oregano
- 4 tilapia fillets (5 ounces *each*)

In a shallow bowl, combine the bread crumbs, Parmesan cheese, garlic salt and oregano. Coat the tilapia fillets in crumb mixture. Place on a baking sheet coated with cooking spray.

Bake at 425° for 8-12 minutes or until the fish flakes easily with a fork. **Yield:** 4 servings.

Nutrition Facts: 1 fillet equals 143 calories, 2 g fat (1 g saturated fat), 72 mg cholesterol, 356 mg sodium, 2 g carbohydrate, trace fiber, 28 g protein. **Diabetic Exchange:** 4 very lean meat.

Turkey Divan

Turkey Divan

(Pictured above)

Prep/Total Time: 30 min.

It looks and tastes decadent...but at just 291 calories per serving, this classic main course from our Test Kitchen staff isn't much of a splurge. Pair it with a side salad and slice of whole grain bread for a complete meal.

1-1/2 cups water
  16 fresh asparagus spears, trimmed
   2 egg whites
   1 egg
   2 tablespoons fat-free milk
1-1/4 cups seasoned bread crumbs
   1 package (17.6 ounces) turkey breast cutlets
 1/4 cup butter, cubed
   8 slices deli ham
   8 slices reduced-fat Swiss cheese

In a large skillet, bring water to a boil. Add asparagus; cover and boil for 3 minutes. Drain and pat dry.

In a shallow bowl, beat the egg whites, egg and milk. Place the seasoned bread crumbs in another shallow bowl. Dip the turkey in the egg mixture, then coat with the bread crumbs.

In a large skillet, cook the turkey in butter in batches for 2-3 minutes on each side or until the meat is no longer pink. Top with a deli ham slice, two asparagus spears and Swiss cheese. Cover and cook for 1 minute or until the cheese is melted. Transfer to a platter; keep warm. **Yield:** 8 servings.

Nutrition Facts: 1 serving equals 291 calories, 12 g fat (6 g saturated fat), 100 mg cholesterol, 595 mg sodium, 16 g carbohydrate, 1 g fiber, 31 g protein. **Diabetic Exchanges:** 3 lean meat, 2 fat, 1 starch.

Basil Parmesan Puffs

(Pictured below)

Prep/Total Time: 20 min.

With pretty flecks of green, these cute little bites are wonderful served with soup, salads or pasta for a meal—or even just as a snack! Minced fresh basil and Parmesan cheese stirred into the dough add fantastic flavor.
       —Amber McKinley, Punta Gorda, Florida

 3/4 cup water
   6 tablespoons butter, cubed
 3/4 teaspoon salt
 3/4 cup all-purpose flour
   4 eggs
   1 cup minced fresh basil
   1 cup grated Parmesan cheese

In a large saucepan, bring water, butter and salt to a boil. Add flour all at once and stir until a smooth ball forms. Remove from the heat; let stand for 5 minutes. Add the eggs, one at a time, beating well after each addition. Continue beating until mixture is smooth and shiny. Stir in basil and cheese.

Drop by rounded tablespoonfuls 1 in. apart onto greased baking sheets. Bake at 400° for 18-20 minutes or until golden brown. Remove to wire racks. Serve warm. **Yield:** about 2 dozen.

Nutrition Facts: 1 puff equals 59 calories, 4 g fat (2 g saturated fat), 41 mg cholesterol, 139 mg sodium, 3 g carbohydrate, trace fiber, 2 g protein. **Diabetic Exchange:** 1 fat.

Basil Parmesan Puffs

Olive Orange Salad

Eggplant Zucchini Bolognese

(Pictured below and on page 258)

Prep: 30 min. **Cook:** 20 min.

Rustic comfort and fresh taste combine in this ground beef dinner. I roast the vegetables while the pasta cooks, making it nice and quick. —*Trisha Kruse, Eagle, Idaho*

- 1 package (16 ounces) penne pasta
- 1 small eggplant, peeled and cut into 1-inch pieces
- 1 medium zucchini, cut into 1/4-inch slices
- 1 medium yellow summer squash, cut into 1/4-inch slices
- 1 cup chopped onion
- 2 tablespoons olive oil
- 2 teaspoons minced garlic
- 1 teaspoon salt
- 1/2 teaspoon pepper
- 1 pound lean ground beef
- 1 can (28 ounces) tomato puree
- 1 tablespoon Italian seasoning
- 1 tablespoon brown sugar
- 8 teaspoons grated Parmesan cheese

Cook the pasta according to the package directions. In a large bowl, combine the eggplant, zucchini, squash, onion, oil, garlic, salt and pepper. Transfer to two 15-in. x 10-in. x 1-in. baking pans coated with cooking spray. Bake at 425° for 20-25 minutes or until tender.

Meanwhile, in a large skillet, cook beef over medium heat until no longer pink; drain. Stir in the tomato puree, Italian seasoning and brown sugar. Drain pasta; stir in tomato mixture and roasted vegetables. Sprinkle with cheese. **Yield:** 8 servings.

Nutrition Facts: 1-1/2 cups equals 395 calories, 10 g fat (3 g saturated fat), 36 mg cholesterol, 378 mg sodium, 56 g carbohydrate, 5 g fiber, 22 g protein.

Olive Orange Salad

(Pictured above)

Prep/Total Time: 20 min.

This simple side salad is fancy enough to serve guests but easy enough to make during the week. It pairs well with spicy dishes such as blackened fish or zesty sausage. —*Carol Gaus, Elk Grove Village, Illinois*

- 6 medium navel oranges
- 6 lettuce leaves
- 6 thin slices red onion, separated into rings
- 6 tablespoons sliced ripe olives
- 6 tablespoons Italian salad dressing

Peel and cut each orange widthwise into three slices. Place lettuce leaves on individual salad plates. Top with orange slices and onion. Sprinkle with olives; drizzle with dressing. **Yield:** 6 servings.

Nutrition Facts: 1 serving equals 138 calories, 7 g fat (1 g saturated fat), 0 cholesterol, 330 mg sodium, 20 g carbohydrate, 4 g fiber, 2 g protein. **Diabetic Exchanges:** 1 fruit, 1 fat.

Eggplant Advice

PLAN to fix Eggplant Zucchini Bolognese (recipe above right)? Select an eggplant with a smooth skin; avoid those with soft or brown spots. Store the eggplant in a cool dry place for 1 to 2 days. To store it up to 5 days, place it in a plastic bag and refrigerate.

Eggplant Zucchini Bolognese

Salsa Chicken Skillet

(Pictured above)

Prep/Total Time: 25 min.

Give dinner a boost anytime with this festive main dish. No one will suspect that the zesty chicken has only 6 g of fat per serving.   —Nancy Daugherty, Cortland, Ohio

   2 cups uncooked instant brown rice
   1 pound boneless skinless chicken breasts, cut into 1-inch cubes
   2 teaspoons canola oil
   1 cup chunky salsa
1/4 cup orange marmalade
   2 tablespoons lime juice
   1 tablespoon brown sugar
1/4 teaspoon ground allspice
   2 tablespoons minced fresh cilantro

Cook rice according to package directions. Meanwhile, in a large nonstick skillet coated with cooking spray, cook chicken in oil over medium heat for 5 minutes or until juices run clear.

Stir in the salsa, marmalade, lime juice, brown sugar and allspice. Bring to a boil. Reduce heat; simmer, uncovered, for 2 minutes. Sprinkle with cilantro. Serve with rice. **Yield:** 4 servings.

Nutrition Facts: 2/3 cup chicken mixture with 3/4 cup rice equals 397 calories, 6 g fat (1 g saturated fat), 63 mg cholesterol, 357 mg sodium, 53 g carbohydrate, 4 g fiber, 27 g protein.

Snow Pea & Carrot Saute

Prep/Total Time: 20 min.

With carrot strips and snow peas, this skillet side from our Test Kitchen staff makes a colorful accompaniment for any entree. If you're short on time, look for matchstick carrots at the grocery store to cut down on prep work.

   1 pound fresh snow peas
   1 tablespoon butter
   2 medium carrots, julienned
   1 garlic clove, minced
   3 tablespoons honey
1/4 teaspoon salt
1/8 teaspoon pepper

In a large skillet, saute snow peas in butter for 3 minutes. Add the carrots and garlic; saute 1-2 minutes longer or until vegetables are crisp-tender. Add the remaining ingredients; heat through. **Yield:** 5 servings.

Nutrition Facts: 3/4 cup equals 108 calories, 3 g fat (1 g saturated fat), 6 mg cholesterol, 155 mg sodium, 20 g carbohydrate, 3 g fiber, 3 g protein. **Diabetic Exchanges:** 2 vegetable, 1/2 starch.

Pork Chops with Mango Salsa

(Pictured below)

Prep: 20 min. + marinating **Grill:** 10 min.

Bits of mango, sweet onion and pineapple make a fresh and fruity topping for these mouth-watering pork chops marinated in bottled Italian salad dressing. For an extra layer of flavor, add chopped cilantro to the salsa.
—Pete Johnson, Chippewa Falls, Wisconsin

> 3/4 cup plus 1 tablespoon Italian salad dressing with roasted red pepper and Parmesan, *divided*
> 6 boneless pork loin chops (5 ounces *each*)
> 1 medium mango, peeled and diced
> 1/2 cup chopped sweet onion
> 1/2 cup chopped fresh pineapple

Pour 3/4 cup Italian salad dressing into a large resealable plastic bag; add the pork chops. Seal the bag and turn to coat; refrigerate for 8 hours or overnight, turning occasionally.

In a small bowl, combine mango, onion, pineapple and remaining salad dressing. Chill until serving.

Drain and discard marinade. Grill chops, covered, over medium heat or broil 4 in. from the heat for 4-6 minutes on each side or until a meat thermometer reads 160°. Serve with salsa. **Yield:** 6 servings.

Nutrition Facts: 1 pork chop with 1/3 cup mango salsa equals 246 calories, 9 g fat (3 g saturated fat), 68 mg cholesterol, 297 mg sodium, 11 g carbohydrate, 1 g fiber, 28 g protein. **Diabetic Exchanges:** 4 lean meat, 1/2 fruit.

Pork Chops with Mango Salsa

Fruited Turkey Salads

Fruited Turkey Salads

(Pictured above)

Prep/Total Time: 15 min.

Here's a lovely salad for summertime luncheons—or to treat yourself! It's bursting with juicy fresh peaches, blueberries, cold turkey and crunchy toasted walnuts.
—Deb Williams, Peoria, Arizona

> 3 tablespoons plain yogurt
> 3 tablespoons orange marmalade
> 4-1/2 teaspoons mayonnaise
> 2 teaspoons lemon juice
> Dash pepper
> 2 cups cubed cooked turkey breast
> 2 medium peaches, sliced
> 1-1/4 cups fresh blueberries
> 4 large lettuce leaves
> 1/4 cup chopped walnuts, toasted

In a large bowl, combine the first five ingredients. Stir in the turkey, peaches and blueberries. Serve on lettuce leaves; sprinkle with walnuts. **Yield:** 4 servings.

Nutrition Facts: 1 cup equals 274 calories, 10 g fat (1 g saturated fat), 64 mg cholesterol, 84 mg sodium, 23 g carbohydrate, 2 g fiber, 24 g protein. **Diabetic Exchanges:** 3 very lean meat, 2 fat, 1 fruit, 1/2 starch.

Onion Ease

TO QUICKLY chop an onion, peel it and cut it in half from root to top. Leaving the root attached, place the flat side down on a work surface. Cut vertically through the onion, leaving the root end uncut. Then cut across the onion, discarding the root end. The closer the cuts, the finer the onion will be chopped.

Chapter 18

◉ *Swift Snacks & Easy Appetizers*

WHY SETTLE for those ordinary, pricey snack foods sold at grocery stores? The homemade recipes in this chapter go together so quickly and easily, you don't have to!

Whether you're looking for wholesome treats to tide over the kids after school, winning munchies for a crowd watching the game on TV or elegant hors d'oeuvres for a holiday party, you'll discover conveniently speedy choices here.

Your family and friends are sure to love finger foods such as Sweet & Spicy Nuts, Cinnamon Baked Pretzels, Cranberry Chili Salsa, Four-Cheese Broiled Tomato Slices, Veggie Tortilla Pinwheels and more.

TIMESAVING TIDBITS. Marinated Sausage Kabobs (p. 280).

Spicy Maple Chicken Wings

(Pictured above)

Prep: 20 min. **Cook:** 10 min./batch

My daughters and I often ask my husband to make his famous chicken wings. They're sweet yet spicy, and we love 'em! —Dona Hoffman, Addison, Illinois

    3 pounds chicken wings
Oil for deep-fat frying
   1/2 cup butter, cubed
   1/2 cup maple syrup
   1/2 cup Louisiana-style hot sauce
   1/4 cup packed brown sugar
   1/2 teaspoon salt
   1/4 teaspoon pepper
    2 tablespoons water
1-1/2 teaspoons cornstarch

Cut chicken wings into three sections; discard wing tip sections. In an electric skillet or deep-fat fryer, heat oil to 375°. Fry chicken, a few pieces at a time, for 8 minutes or until golden brown and the juices run clear, turning occasionally. Drain on paper towels.

In a small saucepan, melt butter. Stir in the syrup, hot sauce, brown sugar, salt and pepper. Combine water and cornstarch; stir into sauce. Bring to a boil; cook and stir for 2 minutes or until thickened. Place wings in a large bowl; pour sauce over and toss to coat. **Yield:** about 2 dozen.

Editor's Note: Uncooked chicken wing sections (wingettes) may be substituted for whole chicken wings.

Flavor Saver

Instead of discarding wing tips when cutting whole chicken wings into pieces, I use them to add flavor to broth and gravy. It's a great no-cost boost—from something I would have otherwise thrown out.
—*Margaret McCully, St. John, New Brunswick*

Kickin' Snack Mix

(Pictured below)

Prep: 20 min. **Bake:** 45 min. + cooling

This combination of cereal with cheddar crackers and mixed nuts puts a new twist on a classic party mix, and cayenne pepper adds an interesting kick. Packed with almonds and pistachios, too, this snack is hard to resist.
—Kim Vogt, Creighton, Nebraska

        3 cups Crispix
        3 cups Wheat Chex
        2 cups cheddar-flavored snack crackers
        1 cup pretzel sticks
        1 cup almonds
        1 cup mixed nuts
        1 cup pistachios
    1/2 cup butter-flavored popcorn oil
        1 envelope ranch salad dressing mix
        1 teaspoon dill weed
        1 teaspoon garlic powder
        1 teaspoon cayenne pepper

In a large bowl, combine the first seven ingredients. In a small bowl, combine the oil, dressing mix, dill, garlic powder and cayenne. Drizzle over cereal mixture; toss to coat.

Transfer mixture to two greased 15-in. x 10-in. x 1-in. baking pans. Bake at 250° for 45-55 minutes, stirring every 15 minutes. Cool on wire racks. Store in an airtight container. **Yield:** 3 quarts.

Mandarin Salsa

Kickin' Snack Mix

Mandarin Salsa

(Pictured above)

Prep/Total Time: 25 min.

Sweet mandarin oranges contrast with the boldness of cilantro, jalapeno and onion in this recipe, creating an impressive and colorful combination. When you're bored with your usual store-bought or homemade salsa, this is the one to try! —Yvonne Opp, Greenville, Pennsylvania

☑ This recipe includes Nutrition Facts and Diabetic Exchange.

        5 plum tomatoes, chopped
        1 large sweet onion, chopped
        2 jalapeno peppers, seeded and chopped
        2 tablespoons sugar
        2 tablespoons minced fresh cilantro
        2 tablespoons lime juice
        1 teaspoon salt
        1 teaspoon minced garlic
        1 can (15 ounces) mandarin oranges, drained
Tortilla chips

In a small bowl, combine first eight ingredients. Gently stir in mandarin oranges. Chill until serving. Drain before serving if necessary. Serve with the tortilla chips. **Yield:** 4 cups.

Editor's Note: When cutting hot peppers, disposable gloves are recommended. Avoid touching your face.

Nutrition Facts: 1/4 cup (calculated without chips) equals 24 calories, trace fat (trace saturated fat), 0 cholesterol, 150 mg sodium, 6 g carbohydrate, 1 g fiber, trace protein. **Diabetic Exchange:** 1/2 starch.

Party Cracker Dip

(Pictured at far right)

Prep: 10 min. + chilling

When I fix this simple appetizer to serve at home or bring to parties, I'm always asked for the recipe. Now I stack copies alongside the dish. It takes only five ingredients and 10 minutes of prep time—and that includes chopping the onion!
—Sue Harville, Orange City, Florida

  1 package (8 ounces) cream cheese, softened
  1 jar (5 ounces) blue cheese spread
  1 jar (5 ounces) pimiento cheese spread *or* sharp American cheese spread
  1 small red onion, finely chopped
  1/4 teaspoon garlic powder
Assorted crackers

In a small bowl, beat the cream cheese and cheese spreads until blended. Stir in the red onion and garlic powder. Cover and refrigerate for at least 2 hours (cheese mixture will be soft). Serve with crackers. **Yield:** 2-1/4 cups.

Zesty Nacho Dip

(Pictured at far right)

Prep/Total Time: 30 min.

With ground beef, this is sure to satisfy. Add more heat by substituting Mexican-style processed cheese and stewed tomatoes. —Denise Hill, Ottawa Lake, Michigan

  2 pounds ground beef
  2 pounds process cheese (Velveeta), cubed
  1 can (14-1/2 ounces) stewed tomatoes, cut up
  2 cans (4 ounces *each*) chopped green chilies
  3 teaspoons chili powder
  3 teaspoons Worcestershire sauce
Tortilla chips

In a Dutch oven, cook the beef over medium heat until no longer pink; drain. Add the cheese, tomatoes, chilies, chili powder and Worcestershire sauce. Cook, uncovered, for 15 minutes or until cheese is melted, stirring occasionally. Serve warm with the tortilla chips. Refrigerate leftovers. **Yield:** 8 cups.

Creamy Chicken Dip

(Pictured above far right)

Prep/Total Time: 15 min.

Bits of water chestnuts bring a nice crunch to this Asian-style dip full of shredded chicken and flavored with soy sauce. —Pamela Luce, Independence, Missouri

  1 cup mayonnaise
  1 cup (8 ounces) sour cream
  1 can (8 ounces) sliced water chestnuts, drained and chopped
  2 tablespoons dried minced onion
  2 tablespoons dried parsley flakes
  1 tablespoon soy sauce
  1 teaspoon garlic powder
  2 cups shredded cooked chicken breast
Assorted crackers

In a large bowl, combine the first seven ingredients. Fold in chicken. Serve with crackers. Refrigerate leftovers. **Yield:** 3-1/2 cups.

Mushroom Onion Dip

(Pictured at right)

Prep: 10 min. + chilling

My husband can't get enough of this tasty dip—he asks for it at least once a month! My late mother-in-law gave me the recipe, and I've shared it many times.
—Teresa Crawford, Indianapolis, Indiana

  2 packages (8 ounces *each*) cream cheese, softened
  1 can (10-3/4 ounces) condensed cream of mushroom soup, undiluted
  3/4 cup milk
  1/4 cup dried minced onion
  2 teaspoons Worcestershire sauce
  1/2 teaspoon garlic salt
Potato chips *or* assorted crackers

In a large bowl, beat the cream cheese, cream of mushroom soup and milk until blended. Add the onion, Worcestershire sauce and garlic salt; mix well. Refrigerate for at least 1 hour. Serve with potato chips. **Yield:** 3-1/2 cups.

Green Chilies and Cheese Dip

(Pictured at right)

Prep: 10 min. **Bake:** 25 min.

With mild south-of-the-border taste, this snack is terrific for everything from Super Bowl gatherings to movie night at home. Tortilla or corn chips are the perfect dippers.
—Linda Webb, Concord, California

  1 cup mayonnaise
  1 cup (8 ounces) shredded Monterey Jack cheese
  1/2 cup grated Parmesan cheese
  3 cans (4 ounces *each*) chopped green chilies, drained
  1 can (11 ounces) Mexicorn, drained
  1 jar (4 ounces) diced pimientos, drained
  2 tablespoons sliced ripe olives
Tortilla *or* corn chips

In a large bowl, combine the mayonnaise and cheeses. Add the chilies, corn and pimientos; mix well. Pour into a lightly greased 2-qt. baking dish. Top with olives.

Bake, uncovered, at 325° for 25-30 minutes or until edges are bubbly. Serve with tortilla chips. Refrigerate leftovers. **Yield:** 4 cups.

BLT Dip

(Pictured above)

Prep: 20 min. + chilling

*When it comes to sandwiches, the bacon-lettuce-tomato
combination is always a popular choice. A spin-off of
the classic BLT, this dip gives you that crowd-pleasing
taste. It was a great success at a friend's party, and now
it's one of my own favorites to serve at get-togethers.*
—*Barbara Schindler, Napoleon, Ohio*

 1 medium tomato, seeded and chopped, *divided*
 1 package (8 ounces) cream cheese, softened
 1/2 cup ranch salad dressing
 8 bacon strips, cooked and crumbled
 1/2 cup finely chopped celery
 3 tablespoons chopped onion
 1-1/2 teaspoons sugar
 Assorted crackers *or* toasted French bread slices

Set aside 2 tablespoons tomato for garnish. In a small
bowl, combine the cream cheese and salad dressing.
Add bacon, celery, onion, sugar and remaining tomato; mix well. Cover and refrigerate for at least 1 hour.

Garnish with reserved tomato. Serve with assorted
crackers or toasted bread slices. **Yield:** 2-1/2 cups.

Simple Seeding

TO EASILY SEED a tomato for recipes such as BLT
Dip (at left), cut the tomato in half and gently squeeze
each half. Seeding a tomato this way not only re-
moves the seeds, but also eliminates some of the juice
that can make a dish too watery. If you don't want to
lose as much juice, try scooping out the seeds with a
small spoon instead of squeezing.

Avocado Shrimp Salsa

(Pictured above)

Prep/Total Time: 25 min.

I love making this special salsa to munch with tortilla chips. But it's so good, sometimes I eat it all by itself!
—*Maria Simmons, Rio Rancho, New Mexico*

☑ This recipe includes Nutrition Facts and Diabetic Exchanges.

- 1 pound cooked small shrimp, peeled, deveined and chopped
- 2 medium tomatoes, seeded and chopped
- 2 medium ripe avocados, peeled and chopped
- 1 cup minced fresh cilantro
- 1 medium sweet red pepper, chopped
- 3/4 cup thinly sliced green onions
- 1/2 cup chopped seeded peeled cucumber
- 3 tablespoons lime juice
- 1 jalapeno pepper, seeded and chopped
- 1 teaspoon salt
- 1/4 teaspoon pepper
Tortilla chips

In a large bowl, combine the first 11 ingredients. Serve immediately with tortilla chips. **Yield:** 6 cups.

Nutrition Facts: 1/4 cup salsa (calculated without tortilla chips) equals 52 calories, 3 g fat (trace saturated fat), 33 mg cholesterol, 133 mg sodium, 3 g carbohydrate, 1 g fiber, 5 g protein. **Diabetic Exchanges:** 1 very lean meat, 1/2 fat.

Surefire Shrimp Hint

TO PEEL and devein shrimp for recipes such as Avocado Shrimp Salsa (at left), start on the underside by the head area to remove the shell from the shrimp. Pull the legs and first section of shell to one side. Continue pulling the shell up around the top and to the other side. Pull off the shell by the tail if desired.

Next, remove the black vein on the back of the shrimp by making a shallow slit with a paring knife along the back from the head area to the tail. Then rinse the shrimp under cold water to remove the vein.

Pork Satay

(Pictured below)

Prep: 20 min. + marinating **Cook:** 10 min.

Our Test Kitchen cooks came up with these impressive skewers. Cilantro gives them freshness, while the sesame oil and Thai chili sauce add layers of Asian flavors that pair perfectly with peanut butter.

☑ This recipe includes Nutrition Facts and Diabetic Exchanges.

> 1/3 cup reduced-sodium soy sauce
> 2 green onions, sliced
> 3 tablespoons brown sugar
> 3 tablespoons minced fresh cilantro
> 3 tablespoons Thai chili sauce
> 2 tablespoons sesame oil
> 2 teaspoons minced garlic
> 1 pound pork tenderloin, cut into 1/4-inch slices
> 1/3 cup creamy peanut butter
> 3 tablespoons hot water
> 2 teaspoons lime juice

In a small bowl, combine the first seven ingredients. Set aside 1/4 cup for dipping sauce. Pour remaining sauce into a large resealable plastic bag; add the pork. Seal bag and turn to coat; refrigerate for 30 minutes.

Drain and discard marinade. Thread pork slices onto 20 metal or soaked wooden skewers. Place skewers on a greased 15-in. x 10-in. x 1-in. baking pan. Broil 3-4 in. from the heat for 3-4 minutes on each side or until meat juices run clear.

Meanwhile, for sauce, combine peanut butter and water in a small bowl until smooth. Stir in lime juice and reserved soy sauce mixture. Serve with skewers. **Yield:** 20 servings.

Nutrition Facts: 1 skewer with 1-1/2 teaspoons sauce equals 73 calories, 4 g fat (1 g saturated fat), 13 mg cholesterol, 172 mg sodium, 4 g carbohydrate, trace fiber, 6 g protein. **Diabetic Exchanges:** 1 lean meat, 1/2 fat.

Pork Satay

Artichoke Crescent Appetizers

Artichoke Crescent Appetizers

(Pictured above)

Prep: 20 min. **Bake:** 15 min.

This is a wonderful appetizer for any gathering. The oven-baked bites are delicious warm, but my family also likes them cold. —Mary Ann Dell, Phoenixville, Pennsylvania

☑ This recipe includes Nutrition Facts.

> 1 tube (8 ounces) refrigerated crescent rolls
> 2 tablespoons grated Parmesan cheese
> 2 packages (3 ounces *each*) cream cheese, softened
> 1/2 cup sour cream
> 1 egg
> 1/2 teaspoon dill weed
> 1/4 teaspoon seasoned salt
> 1 can (14 ounces) water-packed artichoke hearts, rinsed, drained and chopped
> 1/3 cup thinly chopped green onions
> 1 jar (2 ounces) diced pimientos, drained

Unroll the crescent dough and press onto the bottom and 1/2 in. up the sides of an ungreased 13-in. x 9-in. baking dish; seal seams and perforations. Sprinkle with Parmesan cheese. Bake at 375° for 8-10 minutes or until lightly browned.

Meanwhile, in a small bowl, beat the cream cheese, sour cream and egg until smooth. Stir in the dill and seasoned salt. Spread over crust. Sprinkle with the artichokes, green onions and pimientos. Bake 15-20 minutes longer or until edges are golden brown. Cut into squares. **Yield:** about 2 dozen.

Nutrition Facts: 1 piece equals 77 calories, 5 g fat (3 g saturated fat), 19 mg cholesterol, 151 mg sodium, 5 g carbohydrate, trace fiber, 2 g protein.

Cereal Snack Mix

(Pictured at far right)

Prep: 10 min. **Bake:** 30 min. + cooling

I grew up munching on this mix, and now I make it for my husband and kids. They dig into each fresh batch immediately—and eat until it's gone! With a blend of cereal, pretzels, nuts and more, one handful is never enough.
—Becky Larson, Duluth, Minnesota

  9 cups Crispix
  1 cup Cheerios
  1 cup Bugles
  1 cup pretzel sticks
  1 cup salted peanuts
2/3 cup butter, melted
  2 tablespoons Worcestershire sauce
  2 teaspoons celery salt
  2 teaspoons lemon juice
  1 teaspoon garlic powder

In a large bowl, combine the first five ingredients. In a small bowl, combine the remaining ingredients. Drizzle over cereal mixture; toss to coat.

Transfer to two greased 15-in. x 10-in. x 1-in. baking pans. Bake at 250° for 30 minutes, stirring every 10 minutes. Cool completely on wire racks. Store in an airtight container. **Yield:** 3-1/4 quarts.

Corn Salsa

(Pictured at far right)

Prep/Total Time: 25 min.

A friend gave us this recipe, and everyone raves when I bring it to a party or put it out for guests when we're entertaining at home. Convenient canned ingredients make the well-balanced, flavorful salsa a breeze to whip up.
—Dave Kepler, Metamora, Illinois

☑ This recipe includes Nutrition Facts.

  1 can (15 ounces) tomato sauce
  1 can (14-1/2 ounces) stewed tomatoes, cut up
  1 can (11 ounces) Mexicorn, drained
  1 can (10 ounces) diced tomatoes and green chilies
  2 medium tomatoes, chopped
2/3 cup chopped onion
1/2 cup minced fresh cilantro
  2 tablespoons lime juice
  2 tablespoons minced garlic
1/4 teaspoon garlic salt
1/4 teaspoon chili powder
Tortilla chips

In a large bowl, combine the first 11 ingredients. Chill until serving. Serve with tortilla chips. **Yield:** 7 cups.

Nutrition Facts: 1/4 cup (calculated without chips) equals 23 calories, trace fat (trace saturated fat), 0 cholesterol, 216 mg sodium, 5 g carbohydrate, 1 g fiber, 1 g protein.

Summer Fruit Cooler

(Pictured at right)

Prep: 10 min. + freezing

This wonderfully fruity drink is ideal for warm-weather sipping. The sweet-tart taste and lovely color will brighten any occasion.
—Jane Woods, Fort Worth, Texas

☑ This recipe includes Nutrition Facts.

  8 cups ruby red grapefruit juice, *divided*
  2 cups unsweetened pineapple juice
  1 cup orange juice
  1 cup cranberry juice
  4 cups lemon-lime soda, chilled
Orange slices and fresh mint leaves

Pour 3 cups of grapefruit juice into two ice cube trays; freeze until set.

In a large pitcher, combine the pineapple, orange and cranberry juices; stir in the remaining grapefruit juice. Chill until serving. Slowly stir in soda; add the grapefruit ice cubes. Garnish with orange slices and mint. **Yield:** 14 servings (3-1/2 quarts).

Nutrition Facts: 1 cup equals 120 calories, trace fat (trace saturated fat), 0 cholesterol, 9 mg sodium, 30 g carbohydrate, trace fiber, 1 g protein.

Chili Cheese Ball

Prep: 15 min. + chilling

My mother made this appetizer when I was a girl, and it was the one I looked forward to most. Now, I serve it at my own get-togethers. The spicy cheese ball requires just 15 minutes of prep time and spreads easily on crackers.
—Jerrie Denson, Hobbs, New Mexico

  1 pound process cheese (Velveeta), shredded
  4 ounces cream cheese, softened
1/2 cup chopped pecans
1/2 teaspoon garlic salt
Chili powder
Assorted crackers

In a small bowl, combine the cheeses, pecans and garlic salt. Cover and refrigerate for 20 minutes. Shape into a ball. Coat completely with chili powder. Serve with crackers. **Yield:** 1 cheese ball (3 cups).

Keeping Clean

WANT to make Chili Cheese Ball (recipe above)—but want a minimum of mess? Keep your hands and countertop clean by spooning the cheese mixture onto a piece of plastic wrap. Working with your hands on the underside of the wrap, pat the mixture into a ball. Then complete the recipe as directed.

Marinated Sausage Kabobs

Four-Cheese Broiled Tomato Slices

(Pictured below)

Prep/Total Time: 20 min.

Whenever my husband smells these slices cooking, he practically starts to salivate! The recipe is a wonderful use for garden tomatoes. I top them with a mixture of cheese, mayonnaise and spices, then pop them in the oven for a few minutes.
—Jen Low, Buffalo, New York

✓ This recipe includes Nutrition Facts.

1/2 cup grated Parmesan and Romano cheeses
1/2 cup shredded part-skim mozzarella cheese
1/2 cup ricotta cheese
1/2 cup mayonnaise
1 tablespoon dried oregano
1 teaspoon salt
1 teaspoon minced garlic
4 large tomatoes

In a small bowl, combine first seven ingredients. Cut each tomato into five slices. Spread each with 1 tablespoon cheese mixture.

Place on an ungreased baking sheet. Broil 3 in. from the heat for 3-5 minutes or until cheese mixture is golden brown and tomatoes are heated through. **Yield:** 20 appetizers.

Nutrition Facts: 1 appetizer equals 76 calories, 6 g fat (2 g saturated fat), 9 mg cholesterol, 222 mg sodium, 2 g carbohydrate, 1 g fiber, 3 g protein.

Marinated Sausage Kabobs

(Pictured above and on page 270)

Prep: 20 min. + marinating

These flavorful, colorful appetizers are so fun and festive, they're sure to be the talk of the party. No one ever guesses how fuss-free they are to make! Simply marinate the cheese, ripe olives, salami and peppers the day before your get-together and assemble the kabobs the next day.
—Joanne Boone, Danville, Ohio

1/4 cup olive oil
1 tablespoon white vinegar
1/2 teaspoon minced garlic
1/2 teaspoon dried basil
1/2 teaspoon dried oregano
12 ounces cheddar cheese, cut into 3/4-inch cubes
1 can (6 ounces) pitted ripe olives, drained
4 ounces hard salami, cut into 3/4-inch cubes
1 medium sweet red pepper, cut into 3/4-inch pieces
1 medium green pepper, cut into 3/4-inch pieces

In a large resealable plastic bag, combine the first five ingredients; add the remaining ingredients. Seal bag and turn to coat; refrigerate for at least 4 hours. Drain and discard marinade.

For each kabob, thread one piece each of cheddar cheese, ripe olive, salami and pepper onto a toothpick. **Yield:** 3 dozen.

Four-Cheese Broiled Tomato Slices

Mozzarella Sticks

Sweet & Spicy Nuts

(Pictured below)

Prep: 25 min. + cooling

Hot and spicy with a hint of brown-sugar sweetness, these snacking nuts are simply sensational. Keep the quick-and-easy recipe in mind when you need a Christmas stocking stuffer or last-minute holiday gift from the kitchen.
—*Patty Lok, Sherman Oaks, California*

   1/2 teaspoon salt
   1/4 teaspoon ground cinnamon
   1/4 teaspoon ground cumin
   1/4 teaspoon cayenne pepper
   1/4 teaspoon chili powder
   1/4 teaspoon ground chipotle powder
   1/8 teaspoon ground nutmeg
     3 tablespoons unsalted butter
     1 cup shelled walnuts
     1 cup pecan halves
   1/4 cup packed brown sugar
     1 tablespoon water
 1-1/2 teaspoons Worcestershire sauce
Dash Louisiana-style hot sauce

In a small bowl, combine the salt and spices; set aside. In a large heavy skillet, melt butter. Add walnuts and pecans; cook over medium heat until nuts are toasted, about 4 minutes.

Sprinkle toasted nuts with the spice mixture. Add the brown sugar, water, Worcestershire sauce and hot sauce. Cook and stir for 1-2 minutes or until the sugar is melted. Spread on foil to cool. Store in an airtight container. **Yield:** 2 cups.

Mozzarella Sticks

(Pictured above)

Prep/Total Time: 20 min.

It's hard to believe that something this simple can taste so fantastic! The fried cheese sticks are much like the ones you enjoy at restaurants, but you can easily make these in your own kitchen for family and friends. Crunchy outside, gooey inside...it's a snack people of all ages love.
—*Shirley Warren, Thiensville, Wisconsin*

  12 pieces string cheese
  12 egg roll wrappers
Oil for deep-fat frying
Marinara *or* spaghetti sauce

Place a piece of string cheese near the bottom corner of one egg roll wrapper (keep the remaining egg roll wrappers covered with a damp paper towel until ready to use). Fold the bottom corner of the wrapper over the cheese. Roll up halfway; fold the sides toward the center over the cheese. Moisten the remaining corner with water; roll up tightly to seal. Repeat with the remaining wrappers and cheese.

In an electric skillet, heat 1/2 in. of oil to 375°. Fry the wrapped cheese pieces, a few at a time, for 30-60 seconds on each side or until golden brown. Drain on paper towels. Serve the sticks with marinara sauce. **Yield:** 1 dozen.

Sweet & Spicy Nuts

Italian Party Appetizers
Prosciutto Pinwheels
Stuffed Party Mushrooms

Italian Party Appetizers

(Pictured at left)
Prep/Total Time: 30 min.

When you want something quick, effortless and impressive, this is the appetizer to choose. The recipe is easy to double, too. Serve it with a refreshing white wine.
—Heather Nygren, Cumming, Georgia

☑ This recipe includes Nutrition Facts and Diabetic Exchange.

    4 ounces cream cheese, softened
   48 Triscuits *or other crackers*
1/4 cup prepared pesto
1/4 cup oil-packed sun-dried tomatoes, patted dry and thinly sliced

Spread the cream cheese on each cracker. Top with the pesto and a sun-dried tomato slice. Serve immediately. **Yield:** 4 dozen.
   Nutrition Facts: 1 cracker equals 36 calories, 2 g fat (1 g saturated fat), 3 mg cholesterol, 48 mg sodium, 3 g carbohydrate, 1 g fiber, 1 g protein. **Diabetic Exchange:** 1/2 fat.

Stuffed Party Mushrooms

(Pictured at left)
Prep: 55 min. **Bake:** 15 min.

I created these stuffed mushrooms with ingredients I already had in my refrigerator. Now, they're an all-time party favorite. We've tried different kinds of cream cheese in place of the garden vegetable variety, but no matter what flavor I use, I never seem to make enough!
—Tara Sturgeon, Ellsworth AFB, South Dakota

☑ This recipe includes Nutrition Facts.

    2 pounds whole fresh mushrooms
    1 carton (8 ounces) spreadable garden vegetable cream cheese
    4 ounces imitation crabmeat, chopped
1/2 cup shredded cheddar cheese, *divided*
    2 tablespoons mayonnaise
1/4 teaspoon salt
1/8 dash pepper

Remove stems from mushrooms and finely chop 1/4 cup (discard remaining stems or save for another use); set mushroom caps aside.
   In a small bowl, beat the garden vegetable cream cheese until smooth. Stir in the chopped mushroom stems, crab, 1/4 cup cheddar cheese, mayonnaise, salt and pepper. Spoon about 2 teaspoons into each mushroom cap.
   Place on a foil-lined baking sheet; sprinkle with the remaining cheddar cheese. Bake at 350° for 15-18 minutes or until the mushroom caps are tender. **Yield:** about 4 dozen appetizers.
   Nutrition Facts: 1 mushroom equals 30 calories, 2 g fat (1 g saturated fat), 6 mg cholesterol, 59 mg sodium, 1 g carbohydrate, trace fiber, 1 g protein.

Prosciutto Pinwheels

(Pictured at far left)
Prep: 20 min. **Bake:** 15 min.

Fancy-looking and filling, these elegant hors d'oeuvres are a lot simpler to fix than they look. You simply roll up both sides of the dough to create a cute pinwheel shape.
—Kaitlyn Benito, Everett, Washington

☑ This recipe includes Nutrition Facts and Diabetic Exchanges.

    1 sheet frozen puff pastry, thawed
1/4 cup sweet hot mustard
1/4 pound sliced prosciutto *or* deli ham, chopped
1/2 cup shredded Parmesan cheese

Unfold the puff pastry. Spread the mustard over the pastry to within 1/2 in. of the edges. Sprinkle with the prosciutto and Parmesan cheese. Roll up one side to the middle of the dough; roll up the other side so the two rolls meet in the center. Using a serrated knife, cut into 1/2-in. slices.
   Place on greased baking sheets. Bake at 400° for 11-13 minutes or until puffed and golden brown. Serve warm. **Yield:** 20 appetizers.
   Nutrition Facts: 1 appetizer equals 86 calories, 5 g fat (1 g saturated fat), 6 mg cholesterol, 210 mg sodium, 8 g carbohydrate, 1 g fiber, 3 g protein. **Diabetic Exchanges:** 1 fat, 1/2 starch.

Cranberry Chili Salsa

Prep/Total Time: 10 min.

This is a great change of pace because it's very different from the usual salsas. You get a tongue-tingling combination of tart and sweet from cranberries, sugar and lime.
—Mary Guertin, Bourbonnais, Illinois

☑ This recipe includes Nutrition Facts and Diabetic Exchange.

    1 package (12 ounces) fresh *or* frozen cranberries, thawed
3/4 cup sugar
    1 can (4 ounces) chopped green chilies
    3 tablespoons minced fresh cilantro
    2 green onions, chopped
    2 teaspoons lime juice
    1 teaspoon grated lime peel
1/4 teaspoon *each* ground allspice, cinnamon and cumin
Tortilla chips

Place cranberries, sugar, green chilies, cilantro, onions, lime juice, lime peel and spices in a food processor; cover and pulse just until blended. Transfer salsa to a serving bowl; chill until serving. Serve with tortilla chips. **Yield:** 2-1/2 cups.
   Nutrition Facts: 1/4 cup (calculated without chips) equals 78 calories, trace fat (trace saturated fat), 0 cholesterol, 46 mg sodium, 20 g carbohydrate, 2 g fiber, trace protein. **Diabetic Exchange:** 1 starch.

Cucumber Rolls

(Pictured below)

Prep/Total Time: 25 min.

Salmon and cucumber are wonderful together, but it's the presentation of these appetizers that will stop guests in their tracks. And you won't have to do any cooking—just assemble the rolls and watch them disappear.
—Heidi Hall, North St. Paul, Minnesota

✓ This recipe includes Nutrition Facts and Diabetic Exchange.

  1/2 cup cream cheese, softened
1-1/2 teaspoons prepared horseradish
  1/4 teaspoon garlic powder
  1/4 teaspoon curry powder
    1 medium cucumber
  1/2 ounce smoked salmon *or* lox, cut into
      thin strips
Kosher salt
Coarsely ground pepper
Chives

In a small bowl, combine the cream cheese, horseradish, garlic powder and curry; set aside.

    With a vegetable peeler or metal cheese slicer, cut 12 very thin slices down the length of the cucumber; pat dry. Spread about 1 teaspoon cream cheese mixture down the center of each cucumber slice. Roll up.

    Arrange salmon on top of rolls; sprinkle lightly with salt and pepper. Garnish with chives. **Yield:** 1 dozen.

    Nutrition Facts: 1 appetizer (calculated without salt, pepper and chives) equals 40 calories, 3 g fat (2 g saturated fat), 11 mg cholesterol, 54 mg sodium, 1 g carbohydrate, trace fiber, 1 g protein. **Diabetic Exchange:** 1/2 fat.

Veggie Tortilla Pinwheels

Veggie Tortilla Pinwheels

(Pictured above)

Prep/Total Time: 25 min.

These spiral-shaped bites are a guaranteed hit wherever I take them. I love the fact that I can make them ahead of time.
—Lori Kostecki, Wausau, Wisconsin

✓ This recipe includes Nutrition Facts.

    2 packages (8 ounces *each*) cream cheese,
      softened
    1 envelope ranch salad dressing mix
    5 green onions, chopped
    1 can (4 ounces) chopped green chilies,
      drained
    1 can (3.8 ounces) sliced ripe olives, drained
    1 celery rib, chopped
  1/4 cup chopped sweet red pepper
    2 to 3 tablespoons real bacon bits
    8 flour tortillas (10 inches)

In a small bowl, beat the cream cheese and dressing mix until blended. Beat in the onions, green chilies, olives, celery, red pepper and bacon. Spread over the tortillas. Roll up. Cut each into 1-in. slices. Refrigerate leftovers. **Yield:** about 5 dozen.

    Nutrition Facts: 1 piece equals 58 calories, 3 g fat (2 g saturated fat), 8 mg cholesterol, 188 mg sodium, 5 g carbohydrate, 1 g fiber, 1 g protein.

Cucumber Rolls

Nice Slicing

DO YOU PLAN to make refreshing Cucumber Rolls (recipe above left) for your next party? The recipe calls for very thin slices of cucumber. To easily make slices that are the perfect size and thickness for these rolls, slice the cucumber with a julienne peeler.

French Quarter Cheese Spread

(Pictured below)

Prep/Total Time: 20 min.

Topped with toasted pecans, this sweet-and-savory cheese round makes a festive hostess gift for holiday parties. At home, I whip up the spread in advance for convenience, then bring it to room temperature and serve. —Heidi Blaine Hadburg
Safety Harbor, Florida

1 package (8 ounces) cream cheese, softened
1 tablespoon grated onion
1 teaspoon minced garlic
1/4 cup butter, cubed
1/4 cup packed dark brown sugar
1 teaspoon Worcestershire sauce
1/2 teaspoon prepared mustard
1 cup finely chopped pecans, toasted
Assorted crackers

In a small bowl, combine the cream cheese, onion and garlic. Transfer to a serving plate; shape into a 6-in. disk. Set aside.

In a small saucepan, combine the butter, brown sugar, Worcestershire sauce and mustard. Cook and stir over medium heat for 4-5 minutes or until the brown sugar is dissolved.

Remove from the heat; stir in pecans. Cool slightly. Spoon over the cheese mixture. Serve with crackers. **Yield:** 8 servings.

French Quarter Cheese Spread

Cinnamon Baked Pretzels

Cinnamon Baked Pretzels

(Pictured above)

Prep/Total Time: 15 min.

This recipe is almost as fun to make as it is to eat! You need just four basic ingredients, and using packaged frozen pretzels cuts out a lot of the prep work. Try these as a starter for brunch or as after-school snacks for the kids. —Marina Heppner,
Orchard Park, New York

3 tablespoons cinnamon-sugar
2 tablespoons butter
1/4 teaspoon ground nutmeg
1 package (13 ounces) frozen baked soft pretzels
1/2 cup red raspberry preserves, warmed

In a small microwave-safe bowl, combine the cinnamon-sugar, butter and nutmeg. Microwave, uncovered, on high for 30-45 seconds or until butter is melted; brush over pretzels. Transfer to an ungreased baking sheet.

Bake at 400° for 3-4 minutes or until heated through. Serve with preserves. **Yield:** 6 servings.

Chapter 19

⊙ Test Kitchen Secrets

YOU don't have to attend culinary school or become a professional chef in order to work wonders in the kitchen. Our experts show you how in this special chapter!

They reveal their favorite secrets, shortcuts, techniques and tricks of the trade...all for you to put to use in your very own home cooking.

See how our pros make the most of indoor grills...create stunning cake rolls...turn leftover grilled meats into second-day specialties...and serve up burgers that wow the crowd.

With plenty of recipes, how-to photos and step-by-step directions, you'll soon be cooking just like a master!

KEY INGREDIENTS. Antipasto Pasta Salad (p. 297).

Stay Indoors For Grilling

WHEN winter's icy grip takes hold, do you miss firing up the grill? It's never too cold when you have an indoor grill. In fact, this gadget is so handy, you'll want to use it even when the weather's warm!

For success with your indoor grill, rely on these recipes and helpful tips from our Test Kitchen pros.

Greek Chicken Nachos

Apple-Glazed Pork Chops

(Pictured below)

Prep/Total Time: 20 min.

Your pantry probably contains all of the spices needed for these succulent chops from our home economists. The rub is versatile; give it a try on any meat, chicken or fish.

☑ This recipe includes Nutrition Facts and Diabetic Exchanges.

    2 tablespoons brown sugar
    2 teaspoons paprika
    1 teaspoon salt
    1 teaspoon onion powder
    1 teaspoon garlic powder
    1 teaspoon ground mustard
    1 teaspoon dried thyme
  1/2 teaspoon pepper
    4 boneless pork loin chops (1 inch thick and
      6 ounces *each*)
    2 tablespoons apple jelly

Combine the first eight ingredients; rub over both sides of the pork chops. Cook in batches on an indoor grill coated with cooking spray for 5 minutes or until a meat thermometer reads 160°.

In a microwave-safe bowl, heat jelly until warmed; brush over pork chops. **Yield:** 4 servings.

Nutrition Facts: 1 pork chop equals 283 calories, 10 g fat (4 g saturated fat), 82 mg cholesterol, 522 mg sodium, 14 g carbohydrate, 1 g fiber, 33 g protein. **Diabetic Exchanges:** 5 lean meat, 1 starch.

Greek Chicken Nachos

(Pictured above)

Prep/Total Time: 30 min.

These delicious nachos are perfect to share, but don't treat them like an appetizer! Packed with chicken, cheese and all your favorite Greek flavors, they make a hearty and filling meal. —Brenda Murphy, Spokane, Washington

    2 packages (10 ounces *each*) lemon-pepper
      marinated chicken breast fillets
    2 cans (15 ounces *each*) garbanzo beans *or*
      chickpeas, rinsed and drained
  1/2 cup Italian salad dressing
    4 cups coarsely crushed tortilla chips
    1 package (4 ounces) crumbled tomato and
      basil feta cheese
    1 cup chopped tomatoes
    1 cup Greek olives, chopped
    2 cups (8 ounces) shredded part-skim
      mozzarella cheese

Cook chicken in batches on an indoor grill for 6-8 minutes or until juices run clear.

Meanwhile, place garbanzo beans and salad dressing in a food processor; cover and process until smooth. Dice chicken. In an ungreased 13-in. x 9-in. baking dish, layer half of the bean mixture, tortilla chips, chicken, feta cheese, tomatoes, olives and mozzarella cheese. Repeat layers.

Bake, uncovered, at 325° for 8-10 minutes or until cheese is melted. **Yield:** 12 servings.

Apple-Glazed Pork Chops

All-American Rub

(Pictured at right)

Prep/Total Time: 5 min.

This fast, spicy, salt-free rub is great on steaks, pork and chicken—even popcorn! Keep a batch on hand for whenever you need it. —*Heather Bonser, Laurel, Montana*

☑ This recipe includes Nutrition Facts and Diabetic Exchange.

    1/2 cup packed brown sugar
      2 tablespoons dried minced onion
      1 tablespoon garlic powder
      1 tablespoon ground mustard
    1/2 teaspoon cayenne pepper
    1/8 teaspoon ground nutmeg

In a small bowl, combine all of the ingredients; store in an airtight container.

Rub over meat or poultry; cover and refrigerate for up to 4 hours before grilling or broiling. **Yield:** 3/4 cup.

Nutrition Facts: 1 tablespoon equals 43 calories, trace fat (trace saturated fat), 0 cholesterol, 4 mg sodium, 10 g carbohydrate, trace fiber, trace protein. **Diabetic Exchange:** 1/2 starch.

All-American Rub

Salmon with Broccoli and Pasta

(Pictured below)

Prep/Total Time: 30 min.

Save time cooking and eat a little healthier with this terrific fish dinner. The recipe takes just 30 minutes from start to finish. —*Linda Halone, Rochester, Minnesota*

      8 ounces uncooked whole wheat spaghetti
    3-1/2 cups chopped fresh broccoli
      6 salmon fillets (4 ounces *each*)
    3/4 teaspoon seafood seasoning

    2-1/2 cups chopped fresh tomatoes
        1 package (7 ounces) mozzarella and Asiago
          cheese with roasted garlic
      1/4 cup olive oil
      1/2 teaspoon salt
      1/4 teaspoon pepper

In a large saucepan, cook the spaghetti according to package directions, adding the broccoli during the last 5 minutes of cooking.

Meanwhile, sprinkle salmon with seafood seasoning. Cook in batches on an indoor grill for 5 minutes or until fish flakes easily with a fork.

Drain spaghetti and broccoli; transfer to a large bowl. Add the tomatoes, cheese, oil, salt and pepper; toss to coat. Serve with salmon. **Yield:** 6 servings.

Salmon with Broccoli and Pasta

Cooking with an Indoor Grill

- Always use plastic utensils on the nonstick grill surface. Metal utensils may damage it.
- Don't guess. Preheat the grill according to the manufacturer's directions.
- If your recipe includes fish, lean meats or sugary marinades, spray the grill before preheating. Then close the lid and preheat the grill according to the manufacturer's directions.
- Choose thicker cuts of meat or fish (3/4 inch to 1 inch). Thinner cuts may dry out more quickly, and cuts that are less than 1/2 inch thick may not contact the upper grill completely.
- Boneless cuts of meat or poultry that are uniformly thick help to ensure even browning. Chicken breasts may need to be pounded to an even thickness.
- To tell if salmon is cooked properly, simply insert a fork at an angle into the thickest portion of the fish. When it is opaque and flakes easily into sections, it is cooked completely.

Get Cakes On a Roll

FOR ANY OCCASION, cake rolls are an impressive dessert. Think they're complicated? Here's a little secret: they're actually quite easy to make. Read on for some goof-proof hints and spectacular recipes. With our expert techniques, you'll be rollin' in no time!

Orange-Angel Jelly Roll

(Pictured below)

Prep: 25 min. **Bake:** 20 min. + cooling

I came up with this dessert just in time for our Easter Sunday dinner. With its pretty, fluffy orange swirl, the cake was a hit. —Michelle Tokarz, Newport, Michigan

☑ **This recipe includes Nutrition Facts.**

    1 package (16 ounces) angel food cake mix
    1 package (8 ounces) cream cheese, softened
1/4 cup confectioners' sugar
    1 tablespoon orange juice
1/2 teaspoon orange extract
1/2 teaspoon grated orange peel
    3 drops yellow food coloring, optional
    1 drop red food coloring, optional
    1 cup whipped topping
2/3 cup orange marmalade
Additional confectioners' sugar and orange curls

Orange-Angel Jelly Roll

Line a greased 15-in. x 10-in. x 1-in. baking pan with waxed paper; grease the paper and set aside. Prepare cake mix batter according to package directions; spread evenly into prepared pan. Bake at 350° for 18-22 minutes or until cake springs back when lightly touched. Cool in pan for 5 minutes.

Carefully run a knife around edges of pan to loosen cake. Invert onto a kitchen towel dusted with confectioners' sugar. Gently peel off the waxed paper. Roll up cake in the towel jelly-roll style, starting with a short side. Cool completely on a wire rack.

For filling, in a small bowl, beat cream cheese and confectioners' sugar until smooth. Beat in the orange juice, orange extract, orange peel and food coloring if desired. Fold in whipped topping.

Unroll cake; spread orange marmalade to within 1/2 in. of the edges. Spread whipped topping mixture over marmalade to within 1 in. of edges. Roll up again. Place seam side down on a serving platter. Sprinkle with additional confectioners' sugar. Garnish with orange curls. Refrigerate leftovers. **Yield:** 12 servings.

Nutrition Facts: 1 slice equals 279 calories, 8 g fat (5 g saturated fat), 21 mg cholesterol, 345 mg sodium, 48 g carbohydrate, trace fiber, 5 g protein.

Applesauce Cake Roll

(Pictured at right)

Prep: 25 min. **Bake:** 15 min. + freezing

My mother needed a treat for her bridge club on short notice and happened to have this in the freezer. Everyone raved about the apple-flavored cake, vanilla ice cream filling, whipped topping and caramel drizzle. Needless to say, Mom had to hand out many copies of the recipe! —Wendy Curtin, Newtown, Pennsylvania

☑ **This recipe includes Nutrition Facts.**

    3 eggs
3/4 cup sugar
1/2 cup unsweetened applesauce
    1 cup all-purpose flour
1/2 teaspoon baking powder
1/2 teaspoon baking soda
1/2 teaspoon ground cinnamon
1/4 teaspoon salt
1/4 teaspoon ground cloves
    1 tablespoon confectioners' sugar
2-1/2 cups vanilla ice cream, softened
    1 carton (8 ounces) frozen whipped topping, thawed
Caramel ice cream topping, optional

Line a greased 15-in. x 10-in. x 1-in. baking pan with waxed paper; grease the paper and set aside.

In a large bowl, beat eggs for 3 minutes. Gradually add sugar; beat for 2 minutes or until mixture becomes thick and lemon-colored. Stir in applesauce. Combine the flour, baking powder, baking soda, cinnamon, salt and cloves; fold into applesauce mixture. Spread batter evenly into prepared pan.

Bake at 350° for 12-15 minutes or until the cake

Applesauce Cake Roll

springs back when lightly touched. Cool for 5 minutes. Invert onto a kitchen towel dusted with confectioners' sugar. Gently peel off the waxed paper. Roll up the cake in the towel jelly-roll style, starting with a short side. Cool completely on a wire rack.

Unroll the cake; spread vanilla ice cream evenly over the cake to within 1/2 in. of the edges. Roll up again. Place seam side down on a serving platter. Frost the top, sides and ends with whipped topping. Cover and freeze for at least 1 hour. Remove from freezer 10 minutes before cutting. Drizzle with caramel ice cream topping if desired. **Yield:** 10 servings.

Nutrition Facts: 1 slice (calculated without caramel topping) equals 263 calories, 9 g fat (7 g saturated fat), 78 mg cholesterol, 190 mg sodium, 40 g carbohydrate, 1 g fiber, 4 g protein.

Three Steps to Shaping a Cake Roll

1. Cool the cake in the pan for 5 minutes. Turn it out onto a kitchen towel dusted with confectioners' sugar; gently peel off the waxed paper. Roll up the cake in the towel jelly-roll style, starting with a short side. Cool it completely on a wire rack.

2. Unroll the cake and spread the filling evenly over the cake to within 1/2 inch of the edges.

3. Starting with a short side, roll up the cake loosely, pulling away the towel. Place the roll, seam side down, on a serving platter.

Grill Once, Eat Twice

NEXT TIME you fire up the barbecue, why not make the most of all those fantastic, sizzling flavors? Cook a little extra meat for leftovers you can use to jump-start another entree later in the week. Simply use the recipes and hints featured here!

Grilled Lemon Chicken

(Pictured below)

Prep: 15 min. + marinating **Grill:** 10 min.

There's one word to describe this recipe: Yum! It's so easy to prepare when we get home from church on Sunday. Save two of the cooked chicken breasts, and you'll have just the amount needed to prepare Fruited Chicken Pasta Salad (page 293).
—Heather Erb, Milton, Pennsylvania

☑ This recipe includes Nutrition Facts and Diabetic Exchanges.

 1/2 cup plus 1 tablespoon lemon juice
 6 tablespoons olive oil
 3 tablespoons minced fresh parsley
 3 tablespoons grated lemon peel
 1-1/2 teaspoons minced garlic
 3/4 teaspoon salt
 3/4 teaspoon dried thyme
 3/4 teaspoon dried marjoram
 3/4 teaspoon pepper
 6 boneless skinless chicken breast halves
 (6 ounces *each*)

Grilled Lemon Chicken

Hash Brown Pork Skillet

In a small bowl, combine the first nine ingredients. Pour 1/3 cup marinade into a large resealable plastic bag; add chicken. Seal bag and turn to coat; refrigerate for up to 1 hour. Cover and refrigerate remaining marinade.

Drain and discard marinade. Grill chicken, covered, over medium heat for 5-8 minutes on each side or until a meat thermometer reads 170°, basting occasionally with reserved marinade. **Yield:** 6 servings.

Nutrition Facts: 1 chicken breast half equals 258 calories, 12 g fat (2 g saturated fat), 94 mg cholesterol, 256 mg sodium, 2 g carbohydrate, trace fiber, 34 g protein. **Diabetic Exchanges:** 4 very lean meat, 2 fat.

Hash Brown Pork Skillet

(Pictured above)

Prep/Total Time: 25 min.

When you have grilled pork left over from Asian Pork Tenderloins (page 293), use it the next day for this satisfying meal-in-one created by our Test Kitchen cooks. Enjoy it for breakfast, supper...anytime at all!

 4 cups frozen O'Brien potatoes, thawed
 1 cup chopped onion
 1 cup chopped green pepper
 2 tablespoons butter
 2 cups cubed cooked pork
 2 teaspoons chicken bouillon granules
 1/4 teaspoon pepper
 2 teaspoons all-purpose flour
 1/2 cup milk
 3/4 cup shredded cheddar cheese

In a large skillet, cook potatoes, onion and green pepper in butter over medium heat until almost tender. Stir in pork, bouillon and pepper. In a small bowl, combine flour and milk until smooth; add to skillet. Cook on medium-low heat for 5 minutes or until mixture is thickened, stirring frequently.

Sprinkle with cheese. Remove from the heat; cover and let stand until cheese is melted. **Yield:** 6 servings.

Fruited Chicken Pasta Salad

Prep: 25 min. + chilling

This five-ingredient recipe is perfect for summer picnics. It's also colorful, refreshing and a nice way to use up leftovers from Grilled Lemon Chicken (page 292).
—Bridget Francoeur, Adrian, Michigan

  2 cups uncooked bow tie pasta
  2 cups cubed cooked chicken
  1 can (11 ounces) mandarin oranges, drained
  1 cup halved green grapes
1/2 cup ranch salad dressing

Cook pasta according to package directions. Meanwhile, in a large bowl, combine the chicken, mandarin oranges and grapes. Drain and rinse pasta with cold water; add to chicken mixture. Drizzle with salad dressing; toss to coat. Cover and refrigerate for at least 1 hour before serving. **Yield:** 6 servings.

Great Grilled Leftovers

WANT MORE OPTIONS for using up leftover grilled meats? Our Test Kitchen home economists compiled some creative suggestions from fellow busy cooks. Try any of the following ideas to put your extras from the grill to delicious use:

- I buy several pounds of boneless chicken breasts on sale, flatten them slightly, brush them with olive oil and balsamic vinegar and grill them. Then I freeze the leftovers for later meals. Simply defrost as many as needed, cover them with mustard, salsa or bottled gravy, and heat them in the microwave.
  —Thomas Mills, Babylon, New York

- It's easy to make a chef salad using leftover grilled chicken or steak. Toss in shredded cheddar or mozzarella, any on-hand veggies and a few hard-cooked eggs. Sprinkle wheat germ or nuts on top.
  —Kim Lucas, Goshen, Indiana

- When I have leftover grilled ham steaks or chicken, I run the leftovers through the meat grinder, then add pickle relish, mayo, a little sugar, horseradish and mustard for a great ham or chicken salad.
  —Dale Zachary, Indianapolis, Indiana

- We usually buy more fresh salmon fillets than we can eat for dinner, grill all of it and use the leftovers to make salmon cakes the next day. The marinade and spices we use before cooking give the grilled fish great flavor—much better than canned!
  —Bonny Salmeri, Seminole, Florida

Asian Pork Tenderloins

Asian Pork Tenderloins

(Pictured above)

Prep: 10 min. + marinating **Grill:** 25 min.

These mouth-watering tenderloins are a summer favorite at our house and so simple to prepare. Save 1-1/2 of the cooked tenderloins, and you'll have enough to make Hash Brown Pork Skillet (page 292) the next day.
—Joan Hallford, North Richland Hills, Texas

1/2 cup olive oil
1/3 cup lime juice
  2 tablespoons minced garlic
  2 tablespoons minced fresh gingerroot
  2 tablespoons soy sauce
  2 teaspoons Dijon mustard
Dash cayenne pepper
  4 pork tenderloins (3/4 pound *each*)

For the marinade, in a blender combine the first seven ingredients; cover and process until blended. Divide marinade between two large resealable plastic bags; add two tenderloins to each bag. Seal bags and turn to coat; refrigerate for at least 4 hours or overnight.

Coat grill rack with cooking spray before starting the grill. Prepare grill for indirect heat. Drain and discard marinade. Grill pork, covered, over indirect medium-hot heat for 25-35 minutes or until a meat thermometer reads 160°. Let stand for 10 minutes before slicing. **Yield:** 8 servings.

Bite Into Burger Meals

HAMBURGERS truly are an American classic and a grilling staple. Here, our Test Kitchen pros offer their top tips, secrets and shortcuts for making extraordinary burgers. Plus, you'll get recipes for sensational sides to pair with your sandwiches. Enjoy!

All-American Loaded Burgers

(Pictured below)

Prep/Total Time: 25 min.

I first tried these for my daughter's birthday party. I received so many compliments and requests for the recipe that now I don't make hamburgers any other way!
—Marsha Urso, Pittsburgh, Pennsylvania

    1 cup dry bread crumbs
  1/2 cup finely chopped onion
  1/2 cup Italian salad dressing
    2 eggs, beaten
    2 pounds ground beef
    6 kaiser rolls, split
Leaf lettuce, Colby cheese slices, tomato slices, ketchup, prepared mustard and Fried Onion Rings (recipe on p. 296) *or* french-fried onions, optional

In a large bowl, combine bread crumbs, onion, salad dressing and eggs. Crumble beef over mixture and mix well. Shape into six patties.

Grill the burgers, covered, over medium heat or broil 4 in. from heat for 5-7 minutes on each side or until a meat thermometer reads 160° and juices run clear. Serve on rolls with lettuce, cheese, tomato, ketchup, mustard and Fried Onion Rings if desired. **Yield:** 6 servings.

All-American Loaded Burgers

Four Steps to Perfect Burgers

1. **Mixing**
   Mix minimally when making burgers. Over-mixing will result in a burger with a firm, compact texture.

2. **Portioning**
   Portion your patties, making sure they're all uniform in size. Spoon the meat into 1/2-cup measurements before forming.

3. **Forming**
   To ensure the burgers are of uniform doneness, form the patties 1/2 inch thick. Gently pinch to close cracks in the patty.

4. **Cooking**
   Insert the meat thermometer horizontally from the side into the burger's center. Cook ground beef or ground pork burgers to 160°. Cook ground turkey or ground chicken burgers to 165°.

Fried Onion Rings (p. 296)
Swiss Steak Burgers
Asian Pork Burgers

Asian Pork Burgers

(Pictured above)

Prep: 20 min. **Grill:** 20 min.

Give burgers some Asian flair with this recipe featuring hoisin and soy sauces. Bacon and pineapple add even more flavor. —*Terri McKitrick, Delafield, Wisconsin*

  3/4 cup finely chopped green pepper
  1/2 cup finely chopped onion
    2 tablespoons hoisin sauce
    2 teaspoons soy sauce
1-1/2 teaspoons seasoned salt
    1 teaspoon minced garlic
    2 pounds ground pork
    8 pieces unsweetened sliced pineapple
    8 bacon strips
    8 sesame seed hamburger buns, split

In a large bowl, combine the first six ingredients. Crumble pork over the mixture and mix well. Shape into eight patties. Top each with a pineapple slice; wrap with a bacon strip. If grilling the burgers, coat grill rack with cooking spray before starting the grill.

Grill the burgers, covered, over medium heat or broil 4 in. from the heat for 6-8 minutes on each side or until a meat thermometer reads 160° and juices run clear. Serve on buns. **Yield:** 8 servings.

Swiss Steak Burgers

(Pictured above)

Prep/Total Time: 20 minutes

A few years ago, I was introduced to horseradish cheese, and I fell in love! Try horseradish Swiss or any other horseradish cheese on these burgers for a fun alternative. But the classic Swiss called for in the recipe is great as well, especially with the steak sauce and Dijon mustard. —*Greg Dalenberg, Peoria, Arizona*

    4 tablespoons A.1. steak sauce, *divided*
    2 tablespoons Dijon mustard, *divided*
    1 pound ground beef
    4 slices Swiss cheese
    4 hamburger buns, split and toasted

In a small bowl, combine 2 tablespoons of steak sauce and 1 tablespoon Dijon mustard. Crumble the ground beef over the mixture and mix well. Shape mixture into four patties.

Grill the burgers, covered, over medium heat or broil 4 in. from heat for 5-7 minutes on each side or until a meat thermometer reads 160° and juices run clear. Top with cheese. Grill 1 minute longer or until cheese is melted.

Spread buns with remaining steak sauce and mustard; top each with a burger. **Yield:** 4 servings.

Bacon Potato Salad

(Pictured above)

Prep: 30 min. + chilling

My gang was tired of the same old potato salad at family functions, so I decided to do some experimenting with on-hand ingredients to see what I could come up with. This dish with bacon, cheese and ranch dressing was the result. Now I'm asked to bring it to all our get-togethers!
—Tami Gallagher, Eagan, Minnesota

    4 cups cubed red potatoes
    1 cup chopped onion
    7 bacon strips, cooked and crumbled
    2 tablespoons minced fresh parsley
1-1/3 cups mayonnaise
    3 tablespoons grated Parmesan cheese
    3 tablespoons prepared ranch salad dressing
    2 tablespoons prepared mustard
    4 teaspoons white vinegar
  1/2 teaspoon minced garlic
  1/4 teaspoon salt
  1/4 teaspoon pepper

Place the potatoes in a large saucepan and cover with water. Bring to a boil. Reduce heat; cover and cook for 10-15 minutes or until tender. Drain.

In a large bowl, combine the potatoes, onion, bacon and parsley. In a small bowl, combine the remaining ingredients. Pour over the potato mixture; toss to coat. Refrigerate for 1 hour or until chilled. **Yield:** 8 servings.

Fried Onion Rings

(Pictured on page 295)

Prep/Total Time: 25 min.

From our Test Kitchen cooks, these crispy burger toppers and on-the-side snacks are irresistible. Use them to add crunch to your tossed green salads, too.

  1/2 cup all-purpose flour
  1/2 cup water
    1 egg, lightly beaten
    1 teaspoon seasoned salt
  1/2 teaspoon baking powder
    1 large onion

In a shallow bowl, whisk together the first five ingredients. Cut onion into very thin slices; separate into rings. Dip the rings into the batter.

In a deep-fat fryer, heat 1 in. of oil to 375°. Fry the onion rings in batches for 1 to 1-1/2 minutes on each side or until golden brown. Drain on paper towels. Serve immediately. **Yield:** 12 servings.

Antipasto Pasta Salad

(Pictured at right and on page 286)

Prep: 30 min. + chilling

This colorful, hearty pasta salad is ideal for summer picnics because it's mayonnaise-free. It's also a breeze to put together. —Becky Melton, Orlando, Florida

1 package (16 ounces) tricolor spiral pasta
1 jar (16 ounces) giardiniera, drained and cut up
2 cans (one 3.8 ounces, one 2-1/4 ounces) sliced ripe olives, drained
1 jar (5-3/4 ounces) pimiento-stuffed olives, drained and sliced
1 jar (7 ounces) roasted sweet red peppers, drained and chopped
8 ounces summer sausage, cubed
8 ounces pepper Jack cheese, cubed
1 cup Italian salad dressing

Cook pasta according to package directions. Drain and rinse in cold water.

In a large bowl, combine the giardiniera, olives, red peppers, sausage, cheese and pasta. Add the dressing; toss to coat. Cover and refrigerate for 1 hour. **Yield:** 14 servings.

Antipasto Pasta Salad

Mix It Up for Different Burgers

TO MAKE four incredibly different but tasty burgers, try these combos. Each recipe idea yields four patties.
1. In a large bowl, combine the mix-ins, 1/2 teaspoon seasoned salt and 1/4 teaspoon pepper for each burger recipe in the chart below.
2. Crumble 1 pound of ground beef over the mix-ins and mix well.
3. Shape the mixture into four patties. Grill the burgers, covered, over medium heat or broil 4 inches from the heat for 5-7 minutes on each side or until a meat thermometer reads 160° and juices run clear.

BURGERS	MIX-INS			
Horseradish Blue Cheese Burgers	1/4 cup crumbled blue cheese	1-1/2 tablespoons prepared horseradish	1 teaspoon Worcestershire sauce	
Chili Cheeseburgers	1/2 cup shredded cheddar cheese	1/4 cup chili sauce	1/2 teaspoon onion powder	
Spinach Burgers	1-1/2 cups chopped fresh spinach	1/4 cup seasoned bread crumbs	2 tablespoons Dijon mustard	2 tablespoons water
Pepperoni Pizza Burgers	1/4 cup tomato sauce	8 slices turkey pepperoni, minced	3/4 teaspoon Italian seasoning	

Chapter 20

IF YOU'RE LOOKING for a wide variety of recipes, this chapter is for you! We've gathered an array of delicious dishes and organized them by category, so you'll see similar fare together.

Enjoy paging through four different sections—great grilling ideas, small-size recipes for two, suppers from the stovetop and fast favorites that make use of holiday leftovers.

Try Orange-Glazed Salmon for your backyard barbecue... serve up Bacon Jack Chicken when it's just the two of you at the table...pull out a skillet for Hearty Beef and Noodles on a busy weekday...and save your extra Thanksgiving turkey for Broccoli Turkey Casserole.

TASTY FOR TWO. Vegetable Rice Medley and Maple-Glazed Pork Chops (both recipes on p. 305).

Grilled Greats

WHEN summer's in full swing, it's time to fire up the charcoal or flip on the gas and enjoy the taste that only grilling can create. Get your outdoor cooking underway with the standout recipes here, from Barbecued Chicken Pizzas to Orange-Glazed Salmon.

Savory Grilled T-Bones

(Pictured below)

Prep: 15 min. + marinating **Grill:** 15 min.

These marinated steaks are melt-in-your-mouth good and sure to become a favorite. Don't let summer go by without trying this recipe! —Anna Davis, Half Way, Montana

- 1/4 cup chopped onion
- 1/4 cup olive oil
- 2 tablespoons lemon juice
- 2 tablespoons soy sauce
- 1 tablespoon sugar
- 1 tablespoon cider vinegar
- 1 tablespoon honey
- 2 teaspoons minced garlic
- 2 teaspoons Worcestershire sauce
- 1 teaspoon salt
- 1/2 teaspoon pepper
- 6 beef T-bone steaks (1 inch thick and 12 ounces *each*)

In a large resealable plastic bag, combine the first 11 ingredients; add the steaks. Seal bag and turn to coat; refrigerate for 2-4 hours.

Drain and discard marinade. Grill steaks, covered, over medium heat for 6-10 minutes on each side or until meat reaches desired doneness (for medium-rare, a meat thermometer should read 145°; medium, 160°; well-done, 170°). **Yield:** 6 servings.

Savory Grilled T-Bones

Chicken 'n' Veggie Kabobs

Chicken 'n' Veggie Kabobs

(Pictured above)

Prep: 20 min. + marinating **Cook:** 15 min.

I created these skewers for a party, and they were an instant hit. Everyone commented on the meat's tenderness. —Becky Wiesmore, Rochester, New York

- 1 pound boneless skinless chicken breasts, cut into 1-inch cubes
- 1 cup Italian salad dressing, *divided*
- 1/4 cup olive oil
- 1 teaspoon garlic salt
- 1/2 teaspoon dried rosemary, crushed
- 1 medium zucchini, cut into 1/2-inch slices
- 1 yellow summer squash, cut into 1/2-inch slices
- 2 medium onions, quartered
- 1 medium sweet red pepper, cut into 1-inch pieces
- 2 cups cherry tomatoes

In a small resealable plastic bag, combine the chicken and 1/2 cup salad dressing. Seal the bag and turn to coat; refrigerate for 15 minutes. Meanwhile, in a large resealable plastic bag, combine the oil, garlic salt and rosemary. Add vegetables and toss to coat.

Drain and discard marinades. On eight metal or soaked wooden skewers, alternately thread the chicken and vegetables. Grill the kabobs, uncovered, over medium-hot heat for 12-15 minutes or until juices run clear, turning and basting occasionally with remaining salad dressing. **Yield:** 8 kabobs.

Chinese Country-Style Pork Ribs

(Pictured below)

Prep: 25 min. **Grill:** 10 min.

Take a trip to the Far East with these tender, change-of-pace ribs. The tangy Chinese-style glaze featuring hoisin sauce gives them a different and unique taste—and goes together quickly on the stovetop while you're microwaving the meat. Then just toss it on the grill for a great entree.
—Jamie Wetter, Boscobel, Wisconsin

    4 pounds bone-in country-style pork ribs
      (1-1/2-inches thick)
  1/2 cup water
    1 tablespoon Liquid Smoke, optional
  1/2 teaspoon onion powder
  1/2 cup chili sauce
  1/4 cup hoisin sauce
    2 tablespoons honey
  1/8 teaspoon cayenne pepper

Place the pork ribs, water, Liquid Smoke if desired and onion powder in a 3-qt. microwave-safe dish. Cover and microwave on high for 15-20 minutes or until the meat is tender.

Meanwhile, in a small saucepan, combine remaining ingredients. Bring to a boil. Reduce the heat; simmer, uncovered, for 5-8 minutes or until slightly thickened, stirring occasionally.

Coat the grill rack with cooking spray before starting the grill. Drain the ribs. Grill ribs, covered, over medium heat for 4-5 minutes on each side or until browned, basting with the prepared sauce and turning occasionally. **Yield:** 8 servings.

Chinese Country-Style Pork Ribs

Orange-Maple Glazed Chicken

Orange-Maple Glazed Chicken

(Pictured above)

Prep: 25 min. **Grill:** 10 min.

Pick up a medium-size orange for this recipe—the zest and juice from the fruit will combine with maple syrup and balsamic vinegar to lend the chicken outstanding flavor.
—Lillian Julow, Gainesville, Florida

☑ This recipe includes Nutrition Facts and Diabetic Exchanges.

  1/3 cup orange juice
  1/3 cup maple syrup
    2 tablespoons balsamic vinegar
1-1/2 teaspoons Dijon mustard
    1 teaspoon salt, *divided*
  3/4 teaspoon pepper, *divided*
    1 tablespoon minced fresh basil *or* 1 teaspoon
      dried basil
  1/2 teaspoon grated orange peel
    6 boneless skinless chicken breast halves
      (6 ounces *each*)

In a small saucepan, combine the orange juice, syrup, vinegar, mustard, 1/2 teaspoon salt and 1/4 teaspoon pepper. Bring to a boil; cook until liquid is reduced to 1/2 cup, about 5 minutes. Stir in basil and orange peel. Remove from the heat; set aside.

Sprinkle the chicken with the remaining salt and pepper. Grill the chicken, covered, over medium heat for 5-7 minutes on each side or until a meat thermometer reads 170°, basting frequently with the orange juice mixture. **Yield:** 6 servings.

Nutrition Facts: 1 chicken breast half equals 240 calories, 4 g fat (1 g saturated fat), 94 mg cholesterol, 508 mg sodium, 15 g carbohydrate, trace fiber, 34 g protein. **Diabetic Exchanges:** 5 very lean meat, 1 starch.

Barbecued Chicken Pizzas

Barbecued Chicken Pizzas

(Pictured above)

Prep: 25 min. **Grill:** 10 min.

Do you crave pizza—but want something a little bit different for a change of pace? Try this out-of-the-ordinary recipe. Quick and easy to make with a refrigerated crust, this pie will get raves for its hot-off-the-grill taste. It's perfect for a spur-of-the-moment backyard party.
    —Alicia Trevithick, Temecula, California

   2 **boneless skinless chicken breast halves**
     (6 ounces *each*)
 1/4 **teaspoon salt**
 1/4 **teaspoon pepper**
   1 **cup barbecue sauce,** *divided*
   1 **tube (13.8 ounces) refrigerated pizza crust**
   2 **teaspoons olive oil**
   1 **medium red onion, thinly sliced**
   2 **cups (8 ounces) shredded Gouda cheese**
 1/4 **cup minced fresh cilantro**

Coat the grill rack with cooking spray before starting the grill. Sprinkle the chicken with salt and pepper. Grill the chicken, covered, over medium heat for 5-7 minutes on each side or until chicken juices run clear, basting frequently with 1/2 cup barbecue sauce. Set aside and keep warm.

Divide dough in half. On a lightly floured surface, roll each portion into a 12-in. x 10-in. rectangle. Lightly brush both sides of the dough with oil; place on grill. Cover and grill over medium heat for 1-2 minutes or until the bottom is lightly browned.

Remove from the grill. Cut the chicken into 1/2-in. cubes. Spread the grilled side of each pizza with 1/4 cup barbecue sauce; layer with chicken, onion, cheese and cilantro. Return to grill. Cover and cook each pizza for 4-5 minutes or until the bottom is lightly browned and cheese is melted. **Yield:** 2 pizzas (4 pieces each).

Barbecue Beef Kabobs

(Pictured below)

Prep: 25 min. + marinating **Grill:** 20 min.

My husband and sons like these skewers because they're delicious...and I like them even more because they're a breeze to fix! —Karen Engstrom, Glasgow, Montana

   1 **cup ketchup**
 1/3 **cup French salad dressing**
 1/3 **cup soy sauce**
   1 **tablespoon Worcestershire sauce**
   1 **pound boneless beef sirloin steak, cut into**
     1-inch cubes
   1 **cup fresh baby carrots**
   2 **tablespoons water**
   1 **pound medium fresh mushrooms, halved**
   1 **medium green pepper, cut into 1-inch pieces**
 1/2 **medium onion, cut into 1-inch pieces**
Hot cooked rice, optional

In a small bowl, combine the ketchup, salad dressing, soy sauce and Worcestershire sauce. Transfer 1/3 cup to another bowl for basting; cover and refrigerate. Pour remaining marinade into a large resealable plastic bag; add steak. Seal bag and turn to coat; refrigerate for at least 1 hour.

Place carrots and water in a microwave-safe dish. Cover and microwave on high for 4 minutes; drain. Drain and discard marinade. On 10 metal or soaked wooden skewers, alternately thread the beef, carrots, mushrooms, green pepper and onion.

Grill, covered, over medium-hot heat for 18-20 minutes or until the meat reaches desired doneness, basting frequently with the reserved marinade and turning occasionally. Serve with rice if desired. **Yield:** 5 servings.

Barbecue Beef Kabobs

Grilled Vegetable Platter

(Pictured above)

Prep: 20 min. + marinating **Grill:** 10 min.

These veggies are so flavorful. Grilling releases their natural sweetness. —Heidi Hall, North St. Paul, Minnesota

- 1/4 cup olive oil
- 2 tablespoons honey
- 1 tablespoon plus 1/2 teaspoon balsamic vinegar, *divided*
- 1 teaspoon dried oregano
- 1/2 teaspoon garlic powder
- 1 pound fresh asparagus, trimmed
- 3 small carrots, cut in half lengthwise
- 1 large sweet red pepper, cut into 1-inch strips
- 1 medium yellow summer squash, cut into 1/2-inch slices
- 1 medium red onion, cut into four wedges
- 1/8 teaspoon pepper

Dash salt

In a small bowl, combine the oil, honey, 1 tablespoon vinegar, oregano and garlic powder. Pour 3 tablespoons marinade into a large resealable plastic bag; add the vegetables. Seal bag and turn to coat; refrigerate for 1-1/2 hours. Cover and refrigerate remaining marinade.

Place the vegetables on a grilling grid. Transfer to grill rack. Grill, covered, over medium heat for 8-12 minutes or until crisp-tender, turning once. Transfer to a large serving platter. Combine reserved marinade and remaining vinegar; drizzle over vegetables. Sprinkle with pepper and salt. **Yield:** 6 servings.

Editor's Note: If you do not have a grilling grid, use a disposable foil pan. Poke holes in the bottom of the pan with a meat fork to allow liquid to drain.

Orange-Glazed Salmon

(Pictured above)

Prep: 10 min. + marinating **Grill:** 20 min.

Treat guests to this tender salmon in a delectable glaze. They'll love it! —Mildred Sherrer, Fort Worth, Texas

- 1/2 cup barbecue sauce
- 1/3 cup orange juice concentrate
- 7 teaspoons soy sauce
- 4-1/2 teaspoons sherry *or* apple juice
- 4-1/2 teaspoons Dijon mustard
- 1 tablespoon minced fresh gingerroot
- 2 teaspoons brown sugar
- 2 teaspoons red wine vinegar
- 1-1/2 teaspoons canola oil
- 1/2 teaspoon minced garlic
- 1 salmon fillet (2 pounds and 3/4 inch thick)

In a small bowl, combine first 10 ingredients. Set aside 1/2 cup marinade for basting; cover and refrigerate. Pour remaining marinade into a large resealable plastic bag; add the salmon. Seal the bag and turn to coat; refrigerate for 1 hour, turning occasionally.

Coat grill rack with cooking spray before starting the grill. Drain and discard marinade. Place salmon skin side down on grill rack. Grill, covered, over medium heat for 5 minutes. Spoon reserved marinade over fish. Grill 15-20 minutes longer or until fish flakes easily with a fork, basting frequently. **Yield:** 6 servings.

Table for Two

WANT small-yield recipes for just the two of you? You don't have to eat at a restaurant in order to get the right number of servings. With the delectable but down-sized dishes here, you can enjoy home-cooked specialties such as Bacon Jack Chicken, Tangy Deli Melts and Maple-Glazed Pork Chops...without being stuck with a week's worth of leftovers!

Asparagus with Dill Sauce

(Pictured below)

Prep/Total Time: 15 min.

This creamy, fresh-tasting side is terrific alongside fish, but it's also good with a variety of other entrees. The recipe takes just 15 minutes to fix from start to finish, leaving you plenty of time to devote to the rest of your menu.
—Sandy Miller, Wixom, Michigan

✓ **This recipe includes Nutrition Facts and Diabetic Exchanges.**

  1/2 pound fresh asparagus, trimmed
  1/4 cup sour cream
    1 teaspoon milk
  1/4 teaspoon dill weed
  1/8 teaspoon salt
  1/8 teaspoon pepper

Place asparagus in a steamer basket; place in a large saucepan over 1 inch of water. Bring to a boil; cover and steam for 3-5 minutes or until crisp-tender.

Meanwhile, in a small microwave-safe bowl, combine the remaining ingredients. Microwave on high for 30-60 seconds or until heated through. Serve with the asparagus. **Yield:** 2 servings.

Nutrition Facts: 1/4 pound asparagus with 2 tablespoons sauce equals 76 calories, 5 g fat (4 g saturated fat), 20 mg cholesterol, 165 mg sodium, 4 g carbohydrate, 1 g fiber, 3 g protein. **Diabetic Exchanges:** 1 vegetable, 1 fat.

Seasoned Tilapia Fillets

(Pictured below left)

Prep/Total Time: 30 min.

If you need a delicious dinner that's simple and also on the healthier side, you just found it! These restaurant-quality fillets rely on spices to deliver big flavor.
—Dana Alexander, Lebanon, Missouri

✓ **This recipe includes Nutrition Facts and Diabetic Exchanges.**

  2 tilapia fillets (6 ounces *each*)
  1 tablespoon butter, melted
  1 teaspoon steak seasoning
  1/2 teaspoon dried parsley flakes
  1/4 teaspoon dried thyme
  1/4 teaspoon paprika
  1/8 teaspoon onion powder
  1/8 teaspoon salt
  1/8 teaspoon pepper
Dash garlic powder

Place the fillets in a greased 11-in. x 7-in. baking dish. Drizzle with the butter. In a small bowl, combine the remaining ingredients; sprinkle over fillets.

Cover and bake at 425° for 15 minutes. Uncover and bake 5-8 minutes longer or until fish flakes easily with a fork. **Yield:** 2 servings.

Editor's Note: This recipe was tested with McCormick's Montreal Steak Seasoning. Look for it in the spice aisle.

Nutrition Facts: 1 fillet equals 193 calories, 7 g fat (4 g saturated fat), 98 mg cholesterol, 589 mg sodium, 1 g carbohydrate, trace fiber, 32 g protein. **Diabetic Exchanges:** 5 lean meat, 1-1/2 fat.

Asparagus with Dill Sauce
Seasoned Tilapia Fillets

Tasty Twosome

Cooking for two can be a challenge, but I discovered a simple way to reduce the number of servings in some casseroles. Now, I use this idea all the time.

If the recipe calls for a 13-inch x 9-inch baking dish, I reduce the ingredients by half and divide the mixture between two 1-quart dishes. The shallower fill makes it the perfect size for a meal for my husband and me. I bake one casserole for dinner and keep the other in the freezer for a later time—an added bonus!
—Laura Kittleson, Sandy, Utah

Vegetable Rice Medley
Maple-Glazed Pork Chops

Vegetable Rice Medley

(Pictured above and on page 298)

Prep/Total Time: 30 min.

With tons of veggies and tasty rice, this easy side is the only one you need. Pair it with chicken or Maple-Glazed Pork Chops (at right). —Pat Habiger, Spearville, Kansas

  3/4 cup chicken broth
  1/3 cup uncooked long grain rice
    3 tablespoons finely chopped onion
4-1/2 teaspoons butter
  2/3 cup sliced fresh mushrooms
  1/3 cup julienned zucchini
  1/3 cup julienned carrot
  2/3 cup cut fresh asparagus (1-inch pieces)
  1/8 to 1/4 teaspoon dried basil
  1/3 cup grated Parmesan cheese
Dash pepper

Pour broth into a small saucepan; bring to a boil. Add rice. Reduce heat; cover and simmer for 12-15 minutes or until liquid is absorbed.

  Meanwhile, in a large skillet, saute onion in butter for 4-5 minutes or until crisp-tender. Add the mushrooms, zucchini and carrot; saute 3-5 minutes longer or until vegetables are crisp-tender. Add the asparagus and basil; cook, uncovered, over medium-low heat for 5-7 minutes or until asparagus is crisp-tender.

  In a small serving bowl, combine the rice, asparagus mixture, cheese and pepper. **Yield:** 2 servings.

Maple-Glazed Pork Chops

(Pictured above and on page 298)

Prep/Total Time: 30 min.

Just a few basic pantry ingredients make this wonderful entree a frequently requested choice. The slight sweetness from the maple syrup comes through beautifully.
—Athena Russell, Florence, South Carolina

  1/2 teaspoon salt
  1/2 teaspoon paprika
  1/4 teaspoon ground cumin
  1/4 teaspoon ground cinnamon
  1/4 teaspoon pepper
    2 bone-in pork loin chops (7 ounces *each*)
    1 tablespoon maple syrup
1-1/2 teaspoons butter, melted
1-1/2 teaspoons Dijon mustard

Combine the first five ingredients; rub over pork chops. Place in a greased 11-in. x 7-in. baking dish. Bake, uncovered, at 425° for 20 minutes. Combine the remaining ingredients; pour over chops. Bake 5 minutes longer or until meat juices run clear. **Yield:** 2 servings.

Cucumber & Squash Salad
Tangy Deli Melts

Tangy Deli Melts

(Pictured at left)

Prep/Total Time: 10 min.

Here, apricot preserves give ordinary sandwich ingredients a delectable boost. The recipe makes two melts, but you may want extras! —Steve Foy, Kirkwood, Missouri

> 2 tablespoons mayonnaise
> 2 teaspoons apricot preserves
> 1/2 teaspoon Dijon mustard
> 2 seeded hamburger buns, split
> 2 slices deli ham
> 2 slices deli turkey
> 2 slices provolone cheese

In a small bowl, combine the mayonnaise, preserves and mustard; spread over buns.

On each bun bottom, layer a slice of ham, turkey and cheese. Replace tops. Place sandwiches on a baking sheet. Bake at 350° for 5-7 minutes or until cheese is melted. **Yield:** 2 servings.

Cucumber & Squash Salad

(Pictured at left)

Prep/Total Time: 10 min.

I created this recipe one summer when I had too many summer squash. To use them up, I tossed them into a refreshing salad. —Jacqueline Miller, Wooster, Ohio

☑ This recipe includes Nutrition Facts and Diabetic Exchanges.

> 1 cup thinly sliced cucumber
> 1 cup thinly sliced yellow summer squash
> 2 tablespoons chopped green onion
> 1 tablespoon shredded Parmesan cheese
> Dash crushed red pepper flakes
> 2 tablespoons prepared Italian salad dressing

In a small bowl, combine the first five ingredients. Drizzle with salad dressing; toss to coat. **Yield:** 2 servings.

Nutrition Facts: 3/4 cup equals 86 calories, 6 g fat (1 g saturated fat), 2 mg cholesterol, 298 mg sodium, 6 g carbohydrate, 2 g fiber, 2 g protein. **Diabetic Exchanges:** 1 vegetable, 1 fat.

Bacon Jack Chicken

(Pictured at right)

Prep/Total Time: 30 min.

Pepper Jack and Parmesan cheeses add richness to this golden brown chicken topped with tender vegetables and bacon. It cooks in no time at all on the stovetop. —Dawn Jones, Cedar Vale, Kansas

> 2 boneless skinless chicken breast halves
>   (4 ounces *each*)
> 1/4 teaspoon seasoned salt
> 2 tablespoons butter
> 3 bacon strips, halved

> 1/4 cup sliced onion
> 1/4 cup sliced fresh mushrooms
> 3 ounces pepper Jack cheese, shredded
> 1 tablespoon grated Parmesan cheese

Sprinkle the chicken with seasoned salt. In a nonstick skillet, cook the chicken in butter over medium heat for 5-6 minutes on each side or until juices run clear; drain. Remove and keep warm.

In the same skillet, cook the bacon over medium heat until crisp. Remove to paper towels to drain. Saute the onion and mushrooms in the drippings. Return chicken to the pan. Top with the bacon, onion, mushrooms and pepper Jack cheese. Cover and let stand for 2-3 minutes or until cheese is melted. Sprinkle with Parmesan cheese. **Yield:** 2 servings.

Sauteed Zucchini Strips

(Pictured below)

Prep/Total Time: 20 min.

Jazz up zucchini by sauteeing it with just a few everyday items—garlic, lemon juice and Greek seasoning. They all add up to a versatile side dish that's bursting with flavor. —Jeannie Klugh, Lancaster, Pennsylvania

☑ This recipe includes Nutrition Facts and Diabetic Exchanges.

> 3 small zucchini, julienned
> 2 teaspoons minced garlic
> 2 teaspoons lemon juice
> 1/2 teaspoon Greek seasoning
> 2 teaspoons olive oil
> 1/4 teaspoon pepper

In a large skillet, saute the zucchini, garlic, lemon juice and Greek seasoning in oil until tender. Sprinkle with pepper. **Yield:** 2 servings.

Nutrition Facts: 3/4 cup equals 74 calories, 5 g fat (1 g saturated fat), 0 cholesterol, 259 mg sodium, 7 g carbohydrate, 2 g fiber, 2 g protein. **Diabetic Exchanges:** 1 vegetable, 1 fat.

Bacon Jack Chicken
Sauteed Zucchini Strips

From the Stove

PULL OUT a saucepan, pot or skillet, and you'll be well on your way toward serving tonight's dinner. That's because all of the recipes here rely on the convenience and ease of stovetop cooking.

From Curry Shrimp Linguine and Hearty Beef and Noodles to Sweet Potato Pork Skillet and Stovetop Chicken 'n' Stuffing, these fuss-free dishes are sure to please everyone—including the busy cook!

Stovetop Chicken 'n' Stuffing

(Pictured below)

Prep/Total Time: 30 min.

With nothing in mind for dinner one night, I started doing a little experimenting in the kitchen...and this tasty meal-in-one was the result. My entire family loves it.
—Connie Jonas, Eugene, Oregon

- 1 package (6 ounces) corn bread stuffing mix
- 1/2 cup all-purpose flour
- 1 teaspoon salt
- 1 teaspoon ground mustard
- 4 boneless skinless chicken breast halves (6 ounces *each*)
- 1 tablespoon canola oil
- 1 can (10-3/4 ounces) condensed cream of mushroom soup, undiluted
- 2/3 cup chopped onion

Stovetop Chicken 'n' Stuffing

Sweet Potato Pork Skillet

- 2/3 cup milk
- 2 tablespoons crumbled cooked bacon
- 2 cans (14-1/2 ounces *each*) cut green beans, drained
- 1/2 cup shredded Monterey Jack cheese

Prepare stuffing mix according to package directions. Meanwhile, in a large resealable plastic bag, combine the flour, salt and mustard. Add the chicken, a few pieces at a time, and shake to coat.

In a large skillet, cook chicken in oil for 2-3 minutes on each side or until golden brown. In a large bowl, combine the soup, onion, milk and bacon; stir in green beans. Pour over chicken; top with stuffing. Cover and cook for 7 minutes. Sprinkle with the cheese; cook 3-4 minutes longer or until heated through and cheese is melted. **Yield:** 4 servings.

Sweet Potato Pork Skillet

(Pictured above)

Prep: 15 min. **Cook:** 35 min.

Spiced sweet potatoes and tender pork chops pair beautifully in this satisfying dish from our Test Kitchen home economists. With a colorful mix of ingredients, the pretty entree is sure to brighten up an ordinary weekday.

- 4 bone-in pork loin chops (1 inch thick and 8 ounces *each*)
- 1 tablespoon olive oil
- 1 can (20 ounces) pineapple tidbits
- 3 tablespoons brown sugar
- 1/2 teaspoon salt
- 1/2 teaspoon ground cinnamon
- 2 large sweet potatoes, peeled and cut into 1-inch cubes
- 1 medium green pepper, cut into chunks
- 1-1/2 cups uncooked instant rice
- 1 tablespoon cornstarch

In a large skillet, brown pork chops in oil. Meanwhile, drain pineapple, reserving juice; set pineapple aside. In a small bowl, combine brown sugar, salt, cinnamon and 1/2 cup of the reserved juice; stir into skillet. Add sweet potatoes; toss to coat. Bring to a boil. Reduce heat; cover and simmer for 15 minutes. Add green pepper and pineapple; cover and cook for 10-15 minutes or until potatoes are tender.

Meanwhile, cook the rice according to the package directions. In a small bowl, combine cornstarch and remaining pineapple juice until smooth; add to skillet. Bring to a boil; cook and stir for 2 minutes or until thickened and bubbly. Serve with rice. **Yield:** 4 servings.

Curry Shrimp Linguine

(Pictured below)

Prep/Total Time: 25 min.

Curry, cilantro and coconut milk make this shrimp-and-pasta dish an exotic change of pace any night of the week. Also try it with Thai rice noodles or spaghetti in place of the linguine. For a quick and easy side, toss together a green salad.
—Jana Rippee, Anacortes, Washington

1 package (16 ounces) linguine
3 teaspoons curry powder
1 can (14 ounces) light coconut milk
1/2 teaspoon salt
1/4 teaspoon pepper
1-1/4 pounds uncooked medium shrimp, peeled and deveined
1/3 cup minced fresh cilantro

Cook the linguine according to package directions. Meanwhile, in a large skillet over medium heat, toast curry powder for 2 minutes, stirring frequently. Stir in the milk, salt and pepper.

Bring to a boil. Add shrimp; cook for 5-6 minutes or until shrimp turn pink. Drain linguine; toss with shrimp mixture and cilantro. **Yield:** 6 servings.

Curry Shrimp Linguine

Hearty Beef and Noodles

Hearty Beef and Noodles

(Pictured above)

Prep: 10 min. **Cook:** 25 min.

This beef-and-noodle dish is a longtime family favorite. In fact, my children would always ask to bring home friends for dinner on nights I was fixing it! Now my oldest son is in the Army and has had his wife call home to get the recipe. It's filling, home-style food at is best.
—Sylvia Streu, Norman, Oklahoma

1-1/2 pounds boneless beef sirloin steak, cut into 1/2-inch strips
2 teaspoons olive oil
1/2 cup chopped onion
1-1/2 teaspoons minced garlic
1 can (10-3/4 ounces) condensed cream of mushroom soup, undiluted
1 cup water
1 cup half-and-half cream
1/3 cup brewed coffee
2 envelopes brown gravy mix
5 cups uncooked egg noodles
1 cup (8 ounces) sour cream
1/2 teaspoon paprika
1/4 teaspoon pepper

In a large skillet, brown beef in oil on all sides; remove and keep warm. In the same skillet, saute the onion and garlic until tender. Return beef to the pan; stir in the soup, water, cream, coffee and gravy mix. Bring to a boil. Reduce heat; cover and simmer for 20-25 minutes or until meat is tender, stirring occasionally.

Meanwhile, cook the noodles according to package directions. Add the sour cream, paprika and pepper to skillet; heat through. Drain noodles. Serve with beef. **Yield:** 6 servings.

Holiday Extras

Breaded Turkey Sandwiches

ONCE is definitely not enough when it comes to Christmas dinner and other holiday meals. So enjoy your ham or turkey leftovers with the double-take dishes here. You'll find it hard to believe that second-day foods can taste so fabulous!

Ham Fettuccine Bake

(Pictured below)

Prep: 15 min. **Bake:** 25 min.

This is a great way to use up ham in the fridge. I often serve this with a tossed salad, but it can make a meal all by itself. —Cathy Neve, Yakima, Washington

- 1/4 cup dry bread crumbs
- 1/4 teaspoon dried parsley flakes
- 3 tablespoons butter, *divided*
- 2 tablespoons all-purpose flour
- 2 cups milk
- 1-1/2 cups (6 ounces) sharp white cheddar cheese, shredded
- 2 cups cubed fully cooked ham
- 1-1/2 cups cooked fettuccine
- 1 cup frozen peas

In a small skillet, cook the bread crumbs and parsley in 1 tablespoon butter over medium heat for 4-5 minutes or until golden brown. Remove from pan; set aside.

In a large skillet, melt the remaining butter. Stir in flour until smooth; gradually add the milk. Bring to a boil; cook and stir for 2 minutes or until thickened. Stir in cheese; cook 2-3 minutes longer or until melted. Stir in ham, fettuccine and peas. Transfer to a greased 11-in. x 7-in. baking dish; sprinkle with bread crumb mixture.

Cover and bake at 350° for 20 minutes. Uncover; bake 5-10 minutes longer or until bubbly. **Yield:** 5 servings.

Breaded Turkey Sandwiches

(Pictured above)

Prep/Total Time: 30 min.

My son came up with this recipe, and it's become a post-Thanksgiving tradition. The combo is both unique and delicious. For an even "meltier" sandwich, try grilling it. —Shannon Bray, Magnolia, Texas

- 1 egg
- 1/2 cup milk
- 3/4 cup dry bread crumbs
- 1/2 teaspoon salt
- 1/2 teaspoon dried rosemary, crushed
- 1/2 teaspoon pepper
- 1 pound sliced cooked turkey
- 1/3 cup seedless raspberry jam
- 8 slices sourdough bread, toasted
- 8 slices Swiss cheese

In a shallow bowl, whisk the egg and milk. In another shallow bowl, combine the bread crumbs, salt, rosemary and pepper. Dip turkey slices in egg mixture, then bread crumb mixture. Transfer to a greased 15-in. x 10-in. x 1-in. baking pan. Bake at 400° for 15-18 minutes or until golden brown, turning once.

Spread jam over toast; layer four slices with turkey and cheese. Top with remaining toast. **Yield:** 4 servings.

Ham Fettuccine Bake

Chicken Chowder

(Pictured below)

Prep/Total Time: 30 min.

This comforting chowder is wonderful served over tortilla chips or with corn bread...and you can replace the chicken with leftover turkey if you have it on hand. Packed with corn, onion, tomatoes and green chilies, the chunky soup is hard to beat on a cold autumn or winter day.
—Heather Hamilton, Bunker Hill, West Virginia

- 1 can (14-1/2 ounces) reduced-sodium chicken broth
- 1 can (10-3/4 ounces) condensed cream of chicken soup, undiluted
- 1 can (10-3/4 ounces) condensed cream of potato soup, undiluted
- 1-1/2 cups milk
- 2 cans (14-1/2 ounces *each*) diced tomatoes, undrained
- 2 cups cubed cooked chicken
- 1 can (11 ounces) Mexicorn, drained
- 1/3 cup chopped onion
- 1 can (4 ounces) chopped green chilies
- 1-1/2 cups (6 ounces) shredded Monterey Jack cheese

In a large saucepan, combine the chicken broth, cream soups and milk. Stir in the tomatoes, chicken, Mexicorn, onion and green chilies. Bring to a boil. Reduce the heat; simmer, uncovered, for 10-15 minutes or until the onion is tender. Garnish with Monterey Jack cheese. **Yield:** 8 servings (3 quarts).

Chicken Chowder

Broccoli Turkey Casserole

Broccoli Turkey Casserole

(Pictured above)

Prep: 20 min. **Bake:** 25 min.

I've served this creamy dish at after-Christmas luncheons, and I always get recipe requests. French-fried onions add a nice crunch. —Muriel Shand, Isanti, Minnesota

- 1/4 cup chopped onion
- 1/4 cup chopped celery
- 1/4 cup butter, cubed
- 4 cups cubed cooked turkey breast
- 1 package (16 ounces) frozen broccoli florets, thawed
- 1 can (10-3/4 ounces) condensed cream of mushroom soup, undiluted
- 1 can (10-3/4 ounces) condensed cream of chicken soup, undiluted
- 1 cup cooked rice
- 1/2 cup shredded part-skim mozzarella cheese
- 1 can (2.8 ounces) french-fried onions

In a large skillet, saute onion and celery in butter until tender. Stir in turkey, broccoli, soups and rice; transfer to a greased shallow 2-1/2 qt. baking dish.

Bake, uncovered, at 350° for 25-30 minutes or until bubbly. Sprinkle with cheese and onions; bake 5 minutes longer or until cheese is melted. **Yield:** 8 servings.

Frozen for the Future

WANT TO SAVOR your leftover Christmas or Thanksgiving turkey in Broccoli Turkey Casserole (recipe above)—but don't want to eat the casserole right away? This dish freezes well, so just pop the assembled entree in the freezer and bake it on a later day.

Substitutions & Equivalents

Equivalent Measures

3 teaspoons	=	1 tablespoon	16 tablespoons	=	1 cup
4 tablespoons	=	1/4 cup	2 cups	=	1 pint
5-1/3 tablespoons	=	1/3 cup	4 cups	=	1 quart
8 tablespoons	=	1/2 cup	4 quarts	=	1 gallon

Food Equivalents

Grains

Macaroni	1 cup (3-1/2 ounces) uncooked	=	2-1/2 cups cooked
Noodles, Medium	3 cups (4 ounces) uncooked	=	4 cups cooked
Popcorn	1/3 to 1/2 cup unpopped	=	8 cups popped
Rice, Long Grain	1 cup uncooked	=	3 cups cooked
Rice, Quick-Cooking	1 cup uncooked	=	2 cups cooked
Spaghetti	8 ounces uncooked	=	4 cups cooked

Crumbs

Bread	1 slice	=	3/4 cup soft crumbs, 1/4 cup fine dry crumbs
Graham Crackers	7 squares	=	1/2 cup finely crushed
Buttery Round Crackers	12 crackers	=	1/2 cup finely crushed
Saltine Crackers	14 crackers	=	1/2 cup finely crushed

Fruits

Bananas	1 medium	=	1/3 cup mashed
Lemons	1 medium	=	3 tablespoons juice, 2 teaspoons grated peel
Limes	1 medium	=	2 tablespoons juice, 1-1/2 teaspoons grated peel
Oranges	1 medium	=	1/4 to 1/3 cup juice, 4 teaspoons grated peel

Vegetables

Cabbage	1 head	=	5 cups shredded	Green Pepper	1 large	=	1 cup chopped
Carrots	1 pound	=	3 cups shredded	Mushrooms	1/2 pound	=	3 cups sliced
Celery	1 rib	=	1/2 cup chopped	Onions	1 medium	=	1/2 cup chopped
Corn	1 ear fresh	=	2/3 cup kernels	Potatoes	3 medium	=	2 cups cubed

Nuts

Almonds	1 pound	=	3 cups chopped	Pecan Halves	1 pound	=	4-1/2 cups chopped
Ground Nuts	3-3/4 ounces	=	1 cup	Walnuts	1 pound	=	3-3/4 cups chopped

Easy Substitutions

When you need...		Use...
Baking Powder	1 teaspoon	1/2 teaspoon cream of tartar + 1/4 teaspoon baking soda
Buttermilk	1 cup	1 tablespoon lemon juice *or* vinegar + enough milk to measure 1 cup (let stand 5 minutes before using)
Cornstarch	1 tablespoon	2 tablespoons all-purpose flour
Honey	1 cup	1-1/4 cups sugar + 1/4 cup water
Half-and-Half Cream	1 cup	1 tablespoon melted butter + enough whole milk to measure 1 cup
Onion	1 small, chopped (1/3 cup)	1 teaspoon onion powder *or* 1 tablespoon dried minced onion
Tomato Juice	1 cup	1/2 cup tomato sauce + 1/2 cup water
Tomato Sauce	2 cups	3/4 cup tomato paste + 1 cup water
Unsweetened Chocolate	1 square (1 ounce)	3 tablespoons baking cocoa + 1 tablespoon shortening *or* oil
Whole Milk	1 cup	1/2 cup evaporated milk + 1/2 cup water

Cooking Terms

HERE'S a quick reference for some of the cooking terms used in *Taste of Home* recipes:

Baste—To moisten food with melted butter, pan drippings, marinades or other liquid to add more flavor and juiciness.

Beat—A rapid movement to combine ingredients using a fork, spoon, wire whisk or electric mixer.

Blend—To combine ingredients until *just* mixed.

Boil—To heat liquids until bubbles form that cannot be "stirred down." In the case of water, the temperature will reach 212°.

Bone—To remove all meat from the bone before cooking.

Cream—To beat ingredients together to a smooth consistency, usually in the case of butter and sugar for baking.

Dash—A small amount of seasoning, less than 1/8 teaspoon. If using a shaker, a dash would comprise a quick flip of the container.

Dredge—To coat foods with flour or other dry ingredients. Most often done with pot roasts and stew meat before browning.

Fold—To incorporate several ingredients by careful and gentle turning with a spatula. Used generally with beaten egg whites or whipped cream when mixing into the rest of the ingredients to keep the batter light.

Julienne—To cut foods into long thin strips much like matchsticks. Used most often for salads and stir-fry dishes.

Mince—To cut into very fine pieces. Used often for garlic or fresh herbs.

Parboil—To cook partially, usually used in the case of chicken, sausages and vegetables.

Partially Set—Describes the consistency of gelatin after it has been chilled for a small amount of time. Mixture should resemble the consistency of egg whites.

Puree—To process foods to a smooth mixture. Can be prepared in an electric blender, food processor, food mill or sieve.

Saute—To fry quickly in a small amount of fat, stirring almost constantly. Most often done with onions, mushrooms and other chopped vegetables.

Score—To cut slits partway through the outer surface of foods. Often used with ham or flank steak.

Stir-Fry—To cook meats and/or vegetables with a constant stirring motion in a small amount of oil in a wok or skillet over high heat.

General Recipe Index

This handy index lists every recipe by food category, major ingredient and/or cooking method, so you can easily locate recipes to suit your needs.

✓ Recipe includes Nutrition Facts and Diabetic Exchanges

✓ Recipe includes Nutrition Facts and Diabetic Exchanges

✓ Recipe includes Nutrition Facts and Diabetic Exchanges

✓ Recipe includes Nutrition Facts and Diabetic Exchanges

✓ Recipe includes Nutrition Facts and Diabetic Exchanges

✓ *Recipe includes Nutrition Facts and Diabetic Exchanges*

✓ Recipe includes Nutrition Facts and Diabetic Exchanges

✓ Recipe includes Nutrition Facts and Diabetic Exchanges

✓ Recipe includes Nutrition Facts and Diabetic Exchanges

✓ Recipe includes Nutrition Facts and Diabetic Exchanges

✓ Recipe includes Nutrition Facts and Diabetic Exchanges

Pepper Pork Fajitas, 67
Southwest Tortilla Pizzas, 53

PIES & TARTS
Apple-Berry Crumb Pie, 36
Banana Cheesecake Pie, 224
Blueberry Ice Cream Tart, 101
Cherry Chocolate Pie, 241
Easy Cheesecake Pie, 97
Easy Grasshopper Ice Cream Pie, 218
Mud Pies, 18
Pear Custard Pie, 23
Pecan Pumpkin Pie, 39
✓Raspberry-Glazed Pie, 223
✓Tropical Pie, 264

PINEAPPLE
Pineapple Cranberry Ham, 76
✓Pineapple-Glazed Carrots, 59
✓Tropical Pie, 264

PORK (also see Bacon & Canadian Bacon; Ham; Hot Dogs; Pepperoni & Salami; Sausage)
Appetizers
　Party Nachos, 152
　✓Pork Satay, 277
Breakfast & Brunch
　Spicy Sausage Patties, 69
Main Dishes
　✓Apple-Glazed Pork Chops, 288
　✓Apricot Pork Roast, 163
　Asian Pork Tenderloins, 293
　Barbecue Pork and Penne Skillet, 209
　Chinese Country-Style Pork Ribs, 301
　Creamy Pork Potpie, 118
　Crispy Herb-Coated Pork Chops, 58
　Fruit-Glazed Pork Chops, 215
　✓Fruity Pork Roast, 167
　Hash Brown Pork Skillet, 292
　Italian Pork Chops, 65
　Italian Pork Skillet, 133
　Maple-Glazed Pork Chops, 305
　✓Onion-Dijon Pork Chops, 130
　Pear Pork Chops, 52
　Pepper Pork Fajitas, 67
　✓Pork Chops Creole, 240
　✓Pork Chops with Blackberry Sauce, 62
　✓Pork Chops with Mango Salsa, 269
　Pork Roast with Mashed Potatoes and Gravy, 116

Spinach Pork Chops with Lemon Gravy, 127
Sweet Potato Pork Skillet, 308
Teriyaki & Ginger Pork Tenderloins, 31
Sandwiches
　Asian Pork Burgers, 295

POTATOES & SWEET POTATOES
Bacon Potato Salad, 296
Basil Red Potatoes, 29
Beer-Flavored Potatoes, 57
✓Cajun Potato Wedges, 63
Chicken and Red Potatoes, 164
Cordon Bleu Potato Soup, 109
Flavorful Red Potatoes, 140
Garlic Mashed Potatoes, 55
Gruyere Mashed Potatoes, 41
Ham & Cheese Potato Casserole, 236
Hash Brown Pork Skillet, 292
Hot Dog Potato Soup, 73
Mexican Hat Dance Spuds, 209
Peachy Sweet Potatoes, 101
Philly Steak Potatoes, 132
Pierogi Beef Skillet, 121
Pork Roast with Mashed Potatoes and Gravy, 116
Potato Beef Lasagna, 252
Potato-Topped Chicken Casserole, 232
Ranch Potato Cubes, 25
✓Roasted Potatoes with Thyme and
　Gorgonzola, 71
Round Steak with Potatoes, 253
Scalloped Potatoes with Ham & Cheese, 246
Southwestern Shepherd's Pie, 238
Spicy Sausage Hash Browns, 160
Sweet Potato Pork Skillet, 308
Tater Brat Bake, 247

PRETZELS
Blizzard Party Mix, 95
Cereal Snack Mix, 278
Chocolate Pretzel Rings, 46
Cinnamon Baked Pretzels, 285
Kickin' Snack Mix, 273
Pretzel Pumpkin Grahams, 32
Snack Loot, 151

PUMPKIN
Cranberry Pumpkin Bread, 46
Pecan Pumpkin Pie, 39
Pumpkin Mousse, 35

✓ Recipe includes Nutrition Facts and Diabetic Exchanges

✓ Recipe includes Nutrition Facts and Diabetic Exchanges

✓ Recipe includes Nutrition Facts and Diabetic Exchanges

✓ Recipe includes Nutrition Facts and Diabetic Exchanges

✓ Recipe includes Nutrition Facts and Diabetic Exchanges

✓ Recipe includes Nutrition Facts and Diabetic Exchanges

Alphabetical Index

*This handy index lists every recipe in alphabetical order,
so you can easily locate recipes to suit your needs.*

✓ Recipe includes Nutrition Facts and Diabetic Exchanges

Cheeseburger Cups, 87
Cherry Chocolate Pie, 241
Cherry Fluff, 227
Chicken and Artichoke Pasta, 206
Chicken and Pear Salad, 113
Chicken and Red Potatoes, 164
Chicken 'n' Veggie Kabobs, 300
Chicken Cheese Soup, 189
Chicken Chowder, 311
Chicken Cordon Bleu Bake, 234
Chicken Fettuccine Alfredo with Veggies, 14
Chicken-Melon Spinach Salad, 144
Chicken Melts, 108
Chicken Pesto Clubs, 106
Chicken Pesto Sandwiches, 157
Chicken Salad Croissants, 186
Chicken Tostada Salad, 104
Chili Cheese Ball, 278
Chili Cheese Dip, 109
Chili Cheese Dog Casserole, 120
Chili Chicken Sandwiches, 194
Chili Spaghetti with Hot Dogs, 83
Chinese Beef Casserole, 246
Chinese Country-Style Pork Ribs, 301
Chip-Crusted Chicken, 97
✓Chocolate Candy Clusters, 81
Chocolate Chip Dip, 86
✓Chocolate-Mint Truffle Cookies, 49
Chocolate-Orange Scones, 182
Chocolate Peanut Crunch Ice Cream Cake, 228
Chocolate Pecan Waffles, 153
Chocolate Pizza Heart, 23
Chocolate Pretzel Rings, 46
Chocolate Zucchini Cupcakes, 221
Cinnamon Baked Pretzels, 285
✓Cinnamon Candy Cane Cookies, 44
Cinnamon Hot Chocolate Mix, 45
Citrus Chicken, 170
Cobb Salad with Chili-Lime Dressing, 61
Coconut Berry Pizza, 155
Coconut-Layered Pound Cake, 113
Coconut Rhubarb Dessert, 227
✓Confetti Succotash, 26
Cookie Sundaes, 8
Cordon Bleu Potato Soup, 109
✓Corn Salsa, 278
Corned Beef Cabbage Bake, 252
Cornish Game Hens, 256
Couscous with Mushrooms, 141
Crab Pasta Salad, 145
✓Cranberry Chili Salsa, 283

Cranberry Pear Salad, 136
✓Cranberry Pecan Cookies, 223
Cranberry Pumpkin Bread, 46
Creamed Turkey with Puff Pastry, 238
Creamy Beef Enchiladas, 80
Creamy Cauliflower and Bacon Soup, 187
Creamy Chicken Casserole, 239
Creamy Chicken Dip, 274
Creamy Chocolate Mousse, 77
Creamy Pork Potpie, 118
Creamy Spinach Sausage Pasta, 255
Creamy Tomato Shrimp with Penne, 18
Creepy Crawly Cupcakes, 33
Crescent Zucchini Pie, 179
Crispy Chicken Fingers, 87
Crispy Herb-Coated Pork Chops, 58
Crumb-Coated Cube Steaks, 200
Crumb-Topped Baked Fish, 204
Crunchy Walnut Salad, 38
Crustless Chicken Quiche, 175
✓Cucumber & Squash Salad, 307
✓Cucumber Rolls, 284
Curry Shrimp Linguine, 309

E

Easy Caesar Coleslaw, 68
Easy Cheesecake Pie, 97
✓Easy Chicken Strips, 16
Easy Grasshopper Ice Cream Pie, 218
Easy Spanish Rice, 53
✓Easy Tiramisu, 105
Effortless Egg Rolls, 98
Egg Salad & Cucumber Sandwiches, 195
Egg Salad Sandwiches, 192
Eggnog Tube Cake, 40
✓Eggplant Zucchini Bolognese, 267
Eggs Benedict with Jalapeno Hollandaise, 178
Eggs in Muffin Cups, 183
Enchilada Beef, 199

F

Fancy Green Beans, 142
Festive Corn 'n' Broccoli, 144
Fiesta Chicken Burritos, 166
Flavorful Red Potatoes, 140
✓Four-Cheese Broiled Tomato Slices, 280
French Dip Sandwiches, 73
French Onion Cheese Fondue, 98
French Quarter Cheese Spread, 285
Fresh Mozzarella & Tomato Salad, 141

✓ Recipe includes Nutrition Facts and Diabetic Exchanges

✓ Recipe includes Nutrition Facts and Diabetic Exchanges

L

Lasagna Roll-Ups, 248
Lemon Chicken and Veggies, 205
✓Lemon Fluff Dessert, 220
✓Lemon Green Beans, 12
Lemon Ladyfinger Dessert, 26
✓Lemon-Pepper Brussels Sprouts, 41
Lemon-Pepper Chicken, 74
Lime Milk Shakes, 16
Linguine Pesto with Italian Chicken Strips, 202
Loaded Spaghetti Bake, 250

M

Mac and Cheese Chicken Skillet, 205
Macadamia-Crusted Mahi Mahi, 201
Macaroni & Cheese Bake, 82
Macaroni & Cheese Pizza, 81
Macaroni Taco Bake, 89
Macaroni Vegetable Soup, 186
✓Mandarin Salsa, 273
✓Mango Shrimp Pitas, 193
Maple-Glazed Pork Chops, 305
✓Maple Mustard Chicken, 163
✓Maple Nut Truffles, 97
✓Maple Walnut Crisps, 226
✓Marinated Flank Steak, 263
Marinated Sausage Kabobs, 280
Meaty Noodle Casserole, 249
Mediterranean Broccoli Slaw, 157
Mediterranean Green Salad, 147
Mexican Hat Dance Spuds, 209
✓Microwave Apple Crisp, 12
Microwave Marshmallow Fudge, 45
Microwave Veggie Pilaf, 74
Mock Stroganoff, 12
✓Monkey Muffins, 83
Moo Shu Sloppy Joes, 75
✓Mostaccioli Casserole, 241
Mozzarella Sticks, 281
Mud Pies, 18
Muffuletta Pasta, 199
Mushroom Beef Tips with Rice, 112
Mushroom Onion Dip, 274
✓Mushroom-Rosemary Turkey Gravy, 37
Mustard Ham Strata, 178
My Favorite Granola, 177

N

✓Nutty Chocolate Truffles, 22
✓Nutty Orange Snowballs, 219

O

✓Oatmeal Surprise Cookies, 88
✓Olive Orange Salad, 267
Olive Pepperoni Spread, 152
✓Onion-Dijon Pork Chops, 130
Open-Faced Pizza Sandwiches, 189
✓Orange-Angel Jelly Roll, 290
Orange Chicken and Veggies with Rice, 119
✓Orange Cinnamon Rolls, 183
✓Orange Corn Bread, 261
✓Orange-Glazed Broccoli, 58
Orange-Glazed Salmon, 303
✓Orange-Maple Glazed Chicken, 301
✓Orange Rhubarb Sauce, 64
Orange Roughy with Tartar Sauce, 206
Orange Zucchini Muffins, 176
Orzo-Stuffed Peppers, 248
Out-to-Sea Pasta Shell Salad, 150

P

✓Parmesan Breadsticks, 61
Parmesan Cornflake Chicken, 253
Party Cracker Dip, 274
✓Party Meatballs, 161
Party Nachos, 152
Pasta Carbonara, 200
PBJ-Stuffed French Toast, 82
✓Pea Pods and Peppers, 18
Peaches & Cream French Toast, 233
✓Peachy Shrimp Tacos, 113
Peachy Sweet Potatoes, 101
Peanut Butter & Jelly Waffles, 86
Peanut Butter Cake Bars, 219
Peanut Butter Easter Eggs, 27
✓Peanut Butter Turtle Candies, 229
Pear Custard Pie, 23
Pear Pork Chops, 52
✓Pecan Butterscotch Cookies, 156
Pecan Caramel Candies, 46
Pecan Chicken with Blue Cheese Sauce, 251
Pecan Pumpkin Pie, 39
Pepper Pork Fajitas, 67
Pepperoni Pinwheels, 99
Pepperoni Pizza Skillet, 89
Pepperoni Provolone Pizzas, 154
Pesto Chicken Mostaccioli, 247
Pesto Corn, 97
Pesto-Turkey Layered Loaf, 195
Philly Steak Potatoes, 132
Picante Beef Roast, 167

✓ Recipe includes Nutrition Facts and Diabetic Exchanges

Pierogi Beef Skillet, 121
Pineapple Cranberry Ham, 76
✓Pineapple-Glazed Carrots, 59
Pirate Ship Sandwich, 151
Pistachio Pudding Parfaits, 225
✓Pizza Lover's Pie, 255
Pizza Pasta Toss, 8
Popcorn Bars, 153
Poppy Seed Mixed Salad, 73
✓Pork Chops Creole, 240
✓Pork Chops with Blackberry Sauce, 62
✓Pork Chops with Mango Salsa, 269
Pork Roast with Mashed Potatoes and
   Gravy, 116
✓Pork Satay, 277
Potato Beef Lasagna, 252
Potato-Topped Chicken Casserole, 232
Pretzel Pumpkin Grahams, 32
Prime Rib with Horseradish Cream, 40
✓Prosciutto Pinwheels, 283
Pull-Apart Sticky Bun Ring, 181
Pumpkin Mousse, 35

Q

Quick Ghost Cookies, 35

R

✓Radish Asparagus Salad, 143
✓Ramen Broccoli Soup, 92
Ramen-Vegetable Beef Skillet, 212
Ranch Bean Chili, 233
Ranch Chicken Salad, 120
Ranch Potato Cubes, 25
Ranch Turkey Wraps, 110
✓Raspberry Chicken, 198
Raspberry Dessert Sauce, 22
✓Raspberry-Glazed Pie, 223
✓Raspberry Oatmeal Bars, 229
Ravioli Casserole, 245
✓Roasted Potatoes with Thyme and
   Gorgonzola, 71
Roasted Turkey Breast Tenderloins &
   Vegetables, 122
Romaine Pecan Salad with Shrimp
   Skewers, 138
Romaine Salad, 10
Round Steak with Potatoes, 253
✓Rudolph Treats, 44
Rum Banana Sauce, 10

S

✓Salad Greens & Creamy Sweet Dressing, 8
Salads with Pistachio-Crusted Goat Cheese, 142
Salmon with Broccoli and Pasta, 289
Salmon with Lemon-Mushroom Sauce, 117
Salmon with Vegetable Salsa, 214
✓Salsa Chicken Skillet, 268
✓Saucy Beef Patties, 56
Saucy Chicken with Veggies and Rice, 171
Saucy Parmesan Chicken, 245
Sausage & Egg Breakfast Pizza, 180
Sausage & Spinach Calzones, 204
Sausage Skillet Dinner, 208
Sausage Tortellini Soup, 190
✓Sauteed Corn with Tomatoes & Basil, 265
✓Sauteed Zucchini Strips, 307
Savory Grilled T-Bones, 300
✓Savory Onion Chicken, 129
Scalloped Potatoes with Ham & Cheese, 246
Sesame Carrots, 75
✓Seasoned Tilapia Fillets, 304
Shrimp & Broccoli with Pasta, 64
Shrimp Burritos, 124
Shrimp Egg Drop Soup, 132
Six-Cheese Lasagna, 256
Skillet Catfish, 211
Sloppy Joe Calzones, 127
Slow-Cooked Pork & Beans, 168
Slow Cooker Sloppy Joes, 165
Smoked Kielbasa with Rice, 207
Smoked Sausage Gumbo, 164
Smoked Sausage Pasta, 215
✓S'more Bars, 85
Snack Loot, 151
✓Snow Pea & Carrot Saute, 268
Southwest Beef Pie, 130
Southwest Chicken and Rice, 80
Southwest Tortilla Pizzas, 53
Southwest Tuna Noodle Bake, 250
Southwestern Corn Salad, 94
Southwestern Shepherd's Pie, 238
✓Soy-Garlic Chicken, 162
Spiced Cider Punch, 39
✓Spiced Pears, 42
Spicy Maple Chicken Wings, 272
Spicy Sausage Hash Browns, 160
Spicy Sausage Patties, 69
Spinach Pesto, 237
Spinach Pork Chops with Lemon Gravy, 127
Spinach Steak Pinwheels, 93

✓ Recipe includes Nutrition Facts and Diabetic Exchanges

Spinach Tortellini Salad, 146
Spooky Spider Cupcakes, 33
Steaks with Mushroom Sauce, 29
Stovetop Chicken 'n' Stuffing, 308
Strawberries with Chocolate Cream
    Filling, 228
Strawberry Cheesecake Ice Cream, 221
✓Stuffed Party Mushrooms, 283
✓Summer Fruit Cooler, 278
✓Summer Fruit Salad, 175
Summer Squash Casserole, 136
Summer Strawberry Salad, 66
✓Summer Strawberry Soup, 193
Sun-Dried Tomato Chicken Roll-Ups, 251
Sun-Dried Tomato Dip, 108
✓Super Spinach Salad, 140
Sweet and Savory Stuffing, 36
Sweet & Spicy Nuts, 281
Sweet Potato Pork Skillet, 308
Swiss Broccoli Bake, 244
Swiss Steak Burgers, 295
Szechuan Shrimp Salad, 147

T

Taco Salad with a Twist, 139
Taco Turkey Burgers, 191
Tangy Deli Melts, 307
Tangy Pot Roast, 160
Tarragon Corn on the Cob, 30
Tater Brat Bake, 247
Tender Beef Brisket, 171
Teriyaki & Ginger Pork Tenderloins, 31
Teriyaki Chicken, 161
Tex-Mex Beef Barbecues, 168
Tex-Mex Chicken, 107
Tex-Mex Dip, 107
Tex-Mex Seasoning Mix, 107
Thai Barbecued Salmon, 70
Thai Shrimp Linguine, 208
Three-Fruit Smoothies, 182
Tilapia Florentine, 59
Toasted Artichoke Sandwiches, 63
✓Toffee Bars, 226
Tomato-Green Bean Salad, 31

✓Tomato Pasta Side Dish, 93
✓Tomato Zucchini Saute, 261
Tortellini and Ham, 124
Triple Chocolate Cake, 28
✓Tropical Pie, 264
Tuna Mac and Cheese Bake, 254
Tuna Salad in Tomato Cups, 139
Turkey Club Pizza, 212
✓Turkey Divan, 266
✓Turkey Stir-Fry with Cabbage, 263
Turkey Tetrazzini, 234

V

Vegetable Beef Bow Tie Skillet, 126
Vegetable Beef Skillet, 118
✓Vegetable Pasta Salad, 264
Vegetable Rice Medley, 305
✓Vegetable Stir-Fry, 54
Vegetables with Cheese Sauce, 16
✓Veggie Chicken Pitas, 202
Veggie Tortellini Soup, 194
✓Veggie Tortilla Pinwheels, 284

W

Walnut Cheese Crescents, 60
Walnut-Crusted Orange Roughy, 121
✓Watermelon Gazpacho, 262
Wide-Eyed Owl Cupcakes, 32

Y

Yummy Chocolate Dip, 84

Z

Zesty Crouton Salad, 109
✓Zesty Hamburger Soup, 192
Zesty Nacho Dip, 274
Zesty Tacos, 213
Zinfandel Strawberry Trifle, 30
Zippy BLT Wraps, 210

✓ Recipe includes Nutrition Facts and Diabetic Exchanges